The Politics and Strategy of Clandestine War

This collection of new essays on the Special Operations Executive (SOE) sets out to explore the 'non-military' aspects of British special operations in World War II.

SOE was established in Summer 1940 to 'set Europe ablaze', by detonating popular resistance against Axis rule and nurturing 'secret armies'. Based on original archive research, these essays highlight for the first time the numerous other areas in which SOE contributed to the war effort and show that it played a major role in supporting Britain's political, economic, financial and humanitarian interest globally.

By situating SOE within the context of Britain's broader political needs, these essays also demonstrate the extent to which SOE came to epitomise the skills found in today's secret service organisations. SOE showed itself capable of operating on a global scale and developing the necessary expertise, equipment and personnel to conduct activities across the whole spectrum of what we have come to know as 'covert operations'. By bringing SOE's activities into sharper focus and exposing the scale of its involvement in Britain's wartime external relations, this book echoes current thinking on the place of the so-called 'secret world' in international politics. *The Politics and Strategy of Clandestine War* will be of great interest to students of SOE, intelligence studies, World War II and military history in general.

Neville Wylie is Associate Professor of International Relations at the University of Nottingham. His most recent publications include *Britain, Switzerland and the Second World War* (2003) and *European Neutrals and Non-belligerents during the Second World War* (2002).

Studies in Intelligence Series

General Editors: Richard J. Aldrich and Christopher Andrew

ISSN: 1368–9916

Selected titles from the series:

Intelligence and Military Operations edited by Michael I. Handel

Leaders and Intelligence edited by Michael I. Handel

War, Strategy and Intelligence by Michael I. Handel

Strategic and Operational Deception in the Second World War edited by Michael I. Handel

Codebreaker in the Far East by Alan Stripp

Intelligence for Peace edited by Hesi Carmel

Intelligence Services in the Information Age by Michael Herman

Espionage and the Roots of the Cold War: The Conspiratorial Heritage by David McKnight

Swedish Signal Intelligence, 1900–1945 by C. G. McKay and Bengt Beckman

The Norwegian Intelligence Service, 1945–1970 by Olav Riste

Secret Intelligence in the Twentieth Century edited by Heike Bungert, Jan G. Heitmann and Michael Wala

The CIA, the British Left and the Cold War: Calling the Tune? by Hugh Wilford

Our Man in Yugoslavia: The Story of a Secret Service Operative by Sebastian Ritchie

Understanding Intelligence in the Twenty-First Century: Journeys in Shadows by Len Scott and Peter Jackson

MI6 and the Machinery of Spying by Philip H. J. Davies

Twenty-First Century Intelligence edited by Wesley Wark

Intelligence and Strategy: Selected Essays by John Robert Ferris

The US Government, Citizen Groups and the Cold War: The State–Private Network edited by Helen Laville and Hugh Wilford

Peacekeeping Intelligence: New Players, Extended Boundaries edited by David Carment and Martin Rudner

Special Operations Executive: A New Instrument of War edited by Mark Seaman

Mussolini's Propaganda Abroad: Subversion in the Mediterranean and the Middle East, 1935–1940 by Manuela A. Williams

Britain's Secret War against Japan, 1937–1945 by Douglas Ford

The Politics and Strategy of Clandestine War: Special Operations Executive, 1940–1946 edited by Neville Wylie

The Politics and Strategy of Clandestine War

Special Operations Executive, 1940–1946

Edited by Neville Wylie

Routledge
Taylor & Francis Group

LONDON AND NEW YORK

First published 2007
by Routledge
2 Park Square, Milton Park, Abingdon, Oxon OX14 4RN

Simultaneously published in the USA and Canada
by Routledge
711 Third Ave, New York, NY 10017

Routledge is an imprint of the Taylor & Francis Group, an informa business

First issued in paperback 2012

© 2007 Neville Wylie

Typeset in Times New Roman
by Keystroke, 28 High Street, Tettenhall, Wolverhampton

British Library Cataloguing in Publication Data
A catalogue record for this book is available from the British Library

Library of Congress Cataloging in Publication Data
The politics and strategy of clandestine war : Special Operation Executive,
1940–1946 / edited by Neville Wylie.
    p. cm. – (Studies in intelligence series, ISSN 1368–9916)
Includes bibliographical references and index.
1. Great Britain. Special Operations Executive. 2. World War,
1939–1945–Secret service–Great Britain. 3. Great Britain–Foreign
relations–1936–1945. 4. Subversive activities–Great
Britain–History–20th century. I. Wylie, Neville, 1966– II. Title.
III. Series: Cass series on intelligence and military affairs.
Studies in intelligence series.
D810.S7P64 2006
940.54′8641–dc22   2006002155

ISBN13: 978–0–415–39110–8 (hbk)

ISBN13: 978-0-415-65096-0 (pbk)

ISBN13: 978–0–203–96455–2 (ebk)

Contents

Contributors

Roderick Bailey is currently employed as a historian at the Imperial War Museum, London, as a freelance historian and interviewer, running a major project to acquire more material for the Museum's SOE collections. He is a graduate of the universities of Edinburgh and Cambridge and a former Alistair Horne Fellow at St Antony's College, Oxford. His PhD, from Edinburgh, was entitled 'SOE and British policy towards wartime resistance in Albania and Kosovo, 1940–45'.

Kent Fedorowich is a Reader in British imperial history at the University of the West of England, Bristol. He has published extensively on empire migration, Anglo-dominion relations and prisoners of war. His publications include several collections of essays: one co-edited with Martin Thomas on *International Diplomacy and Colonial Retreat* (London: Frank Cass, 2001); and one with Carl Bridge on *The British World: Diaspora, Culture and Identity* (London: Frank Cass, 2003). He has also co-authored with Bob Moore, *The British Empire and its Italian Prisoners of War, 1940–1947* (Basingstoke: Palgrave, 2002).

Matthew Jones is Professor of American Foreign Relations at the University of Nottingham. He is author the of *Conflict and Confrontation in South East Asia, 1961–1965: Britain, the United States, Indonesia and the Creation of Malaysia* (Cambridge: Cambridge University Press, 2002) and *Britain, the United States, and the Mediterranean War, 1942–44* (Basingstoke: Macmillan, 1996).

Saul Kelly is a Lecturer in Defence Studies at King's College, London (Joint Services Command and Staff College). His publications include *The Hunt for Zerzura* (London: John Murray, 2002), *Cold War in the Desert* (London: Macmillan, 2000) and, with Anthony Gorst (eds), *Whitehall and the Suez Crisis* (London: Frank Cass, 2000). His current project is concerned with the 'Great Game' during and immediately after the First World War.

David A. Messenger is an Assistant Professor of History at the University of Wyoming. He is currently completing a book-length manuscript on the subject of French relations with Spain during and after the Second World War and pursuing a new project on the recovery of Nazi assets in Spain.

Christopher J. Murphy is currently an independent scholar. He was formerly Leverhulme Postdoctoral Fellow at the Centre for Contemporary British History at the Institute of Historical Research. His PhD, from the University of Reading, was entitled 'SOE's "missing dimension": an examination of the support organisation and broader internal relations within the Special Operations Executive, 1940–1946'. He has recently completed *Security and Special Operations: SOE and MI5 during the Second World War* (Palgrave Macmillan, forthcoming), a study of the work of SOE's Security (D/CE) Section.

Mark Seaman is a historian with the Cabinet Office. Formerly he was a historian with the Imperial War Museum specialising in the study of the Special Operations Executive and Intelligence during the Second World War. He has just finished editing a collection of essays on SOE written by leading historians in the subject.

Duncan Stuart retired in 1992 after a career in H. M. Diplomatic Service. In 1996, he was invited to become the SOE Adviser at the Foreign and Commonwealth Office. He was the last incumbent of this post, which was abolished in 2002 when the final class of SOE archival files was released to the National Archive: Public Record Office in Kew.

T. C. Wales is the North American editor at the *Oxford Analytica Daily Brief*. His 2005 Edinburgh PhD dissertation, completed under the supervision of Professor Rhodri Jeffreys-Jones and Dr David Stafford, was entitled, 'The Secret War in the South: British and American Intelligence Co-operation and Rivalry in the Western Mediterranean, 1941–1944'. He has written for many academic journals on Cold War, intelligence, and security issues.

Neville Wylie is Associate Professor in International Relations at the University of Nottingham, author of *Britain, Switzerland and the Second World War* (Oxford, 2003), and editor of *European Neutrals and Non-belligerents during the Second World War* (Cambridge, 2002). He has written a number of papers on intelligence and special operations, including '"An amateur learns his job?" Special Operations Executive in Portugal, 1940–1942', *Journal of Contemporary History* 36/3 (2001), 455–471 and 'SOE and the Neutrals', in Mark Seaman (ed.), *Special Operations Executive: A New Weapon of War* (London, 2005).

Acknowledgements

My thanks, as editor, go first and foremost to the contributors, without whose time, patience, and ideas this volume would not have been possible. The majority of the papers published here initially appeared in the journal *Intelligence & National Security*, and I would like to express my thanks to the editorial team, past and present – Wesley Wark, Richard Aldrich, Peter Jackson and Loch Johnson – for their unstinting help and support in bringing this and the *INS*' 'special issue' on SOE (vol. 20, issue 1) to fruition. Thanks are also due to the score of anonymous 'readers', who kindly took the trouble to comment on early drafts of the essays, and to the Imperial War Museum, London, for letting me publish Duncan Stuart's essay (Chapter 1).

Finally, it is a great pleasure to be able to take the opportunity afforded by the publication of this volume to acknowledge my gratitude to M. R. D. Foot and Tony Brooks. It was they who first inspired my interest in the study of special operations, and it has been their writings, views and personal experiences that have more than anything informed my understanding of the extraordinary work and 'world' of SOE.

Neville Wylie
Nottingham

For Olivia and Isabella and 'the bump'

Introduction

Politics and strategy in the clandestine war – new perspectives in the study of SOE

Neville Wylie

Buried amongst the Australian War Memorial's impressive photographic collection is a series of photos taken by W. Mulford, who saw service with Lysander squadrons in Burma at the close of the Second World War. To a casual observer, Mulford's photos might seem unremarkable. Lysanders were a regular sight for British and Commonwealth servicemen during the war, and were found in all theatres in which British troops were engaged. Closer inspection, however, suggests that Mulford's photographs depict scenes that were anything but ordinary. The make of the aircraft itself should at least give us pause for thought. For, although initially designed as army reconnaissance aircraft, Lysanders quickly became a firm favourite in RAF 'special duty' squadrons. What the aircraft might have lacked in space and speed, it made up for in its range and agility. It was found to be particularly well suited for infiltrating and exfiltrating agents from occupied Europe. Good visibility from the cockpit enabled pilots to spot the faint, flickering lights of their reception parties, while the plane's remarkable manoeuvrability meant that it could be safely landed on the unploughed fields or pastures that invariably doubled-up as makeshift airfields for resistance movements during the war. Had the markings of Mulford's aircraft been rather more visible, it would become evident that the Lysanders were IIIAs and belonged to No. 357 Special Duty (SD) squadron. The squadron operated out of Mingaladon airfield in Burma, and was primarily responsible for servicing members of Force 136 – the Special Operations Executive's *nom de guerre* in the Far East – and their allies among the Karen tribes in Burma.

If the provenance of Mulford's aircraft is mysterious, the same might equally be said of the men seen boarding them. One photograph clearly shows parachutes amongst the equipment being loaded into the aircraft. Such were the aerodynamics of a Lysander that anyone attempting to bail out of the cockpit would more than likely find themselves wrapped around the aircraft's tailfin. To make a 'clean' jump, the agents would have to work their way down the ladder on the outside of the aircraft and hope that on letting go, they avoided being sucked into the plane's slip-stream: a technique, one suspects, best not practised too often beforehand.[1] That the men were instructed to proceed in this way is explained by the fact that those directing the operation probably considered them expendable. According to information supplied when Mulford's collection was deposited at the Australian War Memorial, the men boarding the Lysanders were Japanese soldiers who had fallen into Allied hands earlier in the war. If they did indeed exit their Lysander at altitude, it is the only known instance of this procedure being adopted during the entire war.[2] Their mission was also a distinct rarity for SOE. Their task was to intercede on the Allies' behalf and negotiate the surrender of those Japanese forces, still holed up in remote areas of Burma, who were either unaware that the war had ended, or preferred death to the dishonour of falling into 'enemy' hands alive.[3] Sadly, the fate of the men, their aircraft and their mission is not known.[4]

Though faded and grainy, Mulford's photographs capture the essence of much of what historians now know about the work of Special Operations Executive (SOE) during the war. SOE may have been established to 'set Europe ablaze', 'detonate' popular resistance against Axis rule, or nurture 'secret armies', but by the time the war came to a close, SOE's staff had come to embrace a whole raft of different activities, from sabotage and subversion, to political warfare, and, as the case of Mulford's Special Duty squadron suggests, the delicate art of peace-brokering. It was an organisation that acted on a global scale, in some areas dwarfing its 'competitors' in the secret world, and developed the expertise, equipment and personnel to conduct operations across the whole spectrum of what we now, rather loosely, term 'covert activities'. It is these more nebulous aspects of SOE's achievement, and legacy, that the essays in this collection are primarily designed to address. The importance of the subject to the history of special or covert operations, and its contemporary resonance, can scarcely be exaggerated. Though falling out of favour in the final years of the Cold War, there has been something of a renaissance in the use of covert operations in international politics in recent years, not least those undertaken as part of the present 'war on terror'. The vocabulary might be slightly different – with 'regime change' being the most popular of the current buzz-words – but the objectives, and even some of the techniques, have a distinctly older pedigree. Moreover, the activities of secret intelligence agencies have become much more muscular than in the past, with secret service officers working in closer collaboration with their military counterparts. As a recent report on the reform of Britain's Secret Intelligence Service noted, SIS operators in Afghanistan or Iraq have, in some ways, more in common with the behind-the-lines Special Operations Executive 'than with the crypto-diplomatic spies of old. Such conditions are likely to persist, and a new breed of British intelligence officer could develop to match new requirements'.[5] Appreciating SOE's record in covert operations has rarely been as relevant as it is today.

There are, however, important academic reasons for wishing to consider anew the history of SOE. The study of SOE has been transformed in the past few years. This is partly due to the passage of time and the 'maturing' process that takes place whenever any sizeable archival holding is released into the public domain. It is now over ten years since the first SOE files were deposited at the National Archives at Kew, London, and with the arrival of SOE's personnel files, this process is now substantially complete. Quite naturally, the years immediately following the release saw historians rush to answer some of the abiding mysteries that clung to the name of SOE and which had steadfastly resisted attempts at explanation over the previous fifty years. Many of these studies, though necessarily 'cherry-picking' at the archive, and addressing only the more sensational aspects of SOE's war, are nevertheless remarkably good and earn their place in any respectable military history library.[6] Nevertheless, it is only relatively recently that historians – and for the moment I exclude SOE's 'official' historians – have been able to subject the archive to sustained academic research and complete long-term research projects on aspects of SOE's wartime activities. It is no coincidence that three of the contributors to this collection, Roderick Bailey, T. C. Wales and Christopher Murphy, have all recently completed doctoral theses on SOE topics.[7] More established historians – foremost among these, E. D. R. Harrison, Mark Seaman and David Stafford – have also seized the opportunity to immerse themselves in the documents of an organisation which they had come to know, second hand, over the years.[8]

The research agendas pursued by these and other scholars have also come to differ, in certain critical respects, from earlier work on the subject. On the one hand, historians of SOE are tending to address a broader range of issues, and cover a wider canvas, than was the case when the archive first opened its doors. Fresh methodological or intellectual approaches are being brought to bear on the material that raise new questions, and offer new perspectives on the 'SOE phenomenon'.[9] Perhaps more importantly, since access to the SOE archive is no longer the preserve of a few privileged specialists commissioned to write histories of SOE, SOE's papers can now be used to help illuminate other, broader aspects of Britain's wartime activities. It is interesting that under these conditions 'special operations' tend to lose their exotic sheen and come to be seen as one part among many, of Britain's broader political and military effort between 1940 and 1945. The study of SOE is thus a far less exclusive affair than it was in the past, both in terms of those people now able to gain access to the files, and in the way in which contemporary scholars are addressing the whole history of SOE, and evaluating its activities and contribution to the war.

Time and familiarity with the SOE archive have, then, promoted a more nuanced, complex and 'contextualised' understanding of the organisation and its activities than was possible even a few years ago. This 'coming of age' has been hastened by fresh insights into the way in which previous writing on SOE has come about. Though a young field, the study of SOE has already progressed through several distinct phases. The first attempt to make sense of what had occurred took place even before the organisation closed its doors for the last time. A raft of what might be called 'in-house' histories – reports on individual stations, sections or operations – were composed in the final months of the war, frequently by those officers who had been intimately involved in the events they described. The purpose of these reports was partly historical, to inform the work of subsequent 'official' historians, and partly practical: SOE staff were rightly anxious that their hard-learnt lessons were distilled in some form for the benefit of future practitioners. While the standards of objectivity and veracity applied in compiling these reports frequently fall short of what one might have hoped for, this 'first cut' at writing the 'history' of SOE is not without its value. Anyone venturing into the field today will find the reports a useful starting point, especially for the insights they provide into the views of some of the *dramatis personae* and their commentaries on the key events in SOE's record.

The historisation of SOE has been assisted in recent years by the light shed on the attitudes of successive governments towards the whole question of whether or not to allow the writing of *any* accounts of what was, after all, meant to be a secret organisation. This concerned both the production of the 'official history' series, the first volume of which appeared in 1966, and the organisation's own 'in-house' history, written by William Mackenzie between 1945 and 1947.[10] Official attempts to manipulate, or at least control, the historical record by limiting access to the archive and restricting the output of those afforded privileged access are every bit as intriguing as the better known efforts to keep the 'Ultra Secret' from public knowledge. It is particularly revealing in what it tells us about official attitudes towards the retention of 'public records' and the broader political environment within which discussions over the publication of 'official histories' took place.[11] To some, this fascination for the travails of earlier historians may seem rather self-indulgent, but there are important lessons to be learnt from such endeavours. 'Histories of histories' enhance the sense of historical perspective that is so often missing in the writing of contemporary history. They provide historiographical depth to the study of SOE. They remind us too, of how much SOE differed from Britain's other secret services. It was an agency whose actions, for the most part, took place in public view. It was also one whose role was essentially that of a facilitator. Britain's higher military authorities may have dictated SOE's operational priorities, but invariably its success hinged on its ability to collaborate with foreign resistance movements or allied services, who pursued their own national, political or sectional interests with little regard for the wishes of the British government. To a large extent therefore, SOE's war must be judged in terms of its contribution to the national resistance movements in other countries. The need to recognise this achievement, and prevent Britain's allies or rivals laying claim to the historical record, goes a long way to explaining why the government agreed to such unprecedented publicity, and eventually public access, to the archives of one of its secret services.

The importance of official accounts for the study of contemporary history – whether those, like the official history series, designed from the outset for public dissemination, or those, such as Mackenzie's *Secret History of SOE*, destined to remain under lock and key – can scarcely be exaggerated. As Ernest May commented nearly twenty-five years ago, for anyone faced with the task of scaling the towering mass of official documentation on contemporary historical issues, 'official histories' provide an invaluable entrée into the material, without which any attempt to make sense of the immediate past would be well nigh impossible.[12] In terms of its official histories, SOE has, on balance, fared rather well. True, the more 'popular' official histories of SOE activities in Scandinavia and the Far East, written by the late Charles Cruickshank, are generally considered disappointing,[13] and only two of the remaining four histories have yet to see the light of day.[14] Yet to have four, potentially six, official histories appear at all, from a body as addicted to secrecy as the British government, is a boon that we ought not to dismiss too lightly.

It is an abundance of riches in comparison with the official publications on Britain's other secret services. What we know about SOE's sister organisation, the Secret Intelligence Service (SIS), could be put on a postage stamp and most of the other secret services are only marginally better served.[15]

It is the publication of William Mackenzie's 'in-house' history of SOE in 2000, that has provided historians of SOE with their biggest 'windfall' in recent years. As recently as 1959, security and other considerations made Mackenzie's publication 'out of the question': we are fortunate that the passage of time has softened these fears.[16] Mackenzie's focus is, admittedly, a narrow one. His perspective is that of the headquarters staff in Baker Street, not the agent in the field. He is slim on operational details, his narrative ventures only rarely into Africa and the Middle East and passes over SOE's activities in the Far East in complete silence. But his 750 pages of text and supporting documents – many of which are published for the first time – are a masterful account of SOE's war. Historians are much the wiser for being able to read Mackenzie's perceptive and candid judgements on a wide range of SOE's activities. The debt historians of SOE owe to Mackenzie's dedication and scholarship is immense, and the impact of his work on the writing of SOE history is sure to be felt for some time to come.[17]

The essays collected in this issue reflect the debt contemporary historians owe to Mackenzie, but, more importantly, exemplify the changes that have been underway in the study of SOE. They set out to enhance our understanding of SOE by demonstrating the breadth of its activities and the scope of its ambitions over the course of the war. In doing so, most explore aspects of SOE's record that are invariably overlooked in standard accounts of the subject.[18] Our fascination for the more dramatic events in SOE's war record tends to overshadow the fact that by the time the war came to a close, there were few areas of the globe in which SOE was not involved, in some way or other, with the projection of British interests abroad. The form and extent of SOE's contribution varied enormously: in some instances, the Far East being the most obvious example, the scale of SOE operations came to dwarf the activities of Britain's other, more established, secret organisations.[19] But irrespective of the precise nature of SOE's work, there is ample evidence, much of it presented for the first time in this collection, to show that the organisation left an indelible mark on the whole spectrum of Britain's political, economic and military activities during the course of the war.

By bringing SOE's activities into sharper focus and exposing the scale of its involvement in Britain's external relations, the essays echo current thinking on the place of the so-called 'secret world'. As they emerge from the shadows, secret agencies are increasingly being seen not as niche-market service providers – an image which, of course, serves secret agencies well – but rather as forceful and at times central players in the formation of governments' foreign and security policies. SOE may have worked at the margins of Britain's military effort, but its activities were none the smaller for it, nor any less significant for the history of the Second World War. Furthermore, such a reassessment of SOE's record has important implications for those wishing to study the organisation. The larger SOE looms in the formulation and execution of British policies, the greater the need to triangulate the papers found in the SOE archive with those found in other official and unofficial archives, both in the United Kingdom and abroad. No accurate evaluation of SOE's place in the war is possible if we restrict our researches to SOE's papers alone. At the same time, as SOE's footprint is found in ever more areas of British policy, it is clear that the SOE archive is a resource which will attract the attention of more than simply those who specialise in the history of British covert operations. As the thrill of having SOE's files land on our desk gradually wears off, historians, whether military, political or diplomatic, will have to become accustomed to making the 'HS' series a staple hunting ground, much in the same way as the cabinet, prime ministerial, or Foreign Office papers have been used to inform all aspects of historical research on the war since the 1970s.[20]

With this in mind, the collection begins with two essays which are designed to provide a historiographical and administrative context for anyone wishing to work on the SOE papers. The first examines the vicissitudes that befell the SOE archive before it moved to its current resting place in the National Archive. The author, Duncan Stuart, is particularly well equipped to write on this issue. As the last person to occupy the position of 'SOE adviser' in the Foreign and Commonwealth Office, Stuart was responsible for overseeing the transfer of the archive into the public domain. The mantra we instil in our graduate students – 'know your sources' – is especially prescient for those working on the archives of secret agencies. As Richard Aldrich reminds us, while no archive represents an 'analogue of reality', the archives of secret agencies are particularly prone to distortion. The temptation for governments to deliberately subvert the historical record of these organisations through a process of selective archival release, makes it all the more important for historians to appreciate the origins, content and context of the archival material at their disposal.[21] This is especially the case for files relating to SOE. Not only did SOE's staff celebrate 'VE' and 'VJ' Days by incinerating the vast bulk of material in their possession, but by 1946 what remained of SOE's files were turned over to the custody of the SIS, an agency which had, for the best part of five and a half years, been SOE's most implacable domestic opponent. Whether SIS's obedience in complying with Treasury targets for administrative efficiency by butchering the SOE archive were affected by a lingering sense of *Schadenfreude* at their old adversary is a moot point. But, as Stuart's essay explains, the three separate attempts to rationalise and reduce the bulk of SOE's archive were not without result. By the 1970s, no less than 87 per cent of the original archive had been lost to posterity.[22]

The second chapter, a survey of the historical writing on SOE, written by Mark Seaman, has a similar didactic purpose. There can be few secret services as well served by memoir literature as SOE. The outpouring of reminiscences from the 1960s has continued, if in reduced volume, to this day, despite the fact that most of those who served in SOE are long since deceased. Nearly twenty-four years ago, Mark Wheeler calculated that there were somewhere in the order of two hundred books bearing an SOE theme: the number today probably pushes three hundred.[23] Unpublished memoirs and oral history contributions have also increased in number in the past couple of decades, in large measure due to the efforts of the

Imperial War Museum to track down and record the reminiscences of SOE veterans. This project is on-going, and continues to unearth important collections.[24] The haul may well increase if the material assembled by and for SOE's remaining 'official historians' is ever allowed to enter the public domain. The abundance of material has not meant that the writing of SOE's history has been in any way straightforward. The area has attracted more than its fair share of myth- and mischief-makers, and regrettably generated ample opportunity for libel-lawyers to ply their trade. But, as Seaman's chapter shows, there are strong foundations upon which future generations of scholars can build, and plenty of unexplored, or under-explored, aspects of SOE's work awaiting serious scholarly attention.

The next two chapters dwell on one of SOE's most celebrated successes and one of its best-known failures. T. C. Wales' chapter on SOE's Massingham mission builds on the path-breaking work of Jay Jakub on SOE–OSS relations and Martin Thomas on SOE's relations with the French in North Africa.[25] By 1942, special operations had become an inter-allied affair, and while various attempts were made to prevent needless duplication, the field was necessarily a crowded one and rarely free from friction and moments of drama. Yet, as Wales shows, the history of the Massingham mission not only illustrates SOE's capacity to run joint Anglo-American operations – an experience regrettably not always replicated in other theatres – but also in London's willingness to promote the interests of its fledgling American counterpart, the Office of Strategic Services (OSS). By mid-1942, SOE had suffered its own share of grief at the hands of its critics, and one can well imagine the empathy felt for General Donovan, in defending the OSS from the slings and arrows of its many assailers in Washington.[26] 'Offering' Donovan a share in the running of Massingham was perhaps the best way for SOE to support its American ally. Wales' chapter also illustrates the potential for applying social historical approaches in the study of SOE. In illuminating the cultural difficulties that emerged when Britons and Americans were cooped up in a desert training camp for months on end, Wales makes particularly good use of the Imperial War Museum's impressive oral history collection. However, those interested in the cultural or social aspects of SOE's war might find the 12,500 personnel files of SOE officers and agents that have recently been deposited in the National Archive, an equally promising source.[27]

One of the enduring sagas in SOE's history is the question of whether Britain's switch from Mihaliovic to Tito in 1943 was precipitated by the activities of communist sympathizers in SOE's headquarters in Cairo. Although some writers are still attracted to the aura of mystery that surrounds the episode, most scholars explain London's abrupt policy change by reference to the broader strategic considerations facing the British government at the time, and its ability to read German signals traffic which showed the extent to which the partisans' military activity had eclipsed the royalist military effort by early 1943.[28] Rather than revisiting this debate, in Chapter 4, Roderick Bailey asks us to consider how committed communists, such as James Klugmann, a renowned student activist in the 1930s, were recruited into SOE's Cairo headquarters in the first place, and how, once there, they were able to acquire such singularly influential positions within the organisation. James Klugmann's meteoric rise was, Bailey concludes, due to a host of factors, not all of which can be laid on SOE's doorstep. Shear hard work, a quick mind and a gift for difficult languages made Klugmann an indispensable part of Cairo's Yugoslav desk. At the same time, however, as recently declassified Security Service files show, SOE's staff were clearly guilty of complacency, particularly in judging how someone of Klugmann's political conviction could use their position to further their own political agenda. The non-arrival of telegrams from London, detailing the extent of Klugmann's political past, might explain Klugmann's appointment in Cairo, but, as the case of Major Uren – who was caught passing material to the Communist Party of Great Britain – demonstrates, distance alone does not explain SOE's blind spot for communists.[29] SOE was by no means the only agency in the 1940s to take a distinctly cavalier attitude towards its internal security arrangements, but SOE's importance in providing moral and material aid to European resistance movements made it particularly vulnerable to the danger of communist infiltration.

If Wales' investigation into Anglo-American activities in the western Mediterranean paints a favourable picture of inter-allied relations, Chapter 5 by Matthew Jones, which is based on a reading of the OSS records, shows the kind of pressures that can develop when Allies fall out over fundamental issues. In contrast with the western Mediterranean, where Anglo-American relations remained largely amicable, differing attitudes towards how best to respond to the unfolding of events in the eastern Mediterranean saw relations between the two allies quickly sour.[30] The problem was partly historical: Washington was suspicious, and rightly so, about Britain's post-war objectives in the region. It was also, however, partly a result of organisational differences, and an inability to appreciate how each party operated. It was, for instance, difficult for Baker Street to accept OSS's protestations of good faith, when, on being asked to suspend assistance to Mihaliovic's regime, the Americans merely withdrew their special operations agents, and insisted on maintaining a secret intelligence facility with the royalist forces. The tensions that arose between SOE and the OSS over their respective attitudes towards Yugoslavia and Greece are all the more significant given that the absence of Allied ground forces meant that, to a very large extent, Allied policy in the region was dependent on successful collaboration between the two agencies. Jones' study also sheds interesting light on SOE's standing in London. While numerous scholars have emphasised SOE's tetchy relations with the Foreign Office and military establishment, the OSS papers suggest that in American eyes at least, the Foreign Office mandarins were more than capable of upholding the interests, and furthering the ambitions of Britain's secret services.

Taken as a whole, the final five chapters demonstrate the scope of SOE's activities during the war. They address in turn SOE's involvement in 'irregular political warfare', 'psychological warfare', 'economic warfare', and 'financial warfare'. In Chapter 6, I assess SOE's chequered record in the realm of 'irregular political activities'. The political complexion of 'special operations' was widely acknowledged when the possibility of establishing an organisation specialising in 'dirty tricks' was first raised in the summer of 1940. 'Revolutionary warfare', though never properly defined, figured prominently in the thinking of SOE's first minister, Hugh Dalton. Yet while Dalton arguably never lost his faith in the revolutionary potential of the European working class, the aim of fomenting revolution gradually gave way to a more limited conception of political warfare; one which took better account of the political realities in Europe, and sought to complement Britain's broader foreign political objectives towards the Continent. Although SOE enjoyed some noticeable successes, it failed to allay the fears of those who believed its actions would compromise British diplomacy. While much of this work boiled down to political subversion, it also included what Len Scott has recently dubbed 'clandestine diplomacy'; conducting negotiations with foreign elements who, for various reasons, could not be acknowledged by Britain's official ambassadors for fear of compromising British standing abroad.[31]

Saul Kelly's Chapter 7 on the Middle East shows how SOE's political functions dovetailed with its military and propaganda within a single theatre. At an operational level, SOE suffered a 'succession of crises', embarrassing for itself and its staff, and ultimately critical in preventing the organisation from making a significant contribution to Britain's military effort in the region. The responsibility for post-occupational planning, which fell to SOE at an early stage, also proved a mixed blessing. It inevitably led to difficulties with the incumbent regime, and destined SOE to increasing marginalisation within British strategic policy-making once the threat of a German attack had receded. The sense of disillusionment among SOE staff was palpable: one disgruntled officer in the Istanbul station tellingly remarked in late 1942, 'We are wasting money and much hard work begetting and nourishing schemes which are doomed to be stillborn. Personally, I do not wish to spend the remainder of the war in such unfruitful work.'[32] Kelly shows how SOE developed beyond its military remit to develop a position for itself within British diplomacy, by assuming responsibility for the distribution of 'pecuniary inducements' – baksheesh – to those willing to wield influence in Britain's favour. This was not the only region where SOE assumed this role – it was heavily involved in bribery in the Far East and Portugal and contributed to similar schemes in Spain[33] – but, as Kelly shows, in British eyes at least, the political and social fabric of the Middle East made this region particularly well suited to operations of this nature. With hindsight, it could well be argued that SOE's success in this field accounts for the survival of these and other dark arts from SOE's cupboard in British policy in the region into the 1950s and 1960s.[34]

The connection between 'black' propaganda and special operations lay at the heart of SOE from the outset. The administrative arrangement that tried to marry the two concepts within SOE, dividing responsibility between SO1 and SO2, was not, however, without difficulties. The disintegration of the bonds between the two agencies, leading to the creation of an independent Political Warfare Executive (PWE) in September 1941, has been charted elsewhere.[35] SOE's experience with propaganda – and PWE's subsequent work – can hardly be judged a success. Kent Fedorowich's Chapter 8 on the farcical efforts to subvert Italian POWs show why this was the case. Fedorowich gives particular attention to the thorny political problems associated with such activities. With no suitable Italians of their own to enlist in its various campaigns against fascist Italy, Britain was forced to trawl among the large Italian community in the United States. Having recruited Italian-Americans to their cause, however, SOE felt hamstrung in what it could do with them, especially once it became clear that the individuals selected were simply not up to the job. Sending them back home was considered unwise since it threatened to antagonise potential backers in the United States. The entire episode reflects badly on British dabbling in psychological warfare, marred as it was with poor planning and appalling man-management. The potential rewards of mobilising disgruntled, anti-fascist Italian POWs were thus lost and were in many respects a harbinger for the equally disappointing attempts to recruit German POWs, 'Bonzos', for work behind German lines in the final weeks of the war.[36]

David Messenger is one of a small number of scholars who have sought to integrate the work of secret agencies into the history of economic warfare during and after the Second World War.[37] As he shows in his contribution to this collection, SOE's activities in Spain went very much 'against the grain' for an organisation established to create mayhem in occupied Europe. London's determination to avoid any action that might encourage Franco to throw in his lot with the Axis meant that SOE was kept on a very short rein. Yet, like their colleagues in the Middle East, SOE officers in Spain soon found other avenues to develop their talents, in particular, helping to halt the flow of Spanish wolfram crossing the Pyrenees into German hands. Messenger's Chapter 9 highlights the importance of SOE's role in British economic warfare policy, and points the way for future research in this area. It should not surprise us that an agency filled to the brim with men drawn from the commercial or financial world should naturally gravitate towards economic matters, not least since SOE's sister agency, the Ministry of Economic Warfare (MEW), was the principal department responsible for economic policy. SOE's links with the United Kingdom Commercial Corporation, an organisation that was active in most neutral countries during the war, its support for British commercial officials across neutral Europe, and its involvement in tracing Nazi assets fleeing Germany from the summer of 1944 – Operation CODFIELD – all warrant further research. In these activities, SOE's 'H' section, dealing with Iberia, appears to have led the way. As Messenger shows, relations between the representatives of SOE and MEW in Madrid were particularly intimate. Moreover, by late 1944 SOE's successes against Germany's wolfram trade were sufficiently conspicuous that, in this theatre at least, it was able to convince SIS, against its better judgement, to agree to joint intelligence gathering operations against German commercial activities in the peninsular.[38]

The chapters by Wylie, Kelly and Messenger shed considerable new light on SOE's activities in neutral or non-belligerent states. In comparison with its dramatic sabotage operations, or the raising of 'secret armies' in enemy and enemy occupied territory, the work of SOE's stations in these countries might seem rather prosaic. Nevertheless, both the scale of SOE's work and its nature are striking, and while SOE faithfully adhered to a policy of 'no bangs', taken as a whole, its presence in these countries clearly contradicted London's avowed desire to respect the independence, political integrity and neutrality of the countries concerned.

The sensitivity shown towards SOE's various deeds in neutral countries continued after the war. In considering how to respond to the growing clamour for information on SOE's exploits, government officials in the late 1950s were particularly anxious to keep this aspect of SOE's work secret. While there were many 'obvious difficulties and dangers' in publishing 'a full account' of SOE's activities, even more narrowly focused studies would have, it was felt, to be confined in such a way as to avoid any mention of 'operations which had involved violations of neutrality'. The other area of activity deemed too sensitive to divulge in an official history, even tacitly, was SOE's financial dealings.[39] The most celebrated of these was Walter Fletcher's extraordinarily profitable transactions with nationalist warlords in China: 'no C.B.E.', Bickham Sweet-Escott wryly remarked, 'was better earned than Walter Fletcher's'.[40] However, as Chris Murphy's Chapter 10 shows, Fletcher's antics were only one aspect, if a large one, of SOE's financial dealings during the war. Starting in mid-1942, SOE's Finance Section, under John Venner, assumed an increasingly important role in providing the British government with supplies of foreign currencies bought, for the most part, on black markets in Tangiers, Lisbon and Stockholm. Murphy shows how what began as a 'side-line' developed into a core part of SOE's work. These activities were not only valuable in themselves, and allowed SOE to end the war in profit, but were also invaluable in helping SOE 'pay its way' in Whitehall. This was no more so than in the winter of 1943/44, when SOE's many critics came close to forcing the disbandment of SOE altogether, in the wake of revelations about SOE's appalling security lapses in running agents into the Low Countries the previous year. SOE's success in turning its hand to financial affairs might also illustrate a peculiar strength of the organisation, whose staff, drawn for the most part from the City, professions and business world, showed themselves enormously adept in overcoming challenges and responding to new needs and new opportunities as they arose.[41]

Assessments of SOE's record have tended, naturally enough, to focus on its contribution to the major war theatres, where its activities, especially in the last years of the war, had a direct influence on the course of military operations.[42] Outside these areas, there has been a tendency for commentators to belittle, or even disparage, SOE's work. The organisation is frequently castigated for its 'amateurishness', its petty jealousies, its squandering or misuse of resources and its unerring knack of getting people's backs up. In this respect, it is worth recalling the caustic remarks of Churchill's intelligence chieftain, Desmond Morton, who informed Sir Frank Nelson, SOE's director general, in early 1941 that 'the Prime Minister hated Dalton, hated Jebb, hated [Nelson], hated the entire Organisation and everybody in it, and that it was only through [his] efforts . . . that it had been allowed to continue as long as it had'.[43] Yet, the amateurishness for which SOE was routinely maligned had probably as much to do with any innate, or institutionalised incompetence, as with the legendary informality of the organisation and the self-proclaimed 'revolutionary' nature of the warfare it espoused. SOE doubtless suffered more than its fair share of failure, but its record was on the whole little better, and certainly not much worse, than the other secret agencies that prowled the corridors of wartime Whitehall, whose misdemeanours and mistakes remain hidden from view for wont of adequate documentation.[44] The chapters in this collection depict an organisation capable of operating in a wide variety of different contexts. Its methods went beyond the traditional realms of irregular warfare and embraced a raft of operations whose principal focus was political, economic, financial or even psychological. While clearly SOE was unable to demonstrate a proficiency in all of these areas, all of the time, in mastering these arts, it showed itself very much in tune with the context of 'total war' into which it was born. In SOE, 'special operations' became more than simply an adjunct to Britain's military operations, but instead came to embody a distinctly 'modern' approach to secret service activity, an approach which remains as central to a state's politico-military armoury today as it did sixty years ago.

Notes

1   I am grateful to Professor M. R. D. Foot for confirming these details. For SOE's use of Lysanders, see Hugh Verity, *We Landed by Moonlight* (London, 1978) and David Oliver, *Airborne Espionage: International Special Duties Operations in the World Wars* (Stroud, 2005). The photographs can be viewed at the Australian War Memorial website (see especially, Negative Number P022814.012).

2   The rarity of this procedure can be gauged from M. R. D. Foot's remark: 'Agents only jump from Lysanders in fiction.' M. R. D. Foot, *SOE: An Outline History of the Special Operations Executive 1940–1946* (London, 1984), p. 136.

3   For Japanese attitudes towards surrender and captivity, see Ulrich Straus, *The Anguish of Surrender: Japanese POWs of World War II* (Seattle, 2003).

4   For British and American covert operations in the region at this time, see Richard J. Aldrich, *Intelligence and the War against Japan: Britain, America and the Politics of Secret Service* (Cambridge, 2000), pp. 188–213, 340–357, and E. Bruce Reynolds, *Thailand's Secret War: The Free Thai, OSS, and SOE during World War II* (Cambridge, 2005).

5   'Britain's Intelligence Services: Cats' Eyes in the Dark', *The Economist*, 19 March 2005, p. 34.

6   These would include *inter alia* David Stafford, *Secret Agent: The True Story of the Special Operations Executive* (London, 2002), and Ian Dear, *Sabotage and Subversion: The SOE and OSS at War* (London, 1996).

7   Nor are these young scholars alone: see the forthcoming work of Ian Hetherington (de Montfort), Alexandra Luce (Cambridge), Suzanne Hall (Nottingham) and Pia Molander (Exeter).

8   Stafford, *Secret Agent*, Mark Seaman, *The Bravest of the Brave: The True Story of Wing Commander "Tommy" Yeo-Thomas, SOE, Secret Agent, Codename "White Rabbit"* (London, 1997), and E. D. R. Harrison, 'British Subversion in French East Africa, 1941–42: SOE's Todd Mission', *English Historical Review* 114: 456 (April 1999): 339–369; 'The British Special Operations Executive and Poland', *The Historical Journal* 43(4) (2000): 1071–1091.

9   Mark Wheeler, 'The SOE Phenomenon', *Journal of Contemporary History* 16 (1981): 513–519.

10 W. J. M. Mackenzie, *The Secret History of SOE: The Special Operations Executive, 1940–1945* (London, 2000).

11 See Christopher J. Murphy, 'The Origins of SOE in France', *The Historical Journal* 46/4 (2003): 935–952, Richard J. Aldrich, 'Policing the Past: Official History, Secrecy and British Intelligence since 1945', *English Historical Review* 119 (2004): 954–964. The problem was not simply one of how to deal with the existence of Britain's secret organisations. See David J. Reynolds, *In Command of History: Churchill Fighting and Writing the Second World War* (London, 2004), pp. 23–35.

12 Ernest May, 'On Writing Contemporary International History', *Diplomatic History* 8 (1984): 103–113.

13 Charles Cruickshank, *SOE in the Far East* (London, 1983); Charles Cruickshank, *SOE in Scandinavia* (London, 1986).

14 M. R. D. Foot, *SOE in France: An Account of the Work of the British Special Operations Executive in France, 1940–1944* (London, 1966, with new revised edition, 2004). M. R. D. Foot, *SOE in the Low Countries* (London, 2001). We are told that Ian Wood's history of Italy and Mark Wheeler's history of Yugoslavia are some way off.

15 See F. H. Hinsley *et al.*, *British Intelligence in the Second World War*, vols 1–3 (London, 1979–1988). For MI9, the escape and evasion organisation, see M. R. D. Foot and J. M. Langley, *MI9: Escape and Evasion* (Boston, 1980), for strategic deception, Roger Hesketh, *Fortitude: The D-Day Deception Campaign* (London, 2000) and Michael Howard, *British Intelligence in the Second World War*, vol. 5 *Strategic Deception* (Cambridge, 1990), and for PWE, David Garnett, *The Secret History of PWE: The Political Warfare Executive* (London, 2002).

16 Sir Edward Hale (Cabinet Office, Historical Section) to Burke St J. Trend (Treasury), 10 June 1959. The National Archive, Public Record Office (hereafter PRO) T220/1388.

17 St Ermin's Press should be applauded for publishing an unabridged text.

18 For a more comprehensive account of SOE's war, readers should consult Mackenzie, *Secret History of SOE*, M. R. D. Foot's *SOE: An Outline History*, David Stafford's *Britain and European Resistance. 1940–1945: A Survey of Special Operations Executive with Documents* (London and Toronto, 1980), whose penetrating insights of the organisation and its place in British strategy have more than stood the test of time, Nigel West's *Secret War: The Story of SOE, Britain's Wartime Sabotage Organisation* (London, 1992), or the proceedings of a conference on SOE hosted by the Imperial War Museum and scheduled for publication in the near future: Mark Seaman (ed.), *SOE: A New Instrument of War* (London, 2005).

19 In the Far East, SOE personnel outnumbered SIS by ten to one.

20 A total of 28,090 SOE records were ordered by readers at the PRO between 1999 and 2004, representing 0.87 per cent of the total number of ordered over this six-year period. The numbers per annum were 1999, 4,326; 2000, 5,544; 2001, 3,838; 2002, 5,078; 2003, 5,035; 2004, 4,269. Of these, HS6, Western Europe, was the most frequently requested series (with 5,488 orders), however, HS4, Eastern Europe (3,555), HS5, the Balkans (4,252), HS7, war diaries (3,988) and HS8, headquarters (3,381) were also popular, and HS1, Far East (1,321), HS2, Scandinavia (1,878) and HS3, Africa and the Middle East (1,601) attracted significant numbers. HS11–20 were only released in late 2004. My thanks to Howard Davies of the Records Management Department at the National Archive for providing this information.

21 For Aldrich's thoughts on 'historians of secret service and their enemies', see Richard J. Aldrich, *The Hidden Hand: Britain, America and Cold War Secret Intelligence* (London, 2001), pp. 1–16.

22 One can only guess at whether SIS's own wartime archive suffered the same fate.

23 Mark Wheeler, 'The SOE Phenomenon', *Journal of Contemporary History* 16 (1981): 513–519.

24 The IWM's catalogue, *Special Operations Executive: Catalogue of Oral History Recordings* (London, 1998), though useful, should not be taken as a complete inventory of the museum's holdings.

25 Jay Jakub, *Spies and Saboteurs: Anglo-American Collaboration and Rivalry in Human Intelligence and Special Operations, 1940–1945* (London, 1999); Martin Thomas, 'The Massingham Mission: SOE in French North Africa, 1941–1944', *Intelligence & National Security* 11/4 (1996): 696–721.

26 For a perceptive new study, see Christof Mauch, *The Shadow War Against Hitler: The Covert Operations of America's Wartime Secret Intelligence Service* (New York, 2003).

27   SOE Personnel Files are filed in PRO HS9.

28   See *inter alia*, Ralph Bennett, Sir William Deakin, Sir David Hunt, Sir Peter Wilkinson, 'Mihailovic and Tito', *Intelligence & National Security* 10/3 (1995): 526–528, Heather Williams, *The Special Operations Executive (SOE) and Yugoslavia, 1941–5* (London, 2002), and Sebastian Ritchie, *Our Man in Yugoslavia* (London, 2004).

29   See Christopher Andrew and Oleg Gordievsky, *KGB: The Inside Story of its Foreign Operations from Lenin to Gorbachev* (London, 1990), p. 306.

30   For a comparison between resistance movements in the Mediterranean see Tony Judt (ed.), *Resistance and Revolution in Mediterranean Europe 1939–1948* (London, 1989).

31   For a stimulating study of the concept of clandestine diplomacy, see Len Scott, 'Secret Intelligence, Covert Action and Clandestine Diplomacy', in L. V. Scott and P. D. Jackson (eds), *Understanding Intelligence in the Twenty-First Century: Journeys in Shadows* (London, 2004), pp. 162–179.

32   Minute by 'DH44', 1 Dec. 1942, PRO HS3/222.

33   For Spain, see Denis Smyth, 'Les Chevaliers de Saint-George: la Grande-Bretagne et la corruption des généraux espagnols (1940–1942)', *Guerres mondiales et conflits contemporains* 162 (1991): 29–54, and for Portugal, see Neville Wylie, '"An Amateur Learns his Job?" Special Operations Executive in Portugal, 1940–1942', *Journal of Contemporary History* 36/3 (2001): 455–571.

34   See Aldrich, *The Hidden Hand*, p. 76. For a particularly graphic illustration of this see, Matthew Jones, 'The "Preferred Plan": The Anglo-American Working Group Report on Covert Action in Syria, 1957', *Intelligence & National Security* 19/3 (2004): 401–415; Clive Jones, *Britain and the Yemen Civil War, 1962–1965: Ministers, Mercenaries and Mandarins – Foreign Policy and the Limits of Covert Action* (Brighton, 2004).

35   See most recently Garnett, *Secret History of PWE*, and Michael Stenton, *Radio London and Resistance in Occupied Europe* (Oxford, 2000).

36   Mackenzie, *Secret History*, p. 712. See also AD/X1 to D/CE 12 Dec. 1944, PRO HS8/883.

37   See David Messenger, 'Fighting for Relevance: Economic Intelligence and Special Operations Executive in Spain, 1943–1945', *Intelligence & National Security* 15/3 (2000): 33–54.

38   For these arrangements, see minutes of inter-departmental meeting, 17 Oct. 1944, PRO HS8/355.

39   Memo, 'Official History of SOE: Further Report by a Working Party, Secret', 22 May 1959, PRO T220/1388.

40   Bickham Sweet-Escott, *Baker Street Irregular* (London, 1965), p. 254. See Robert Bickers, 'The Business of a Secret War: Operation "Remorse" and SOE Salesmanship in Wartime China', *Intelligence & National Security* 16/4 (2001): 11–36.

41   This flexibility is no better illustrated than in SOE's work on behalf of prisoners of war: see Suzanne Hall, 'The Politics of Prisoner of War Recovery: SOE and the Burma-Thailand Railway during World War II', *Intelligence & National Security* 17/2 (2002): 51–80.

42   See, for instance, M. R. D. Foot, 'Was SOE Any Good?', *Journal of Contemporary History* 16/1 (1981): 167–181.

43   Memo by Sir Frank Nelson (CD) 17 Feb. 1941, PRO HS6/309 SOE France No. 1, Vol. 2. I am indebted to David Stafford for drawing this document to my attention.

44   There is more than a suspicion that the gusto with which SOE's critics routinely recited its shortcomings reflected institutional pique at the emergence of a new and potent agency, and a desire to mask their own palpable shortcomings and inability to change with the times.

1 'Of historical interest only'

The origins and vicissitudes of the SOE Archive

Duncan Stuart

The two most authoritative descriptions by historians of the condition of the SOE Archive as they found it at different dates are those of William Mackenzie in the Preface to his History of SOE, written for the Cabinet Office in 1948, and of Michael Foot in his Appendix on Sources (A (i)) to *SOE in France*, published in 1966.[1] Both are accurate within the limits of contemporary security inhibitions. The latter is more informative in its detail. But I quote the former for its succinctness:

> This material is in great confusion. Partly through inexperience, partly for reasons of security, SOE began life without a central registry or departmental filing system. Each branch kept its own papers on its own system, from the Minister down to the sub-sections of the Country Sections; if a paper existed in a single copy, it might come to rest anywhere in this hierarchy of separate archives. The original confusion was made worse because in 1945, when the end was in sight, SOE made a resolute attempt to impose on the existing chaos a proper system of departmental filing by subject. This was an immense task which was scarcely begun when the department officially came to an end: the registry staff was kept in being for some time, but the work was eventually stopped on grounds of economy when it was about a quarter done. One has therefore to cope with two superimposed systems of filing, both radically imperfect.[2]

These two descriptions are essentially confirmed by a third, the report on the Archive written in late 1974 by a professional archivist from the PRO, Bernard Townshend, after he had spent five years reorganising the files into their present form: the third superimposed system. When he started work, he found that the Archive consisted of

> the surviving files of a collection of files of which we have documentary evidence that at least 87% were destroyed in London between 1945 and 1950. They are in a confused state as a result of a number of ill-conceived attempts at their reorganisation by, for the most part, inexperienced archival staff with neither the time nor the knowledge to successfully complete the task . . . The

only list of SOE files available in January 1970 was that contained in the SOE Subject File Index, a list which did no more than describe the files by the 1945 subject headings.[3]

If the processes which produced this 'confused state' were lamentable, they are not hard to understand. From its inception, SOE was a poor record-keeping organisation by the standards of normal government departments. It inherited the administrative and operational attitudes of its predecessors, Section D of the Secret Intelligence Service (SIS) and the War Office's Department MI(R). Sections worked independently and were led by action-orientated individualists with a keen appreciation of the operational needs for close control and restrictive security but little concern for filing systems. There was, initially at least, no infrastructure of experienced bureaucrats, and support staff were at a premium. And the bugles were urgently sounding. As Foot puts it: 'security married with haste to beget filing by Country Sections or even smaller sub-divisions, who all kept their papers in separate places, classified on individual plans'.[4] In the judgement of a later archivist, 'some of these [filing systems] were good, some were appallingly bad'.[5]

There were also institutional biases, common to most secret services, against more than minimal record keeping and in favour of the destruction of all papers judged operationally inessential. SOE's security regulations were quite explicit on these points[6] and, among other SOE veteran writers, Sir Douglas Dodds-Parker recalls them in his *Setting Europe Ablaze*, where he writes of the Massingham (Algiers) Mission: 'by standing orders and sensible self-protection as our base was on a deserted sea-shore, records were minimal and destroyed as long as they were no longer of immediate use'.[7] I have sometimes suspected that a degree of prudent self-censorship may have prevented details of some more sensitive operations from being committed to paper at all.

In the summer of 1944, the leadership of SOE began seriously to consider what was likely to happen to the Service at the end of the War and how best to set about preserving its experience in forms which might be of use in future conflicts. In mid-August 1944, General Gubbins' Deputy and Director of Staff Duties and Administration, M. P. Murray (D/CD),[8] issued an instruction to all Directors, Regional Heads, Section Heads and Heads of Country Establishments to conduct a survey of documents 'so as to decide what is to be retained permanently, what can be given a more limited "life", and what can be moved immediately to a Central Archives Section'.[9] A follow-up circular dated 19 August 1944 defined the categories into which documents for retention or destruction should be placed according to the degree of their historical significance or future utility. It went on to describe how the survey should be conducted, acknowledging that it would be 'a long and tedious occupation for all concerned'.[10]

On 29 August 1944, the SOE Council considered a paper by Col. Dick Barry (CD/S), which outlined proposals for the preparation of a Handbook of SOE Work, or 'Manual of Subversive Warfare', and a History of SOE. In discussion, Gubbins emphasised that distinctions should be made between the SOE Handbook, the Official History and 'any history which might be written for public consumption', giving as an example of the latter 'the story of the French Resistance'.[11] There was further discussion of all these initiatives in subsequent Council meetings.

The survey of documents continued into the autumn of 1944 and, in parallel, sections were winding up and preparing material for the Handbook and for their Section Histories. The requirements of the sections and of the future Central Archives Section were thus to some extent in conflict: both presupposed use of the same documents. So progress towards the actual creation of the Central Archives Section was not rapid.[12]

Nevertheless, on 25 October 1944, in a letter to Brig. Latham of the War Cabinet Offices, Murray was able to outline the steps already taken and those planned 'to centralise our historical records and to ensure that, after use for current operational and security purposes, they are available for research and are then finally housed in proper conditions'. He envisaged that, after the operational sections had sorted their material and 'written up certain portions of it before memories fade', the records would gradually be centralised and would then be indexed to help a future official historian. Simultaneously, syllabuses for future training purposes would be laid down and material in the Handbook and the History would be cross-referenced for the use of future instructors. He did, however, admit that the records were not yet in a convenient form for an external historian, adding 'we are indeed less conversant with them ourselves than we would like to be. We are also uncertain as to what will be destroyed'; and that 'the ultimate disposal of the records depends to some extent on the future of this organisation'.[13]

While preparatory work continued on all these fronts, minds and responsibilities became clearer as the nature and size of the problems to be faced became more apparent.[14] In January 1945, the Central Archives Section was launched with an initial staff of six under S/Officer Jean Woollaston (C/A). Its mandate was to create a Central Archive 'for the needs of any future SOE and the official Historians'. This was to be achieved by putting all SOE paper thought worth keeping into a central system of filing, indexed and designed to satisfy any requirement laid on it.

The new filing system was designed from the top down. It required the physical transfer of papers from their existing files to fresh ones newly specified by deduction from general SOE experience. The papers were to be carefully studied by readers and then marked to be sorted first by countries; next to one of forty main subject headings; and finally to specific subjects. Each paper was to be marked with a three-figure reference (e.g., 3/210/11 = France/Air Operations, Dropping/Successful) which established its place in the new filing universe, but provided no indication of its provenance. Among the, presumably unintended, consequences of this reorganisation was that the bulk of the Directorate files disappeared altogether, as also did most of those of the Specialist Sections; and there remained a great number of files containing material for which no subject heading had been allotted.

The method was reasonably sound, if over-systematic and over-ambitious: it demanded a large staff and a longish period of time before results became apparent. In its first nine months, the staff of the Section grew from six to nearly sixty. At first, papers came in from the Country Sections rather slowly, since they were finishing their own histories. But, towards the end of 1945, with the end of the war in Europe followed by that in the Far East and the consequent rapid disbandment of SOE, the Section began to diminish in size (to thirty staff by the end of December 1945), while the volume of paper handed to it greatly increased.

As SOE's overseas missions were about to be closed, instructions were issued for all their surviving papers to be sent home after first being weeded of ephemeral material. Townshend later commented: 'It is to be feared that some officers took advantage of the instructions to dispose of material which they thought would prove unduly sensitive should their contents ever be disclosed.'[15] Whatever the truth of this unsupported comment, there were known end-of-war bonfires of virtually all the records of the British Security Organisation in New York (carried out at Camp X in Canada) and of the Records of the Special Training Schools in the UK. There were certainly others both in the UK and overseas.

Thoughts of incendiarism lead naturally to the far-famed fire at Baker Street. There seem to be no surviving contemporary documents about this. Townshend wrote in 1974 that it 'destroyed an unknown quantity of records the subject of which it has been impossible to trace . . . some maintain that only finance files were destroyed (and certainly these are conspicuous by their absence)' but he added that Col. H.B. Perkins, the former Head of the Polish Section, complained after the war that 'a great number of my records have been destroyed by fire'.[16]

One of my predecessors as SOE Adviser said that he had been told that the fire started in a waste-paper basket in the Belgian Section. Michael Foot reported that, while working on his history of SOE in the Low Countries, he found some Belgian papers charred at the edges. Some records of First Aid Nursing Yeomanry (FANY) staff now in FANY H.Q. are similarly singed. Norman Mott, Head of the SOE Liquidation Section in Baker Street, known as MO1SP, in a letter dated 12 April 1946 on a naturalisation case, wrote: 'unfortunately, the greater part of my papers dealing with naturalization cases were burnt up in a fire which we had in the office here a few weeks ago . . .'.[17]

Ten years later, Mott recalled that the fire had broken out in February 1946 in his offices on the top floor of Baker Street

> in a stationery store situated between my own office and the remainder of the wing which was occupied by the F.A.N.Y. Administration Section. The whole floor was practically gutted and a large proportion of the F.A.N.Y. records were destroyed together with the entire contents of my own office where I was holding a considerable number of operational files. Some of the latter related to the activities in the field of SOE F.A.N.Y agents. In addition, all the handing-over briefs from the SOE Country Sections were destroyed as well as a good deal of material relating to investigations into blown *réseaux*.[18]

This is the most detailed and authoritative statement I have found of what occurred. It confirms that the fire was seriously destructive but not as all-consuming as its mythology suggests.

There were earlier losses too. In early and mid-1945, the staff of the Central Archives Section was augmented by some young officers just returned from abroad and awaiting out-posting from SOE. There is reliable anecdotal evidence that not all of these attended to their duties with appropriate diligence. Two of them, indeed, competed in joyously tossing whole files, unread, into a waste-bin situated between them.[19]

By the end of 1945, the twin pressures of reducing staff and increasing accession of material had slowed progress in reading and re-filing papers. Less than half the papers held by the Central Archives Section had been processed, but it was still hoped that the task could be finished by August 1946.

When SOE was formally terminated in January 1946, various relic organs continued to carry out their respective functions for several months. Among these were the Liquidation Section, the War Diary Section and the renamed Special Operations (SO) Archives Section, all now paid for out of the SIS budget.

In a review dated 25 April 1946,[20] the Head of the SO Archives Section reported that it now consisted of only four officers and eighteen secretaries and clerks and that its holdings were as follows:

steel filing cabinets	214
steel cupboards	81
wall safes	7
no. of files approx.	66,000
total weight of paper approx.	30 tons

Of these, for example, the French files made up fifteen cabinets. Two more tons of paper were expected from the Far East and another seven cabinets from the Liquidation Section.

Meanwhile, the nature of the SO Archives Section's work had begun to change. One of its secondary functions, to answer enquiries about SOE matters, had begun to assume major importance. Requests were increasing from various government departments for information relevant to claims, to war crimes, to security investigations, etc., and were averaging about twenty-five a week.

This all militated against the section completing its task by August 1946. So it was proposed to change its method of work to a less thorough but more expeditious one: both sorted and unsorted papers were now to be put roughly into the filing system by country without being read first. Once this had been done, the papers would be 'looked through with some care, anything unnecessary being destroyed, then indexed and made to function as precisely as possible within the Central Filing System'. This method, it was stated, 'will not be as meticulously accurate as the previous method of working but . . . it will suffice and with good indexing be a workable reference library . . . it will certainly prove quicker and more expedient in answering the present day to day enquiries'.

The questions of defining the future utility of the material in the Archive and of the various handbooks and histories which were still in preparation were also addressed in early 1946 by an SIS officer.[21] He concluded that Mackenzie's work on the Official History, which he hoped to have in final draft by the autumn of 1947, must clearly continue. Mackenzie himself thought that he would continue to need support from the SO Archives Section until the end of 1948. It was also proposed that the compilation of the handbooks, estimated still to need another year's work by one person, should continue. Two further staff should be allocated to it and the work be completed within three months.

The War Diary, however, on which one Major, eight other officers and six secretaries were engaged and which was 'exceedingly behindhand', was judged to be without real value. It was described as 'purely academical past history'.[22] Work on it should cease. So should work by individual officers on books such as those on 'Agent Technique' (Col. Woolrych) and 'Special Duties Operations in Europe' (Jean Woollaston). Books already written should be held in the SIS Library.

By mid-1946, plans were being made for the eventual move of the SO Archives Section to an SIS building, but it was seen as necessary, before this could take place, further to reduce the amount of paper held. The Archivist was therefore instructed to step up the rate of weeding and destruction and to report progress monthly. In the event, between August 1946 and the end of May 1947, holdings were reduced to 169 filing cabinets, nine cupboards of files and four cupboards of card indexes.

Among the papers destroyed in this period, it is worth noting the following total categories and amounts (expressed in filing cabinets or equivalent):[23]

Stores and Supplies		20
Middle East		20
Signals and Telegrams		14
Training		14
Admin and Organisation		11
Far East		9
War Diary		9
French		7
European Countries General		6
Scandinavian		3
Central Europe, Italian	each	2
Belgian, Dutch	each	1

It is not recorded how carefully or systematically the weeding process was conducted but the Archives Section was under constant pressure to meet the move deadline and judgement was apparently sacrificed to speed. It was estimated in late 1949 that, overall, 'something like 100 tons of material was destroyed, . . . more by destruction of categories of material than by removal of redundant material from individual files'.[24] The bald lists on file of the categories destroyed seem to bear this out.

With the winding-up of the SOE Liquidation Section in the late 1940s, the files it had kept for its own use passed, unweeded, to the SO Archives Section.

These comprised some finance, personnel, security and investigations papers. No record remains of their precise volume, but that it was not inconsiderable, even after the fire, can be inferred from some figures which appear in a review of early 1950: '36 4-drawer cabinets of AG or MO1SP material';'there is also MO1SP material in some of the 9 cupboards in room . . .'. In a long list of other unweeded files, there were still '14 4-drawer filing cabinets and 17 cupboards of finance records' and '65 <u>unopened</u> crates and tin boxes'.[25]

This review of early 1950 was conducted by an SIS officer concerned with War Planning following a 'fateful meeting . . . at which it was discovered that practically no progress at all had been made in weeding out SOE files in the last 18 months'.[26] Its aim was to determine what of the material remaining in the Archive should be kept, and for what purposes, and what should be passed to other departments. The introductory paragraphs of the reviewer's report are instructive, containing as they do a good measure of respect for the Archive with a barely audible undertone of despair:

> So wide was the range of subjects covered by SOE and, in consequence, by the Archives, that it is physically impossible for one person to make a comprehensive list of what should be retained and what should be destroyed. One of the contributory factors is the absence of any complete catalogue of file contents, i.e., although there is a file classification system, very few files contain a list of the documents which are in them. This means that <u>if the job of screening is to be done properly, every file must be read through carefully from cover to cover.</u>
>
> The Archives represent the only material available on what was in fact a new form of warfare, or, as it was sometimes described, 'The Fourth Arm'. For this reason, if for no other, one is chary of advising wholesale destruction even though it is unlikely that Special Operations in a future War will be waged on similar lines . . .
>
> Without the availability of something like the SOE Archives, in some manageable and accessible form, much time is liable to be wasted by inexperienced personnel who make mistakes which others made before and from which mistakes those others learnt.

The reviewer went on to list the value of the Archives under the following headings:

> **Historical**. Observations on the value of the Archive made by Mackenzie in the preface to his History were cited as a caution against destruction without consultation with other Departments and he was credited with having marked files and papers with the now familiar yellow stickers reading 'Historical Document. Permanent Preservation'. [Michael Foot later added more of these.]
>
> **Planning**. 'There are innumerable examples of plans prepared to meet various situations, which both in form and content serve as admirable guides to the preparation of similar plans . . .'

Background material. '[E]xtremely useful and readable reports covering almost every type of SO operation in almost every country in the world where SO was carried out, which provide most useful local colour and give non SO experienced personnel the "feel" of Special Operations . . .'.

Names. 'of people who worked in or for SOE, or with whom SOE had contacts in foreign countries . . .'.

Intelligence. While most of the reports on economic subjects had already been extracted for use elsewhere, there was much potentially useful topographical material and reports on minorities, populations, dropping zones, landing grounds, beaches, etc., much of which did not exist elsewhere.

Casework. Files existed relevant to cases for compensation, to security investigations, etc., to which reference would no doubt have to be made for 'some considerable time . . . though we may wish to put an end to such problems . . .'.

Histories. There were useful summary Histories of SOE's individual Sections and Branches.

The reviewer outlined the system of file classification which had been adopted and pointed out its failings, adding that there were still 'a large number of crates containing papers from the Middle and Far East which have never been opened'. He went on to make proposals for continuing the work of the Archives Section, both of destroying unnecessary papers and of classifying and carding useful ones. His review gave rise to a good deal of internal minuting which, among other things, mentioned that there were now only two staff in the Section, who had been prevented from carrying out their primary function of weeding and classifying since they were 'entirely occupied in answering enquiries and requests for trace'. It was duly recommended that there should be 'maximum possible destruction and reduction' of material in unwanted categories but that increased effort should be allocated to the creation of an index of SOE agents, of whom 40,000 were estimated to be on record, only some 4,000 of whom were 'sufficiently trained and experienced to be of possible use in a future war'. In this connection, it was recorded that the archives still held twenty-four volumes of SOE training reports arranged alphabetically 'in extremely good order', the first volume of which contained reports of 175 agents of seventeen different nationalities. Hence, presumably, the estimate of 4,000 'sufficiently trained' ones.[27]

It has not been possible to locate more than a few scattered references to policy and practice on the Archives during the twenty years between 1950 and 1970. From these, however, it is clear that weeding continued, exacerbated by problems of accommodation. ('The object of weeding is to get rid of unwanted paper and to delete the vast number of "dead wood" names at present carded'; 'cut away dead wood and clear cellars of unwanted paper' – July 1957).[28] But so did the carding and organising of what remained.

During the 1950s, pressure grew from former members of SOE and other authors for information from official records to help with books they wanted to write. This pressure was at first firmly resisted on security grounds. But the determined campaign by Miss (later Dame) Irene Ward, waged both in and out of Parliament, for the release of SOE records, first for her own book *F.A.N.Y. Invicta* and then for an official history of SOE, and publicity generated by other writers gradually wore down official obduracy.[29]

One result was the appointment as the first SOE Adviser of Lt. Col. Eddie Boxshall, a former SOE officer, in early 1959 'to advise and assist enquirers on matters connected with the wartime operations of SOE and to deal with questions regarding the release of information on them'.[30] Boxshall's (unpublished) instructions were precise and restrictive in respect of the security limitations placed upon him and it thus seemed to some that his main function was to ensure that as little information as possible was given out.

The other result was the appointment in 1960 of Michael Foot to write the first public history of SOE's operations in France. Following the publication of *SOE in France* in 1966, the trend towards greater openness persisted. More official histories were duly written and successive SOE Advisers were able to be increasingly forthcoming to authors, researchers and the media. Eventually, following the Waldegrave Initiative, it was agreed that the Archive could be released to the PRO.[31]

To return to what I wrote above: the SOE Archive which has been released is in a form which was the result of five years of admirably industrious and professional work by Bernard Townshend. He was appointed with the brief 'to put into the existing files as much order as is still possible' and 'to smooth the path of a tentative [*sic*] historian'. This brief, as he himself put it:

> posed a most perplexing problem which was in no way eased by the knowledge that work on the compilation of a card index to personnel was already well under way. The existence of this vast (albeit uncompleted) index meant that little, if any, alteration could be made to the existing file order. The difficulty therefore lay not in devising a system which could be regarded as reasonably correct but in finding one which would prove the least incorrect.[32]

Townshend went on to list the problems and weaknesses of the Archive which he had found and wherever possible rectified:

a. Whereas duplicated material and carbon copies abound, very few original papers have survived. This is remarkable in that most SOE correspondence was internal.

b. A very large proportion of the files were not in chronological order.

c. Enclosures had been removed from covering letters and filed by date. A great number of these enclosures are now untraceable.

d. Files had been added to various series without first ascertaining whether copies already existed elsewhere in a more logical home.

e.   Lists had been altered without all interested parties being notified.

f.   Papers had been removed from files for reference purposes.

g.   Files had been reorganised (some many times) within the same numerical sequence.

h.   Papers from other departmental files had been collated within SOE files.

i.   A great many papers refer to the activities of secret services other than SOE.

j.   Files quoted in the SOE Histories and War Diaries had either been destroyed or dispersed. Most quoted references can no longer be traced.

k.   'Historical Document' labels appear to have been used indiscriminately. (On one file a carbon copy had been granted a label while its signed original had been ignored.)

l.   A number of files have been mutilated by inked marginal notes, annotations and underlinings.

m.   Flammable material had been used for the protection of papers in an advanced state of deterioration.[33]

It is not useful to give a detailed description of the way in which Townshend reorganised the Archive. It is now in the National Archives so anyone who is interested can easily discover the results. The prime categorisation is geographical, by region and country. Within countries, the files are grouped in fairly coherent runs, usually beginning with the more general policy files, working through specific operations and reports and on to lists of personnel and awards. The papers in each run are in (sometimes rough) date order. In addition, there are various categories of more general files (e.g., Headquarters files, Lord Selborne's papers), some specialist files (e.g., Air, Naval, Security, Liquidation) and the Section Histories, War Diaries and Symbols Lists. There are also some 12,500 surviving Personal Files of SOE staff and agents, which contain mainly administrative papers but also occasionally and unpredictably copies of operational papers, some of which are to be found nowhere else.

Townshend ended his report by expressing his thanks for having been granted 'the opportunity to have taken up what must surely prove to be the most challenging task of my career'. It is, on the contrary, we who owe him a great debt of gratitude for rationalising the SOE Archive. The damage done to it occurred well before his time – and I have shown how enormous that damage was over the years. The tale is a sad one for historians. But they may conclude from the reasonably complete and coherent picture of SOE and its operations which has survived successive waves of destruction that the process was not entirely ill-judged. And they should remember that, in the British secret services, until relatively recently, records were regarded primarily as an aid to operations and of little interest from any other point of view.

Which is why I took the title of this article from a note marked on a file discovered by one of my predecessors as SOE Adviser: 'Of Historical Interest Only'.

Notes

1 M. R. D. Foot, *SOE in France: An Account of the Work of the British Special Operations Executive in France, 1940–1944* (London, 1966, with new revised edition, 2004).

2 W. J. M. Mackenzie, *The Secret History of SOE* (London, 2000), p. xxvii.

3 C. B. Townshend's report of 17 Dec. 1974, held by the Secret Intelligence Service (SIS).

4 Foot, *SOE in France*, p. 449.

5 The National Archives, United Kingdom, Public Record Office (hereafter PRO) HS8/443 (retained by Department) Archivist's report of 25 Apr. 1946.

6 Instructions of Nov. 1941, PRO HS8/866.

7 Sir Douglas Dodds-Parker, *Setting Europe Ablaze* (Windlesham, 1983), p. 163.

8 The SOE system of symbols to designate posts in the organisation and/or the staff who held them was idiosyncratic and inconsistent but pragmatic. It was born of both SIS and military staff practice. A few symbols were directly inherited from Section D of SIS. Thus CD for the Chief of SOE was analogous to 'C' for the Chief of SIS plus D for D Section. CD's closest staff usually had symbols which indicated either their status (V/CD for Vice, D/CD for Deputy) and/ or their function (D/FIN for Director of Finance, CD/S for Chief Staff Officer). Some symbols were simply acronyms for job titles (C/A for Head of Central Archives, A/DN for Assistant Director Naval); some deliberately obscured geographical responsibilities (X for Germany, H for Iberia, T for Belgium) but others revealed them (SN for Scandinavia/Norway and F for the French Section, some members of which had symbols which incorporated their initials: FB for Nicholas Bodington, FV for Vera Atkins, FM for Gerry Morel). Symbols for staff and agents overseas were always obscurantist (BB 100 for the Head of Force 136) and followed differing patterns of numerical hierarchy. To make matters worse, a few of the more long-standing staff, for no obvious reason and untypically, retained their symbols even when they changed jobs. Symbols proliferated and mutated with jobs over the course of the war. Not surprisingly, secretaries became confused by them and often produced typographically varying versions of the same symbol (F Recs, F.Recs, F/Recs). Reasonably complete list of symbols used in SOE can be found at PRO HS8/965–986.

9 The instruction itself appears to have survived. It is summarised in ADB/270 of 19 Aug. 1944, PRO HS8/868.

10 Ibid.

11 Minutes of SOE Council Meeting, 29 Aug. 1944, PRO HS8/201.

12 Various papers in PRO HS8/443.

13 Letter of 25 Oct. 1944. Ibid.

14 See, for example, minute by DCD/542 to CD of 17 Dec. 1944. Ibid.

15 Townshend's report of 17 Dec. 1974, held by SIS.

16 Ibid.

17 PF of Miss Gertrude Ornstein, PRO HS9/1125.

18 Correspondence dated 5 June 1956, PRO HS8/443.

19 Private information from SOE veteran.

20 PRO HS8/443.

21 Ibid.

22 Ibid.

23 These figures are totals derived from a series of monthly returns on an SIS file.

24 Minute of 22 Dec. 1949, PRO HS8/443.

25 Minute of 21 Feb. 1950, PRO HS8/443. Emphasis in original.

26 Ibid.

27 Subsequent minuting, PRO HS8/443.

28 Ibid.

29 *F.A.N.Y. Invicta* (London, 1953).

30 Boxshall's appointment with the quoted description of his remit was announced

in Parliament by John Profumo on 15 December 1958 and is recorded in Hansard Col. 757/758 for that day.

31 The Waldegrave Initiative in 1992, and the Open Government White Paper, which followed in 1993, paved the way for the transfer of much of the SOE Archive to The National Archive: Public Record Office. See Wesley Wark, 'In Never Never Land? The British Archives on Intelligence', *The Historical Journal* 35/1 (1992): 196–203; Richard J. Aldrich, 'Never Never Land and Wonderland? British and American Policy on Intelligence Archives', *Contemporary Record* 8/1 (1994): 133–152, and Aldrich, 'The Waldegrave Initiative and Secret Service Archives: New Materials and New Policies', *Intelligence & National Security* 10/1 (1995): 192–7.

32 Townshend's report of 17 Dec. 1974, held by SIS.

33 Ibid.

2 A glass half full

Some thoughts on the evolution of the study of the Special Operations Executive

Mark Seaman

In his memoir, *Setting Europe Ablaze*, Douglas Dodds-Parker, the head of 'Massingham', the Special Operations Executive (SOE) base in North Africa, wrote:

> By standing orders, and sensible self-protection as our base was on a deserted seashore, records were minimal and destroyed as soon as they were no longer of immediate use. After France was liberated, the Club des Pins was closed down. A FANY [First Aid Nursing Yeomanry] said to me that as she saw the last paper curl up in flames she realised that with it went the only record of two years of great interest and effort. It must be hoped that one day a senior Massingham officer will find time to record his or her memories.[1]

This evocative image of burning files and a loyal subordinate's belief that a senior officer (time permitting) would write a suitable historical record encapsulates many of the difficulties in producing SOE's history. There is no question that the records of 'Massingham' were destroyed but is Dodds-Parker's book an adequate alternative? Fortunately, not all of SOE's documents were as comprehensively eradicated as those of its Algerian headquarters and, some sixty years after SOE's demise, most of the surviving records are now available for perusal. Nevertheless, any serious student of SOE will find him or herself required to ply a difficult course through a sea of patchy paperwork and a host of personal accounts of uncertain accuracy. Dodds-Parker might have sought to make his book the realization of the FANY's hopes but were his efforts sufficient to meet the demands of serious scholars of SOE's history? His account provides a significant illustration of the perennial problems facing any would-be student of SOE's history. How accurate is the record to be found in published personal accounts and, with so many of the official papers destroyed, can we ever hope to get close to a meaningful perspective?

There are many factors that made the Special Operations Executive (SOE) unique among the United Kingdom's other secret agencies. Perhaps the most obvious is that, unlike its sister services, it enjoyed only a short life span. By the outbreak of the Second World War, the Secret Intelligence Service (SIS) and the Security Service (MI5) had already been in existence for thirty years and have endured to the extent that in 2009 they will attain their centenaries. In contrast, SOE was a purely wartime phenomenon, its formation being approved by the War Cabinet on 22 July 1940 and its formal closure taking place on 15 January 1946.[2] While short-lived and frequently (and inappropriately) labelled 'amateur' by its detractors, SOE nevertheless acquired a prominent position in most theatres of operations and exerted British influence on a truly global scale. Its colleagues (and sometime rivals) in SIS and MI5 of course maintained their own connections with Allied intelligence services, military high commands and elements within resistance movements. However, the sheer scale and diversity of SOE's control and support of myriad resistance groups from Norway to Malaya were vastly different to the endeavours of its counterparts. Its range of operations encompassed urban groups of undercover agents through para-military *coup de main* parties to large-scale guerrilla formations acting in concert with conventional Allied units. Not surprisingly, SOE's staff was greater than the other organizations comprising, 'just under 10,000 men and some 3,200 women' with tens of thousands of resistance fighters operating under its command.[3] All these factors contributed in large part to SOE being the least secret of Britain's secret services. It was therefore no surprise that SOE was the first secret service to acquire an official history intended for a public readership and that its surviving papers were the first Second World War secret service records to be released into the Public Record Office.[4]

During its existence, the very use of SOE's real name was considered a breach of security and the cover titles 'Inter-Services Research Bureau' and 'MO1(SP)' were employed on documents read by outsiders. Nevertheless, there were, inevitably, leaks. One MP learned a little of SOE's existence and sought to ask potentially embarrassing questions in the House. The files record that his intrusive nosiness was effectively discouraged.[5] The SOE Security Section appears to have coped well and the post-1945 proliferation of public disclosures should not obscure the existence of a highly effective security blanket during the war. However, even as the war in Europe was drawing to a close, there was a strong impetus from within SOE that an appropriate record of its achievements should be left for posterity. The main rationale was two-fold. There was an understandable desire that the hard work and sacrifice of five years should not be neglected and, moreover, that SOE's achievements not be airbrushed out of the record by its rivals. Similarly, SOE's leaders considered that the lessons learned from the revolution in special operations and irregular warfare that had been carried out by SOE ought to be of use to British commanders in a future war. The first step to maintaining a record was the commissioning of internal histories of the various Country Sections. These accounts, mostly completed before SOE's demise, were of very uneven quality and relied heavily upon the calibre of the individual officer detailed to complete the task. Two examples might suffice to illustrate the dilemma. The RF (Gaullist French) Section history was written by one of its members, H. H. A. Thackthwaite, who, as a schoolmaster, might have been expected to exhibit sound historical techniques. However, the work shows little evidence of a genuine attempt to narrate the full story and the details of Thackthwaite's own war loom disproportionately large in the account.[6] In contrast, R. A. Bourne-Paterson of F Section was given a more pragmatic brief and produced a record of its activities in order to apprise British post-war representatives in France of what had passed. As well as a sound historical record, it was intended as a guide to diplomats who might be called upon to investigate a local dispute over SOE/resistance work. Meanwhile, senior members of SOE wanted to have the contribution that the organization had made to the Allied victory properly chronicled in a major historical work. Major-General Sir Colin Gubbins, SOE's leading light throughout its existence, was a strong advocate of a controlled release to the public of certain aspects of SOE's work but, at the same time, he also promoted a classified history for internal, governmental purposes. With hindsight, this dual perspective emerges as, at best, difficult and, at worst, impossible to achieve. Perhaps only Gubbins could be the arbiter of what the public could be permitted to know and what had to remain within government circles. As a result of these difficulties, Gubbins's hopes for a popular history came to nought but he attained his other objective with the appointment of William Mackenzie to write a classified history. Mackenzie, a political historian and wartime civil servant with the Air Ministry, was accorded privileged access to SOE's surviving archives that were closed to anyone other than government officials.[7] By 1948, Mackenzie had completed his task and Gubbins had a fine testament to SOE's work and achievements. However, there was no denying the drawback that for the next fifty years the book was to have the most limited of readerships. Gubbins thereafter made a personal commitment to promulgating the historic importance of resistance and SOE's contribution towards it, exemplified by his lecture, 'Resistance Movements in the War', given at the Royal United Services Institution on 28 January 1948. He remained SOE's most potent ambassador for the rest of his life, lecturing, writing introductions to the published memoirs of SOE agents and taking a leading role in the creation of the Special Forces Club. In short, Gubbins was almost as active in perpetuating the memory of SOE as he had been in directing its work during the war.[8]

Given the British public's voracious appetite for tales of spies and operations behind enemy lines, it was inevitable that an account written by one of SOE's agents would eventually appear in print. The first 'approved' SOE memoir is generally ascribed to pre-war journalist George Millar who wrote an account of his experiences as an SOE agent almost as soon as he returned from France in the autumn of 1944. The typescript had to be submitted to SOE for approval and eventually emerged 'mangled in the text and with many deletions' before being cleared by the War Office and published as 'Maquis' with a 70,000 hardback print run.[9] Further public prominence was soon given to SOE as a result of the award of the George Cross to a small number of its personnel. The bulk of these gallantry awards went to agents who had operated in France but other recipients included Colonel Arthur Nicholls (Albania) and Major Hugh Seagrim (Burma). Although SOE was not named in the citations for the awards, the organization and its deeds inevitably were nudged a little closer to the limelight. It was not just the citations that announced the existence of these valiant men and women and most of them became the subjects of hugely successful biographies. The first, *Odette*, the story of Mrs Odette Sansom, was a virtual hagiography of the agent. Surprisingly, and in contravention of the embargo placed on the files, the author was able to gain access to some SOE documents and even reproduce some of them, 'I am deeply indebted to the War Office and particularly to Major Norman Mott who put files at my disposal and who helped with such genial patience'.[10] Sadly, the opportunity to consult the records did not prevent the author drifting into a cloying narrative. Two of the other George Cross recipients, Noor Inayat Khan and Wing Commander F. F. E. Yeo-Thomas, were soon the subjects of biographies, *Madeleine* and *The White Rabbit*, while a posthumous work on Violette Szabo did not appear until 1956. A rather more restrained biography of Seagrim was published in 1947 while a full account of Nicholls's life awaits to be written.[11]

In parallel with the idealized biographies and ghosted autobiographies of agents, a more probing form of research began in the mid-1950s notably regarding allegations that SOE activities in France had been mishandled. British and French newspapers found that revelations and controversies about SOE made good copy and exposés and serializations of books became frequent features in the press in the 1950s and 1960s. The most persistent and resonant topics concerned the fate of captured F Section women agents, the activities of double agents and the alleged incompetence of SOE staff officers in London.[12]

The growing public furore surrounding F Section and the increasing threat of government embarrassment at home and abroad demanded that an authoritative voice be heard on SOE matters. The result was the creation of the somewhat unusual post of 'SOE Adviser'. The appointment was announced in the House of Commons on 15 December 1958 when Dame Irene Ward, an inveterate agitator for greater access to SOE's history, 'asked the Secretary of State for Foreign Affairs, whether he will make arrangements for information contained in the files of the Special Operations Executive to be made available to those interested in them'. John Profumo, Parliamentary Under Secretary of State for Foreign Affairs, replied that direct access to the papers would still not be possible but

> Arrangements are accordingly being made in the Foreign Office to assign a former officer with war-time experience of the Executive to advise and assist inquirers and in general to deal with questions regarding the release of information on the Special Operations Executive.[13]

From the outset, the Adviser's role seemed as much to monitor research as to 'advise and assist' those engaged in it. Such caution was not merely bureaucratic obstructionism. In the first decades following the end of the war, the impact of SOE's activities was still evident and had a clear, contemporary relevance. The first Adviser, Lieutenant-Colonel E. G. Boxshall, certainly seemed aware of his responsibilities and consequently pursued a brief to limit the dissemination of information wherever possible. Boxshall, a First World War member of British Intelligence and wartime SOE staff officer, stayed in harness until his death in 1984, apparently without any significant mellowing of his attitude. In great contrast, his successors, Christopher Woods, Gervase Cowell and Duncan Stuart each made a remarkable contribution to the development of the study of SOE. Open and helpful, they accommodated the broadest spectrum of researchers and their detailed correspondence and briefings had the effect of making segments of the closed SOE archive available by proxy. There are many books that were published during their periods in office that would either not have appeared or would have been greatly inferior without their assistance.[14]

Much of SOE's early, public history featured popular accounts of secret agents with publishers seeking to sell the books as out and out adventure stories. Market forces seem to have ensured that it was better to offer a ripping yarn rather than attempt to provide a serious, accurate account of operational activity. The literary style was not confined to the agents and when staff officers wrote, they, too, were encouraged to let the 'action' dominate. The two books written by the head of F Section, Maurice Buckmaster, concentrated upon drama at the expense of veracity but at least the author had the good grace to admit it, 'I do not claim that the incidents described in these pages are completely factually accurate.'[15] Only some time later did more measured accounts of behind the scenes activity emerge from leading SOE personalities such as Bickham Sweet-Escott, J. G. Beevor and Donald Hamilton-Hill.[16]

While personal accounts continued to appear courtesy of the British public's fascination with secret agents, in the late 1950s Whitehall took the momentous step to commission an official history.[17] The gestation of the work merits a book in itself. SOE's activities in France had continued to maintain a particularly high level of notoriety. A succession of books had suggested maladministration by F Section and a negligent attitude to investigating the fate of missing agents. Meanwhile, Whitehall was concerned at the lack of recognition in France of Britain's contribution to the resistance and, equally, that the communist elements of the resistance were receiving a disproportional amount of credit. Throughout 1959, civil servants and some of SOE's former staff officers deliberated on whether to recommend that a general history of SOE or a 'pilot project' focusing on one country be commissioned. In the event, the latter alternative got the nod and an Oxford academic, M. R. D. Foot, was appointed as an official historian charged with writing the history of SOE in France. It was a daunting project with the author not merely having to master a confusing mass of files – abundantly strong in some places, lamentably weak in others – but also to satisfy the demands of his sponsors and those SOE veterans with an understandable interest in how their own history was to be represented. While granted full access to the surviving SOE archive, Foot was denied permission to interview all but a very few of the participants. As a result, a groundswell of resentment and suspicion built up among many of the veterans:

> It was inevitable that not a few of the personalities featured in his text were aghast that a major work was on the verge of publication without their having been consulted. Among the most vociferous was Buckmaster [the wartime head of F Section] who, when he was given sight of the galley proofs, declared himself 'utterly horrified' and 'amazed by the number of mistakes'.[18]

There was still time for the 'mistakes' to be rectified and Foot was able to incorporate Buckmaster's thirty-five pages of comments, together with the observations of some thirty to forty other interested parties who were shown the draft, into his revisions. Nevertheless, when eventually published in 1966, *SOE in France* excited a great deal of controversy. The book was a remarkable achievement with a complex but coherent story emerging out of the inchoate files. Moreover, it proved a watershed in the historiography of SOE, at last elevating the literature out of the sole province of fictionalized memoirs and providing a well-argued, well-documented history. Unfortunately, Foot's uncompromising and profoundly iconoclastic approach veered on occasion into some ill-judged observations. While attempting to dispel some of the myths and resolve some of the *causes célèbres* surrounding *SOE in France*, Foot (perhaps inevitably) ended up by creating a whole new set of controversies. Two legal actions were taken against him and the publishers with the result that substantial damages were settled out of court and the book was withdrawn. A second impression appeared two years later with the offending passages removed and several other amendments.

Meanwhile, in addition to the continuing quota of tales of derring-do, at least a few historians were beginning to analyse previously neglected aspects of SOE's history. Foremost was David Stafford who, in 1975, posted a notice of intent with an article, 'The Detonator Concept: British Strategy, SOE and European Resistance After the Fall of France'.[19] From this brief work later emerged a far more substantial volume, *Britain and European Resistance*, that in its own way made almost as great a contribution to the subject as Foot's official history.[20] Without the benefit of access to closed, still secret archives, Stafford perused official documents that had been released into the Public Record Office, especially the Chiefs of Staff papers, to plot SOE's role and the impact it had had on Allied strategy. At last, a perspective was offered that neither concerned itself primarily with the bravery of secret agents nor focused on specific regional/national emphases.

The controversy over *SOE in France* seems to have left a little too much scar tissue in Whitehall to permit the adoption of the contemplated series of SOE histories. It was therefore not until 1980 that a second official history was commissioned, this time dealing with the Far East, a theatre of operations where the work of SOE found itself almost as overlooked as the famously 'forgotten' 14th Army itself. The author, Charles Cruickshank, produced a worthy, if workmanlike, book that showed little sign that the study of SOE's history had significantly advanced in the two decades that had elapsed since Foot's history.[21] Instead, in his Preface, Cruickshank bemoaned the perceived disadvantages that he faced in comparison to his predecessor:

> The research for *SOE in the Far East* was carried out twenty years later than that for *SOE in France*, with inevitable consequence that the number of survivors who could provide evidence was much reduced. On many occasions I have hoped to discuss an operation or a policy decision with one or other of the principal actors, only to find that they had disappeared from the stage.[22]

Any sympathy the reader might have felt for Cruickshank would probably have been dispelled by recourse to Foot's comments on his own, limited, opportunities to speak to veterans:

> Similarly, my access to former staff and agents of SOE was severely limited: till it had been decided that this pilot study was to appear, much importance was attached to keeping the author out of the way of interested parties. Once the decision to publish had been made, more than a year after the bulk of the book had been completed, it seemed more important to publish as soon as possible than to make perfectionist attempts to polish and re-polish a tale that in many ways is bound to remain craggy and imperfect. I would have liked to talk to all the survivors; but owed it to them, and still more to their dead companions, to get something into print quickly to show that the dead deserve honour and that SOE's efforts was not made in vain.[23]

Clearly, Cruickshank's conclusion that the passage of time had deprived him of a resource that had been available to Foot was wrong.

The next official history, once again by Cruickshank, proved far less satisfactory than his earlier volume. *SOE in Scandinavia* employed a similar template to that adopted for *SOE in the Far East* and it did not work.[24] The limited range of English language sources that had proved adequate to supplement the SOE files on the Far East were in marked contrast to the abundance of Norwegian, Danish and Swedish archival and secondary sources relating to SOE's work in Scandinavia. Cruickshank seems merely to have contented himself with the closed SOE archive, a few PRO files and a small selection of English language secondary sources. In his very brief Preface, the author acknowledged the help of two senior members of the Danish and Norwegian resistance (Ole Lippmann and Jens Christian Hauge) but he did not appear to have gone in search of the range of distinguished SOE personnel who, he so lamented, were unavailable to him for his work on the Far East.[25] Hardly surprisingly, Cruickshank's approach did not endear him to Scandinavian authorities on the subject and from at least one of them, the distinguished Norwegian historian, Olaf Riste, he received a swingeing criticism. The impact of Riste's comments were all the greater in that he was not an embittered veteran bemoaning a failure to consult but rather that Cruickshank had written inadequate history. Among the more incisive comments was Riste's description of the book as 'a haphazard collection of cloak and dagger stories that are often seriously at variance with the painstakingly researched studies already available'.[26] A subsequent assessment of the book by a leading Danish historian was equally scathing:

> As a trusted government historian, Cruickshank had almost unrestricted access to the SOE archives and his work is presented as 'the official history'. But perhaps he was too strongly influenced by the burden of discretion; perhaps a lack of fluency in Danish ruled out a consideration of Danish research. For whatever reason, the result is remarkably bland and, to some extent, misleading.

The work, which is based exclusively on papers in the SOE archives, is full of references to related documents, stereotyped, and without depth. Its usefulness is further reduced by an absence of direct references to the archives. It has the hallmark of an official report; there are very few real evaluations, and it does not reveal a great deal when one considers the mine of information he could draw on. Finally, the work labours under the drawback that, in seeking to deal with the whole of Scandinavia, the author bit off more than he could chew, and he thereby obscures significant differences in the circumstances which prevailed in the countries within Scandinavia during the war.[27]

In spite of the adverse reviews of *SOE in Scandinavia*, a whole programme of further SOE histories was soon approved by Whitehall. Richard Clogg was to tackle Greece and Mark Wheeler took on the hottest of potatoes, Yugoslavia. Christopher Woods (a wartime SOE British Liaison Officer who had been parachuted into German-occupied Veneto and, later, was the second SOE Adviser) was entrusted with Italy and M. R. D. Foot was given the opportunity of his second official history, examining SOE's effort in the Low Countries. Although carrying the imprimatur of 'official' – without it access could not have been given to still classified files – the authors were not obliged to sign up with HMSO and were free to find themselves their own publishers. Since the appointments some twenty years ago, only one of the four has appeared. M. R. D. Foot's *SOE in the Low Countries*, was published in 2001, the author explaining 'This book was finished two and half years ago; needed time to be cleared by various authorities; and has had to wait its turn to be published.'[28] The three absentees were to be overtaken by a late addition to the list, Brooks Richards's *Secret Flotillas* that, strictly speaking, was not an SOE history for it was just as much concerned with SIS and MI9 sea communications.[29] The failure of the SOE histories to appear did not excite too much comment. In part, this might be explained by the publication of other official accounts of the 'secret' story of the Second World War. The first of F. H. Hinsley's magisterial volumes on *British Intelligence in the Second World War* was published in 1979 and subsequent tomes thereafter regularly appeared over the next decade.[30]

By the 1980s, many aspects of SOE's history were firmly in the public domain but the SOE Archive remained classified and unobtainable. Those seeking to carry out research had to adopt an oblique approach, similar to Stafford's, by scouring the archives of other government departments. Patience and hard work in Foreign Office and armed forces records revealed references to joint operations and not a few details of SOE activity. An indication of the breadth of these files is provided by a 1998 PRO Source Sheet entitled 'Special Operations Executive' that lists numerous Air Ministry, War Office, Foreign Office and Prime Minister's Office files that contain important references to the organization. Among the many small insights into SOE activity afforded by open sources were the Squadron Operations Record Books of the Special Duty squadrons that handled clandestine flights. These provide an empirical record of supply and agent infiltration. Although the details are sometimes sparse – 'Operations' and little more is a frequent description of a sortie – they nevertheless help in the creation of chronologies and assessments of the scale of supply to SOE networks.

At last, on 21 October 1993, the first release of SOE documents into the PRO appeared under the auspices of the Waldegrave Initiative on Open Government. Sensibly, the decision-makers eased their way gently into the uncharted waters by electing to make the first release of papers one that had already been the subject of an official history – 'SOE in the Far East'. The release was accompanied by the first of a series of PRO guides to the documents that helped the researcher to know what to expect from the SOE records and where to find it.[31] Thereafter, a succession of releases of files arrived at the PRO, the first few tranches being accompanied by other guides. The last major group of files to reach Kew, the Personal Files of SOE staff and agents, proved to be among the most problematic. The provisions of data protection legislation, together with what appear to be a perplexing archival policy, resulted in a cumbersome process for granting access to individual records.[32]

Certain SOE documents have been retained under Section 3(4) of the Public Records Act. Documents too heavily saturated with SIS or MI5 papers seem to be the major victims of the reviewer's blue pencil. Intimate personal details contained in a file or unsubstantiated allegations of misconduct would appear to have been other areas of concern. There is no question that some anomalies have appeared, not least as a result of the release of related files, in particular, those of MI5 and the War Office. Doubtless hardy individuals have expended much time measuring the gaps left by redacted words and scouring parallel documents in other files to discover any flaw in the weeders' procedures.[33] As well as providing anomalies, many of the MI5 files throw much light on SOE's activities and its relations with other government bodies. The diaries of Guy Liddell, the head of MI5's B Division, positively groan under the weight of references to SOE.[34]

A more significant anomaly than the unintended release of an individual's name involves the presence in the SOE files of papers generated by SIS's Section D. SIS records constitute now (2006) the only Second World War British secret service whose files have not seen the light of day. One must assume that a great many of Section D's files were acquired by SOE when the former body was subsumed into the latter. The reviewers presumably considered that there was little merit in extracting all pages with an SIS origin from SOE records although some names have been redacted.[35]

The SOE archive has proved something of a draw for the Public Record Office National Archive in London both in terms of use of the records and in generating media interest in official records. Between 1994 and 1998 before the bulk of the archive had been released, the number of SOE files produced for readers was 14,934 out of around 2,300,000 total productions during the same period.[36] The PRO/TNA has sought to promote their SOE holdings as much as possible. The media frenzy surrounding the successive releases of the SOE archive indicated that there was a publishing opportunity (sadly one not tied into the release but subsequent to it). Thus, the extensive interest in the release of one of SOE's least thought-through plans, Operation FOXLEY – the plan to assassinate Hitler, led to the reproduction in full of the file.[37] Similarly, other SOE records with a broad public appeal including a catalogue of 'Special Devices and Stores' and a training syllabus from SOE's Camp X in Canada were published to some success.[38]

Whereas the arrival of the SOE files at the National Archive marked the greatest contribution to the study of the subject, other public institutions have also made substantial efforts to develop non-official SOE archival holdings. The London School of Economics has for long held the papers of Hugh Dalton, while the Liddell Hart Collection possesses papers by a substantial number of SOE figures including C. M. Woodhouse and E. C. W. Myers. However, the Imperial War Museum (IWM) has developed the strongest range of research collections relating to SOE. The Museum's general terms of reference – tri-service and civilian – made it eminently suitable as a repository for SOE's peculiar, hybrid ancestry. The IWM's Sound Archive interviewers had begun recording the experiences of members of SOE since at least the early 1980s. The project expanded over the years to encompass the broadest range of SOE personnel from cipher clerks to secret agents from secretaries to wireless operators.[39] The IWM's current collections include over 300 interview recordings and more than 150 individual holdings of personal and private papers that relate to SOE and its operations worldwide. In addition, the IWM has built a substantial collection of SOE memorabilia, equipment, firearms, photographs and film. False identity cards, concealing devices, lethal tablets, thumb knives and sabotage material constitute just a fraction of the range of artefacts, many with detailed, personal provenance. Among the most remarkable of acquisitions is black and white and colour film footage of agents undergoing sabotage training at an SOE school in Hertfordshire.[40] The IWM's Department of Documents has made a concerted effort over some two decades to acquire the private papers of SOE personnel. The list is now most impressive and among the collections of papers are those of Colin Gubbins, Peter Wilkinson, Frank Nelson, Vera Atkins, Neil 'Billy' MacLean and David Smiley. The Museum has enjoyed a very close relationship with the Special Forces Club, the old comrades association of SOE, and benefited from the munificence of the late Sir Paul Getty and the Gerry Holdsworth Special Forces Charitable Trust. Getty funded the establishment of a permanent gallery, 'Secret War', that chronicled the story of the United Kingdom's secret agencies and that features a substantial section devoted to SOE. In turn, the Trust financed a three-day conference on SOE held at the Imperial War Museum in October 1998. This occasion brought together many, if not most, of the leading historians in the field and, just as importantly, a constellation of SOE veterans to offer their own testimonies and comment on the offerings of the historians. The proceedings were published in 2005.[41]

SOE has achieved a certain public reputation through film and television representation. Among the first and certainly one of the most important was the RAF Film Production Unit's 1946 'docu-drama', *Now It Can Be Told*. Whatever this film lacked in script, direction and, most of all, acting talent, it made up in offering a virtual documentary on SOE operations in France. While the two dramatic leads, Harry Rée and Jacqueline Nearne, were evidently better secret agents than thespians, the film offers intriguing, detailed sequences on training, tradecraft, agent infiltration and airborne supply. Not surprisingly, its footage has formed a staple feature of most television documentaries on SOE and other wartime clandestine organizations.[42] A review of feature films on SOE awaits another paper but the kindest overall description is that the quality is uneven. The two films based upon the biographies of two of the George Cross recipients, *Odette* and *Carve Her Name with Pride* were hugely successful at the box office and reinforced the enduring fascination exhibited by the British public for tales of women agents in France. Several real SOE operations have been rendered in dramatized film versions while various fictional dramas inspired by SOE's activities have appeared over the years.[43] Women agents in France have continued to exert a hold exemplified by David Hare's play 'Plenty' and the subsequent film released in 1985. 'Plenty' sought to examine the stress of clandestine life and in large measure managed to reflect the mental scars that the war had left upon some of the agents. In contrast, Sebastian Faulks's novel *Charlotte Gray*, in spite of its commercial success, did not illustrate many of the truths of SOE agents' lives. Neither book nor film did much to provide a new insight into the reality of SOE's work and, apart from depicting a rather more lively sex life for the heroine than had been present in earlier films.[44]

In 1984 a major BBC documentary series produced by Dominic Flessati was made at a time when many of SOE's major players were still around to be interviewed and even taken back to their operational locations. The passage of time has begun to restrict the opportunity for filmmakers to question the participants but several series have endeavoured to record the experiences of surviving SOE agents and staff: *Secret Agent*, *SOE: Churchill's Secret Army* and *The Real Charlotte Grays*. The BBC *Timewatch* programme has paid several visits to SOE and Operation FOXLEY merited a hybrid programme that comprised a mix of 'docu-drama', dramatized speculation of the assassination plan being put into effect and a roundtable discussion carried out by sundry 'experts'.

There clearly remains a public readership for books on SOE although the publishers' interest remains largely confined to controversy or an action story. Nevertheless, some books of real historical worth have emerged. Among the most important was a biography of SOE's driving force, Colin Gubbins.[45] Peter Wilkinson and Joan Bright Astley were able to infuse their scrupulously researched work with their own intimate knowledge of their subject. Almost as important was Wilkinson's own memoir, *Foreign Fields* in which his outstanding qualities were subtly and almost disingenuously displayed.[46] In addition to the abundance of books on France, a significant number of memoirs have appeared over the years describing SOE's efforts in the Balkans and Italy. Those not operating behind enemy lines have also written of their works.[47] Peter Tennant has provided a welcome insight into SOE's role in carrying out a propaganda war in a neutral state. Leo Marks's long-awaited memoir was a commercial success but its value as a major historical source remains questionable. Its style was redolent of the bad old days of reconstituted dialogue and, in spite of the author evidently having consulted contemporary documents, the reader was left with an uneasy feeling regarding its veracity.[48]

So where do we now stand? Most of the SOE papers are now safely deposited at the National Archives apart from those retained under the Act and those personal files closed for other more general reasons. It seems unlikely that the papers that have been retained will radically alter perceptions already formed by the available records. While SOE topics have been the focus of doctoral theses and numerous articles have been written for academic journals, there have been disappointingly few substantial works based on the SOE archive. Instead, a few new editions of old books have been published recently. Although there had already been two editions of *SOE in France* in 1966 and 1968, a third version appeared in 2004.[49] A classic history has been little improved by a little tinkering with the text, an expanded bibliography and some additional footnotes. Foot's 1978 *Six Faces of Courage* that included biographical sketches of three personalities with strong SOE connections, has also undergone a partial facelift.[50] Sadly, it shows little sign of the new archival material having been incorporated in the revised, updated edition. At the same time as the third edition of *SOE in France* appeared, an expanded, two-volume version of Brooks Richards's *Secret Flotillas* was posthumously published. This included additional new material on naval operations in the Mediterranean.[51]

In spite of the SOE Archive at Kew, the need for researchers to continue to look elsewhere for material is as great as ever. There is no guarantee, however, that the missing pieces of the jigsaw are to be found in foreign archives and, for example, Knud J. V. Jespersen's *No Small Achievement: Special Operations Executive and the Danish Resistance 1940–1945*, suggests that there is only a limited number of papers in Denmark to supplement those available at Kew.[52] In contrast, a host of Norwegian files relating to SOE are to be found in abundance at the Norges Hjemmefrontmuseum, Oslo. Encouragingly, it even seems as if some papers covering SOE's limited work in Czechoslovakia may have survived the depredations of the communist regime. Prominently displayed in a recent exhibition on the assassination of Reinhard Heydrich was an SOE training report of one of the assassins.[53] Further afield, there is evidently an abundance of SOE files to be found in Australia evidenced by two excellent works on the war in the Far East.[54]

Informed researchers into SOE's history must be reconciled to the fact that the ravages of time and policy have ensured that the archives are unlikely to provide all that is required. However, those of a certain age, unlike their younger colleagues, will perhaps be able to indulge themselves with the pleasant reflection that they are now using files that they were once told would always to be denied them. There is much work to do. There are whole areas of SOE's work that remain unexplored. But perhaps there is some cause for considering that the glass is half full rather than half empty.

Notes

The views expressed in this article are those of the author alone and do not represent the opinions of the Cabinet Office.

1   Douglas Dodds-Parker, *Setting Europe Ablaze* (Windlesham, 1983), pp. 163–164.
2   William Mackenzie, *The Secret History of SOE* (London, 2000), p. 715.
3   M. R. D. Foot, *SOE in France* (London, 1966), p. 14.

4   Ibid.

5   The National Archive, United Kingdom, Public Record Office (hereafter PRO) HS8/835.

6   PRO HS7/123.

7   Mackenzie, *Secret History*. M. R. D. Foot's Introduction provides some helpful details of the evolution of Mackenzie's work. The original text can be found at PRO CAB102/649–652.

8   Gubbins's commitment is evident in the post-war correspondence now held by the Imperial War Museum and in Introductions to works such as Knut Haukelid, *Skis Against the Atom* (London, 1954) and Richard Heslop, *Xavier* (London, 1970).

9   George Millar, *Road to Resistance* (London, 1981), p. 405; George Millar, *Maquis* (London, 1945).

10 Jerrard Tickell, *Odette* (London, 1949), p. 10.

11 Jean Overton Fuller, *Madeleine* (London, 1952); Bruce Marshall, *The White Rabbit* (London, 1952); R. J. Minney, *Death Be Not Proud* (London, 1956), and Ian Morrison, *Grandfather Longlegs* (London, 1947).

12 See Mark Seaman, 'Good Thrillers, but Bad History: A Review of Published Works on the Special Operations Executive's Work in France during the Second World War', in K. G. Robertson (ed.) *War Resistance and Intelligence: Essays in Honour of M. R. D. Foot* (Barnsley, 1999), pp. 119–133.

13 *Hansard, House of Commons Debates, 15 December 1958* cols 757 and 758. A dissenting voice was offered by Lieutenant-Colonel John Cordeaux MP, a former member of SIS, who questioned whether Dame Irene Ward's suggestion

> has really gone beyond a joke, in view of the harm already done by these amateur spies cashing in on their war experiences by turning amateur authors? Will he [Profumo] ensure that what has not yet been disclosed of Services technique and practice remains secret from now on? Will he deny access to these files to all historians, professional or amateur, or other unauthorised persons?

14 Nigel West, *Secret War: The Story of SOE Britain's Wartime Sabotage Organisation* (London, 1992), Pierre Péan, *Vies et Morts de Jean Moulin* (Paris, 1997) and Mark Seaman, *Bravest of the Brave* (London, 1997) are but a few of the many works on SOE that feature the indebtedness of their authors to the contribution made by the Advisers.

15 Maurice Buckmaster, *Specially Employed* (London, 1952), p. 7; Maurice Buckmaster, *They Fought Alone* (London, 1958).

16 Bickham Sweet-Escott, *Baker Street Irregular* (London, 1965); J. G. Beevor, *SOE Recollections and Reflections 1940–45* (London, 1981); Donald Hamilton-Hill, *SOE Assignment* (London, 1973).

17 A detailed exposition of Whitehall's handling of the broader, knotty problem of 'secret' history and specifically of *SOE in France* is provided in Richard J. Aldrich, 'Policing the Past: Official History, Secrecy and British Intelligence since 1945', *English Historical Review* 119 (2004): 922–953.

18 Seaman, 'Good Thrillers but Bad History', p. 127.

19 David Stafford, 'The Detonator Concept: British Strategy, SOE and European Resistance After the Fall of France', *Journal of Contemporary History* 10/2 (April 1975): 185–217.

20 David Stafford, *Britain and European Resistance 1940–1945: A Survey of the Special Operations Executive, with Documents* (London, 1980).

21 Charles Cruickshank, *SOE in the Far East* (Oxford, 1983). The select bibliography is less a reflection of lack of industry by its author than an indication of the shortage of histories and memoirs on this subject. Cruickshank was a former Foreign Office official and author of an official history, *The German Occupation of the Channel Islands* (Oxford, 1975) and *The Fourth Arm: Psychological Warfare 1938–1945* (Oxford, 1981).

22 Cruickshank, *SOE in the Far East*, p. v.

23 Foot, *SOE in France*, pp. 452–453.

24 Charles Cruickshank, *SOE in Scandinavia* (Oxford, 1986).
25 A host of SOE veterans intimately involved with SOE's activities in Scandinavia were available to him including, to name but a few, Reginald Spink, Ralph Hollingworth, Joachim Ronneberg, Knut Haukelid and Gunnar Sonsterby.
26 *The Times*, 10 June 1986.
27 Knud J. V. Jespersen, *No Small Achievement: Special Operations Executive and the Danish Resistance 1940 1945* (Odense, 2002), pp. 17–18.
28 M. R. D. Foot, *SOE in the Low Countries* (London, 2001), p. xiv.
29 Brooks Richards, *Secret Flotillas: Clandestine Sea Lines to France and French North Africa 1940–1944* (London, 1996).
30 F. H. Hinsley *et al.*, *British Intelligence in the Second World War*, five vols (London, 1979–1990).
31 Louise Atherton, *SOE Operations in the Far East: An Introductory Guide to the Newly Released Records of the Special Operations Executive in the Public Record Office* (London, 1993).
32 PRO HS9. One of the criteria for release is proof that the subject has died. It might have proved useful to refer to 'In Memory', a Roll of Honour produced by a former SOE Adviser to coincide with the unveiling of a memorial plaque in Westminster Abbey on 13 Feb. 1996. It provides the names of some 800 of SOE's war dead.
33 One example of such an anomaly exists over the SOE and Security Service files, HS6/422–3 and KV6/17–18 covering the 'Bishop' investigation. The name of an investigating officer, Wethered, has been redacted from the SOE files but included in the MI5 record.
34 PRO KV4/185–196.
35 Notably PRO HS 7/3–5 but also liberally sprinkled throughout the Archive.
36 Statement made by Louise Atherton of the Public Record Office at the Imperial War Museum SOE Conference, 29 Oct. 1998.
37 Mark Seaman, 'Introduction', in *Operation Foxley: The British Plan to Kill Hitler* (Kew, 1998).
38 Mark Seaman, 'Introduction', in *Secret Agent's Handbook of Special Devices* (Richmond, 2000) and Denis Rigden, 'Introduction', in *SOE Syllabus: Lessons in Ungentlemanly Warfare, World War II* (Richmond, 2001).
39 A catalogue, *The Special Operations Executive Sound Archive Oral History Recordings* (London, 1998), gives an insight into the programme. The number of interviews has, of course, substantially increased in the intervening period.
40 IWM Major C. V. Clarke collection, MGH 4321.
41 Mark Seaman (ed.), *Special Operations Executive: A New weapon of war* (London, 2005).
42 Imperial War Museum ID Number: RMY 78. The real-life F Section agents, Harry Rée and Jacqueline Nearne, took the leading roles. Rée had run the 'Stockbroker' circuit from April to November 1943 when, wounded, he had to flee to Switzerland while Nearne was a courier for the 'Stationer' circuit from January 1943 to April 1944. The film does not mention SOE specifically but the cast is littered with the organization's personalities including Robin Brook, Dick Barry and Brian Stonehouse. Not surprisingly, it also features many of the RAF personnel who were either seconded to SOE or worked closely with the organization in the Air Ministry or at RAF Tempsford.
43 *Odette*, director Herbert Wilcox, 1950, *Carve Her Name with Pride*, director Lewis Gilbert, 1958. Other operations include the kidnapping of General Kriepe on Crete (*Ill Met by Moonlight*, director Michael Powell/Emeric Pressburger, 1956), the sabotaging of the Norsk Hydro 'heavy water' plant (*The Heroes of Telemark*, director Anthony Mann, 1965) and the assassination of Reinhard Heydrich (*Operation Daybreak*, director Lewis Gilbert, 1975). Fictional movies that deal with, usually unnamed, SOE are *The Guns of Navarone* (director J. Lee-Thompson, 1961) and *Where Eagles Dare* (director Brian G. Hutton, 1969).

44 Sebastian Faulks, *Charlotte Gray* (London, 1999). The author cannot disassociate himself from all culpability having been 'technical adviser' on the film.

45 Peter Wilkinson and Joan Bright Astley, *Gubbins and SOE* (London, 1993).

46 Peter Wilkinson, *Foreign Fields* (London, 1997).

47 Those who made a perilous descent into enemy territory include Brigadier 'Trotsky' Davies, *Illyrian Adventure* (London, 1952); Basil Davidson, *Special Operations Europe: Scenes from the Anti-Nazi War* (London, 1987); E. C. W. Myers, *Greek Entanglement* (Gloucester, 1985); David Smiley, *Albanian Assignment* (London, 1985); and Charles Mackintosh, *From Cloak to Dagger: An SOE Agent in Italy 1943–1945* (London, 1982).

48 Peter Tennant, *Touchlines of War* (Hull, 1992); and Leo Marks, *Between Silk and Cyanide: The Story of SOE's Code War* (London, 1998).

49 M. R. D. Foot, *SOE in France* (London, 2004).

50 M. R. D. Foot, *Six Faces of Courage* (London, 1978), revised edition (Barnsley, 2003).

51 Brooks Richards, *Secret Flotillas.* vol. I: *Clandestine Sea Operations to Brittany, 1940–1944*, vol. II: *Clandestine Sea Operations to the Mediterranean, North Africa and the Adriatic, 1940–1944* (London, 2004).

52 Jespersen, *No Small Achievement.*

53 Reproduced along with other related documents in Michal Burian, Aleš Knízek, Jirí Rajlich, Eduard Stehlík, *Assassination: Operation Anthropoid 1941–1942* (Prague, 2002).

54 Alan Powell, *War by Stealth: Australians and the Allied Intelligence Bureau, 1942–1945* (Carlton South, 1996), and Richard J. Aldrich, *Intelligence and the War Against Japan: Britain, America and the Politics of Secret Service* (Cambridge, 2000).

3 The 'Massingham' mission and the secret 'special relationship'

Cooperation and rivalry between the Anglo-American clandestine services in French North Africa, November 1942–May 1943

T. C. Wales

Cloak-and-dagger social history

Recent archival releases – and discoveries – now allow for a case study to be conducted of the cooperative enterprise at 'Massingham', the principal Allied 'dirty warfare' base in the Western Mediterranean from November 1942–May 1945. Housed for the bulk of its existence in a former French 'adult play area' 20 kilometres west of Algiers, 'Massingham' served as the main command, communications, supply and training centre for clandestine operations into south-western Europe after the North African TORCH landings in November 1942. It was one of the most conspicuously successful Allied special operations (OSS-SO and the British Special Operations Executive – SOE) field stations of the war and one of the few that achieved a complete merger of Anglo-American operations.[1] By the autumn of 1944, 'Massingham' had played a major role in the liberation of Corsica, facilitated the secret armistice negotiations that led to the Italian surrender in September 1943, helped pave the way for the ANVIL landings in the south of France, and instigated several massive guerrilla uprisings behind Axis lines. In France alone, it airdropped more than 400 agents, 14,000 crates of arms and 7,500 miscellaneous supply packages.[2] Colonel Douglas Dodds-Parker, the senior SOE officer at 'Massingham' for most of its history, estimates that his base accounted for 40 per cent of all the material secretly infiltrated into France over the course of the war.[3] Although this latter number may be an exaggeration, it is still an amazing figure for an establishment that is barely mentioned in the official histories.

Since the publication of M. R. D. Foot's ground-breaking *SOE in France* in 1966, historians have lamented the lack of documentary evidence of the base – Dodds-Parker and his associates were assiduous in carrying out their orders to burn the record of their activities. Some recent determined digging in the UK and abroad has unearthed a small trove of new information, however. Jay Jakub, a former staff member of the US House of Representatives' Permanent Select Committee on Intelligence, turned up considerable extant cable traffic between 'Massingham', SOE's London headquarters in Baker Street, and British intelligence in North America.[4] Martin Thomas provided a fine introduction to the history of the base in a journal article – particularly regarding how the Giraud/De Gaulle political controversy stoked tensions between OSS and SOE.[5] The author's own research has discovered that prior to the destruction of the operational record a fairly comprehensive synopsis of Allied activities at 'Massingham' was recorded by a member of the base's First Aid Nursing Yeomanry (FANY) contingent, Captain Jacky Porter. Porter's piece was subsequently misfiled at the PRO, where it languished for sixty years.[6]

The aim of this chapter is to synthesize these new discoveries through a study of the mission's fractious first six months: from the chaos of the British-American invasion of the Magreb (Morocco, Algeria, Tunisia) in November 1942 until Charles de Gaulle's May 1943 arrival in Algiers heralded an end to political instability. During this period three wide-ranging disputes – precipitated by organizational self-interest, the French political situation and cultural irritants, respectively – strained relations between the Anglo-American secret warfare agencies. Initially, cooperation looked neither possible nor desirable, particularly from the OSS perspective. The near-total integration finally achieved was the result of a determined effort by a few individuals who recognized that an overall convergence of vital interests outweighed short-term aggravations.

Martin Thomas rightly notes that Franklin Roosevelt's decision to prop up the Darlan/Giraud regime in Algiers against the challenge to its legitimacy by the Fighting French, and the requirement that SOE cooperate with OSS, initially stymied British efforts to make 'Massingham' an effective staging area for European resistance.[7] As we shall see, however, despite this policy, senior officials at SOE made a conscious decision to sacrifice short-term operational effectiveness in order to aid the US clandestine service. During the winter of 1942/1943, OSS faced a serious attempt to dissolve the agency in Washington. Its flamboyant Director, William Donovan, desperately needed to prove OSS was capable of staging independent operations. The SOE leadership agreed to temporarily cede a lead role in North Africa to their US counterparts, correctly assuming that they could eventually reclaim *de facto* primacy in the region. Their ploy worked perfectly: OSS was given cover against its bureaucratic rivals, and SOE's grand ambitions for 'Massingham' were not cancelled, but merely postponed until later in 1943. In the interim, Dodds-Parker and his colleagues established a strong working relationship with their American counterparts, which proved the foundation of the mission's eventual success. The quasi-mystical, sentimentalized sense of pan-Anglo-Americana that occasionally bedazzles some contemporary political scientists clearly had little influence with the men who made these practical wartime calculations.[8]

The Establishment Controversy – November 1942

Until late 1942, SOE had played an unusual second-fiddle role to OSS in French North Africa. After 1940, Britain was excluded from the region due to political tensions with the French government at Vichy, while the United States parleyed continued diplomatic relations with Pétain's regime into an effective informal intelligence network of 'vice-consuls' in the Magreb. Run jointly by Colonel William Eddy, OSS Director William Donovan's representative in Tangier, and Robert Murphy, President Roosevelt's personal plenipotentiary in French North Africa, the consular web became the most effective Allied intelligence-gathering operation in the region. By November 1942, it was sophisticated enough to provide Allied military planners with vital geographical, logistical and French order of battle data prior to the TORCH landings. It also touched off an abortive coup in Algiers that, while mostly unsuccessful, earned OSS considerable credit with Allied army commanders and the American Joint Chiefs of Staff (JCS).[9]

For OSS Director William Donovan, this success came at a crucial time. In Washington, a series of midwinter bureaucratic challenges to OSS's existence came within a whisker of precipitating Donovan's resignation and the absorption of his overseas operations by the US Army's Military Intelligence Division (MID, or 'G-2').[10] Donovan's record of operational success in the Magreb – and the ammunition this gave him against the institutional enemies of his organization – invested OSS's presence in the region with vital importance.

TORCH also re-ignited Britain's – particularly SOE's – interest in French North Africa. It opened up the possibility of realizing the War Office's favoured strategy, an advance north into the 'soft underbelly' of Europe through Italy or the Balkans. SOE would certainly have a role fomenting native 'fifth columns' ahead of the advancing Allied armies; the Magreb could also serve as a forward staging area for clandestine work into France.[11] With TORCH in prospect, SOE's then-Assistant Director Brigadier Colin Gubbins drew up plans to address these possible opportunities in August 1942. By late October, General Eisenhower had been successfully petitioned on the subject; he had assented to the establishment of an 'advanced operations base' for SOE outside Algiers following a successful Allied landing.[12] This base, code-named 'Massingham', would serve as a training centre, holding area and launch pad for secret agents slated for insertion into a vast swathe of fascist Europe: Spain, Italy and France.

Unfortunately for inter-Allied comity, the Americans believed SOE had already ceded them an exclusive franchise in French North Africa. At a secret London meeting in June 1942, SOE and the Office of Strategic Services-Special Operations Branch (OSS-SO) had agreed to split their global responsibilities. Donovan and Sir Charles Hambro (Director of SOE or 'CD') divided the world into spheres of 'primary', 'secondary', and 'joint' control. The only significant regions where OSS secured primary responsibility for special operations were China and French North Africa.[13] The former became a great disappointment: Chiang Kai-shek did not cooperate effectively with the Americans on intelligence matters.[14] The latter proved fertile ground for Eddy, Murphy and his amateurish 'apostles' (as the vice-consuls became known). Ambitious OSS expansion plans were in the works; Eddy had picked out a large pseudo-Moorish mansion overlooking Algiers called the Villa Magnol as his new headquarters. More importantly, the OSS 'success' in North Africa became an effective wedge Donovan used to pry money and support from the JCS, and a mantra he used to fend off his bureaucratic foes at MID.

When the dust had settled after TORCH, and OSS learned of the British ambitions in North Africa – its area of 'primary responsibility' – there were predictably serious high-level ructions. Donovan had staked OSS's prestige on North African-based operations and was unwilling to cede the region to the British; but the Magreb was also an integral part of SOE's plans for French resistance.

Bickham Sweet-Escott, acting as part of SOE's liaison mission in the United States, found himself in the eye of the ensuing storm. Summoned before the Director in Washington on 10 November, the British bank executive found Donovan in a 'towering rage'. Having read the Baker Street telegram informing OSS that the British were, with Eisenhower's permission, establishing a major clandestine base in the Magreb, Donovan 'was convinced he had been double-crossed'. Sweet-Escott, who confessed to having 'a good deal of sympathy for him' rushed off to inform the head of the SOE mission in Washington, Barty Pleydell-Bouverie. After a quick huddle, they decided that the only solution was to try to get Bill Stephenson to come down from New York and mediate.[15]

William Stephenson was the Canadian millionaire who headed British Security Co-Ordination (BSC) – the proxy for all British intelligence agencies in the Western Hemisphere. An esoteric character even for a spy, Stephenson had become a close associate of his US counterparts; indeed, despite the outlandishness of the 'quiet Canadian's' later claims to fame, Thomas Troy has presented convincing evidence that Stephenson had a major hand in fostering OSS within the US government bureaucracy.[16] Therefore, cognizant of the political pressure Donovan faced, he regarded the young American agency with a vaguely paternal instinct. Stephenson's involvement produced a flurry of telegrams between Washington, BSC head-quarters in New York, and Baker Street.[17] These exchanges, principally in the form of personal messages between Hambro and the BSC Chief from 8 to 20 November, brought Baker Street up to speed on the weakness of OSS's position in Washington. While this ultimately led to a compromise on SOE/OSS cooperation in French North Africa, it also exposed Baker Street's frustrations with the 'teething trouble' experienced by the new US agency.

Setting aside his regular duties in New York, Stephenson decamped to the capital. After a briefing from his colleagues, he had a long talk with Donovan. Although no detailed record of their conversation exists, it's clear that it made Stephenson very angry. Having spent countless hours encouraging the growth of an American central intelligence organization, cultivating Donovan, and helping stave off the jealousies of established agencies in the American bureaucracy, Stephenson was not about to let bungling at Baker Street jeopardize the relationship.

These sentiments were expressed in the cipher telegram he dispatched that day to Hambro in London.[18] Noting that both Donovan and the OSS-SO chief Ellery Huntington were incensed, Stephenson described his own distress:

I find it difficult to understand why arrangements [with Eisenhower] were completed in [London] without either ourselves [BSC] or [Donovan] being informed . . . We received no communication from you . . . As regards [the] question of operations [into Europe] based [in North Africa] it was I think obvious from my [earlier communications] that [OSS] expected to operate in this area at least on an equal basis.

The entire SOE liaison staff in Washington shared Stephenson's sentiments. Stung after being cut out of the loop on negotiations for a North African base with Eisenhower, station chief Pleydell-Bouverie asked to be recalled.[19] Discussing the debacle years later, Sweet-Escott was equally blunt: 'I was never quite clear whether [OSS] suspected our integrity or our competence. Whichever it was, it did not help us'.[20]

Faced with a rebellion by its representatives in America, SOE took a conciliatory line; and did what it should have done long before – ask its officers in the USA for advice about OSS's concerns. Hambro, however, informed Stephenson that he was unwilling to abandon plans for 'Massingham', which was absolutely essential for future subversion in occupied Europe. Furthermore, 'the door is wide open for OSS co-operation if they will come in and work with us: the quicker the better for all concerned'. The need for haste became one of the major themes in Hambro's debate with Stephenson, which continued in this vein for another week. CD emphasized that SOE could not dawdle while OSS put its house in order: 'we . . . cannot be inactive, but must sail with the tide'.[21]

Yet CD also accepted the validity of Stephenson's concerns, and sent a statement of regret to Donovan on 11 November.[22] There was a lively discussion within Baker Street about how to accommodate OSS's wish for its own autonomous base in North Africa given what SOE saw as an imperative need for joint activity to ensure 'efficiency' – a euphemism for British leadership. Anticipating, correctly, that 'the Allied Commander [Eisenhower] will . . . insist on dealing with one authority for Special Operations', Hambro felt that OSS and SOE would be thrown together regardless of Donovan's objections.[23] If this occurred, the good of the overall war effort dictated that SOE must assert controlling authority. Brigadier Colin Gubbins summarized the British attitude when he wrote that 'I feel strongly that until OSS can produce men with experience, the head [of the North African mission] should be from SOE.'[24]

Yet compromise was unavoidable. A memo from the SOE Washington office convinced Baker Street that OSS was in dire straits:

For a considerable time Donovan has occupied a unique position [*vis-à-vis* the President] and a number of people have long been anxious to dislodge him from it . . . Now . . . it is necessary for Donovan to justify [OSS and] one of the ways he intends to do it is to create an impression in the minds of his adversaries that he . . . is responsible for a big SO organization . . . [in] North Africa.[25]

Stephenson was not the only one who viewed the possible demise of OSS with horror; it was the last thing anyone in SOE wanted to see happen. A proprietary instinct prevailed: they had helped to make OSS and Donovan was 'their man'. Thus, Hambro allowed that OSS should have separate facilities in North Africa – for now. Ultimately, however, no one at Baker Street expected this situation to last: the 'facts on the ground' would 'force' OSS 'into some form of joint mission' controlled by the British.[26] Donovan and Stephenson were ceded a pyrrhic victory.

In time it would become clear that Donovan's differences with the British were less significant than they seemed. He had no objection to joint operations at 'Massingham' – or even a subordinate position in the field to SOE. As long as OSS *appeared* to be independent and strong, thereby solidifying its political position in Washington, Donovan allowed his theatre commanders to operate as they saw fit. It was up to Colonel Eddy and his British counterparts in the field to make 'Massingham' a cooperative enterprise.

Operational frustration and the assassination of Jean Darlan, December 1942

While the 'Massingham' wrangle played out during the first three weeks of November, TORCH fighting in the Magreb between the Anglo-American invaders and French forces loyal to Marshal Pétain ended in an awkward truce. Robert Murphy's OSS plotters had hoped that the exhortations of General Henri Giraud – a pliant officer untainted by association with the Vichy government – would induce the defending troops to assist the Allies. When this plan failed, Murphy turned to Admiral Jean Darlan, who was serendipitously visiting Algiers. Darlan had served as Vichy premier under Pétain from February 1941 until Pierre Laval's return to power in April 1942, when he assumed command of all French military forces. During his stewardship of unoccupied France, Darlan had bent over backwards to accommodate the Germans, at one point offering to provide major aid to Rommel's campaign in Libya. The conspirators OSS recruited for its partially successful Algiers putsch loathed him. Murphy, however, felt his authority could salvage the situation for the Allies. The French high command in North Africa would defer to the 'little Admiral's' orders.[27]

Darlan's self-interested pragmatism made him receptive to the idea. Having ascertained the size of the Anglo-American invasion force and the ultimate hopelessness of resistance, he decided to cooperate. In exchange for his appointment as French High Commissioner for North Africa, Darlan ordered all French forces to cease-fire. Although the military effect of his intervention was relatively limited, it avoided prolonging the bloodshed. In the end, 479 Allied and 1,346 French soldiers died during the TORCH operation: a toll that would have been much higher without the deal with Darlan and the OSS-sponsored subversion around Algiers.[28]

The agreement with Darlan was formalized on 12 November. Major-General Mark Clark, who had flown from Gibraltar to help Murphy negotiate with the

French, signed on behalf of General Eisenhower. With the agreement the US military got a pledge of full cooperation from the French political and military bureaucracy in North Africa: aid that it hoped would facilitate a quick strike at the rear of Rommel's Afrika Corps through Tunisia. In return, the Vichy status quo was essentially preserved.[29] Opponents of the regime remained imprisoned in desert camps, anti-Semitic legislation stayed on the books, and Darlan – a man who had abetted the creation of Hitler's 'New Order' in Europe – became the most important French figure.

At the time of the Clark–Darlan accord, the Americans did not appreciate how seriously it damaged their ambition to support 'fifth column' resistance in metropolitan France. Murphy tried to placate the supporters of OSS's Algiers putsch by stipulating in the agreement that Darlan would appoint General Giraud commander of all French forces in Africa. While this may have mollified some right-wing French opinion-makers in the Magreb, it ignored Charles de Gaulle's growing stature within the French underground. This oversight would plague all OSS and SOE activities for the next seven months.

In the interim, the 'Massingham' plan went forward. On 17 November, SOE's first representative entered Algiers. Lieutenant Colonel J. Keswick, RA, the executive officer for the new 'advance base', bore a letter of introduction from Hambro to General Eisenhower. His first stop was the Hotel St Georges, the large second empire vintage structure where Eisenhower had established Allied Forces Headquarters (AFHQ) after the Clark–Darlan agreement. CD's missive reminded the General of his commitment to an SOE redoubt in the region, and sketched its mission parameters: carrying out subversive activities in southern France, Corsica, Sicily, Sardinia and mainland Italy.

After noting that these activities would be carried out while working 'as closely as possible' with OSS, it concluded by soliciting permission to requisition a headquarters somewhere in the near environs. Keswick and AFHQ agreed that the new clandestine base would be formally assigned the banal moniker Inter-Services Special Unit 6 (ISSU 6). Its informal code-name was 'Massingham'.[30]

With Eisenhower's assent, Keswick selected Cap Matifou, a rocky peninsula that jutted out into the Mediterranean east of the capital, as the site for 'Massingham'. A platoon of radio operators, the vanguard of a field large staff Gubbins had organized in Baker Street, joined him on 20 November. Although they were somewhat sullen from their stormy, U-boat-plagued sea passage, Keswick put the men to work building radio 'masts', designed to amplify weak radio signals transmitted by SOE agents in occupied Europe.[31] Over the course of the next three weeks the rest of the 'Massingham' officer corps flew into Algeria: including the commander, Colonel James Munn, and Major Douglas Dodds-Parker, the head of operational plans. Munn, fresh from a long stint working with OSS at SOE's top-secret training area near Oshawa, Ontario, was ideally suited for his demanding new job. It was his subordinate, however, who would play a more significant role in the history of 'Massingham'.

Dodds-Parker was the son of an Oxford surgeon of modest means. Though no intellectual, the elder Dodds-Parker had an old Oxonian's taste for the scholarly milieu. His father's son, Douglas also enjoyed the routine of life in a college town; he remembered a childhood 'enriched by the annual influx of the young, especially the Rhodes Scholars'.[32] Influenced, perhaps, by the Rhodesian political outlook, he became a lifelong friend of the United States, convinced that America was indeed the 'arsenal of democracy' and future 'guarantor' of Britain's 'freedom'.[33] 'The most deplorable date in the history of Western Civilization was 4 July 1776', he once quipped.[34] In Algiers this attitude helped disarm his OSS counterparts and – coupled with an even temper – prevented many small disputes from getting out of hand.

Soon after their arrival, Munn and Dodds-Parker convinced Keswick that Cap Matifou was hardly an ideal spot for 'Massingham'. In late December the Colonel's attention was drawn to a secluded site 20 kilometres up the coast west of Algiers. Located amidst a copse of pine trees was a charming cluster of buildings called the Club des Pins – a former French beach-club.[35] With its secluded beach, nearby verge with large sand dunes, and belt of luxurious villas, the Club seemed designed for seaborne operations, parachute training and a large staff. The presence of the airfield at Blida three kilometres to the southwest was an added bonus. Shifting from Cap Matifou took time[36] – but 'Massingham' had found its home.

With the base established, Munn's next task was to achieve an effective parley with the Villa Magnol. Contrary to expectations, Eddy was more than willing to consider an informal merger of OSS and SOE operations – so long as the agencies retained separate headquarters. Writing to explain the relationship between the Anglo-American services to a member of Darlan's intelligence section on 10 December, Eddy noted: 'The Office of Strategic Services [in French North Africa] is part of a *joint Anglo-American mission* . . . to prepare for advance . . . operations in future theatres of war outside North Africa' [italics added].[37] In a stroke, Eddy gave away the principle that Donovan had spent weeks fighting for: OSS autonomy. Yet from Washington's perspective, OSS's mission remained independent – as the Director intended.

Under this *ad hoc* arrangement, the Anglo-American sabotage services settled down to business, only to confront serious new difficulties. There was a dire short-age of transport. In order to make contact with the resistance in occupied Europe, SOE and OSS needed dedicated airplanes or the use of submarines. In December 1943, they had neither; indeed, OSS did not even receive official sanction from the JCS for post-TORCH operations until late December. (This was a by-product of MID's continued obstructionism and anti-OSS campaign.[38]) SOE had been promised a RAF squadron, but it would not arrive until the New Year. In the interim, the Anglo-Americans might have been stymied completely were it not for the appearance of the submarine *Casabianca*.

The submarine's captain, an eccentric French patriot named Jean L'Herminier, had been interned with his ship in Toulon after the collapse of 1940. Under the nose of the Italian Armistice Commission, however, he and his crew managed to hoard fuel in the forlorn hope of affecting a breakout. When the Germans occupied Vichy in the wake of TORCH, Pétain ordered the French fleet to scuttle itself. Instead, L'Herminier cut his moorings, steamed into the Gulf of Lyons, and crash dove in order to avoid an attack by Luftwaffe dive-bombers. When the Germans gave up the chase, Herminier slipped away to join the Allies in Algiers. Despite this heroic display, Darlan's authorities refused to clear the *Casabianca* for patrol duty due to some of its officers' ideological leanings. Seizing the opportunity this presented, SOE approached L'Herminier while OSS paid off Darlan's cronies for the use of the submarine.[39]

This deal – whereby the *Casabianca* would carry men, arms and explosives to Europe – facilitated the beginning of the OSS/SOE campaign in Corsica. In mid-December, OSS set up a 'listening post' code-named 'Pearl Harbor' in the north of the island. Manned by several of Darlan's intelligence agents and an OSS officer, it monitored shipping off the Gulf of Lyon and Italian troop movements. Although 'Pearl Harbor' served as an effective bolt-hole and intelligence gathering station, it did not become a regular contact point for funnelling arms to the local Resistance. Its failure in this respect was caused by the growing international backlash against the Clark–Darlan agreement: many Corsicans viewed the 'Pearl Harbor' agents' connection to Darlan with distaste.[40] This attitude was a harbinger of further strife. The British–French–American political wrangle that developed in Algiers played even greater havoc with OSS and SOE's 'fifth column' ambitions than the inter-Allied controversy that had gone before.

It was vital for European resistance movements to believe that collaborationist regimes would be overthrown by the Allied armies, otherwise – as events in North Africa soon demonstrated – they would be liable to reprisals. The moral hazard to the Allied cause was extreme. Lord Selborne (the minister responsible for SOE) reported that the Darlan agreement 'produced violent reaction among all our subterranean organizations in enemy occupied countries, particularly in France'.[41] Although these sentiments were widely shared by others within the British foreign policy establishment, AFHQ – particularly Robert Murphy – had decided that Darlan was the indispensable linchpin between Allied Headquarters and the colonial bureaucracy that ran civil affairs in the Magreb. The chorus of anti-Darlan voices were ignored; AFHQ warned that any Allied agency caught plotting to liquidate the Admiral would be expelled from North Africa.[42]

This decision increased political tensions in the region throughout December, hurt 'Massingham''s nascent programme in Corsica, and failed to protect the Admiral. On Christmas Eve, Darlan was accosted and shot to death at close range while returning to his office at the Palais d'Eté in Algiers. The assassin, a young, Gaullist, French Army officer named Fernand Bonnier de la Chapelle, had received weapons training from both OSS and SOE; although neither agency has ever been directly implicated in the assassination scheme. Bonnier, who expected to be hailed as a hero, was summarily executed by a French Army firing squad.[43]

Eisenhower and de Gaulle: a new landscape for clandestine operations, January 1943

Darlan's removal did not lead to a more convivial political atmosphere for the Anglo-American intelligence services in North Africa. At Murphy's suggestion,

Roosevelt approved General Giraud's elevation to High Commissioner. Untainted by service in Vichy, Giraud might have chosen to help reconcile anti-German French opinion. As a vain man of reactionary views and little political acumen, however, he was incapable of regarding de Gaulle as anything other than a dissident officer junior to himself. Rejecting friendly overtures from the Free French, Giraud elected to retain Darlan's cadre of Vichy administrators; fascist legislation remained on the books. Tainted by association, the Anglo-American clandestine services – particularly OSS – lost standing with the Resistance.[44]

In the near term, there were even more pressing concerns. General Eisenhower intended to make good on his threat to expel the Allied espionage agencies (both OSS and SOE had given weapons to Bonnier); but it was discovered that the pistol used to kill Darlan had come from a third party.[45] Instead, he was merely enraged: Colonel Munn was declared *persona non grata* and directed to leave North Africa, while Donovan and Brigadier Gubbins were forced to plan personal trips to Algiers in January for damage control.

In early January, General Eisenhower convened a joint meeting with representatives from the Club des Pins and the Villa Magnol. Eddy and Dodds-Parker (who replaced Munn as the Algiers SOE chief) were joined by Donovan and Gubbins for a long *ad hoc* session at the Hotel St Georges. Eisenhower, who had much more important things on this mind (namely the fierce struggle with Rommel's troops in Tunisia), was tired of the inter-service wrangling. OSS and SOE, he declared, bringing his hands together forcefully for emphasis, must 'work together 100 percent'. OSS was ordered to place its entire organization under 'Massingham' at the Club des Pins.[46]

Donovan was not resigned to the situation. In late January, he arranged for a private repast with Dodds-Parker. After sharing a cordial meal, the Director told 'Massingham's commander that he had no intention of obeying General Eisenhower's orders. As Dodds-Parker recalled:

> Donovan told me that if he went to the President and told him that he was merely supporting another half a dozen British operations he wouldn't get the support that he would have to get . . . I fully agreed with that and said that I would do my best to help him to find methods of having wholly American operations . . . although I realized that I would have to 'carry the can' if things went wrong.[47]

With this agreement, Donovan effectively formalized the understanding that Munn had established with Eddy. There would be an effective pooling of resources under British command. From Washington's perspective, however, OSS would appear to run its own, independent show at the Villa Magnol.

Dodds-Parker acceded to this extraordinary request for personal and practical reasons. He was philosophically inclined to support an increased role for the United States in world affairs, and the younger man revered General Donovan.[48] Yet it was also a rational compromise designed to put 'Massingham' on firmer footing. It reduced OSS–Baker Street friction and promised an increased ability to tap American sources of men, material and expertise.

Bureaucratic infighting drove Donovan's appeal to the 'Massingham' commander. In late December, MID's General Strong had officially demanded that JCS fold OSS into his outfit; OSS had barely survived. Now Elmer Davis, head of the Office of War Information (OWI), was manoeuvring to appropriate OSS's foreign propaganda function; Strong waited in the wings to snap up the remaining 'carcass'. This new power-play represented a serious political threat to OSS's existence: Davis was a Democrat intimate with many leading figures within FDR's New Deal establishment. As a Republican, Donovan felt threatened. Only by proving that OSS had an effective, independent organization in North Africa could he avoid partisan vultures.[49]

Shortly after Donovan's return to Washington from North Africa in early February, rumours circulated that the President had issued a directive dissolving OSS. Donovan drafted a letter of resignation.[50] The note was never submitted, thanks in no small measure to Dodds-Parker's compromise with OSS. Once again, SOE had defended the short-term interests of 'their man'. In the long run, however, the effectiveness of the Anglo-American secret agencies in the Magreb depended on how well the Allies could work together in the field.

In this, however, they were severely hampered by the on-going conflict between Giraud and General de Gaulle. While Eisenhower brought OSS and SOE together in Algiers, Roosevelt and Churchill had failed to secure similar comity between the French factions during the Allied Casablanca conference. Giraud agreed to talk, but de Gaulle was considerably more reluctant, fearing that he might come under pressure to accept a compromise with the Vichyite administration in North Africa. He also objected in principle to discussing purely French matters 'in a barbed-wire encampment surrounded by foreign powers'.[51] This stance caused the British authorities considerable embarrassment, as Harold Macmillan, His Majesty's political representative in the Magreb, recalled: 'Here was our great hero, the winning horse that we had bred and trained in our stable; and when the great day came it refused to run at all.'[52] It was only under British pressure that de Gaulle agreed to fly to Casablanca on 22 January, shake hands with Giraud and pledge solidarity. Yet privately 'the temperamental lady de Gaulle ... [showed] no intention of getting into bed with Giraud',[53] and no real accord was reached.

FDR blamed the whole fiasco on de Gaulle's rampant egoism. 'Yesterday he wanted to be Joan of Arc – and now he wants to be a somewhat more worldly Clemenceau.' Giraud thus remained entrenched in Algiers with US support. Seemingly chastened, de Gaulle returned to London.[54]

General de Gaulle, however, realized that he had never been in a stronger position. In the darkest days of 1940 he had possessed the imagination to see a future Europe free of Nazi dominion. This inspirational vision, coupled with a total rejection of the dubious moral compromise represented by Pétain, had earned the Free French movement considerable esteem within the Resistance. Initially, a demoralized public in metropolitan France had little sympathy for such idealism.[55] By mid-1942, however, when Laval dispatched the first mass consignment of forced labourers to Germany, sentiments had begun to change. De Gaulle's envoy to the Resistance

Jean Moulin – who had been transported to France by SOE – found a receptive audience when he offered guns and guidance through SOE's RF section.[56]

This shift in public opinion, coupled with his rejection of British control at Casablanca, greatly enhanced the legitimacy of his movement. Vichy might have *de jure* authority, but it had become a creature of Germany. Giraud commanded the loyalty of the army in the Magreb, but he was an American stooge. If the Resistance rallied collectively to the Free French, de Gaulle's movement could claim to legitimately represent the interests of the people.[57] This would allow France a much more powerful voice at Allied councils and perhaps enable her to retain the trappings of great power status during any post-war settlement.

Thus, when de Gaulle returned to London after Casablanca, he immediately made plans for a united Resistance council. Writing to former French premier Léon Blum on 10 February 1943, the General claimed that such a body would undermine 'attempts at division and confusion attempted by some among the Allies [the United States] with the assistance of French clients [Giraud]'. The Council would encompass both representatives of the Resistance movements themselves and extant political parties. These new instructions were entrusted to Moulin, who returned to France on 19 March, and conducted a series of clandestine negotiations from late March to mid-May 1943. Moulin's efforts convinced the entire spectrum of dissident bodies in France to form a National Resistance Council (CNR) under de Gaulle's leadership. Although the Gestapo captured Moulin shortly afterward in Lyon, he had ensured de Gaulle's gamble paid off. After the CNR's first meeting on 27 May, the Council spoke for the Resistance; the Resistance had become France.[58]

In the long run, de Gaulle's triumph strengthened the French Resistance and aided the OSS/SOE 'fifth column' effort. During the first four months of 1943, however, his gambit seemed rash and irresponsible. It produced high-level tension between Britain and the United States and further destabilized the political landscape in North Africa. Recruiting French intelligence agents became extremely difficult. In this context, the increasingly intimate cooperation between OSS and SOE in the field was remarkable. The mutual dependency created by de Gaulle's play reinforced the Anglo-American secret alliance.

A school for spies: The 'Massingham' mission at the Club des Pins, February–March 1943

By late January 1943, the Club des Pins had shed its frivolous trappings and was prepared to host the players of a much deadlier game. The upheavals that followed Admiral Darlan's murder and Munn's expulsion delayed SOE's move from Cap Matifou; at the end of the month only one of the villas was occupied. Captain Michael Gubbins – who had contacts with the Admiral's assassin Bonnier – taught weapons and 'methods of killing' to a small group of potential French recruits. By February, this sprinkling of men was subsumed in an eclectic deluge of humanity. Dodds-Parker, Keswick and the rest of the SOE command were joined by veteran radio operators from Cap Matifou, representatives of the Giraudist intelligence service and a team of technical sergeant-instructors from Baker Street. Reinforcements also included an initial detail of twelve British First Aid Nursing Yeomanry (FANY) officers who had been personally recruited by Brigadier Gubbins for their W/T skills. They were the vanguard of an increasingly important element at 'Massingham': women would ultimately comprise more than a quarter of the permanent staff – nearly 250 FANYs.[59]

Eddy kept the Villa Magnol as his headquarters, but Donovan's 'understanding' with Dodds-Parker led to a substantial OSS presence at the Club des Pins. A parachute training company under the command of Major Lucius O. Rucker was in the American vanguard; they claimed the largest chalet adjacent to Dodds-Parker's villa. Many of the 'apostles' also moved into the base as they followed their agents' progress in training. With the arrival of a large group of Spanish Republican security officers (newly 'liberated' from Darlan's old desert concentration camps by OSS officer Donald Downs), the Club des Pins reflected the diversity of the world coalition against fascism.[60]

Pluralism, however, can also breed discord; cultural misunderstandings often flared at 'Massingham'. That they did not get out of hand was partially attributable to the commandant's sure touch: Dodds-Parker had cut his teeth as a political officer in the Sudan and knew how to deal with obstreperous sniping.[61] Yet real tolerance was mostly a product of time and shared experience. Even as their leaders jockeyed fiercely for political position, the men and women of 'Massingham' laid the foundations for future success in their growing mutual trust and esteem.

The culture clash at 'Massingham'

As the officer corps at the Club des Pins underwent a major expansion in February and March, the new arrivals from London and Washington produced a strained atmosphere. Major Peter Murray Lee was dispatched from Baker Street by Gubbins to serve as 'Massingham''s security chief. As soon as he alighted from his jeep in the camp's focused chaos, he was confronted with the distasteful prospect of commanding Downes' escaped 'Spanish communists'. Lee thought they were like 'tiny hens' because they 'saluted with a closed fist' and 'none of them were more than five feet tall'. Now he was expected to turn these exotic, politically suspect midgets into proper British security guards![62]

Lee's biggest headache, however, was dealing with the Americans. Like many of his fellow SOE officers, he was appalled by 'the extraordinary agents' recruited by the Villa Magnol, 'who had absolutely no chance of survival [behind enemy lines] at all'. He attributed these shortcomings to the 'terribly green' OSS officer corps – conveniently forgetting the poisonous political conditions under which the Americans operated and the enormous advantage SOE enjoyed with long-established agent networks in France (F and RF sections).[63]

The disdain that Lee and other British officers had for OSS was rooted in cultural misunderstanding. One particular incident is telling: in order to establish a convivial social atmosphere between the British and American contingents, Dodds-Parker arranged for a joint soirée at a nearby French restaurant. As Lee remembers it:

We had this . . . drunken orgy, but I don't think it really did very much [for inter-service solidarity] because American ways of amusing themselves are not quite the same as English ways [and the Americans] were really rather an unsophisticated lot.[64]

Not all OSS officers were tarred with the same brush. Anglophiles escaped censure, as did exceptional individuals who manifested traditional 'English' traits – a dry sense of humour, appreciation of 'classical virtues', respect for authority. Douglas Fairbanks, Jr. (the famous actor) and a few other 'worldly' OSS personnel at 'Massingham' met the standard; but initially the British officer corps functioned as a private club that only a select few were allowed to join.

Many of his American counterparts repaid Lee's scorn in kind. Lieutenant Max Corvo, who came to the Club des Pins as part of the planning team for future Italian operations, was very suspicious of the British. Their controlling instinct was 'intolerable' given that this malign influence prevented OSS from establishing a service that 'would reflect the principles expressed by [the American] way of life'.[65]

If relations within 'Massingham''s Anglo-American officer corps were initially strained, at least the bad blood usually remained hidden beneath the surface. Among the enlisted men a rather *opera bouffa* rivalry developed. Again, cultural crossed wires played a role; ignorance, drink and youthful naïveté exacerbated the ill will. The young men who did yeoman's tasks at 'Massingham' – construction, maintenance, basic radio (W/T) operations, chauffeur duty – were from working-class backgrounds. They had very little experience outside their home countries. Thrust into an exotic land, expected to operate 'hand-in-glove' with foreigners, they were subject to many new temptations – including the urge to lash out at the unfamiliar.

For Harry Hargreaves, a private from the Midlands who had just turned 19, assignment to SOE 'Massingham' offered all sorts of potential diversions. Although there was an occasional German bombing run on Algiers, in the paradisiacal way station of the Club des Pins it was difficult to believe that the war lurked just over the horizon. Hargreaves and many other British soldiers, including his principal mate, William Pickering, would amuse themselves by 'pinching plastic explosive' and using it to fish in the cove. The security chief, Major Lee, who feared the ruckus might attract German U-boats, did not look kindly on this little hobby.[66]

Algiers' ancient Casbah quarter also offered many charms to the nascent orientalist. The strange traditional music of the Magreb and the seductive Arab-Berber women were the subject of much attention; Hargreaves and his credulous confederates were as mesmerized by the North African ephemera as any Victor Hugo or Jean-Léon Gerome. Yet while they shared the fascination of their great European predecessors, they lacked their experience: the ordinary SOE soldier's greatest weakness was not woman or song, but wine. During the early 1940s, the nectar of Bacchus was not the common commodity it is today; until his arrival in Algeria the only wine Hargreaves had ever experienced was his mother's Christmas tipple, 'Whiteway's English sherry'. Algeria, however, was the home

of an 'easy-sipping' viniferous tincture the men dubbed 'red bidet'. It was too much
for the young Englishmen:

> [I was fond of] that horrible red Bidet. We got our bellyful of this and needless
> to say, the ones that we picked on was [*sic*] always the Americans. There was
> a deadly feud between the British and the Americans as far as being out on
> the 'razzle' and Algiers was quite a place.[67]

In the hothouse environment of the camp these nocturnal ructions frequently spilled
over into the working day. The chief problem was that early in 'Massingham's
history, before the British and Americans had much experience with each other,
any little quibble could rapidly spin out of control. Even a silly dispute between
soldiers over the proper name for an undershirt – the American 'T-shirt' or British
'vest' – could generate trouble.[68]

Finally, Dodds-Parker had enough. Serious hotheads like Hargreaves and
Pickering were thrown in the brig – Harry drew twenty-eight days in the 'cooler'
for his various international misdemeanours. The commandant could present carrots
with as much aplomb as he wielded the stick, however. When he went out of his
way to help assuage tension and clear up misunderstandings, Dodds-Parker's
skill at empathy told. 'Douglas' political service . . . and tact made him a marvellous
pourer of oil on troubled waters', Lee observed.[69] William Donovan would have
certainly agreed.

As the winter wore on and activity at the Club des Pins settled into a semblance
of routine, Dodds-Parker's sure diplomatic touch became less essential. Working
together on missions where failure could be deadly, petty rivalries were forgotten.
This was well, for the patience of their political masters was not infinite.

Corsica in the stars: operational success at 'Massingham', March 1943

By early March the Anglo-Americans at 'Massingham' faced great pressure from
London and Washington to produce results quickly. France was the most important theatre for subversion and the failure to establish a viable network there from
North Africa was both conspicuous and humiliating. In late February, the Italians
had broken up OSS's small outpost in Corsica, 'Pearl Harbor'. SOE's attempts
to establish a viable presence on the island had failed completely; its case officer
had committed suicide in prison to prevent the fascists from extracting information
under torture.[70]

Just when the Corsican guerilla campaign seemed destined for total disaster,
aid arrived via a highly unusual source – an Arabic seer. The commandant of the
Algiers gendarmerie, a native Corsican by the name of Paul Colonna d'Istria, had
a superstitious streak. Prior to TORCH in November he had gone to an astrologer
in the city's old quarter for his annual reading. The stargazer informed him that
he was destined to make dangerous journeys to his native land during the coming
year. At the time this seemed a ridiculous prediction – the island was an easy ferry
ride from Algiers. Only after TORCH, when the Germans occupied Vichy France

and the Italians seized Corsica, did the seer's meaning become apparent. In March, the credulous gendarme offered his services to SOE.[71]

Colonna d'Istria was uniquely suited for his self-appointed task. Although no Gaullist (indeed, his position as a police captain under Giraud would have otherwise been untenable), he had small ties with the military regime in the Magreb. This apolitical stance, coupled with his status as the scion of an old and respected Corsican family, gave him automatic currency with the islanders. Furthermore, his standing as a gendarme and contacts within the Corsican police establishment gave him a superb official cover. At least initially, it would be possible for him to move around relatively freely – and carry weapons openly.[72]

In late March, the British submarine *HMS Trident* was detailed to take Colonna to a prearranged estuary on the east coast of Corsica. Met by representatives of the fragmented resistance movement, he disappeared into the rocky, *maquis*-covered hills. Over the course of the next several months, the former lawman forged a powerful 'fifth column' on the island. As the strongest extant Resistance cadre, the communist *Front National* initially served as the movement's hard core. Over time, however, Colonna brought together *Maquisards* from across the entire political spectrum – including the indigenous criminal Mafia. The former gendarme became SOE's godfather for the Corsican underground.[73]

OSS played an important role in the campaign. Colonel Robert Pflieger, Eddy's newly appointed deputy for special operations, worked closely with SOE's Jacques de Geulis to ensure Colonna's men had all the arms, money and supplies they needed. It was a tricky task. The island's small size and mountainous terrain made air drops dangerous and the Italian Army was vigilant. *Casabianca*, *Trident* and other British submarines made frequent 'milk runs' for the guerillas. One evening Colonna's party was spotted offloading guns on a beach and only escaped after a wild gun battle with the *carabinieri*. On another occasion a patrol flushed Colonna out into a field – only to lose the commandant when he crawled through a herd of goats on his belly. The Anglo-American intelligence services had scored their first major success.[74]

The Corsican campaign became the prototype for effective OSS/SOE operational cooperation in an uncertain political environment. During the early months of 1943 – as the French struggled to contain their bitter divisions, operations in Italy were delayed by the slow Tunisian campaign and Donovan tried to ensure OSS's viability in Washington – cooperation between regional commanders played a key role in fostering the Anglo-American secret alliance. A pragmatic attitude toward cooperation by Eddy and Dodds-Parker adopted a pragmatic approach that helped to contain disputes and finesse political considerations.

Training agents, winning trust

With a transportation shortage and the serious difficulties they faced recruiting prospective agents crippling operations beyond Corsica, necessity forced Dodds-Parker's men to focus on 'Massingham''s other main directive – training men and women for 'fifth column' activities in occupied Europe. Many individuals with the skills to teach this 'tradecraft' were on hand and an increasing number of raw recruits turned up at the base from late March onward. Initially this 'new meat' was composed of Downes' former concentration camp inmates and returnees from SOE's 'Brandon' mission in Tunisia. They were followed by groups of Italian-Americans in April and increasing numbers of Frenchmen from May and June. By chance, the instructors with the greatest expertise in the subjects that would compose the 'curriculum' were divided relatively evenly between OSS and SOE. Thus, cooperation became obligatory.

An informal division of labour emerged. As the dominant military presence in the theatre, there were many US personnel available to teach weapons and guerilla tactics; OSS's Major Rucker handled parachute training. SOE had men with years of experience running small boat missions from Gibraltar and infiltrating operatives into German-controlled territory via submarine, so naval instruction came under its purview. Clandestine experience in France and elsewhere in Europe also gave the British an edge *vis-à-vis* an agent's stock in trade: explosives, 'silent killing', and clandestine communications.

OSS Major Lucius Rucker was the earliest and most enthusiastic proponent of a joint effort on the American side. When the parachute school at the Club des Pins began operating in February, Rucker worked side by side with his SOE counterpart Major Wooler to produce a viable jumping programme. Modelled on the US Army airborne infantry school at Fort Benning, Georgia, it involved ground exercises where the students familiarized themselves with the equipment, learned technique, and otherwise worked to overcome their fear; three live jumps followed. To facilitate the first segment of training, several old aircraft fuselages were dragged into camp. Rucker had the recruits simulate jumps by throwing themselves out of the cabin door utilizing the 'tumbling roll' – designed to help them avoid hurt if they landed on uneven ground. The actual jumps took place from DC-3s based at RAF Blida; the students aimed for sand dunes on the outskirts of the Club des Pins, which were less punishing on the novice paratrooper. Practice drops at night and over water were scheduled for trainees whose missions might require special skills.[75]

Perhaps influenced by Wooler, Rucker adopted a semi-British marking system for his students: first class, second class, or third class (failed). Assessment was based upon formal criteria including technical skill, a written exam and attitude aboard the airplane. The forthright American did not stop there, though. He also went out of his way to critique the men's more ephemeral qualities: capacity for leadership, courage, resourcefulness and determination. Rucker's 'report cards' to Colonel Eddy were sometimes laced with caustic comments on a student's laziness, stupidity, fear, or inability to connect with the rest of the team. 'Untrustworthy' was the ultimate opprobrium. Conversely, he went out of his way to cite those with a special 'capacity for leadership' or an otherwise beneficial effect on the rest of the team. These additional observations, designed to weed out men unsuited to the exigencies of life as a secret agent, were soon adopted by the other 'Massingham' trainers.[76]

Rucker's outfit became the most conspicuously successful OSS training section at the Club des Pins.[77] The Americans also contributed several instructors in weapons and irregular warfare. Classes addressed the efficient use of knives, effective ambush techniques, and how to use captured German or Italian firearms. When prospective operatives had mastered several disciplines their knowledge was tested through war games.

On the night of 18 March the entire camp was rousted from bed by a massive explosion. Fortunately for Major Lee, the bedlam was not caused by shells from a German submarine: a training operation had 'attacked' the Club des Pins. At dusk a combined British-American team had parachuted into 'Massingham's dune perimeter, gone to ground until nightfall, and then advanced to screen the 'enemy' camp from its 'ammunition dump' (a large piece of scrap metal hidden in some trees). A two-man patrol was then dispatched to destroy the target – to spectacular effect. The password-exchange the 'agents' used to mark their return to base was a whispered 'VIVRE' answered by 'LA FRANCE'.[78]

The SOE course in 'small boat landings' completed a new recruit's basic training. Founded by the ubiquitous Michael Gubbins and refined under Captain Andrew Croft, it involved learning to pilot small boats from an offshore ship or submarine to a beach without attracting enemy attention. This sounds much easier on paper than it was in practice. The collapsible canoes (or folboats) that were kept for this purpose by the Royal Navy's submarines were awkward, unsteady little tubs and the containers of arms the men carried with them weighed hundreds of pounds. Moreover, the presence of shoals often meant the supply submarine had to disgorge the men several miles from shore; none of the folboats carried outboard motors because of the noise. Croft emphasized to his students how hazardous this made landing in the face of tide, rocks, or bad surf; efficient paddling and teamwork could mean the difference between successful contact with the Resistance's 'reception committee' on the beach and a watery grave.[79]

Trainees who survived the Rucker–Croft gauntlet of technical assessment and close personal evaluation were given advanced instruction in secret operations by SOE. British Army Captains Milner and Hoggart established themselves at another of the vacant chalets in camp. Adjacent to this structure (where classes were conducted under conditions of maximum security) a Nissen hut was erected, dubbed 'The Museum', and endowed with a collection of spy paraphernalia. This included displays of itching powder for distracting Nazi guards and a silenced, single-shot .22 calibre pistol that could fit under the ring finger. When the victim leaned forward to shake hands with the agent, the 'stinger' would be discharged into his heart.[80] The Milner–Hoggart team also handled formal training in explosives. Students were taught how to handle the standard tools of sabotage: limpet mines designed to destroy ships and plastic explosive that could be moulded into railroad tracks. Much time, however, was also spent teaching how to improvise bombs from ordinary ingredients. If OSS and SOE had difficulty supplying their agents in the field, these crude explosives might allow the men to complete their missions.[81]

Exotic weapons, stealthy forms of transport and bomb-making skill are renowned aspects of a spy's 'tradecraft'. Yet as Sun Tzu realized 2,500 years ago, simple information is the most vital element of espionage. Thus, the largest SOE training section was devoted to cipher communications with agents in the field – and many of the instructors involved were FANYs. An agent's lifeline was his portable radio. With it he could report on the status of his mission, request additional supplies (via submarine or air-drop), or abort and request 'extraction' from enemy territory. Without it he was essentially helpless; barring aid from indigenous resistance forces, it was unlikely his comrades would ever see him again. Operating a radio from Nazi-occupied Europe was an incredibly dangerous task. By 1943, the Gestapo had sophisticated direction-finding equipment, which meant that broadcasting from the same location for too long invited capture and death. Messages to 'Massingham' had to be brief and unobtrusive: furtive transmissions on prearranged frequencies at odd hours. They also had to be powerfully enciphered to befuddle eavesdroppers.[82]

The task of receiving, rapidly deciphering and replying to these often desperate communiqués fell upon the cipher corps at the Club des Pins. This tight-knit group included some men, but was mostly composed of a dedicated, meticulous group of FANY technicians. It was arduous work. Incoming messages had to be received in Morse code, decrypted, analyzed, and reported to the responsible country section officers for action. Any reply would then be broken down, enciphered, translated back into Morse and transmitted to the field. Error or delay could mean the loss of many lives. During periods when incoming radio traffic was intense, FANYs would sleep next to their radios.[83]

Mastering the technical aspects of enciphered Morse code was difficult enough; but the art of recognizing an agent's personal coding was also crucially important. When the Gestapo overran a SOE unit 'in country' they would usually attempt to 'turn' the W/T operator (through torture) or have one of their own officers use the captured cipher-key books to simulate the agent's presence. Additional men and supplies that were sent to a network 'gone bad' met a gruesome fate. In this case, only the skill of the radio operator could avert disaster. Former SOE FANY officer Peggy Widgery recalled that the idiosyncrasies of an operative's individual Morse messages were almost 'like a style of writing'. If something 'didn't seem quite right' about an agent's 'signature' their responses would be 'tested' to make sure there wasn't a German fly in the ointment. Eventually the need for W/T FANYs adept at this advanced technique became so great that a special advanced class was created at the Club des Pins.[84]

Partners

Several months of close proximity, determined work and shared hardships produced a sea change in 'Massingham's environment. Old squabbles between the Anglo-Americans were forgotten as both sides faced up to the enormity of the collective task. The Club des Pins had a unique capacity to foster solidarity in this respect: it was the only area in the world where OSS and SOE members underwent training, planned missions, and communicated with their colleagues in the field as an integrated unit. One particularly striking incident recalled by Major Lee is illustrative:

I remember one appalling evening when all the FANY wireless operators, and quite a lot of the male staff of all ranks were watching practice jumps. One wretched chap . . . did what they called a 'roman candle' – the slipstream [made] a [mess] of the parachute cords and the parachute . . . [knotted] in the cords. You go straight down. Even though he was going straight into the sand dunes he was killed outright. It was . . . pretty grisly, that.[85]

In such an atmosphere it became nearly impossible to maintain extraneous cultural or social animosity. Even American peanut butter began to taste better to the SOE contingent.[86] By early May 'Massingham' had become a *de facto* joint operation.

Shortly thereafter, William Donovan formally recognized a new, openly collaborative approach to Anglo-American clandestine operations from North Africa. The trigger came from OSS Special Operations chief Ellery Huntington, who complained on 5 May that SOE had failed to ensure that to '*all outward appearances*, at least, we would have the semblance of [independently] handling and directing certain small organizations on the continent' [from North Africa]. This was, in fact, the same issue that Donovan and Stephenson had fought over with Hambro. Huntington wanted to know if he should 'force the issue' again with Baker Street.[87] The Director said no. In his reply to Huntington he emphasized that 'I don't think that we want to keep stressing these questions with [SOE] indefinitely. Besides, we can take it up directly with Bill Stephenson and not conduct ourselves so that it would create suspicion in the minds of our [British] colleagues.'[88] The desire to secure operational independence for OSS was still there, but Donovan had moderated his hard-line stance against a subordinate role for his agency in the near term.

Donovan's change of heart on this issue was attributable to OSS's firmer political standing in Washington. In late April he had emerged victorious from his internecine battles with MID and OWI. The position of OSS within the JCS structure had been regularized; the Director had been promoted to Brigadier General in early March. From this stronger position, Donovan could compromise with the British on joint operations without giving the appearance of weakness within the Washington bureaucracy.[89]

The new American policy came at an auspicious time. In May 1943, de Gaulle was in the final stages of uniting the French Resistance under his banner; the General would arrive in Algiers himself on the 30th. With his return, the Anglo-American clandestine services began to have a much easier time dealing with the *Maquis* from North Africa. Likewise, the deluge of Italian-American recruits that flooded the Club des Pins offered the possibility of fostering subversive activities in Italy.[90]

More than any other single factor, however, it was the experience of OSS/SOE relations since TORCH that laid the groundwork for the future success of Anglo-American work with the European 'fifth column'. The Hambro–Stephenson decision to help foster OSS through its difficult winter teething period in Washington; and Donovan's pragmatic understanding with Eddy and Dodds-Parker helped to get the relationship up on its feet. The true basis for cooperation, however, was forged through many individual friendships at Massingham.

Conclusion

The secret 'special relationship' between the United States and Great Britain was inaugurated at the highest political levels – through a personal understanding between the President and the Prime Minister over the sharing of signals intelligence in August–September 1940. The two chief executives later broadened this collaboration to encompass special operations and took a personal hand in fostering the early stages.[91] Yet, close cooperation in a field as sensitive as intelligence requires more than a simple directive from on high: the overall relationship had to be built through a series of small steps, as people connected to each other and began to establish an individual rapport with colleagues.

Activities in French North Africa were an essential part of this process for OSS and SOE. During the six-month period from TORCH (November 1942) through de Gaulle's arrival in Algiers (May 1943) the Anglo-American secret warfare agencies experienced one frustrating failure after another. Martin Thomas rightly points out that SOE's 'Massingham' officers – particularly Major Keswick – initially resented having to cooperate with OSS because America's alliance with Darlan hurt their standing with the French underground.[92] Indeed, as we have seen, these differences went deeper than an overt dispute over policy – there were also strong undercurrents of cultural friction. OSS and SOE were able to overcome these issues and transform 'Massingham' into a success because, as Jay Jakob's work reveals, the top brass at Baker Street decided that preserving Donovan's political viability in Washington was worth sacrificing short-term operational efficiency in Algiers. Charles Hambro's intelligent compromise on this issue, and Douglas Dodds-Parker's diplomatic leadership on the ground, helped to ensure that near-term political tension did not jeopardize Massingham's eventual success. The close personal contacts that began in this often-poisonous environment eventually provided a fertile ground for trust – over time it blossomed into a rich partnership.

In May 1943, when Donovan gave his blessing to closer OSS/SOE integration in the field and the French began to escape from their political quagmire, the framework of confidence that had been established at 'Massingham' was put to the test. While the number of secret operations launched from the Club des Pins during the preceding six months can be calculated on one hand, over the course of the next year 'Massingham' became perhaps the most active OSS/SOE base in the world outside Britain. By the autumn of 1944, the Algerian 'Club' had played a major role in the liberation of Corsica, facilitated the secret armistice negotiations that led to the Italian surrender in September 1943, helped pave the way for the ANVIL landings in the south of France and instigated several massive guerilla uprisings behind Axis lines.[93] Moreover, it set the precedent for the increasingly close Anglo-American secret intelligence relationship that developed on a global scale. It is difficult to imagine that the 'Jedburgh' programme of 1944 – where integrated commando teams composed of American, British and French officers were parachuted into France prior to the invasion of Normandy – would have been possible without the North African experience of 1943.

Notes

1 In May 1944, 'Massingham' and other regional OSS elements were merged to form the Special Projects Operation Centre (SPOC). See M. R. D. Foot, *SOE in France: An Account of the Work of the British Special Operations Executive in France, 1940–1944* (London, 1966), p. 32.

2 Captain Jacky Porter, 'FANY: The History of MASSINGHAM' (unpublished: 15 Sept. 1945), Part I, p. 3, the National Archive, Kew, United Kingdom (formerly known as the Public Record Office, hereafter PRO) HS 7/169 – mistakenly filed as the *History of SOE in Corsica*, with cover letter, notes, and appendices.

3 Sir Douglas Dodds-Parker, Reel 2, SOE Oral History Collection, Imperial War Museum, Lambeth, London (hereafter IWMOH).

4 Jay Jakub, *Spies and Saboteurs: Anglo-American Collaboration and Rivalry in Human Intelligence Collection and Special Operations, 1940–1945* (London, 1999), pp. 74–79.

5 Martin Thomas, 'The Massingham Mission: SOE in French North Africa, 1941–1944', *Intelligence & National Security* 11/4 (1996): 696–721.

6 Porter, *FANY*, PRO HS 7/169.

7 Thomas, 'Massingham Mission', p. 717.

8 John Dumbrell, *A Special Relationship: Anglo-American Relations in the Cold War and After* (London, 2001), p. 2.

9 Bradley F. Smith, *The Shadow Warriors: OSS and the Origins of the CIA* (London, 1983), pp. 165–167.

10 Thomas Troy, *Donovan and the CIA: A History of the Establishment of the Central Intelligence Agency* (Frederick, MD, 1981), pp. 179–199.

11 William J. M. Mackenzie, *The Secret History of SOE: The Special Operations Executive, 1940–1945* (London, 2000), pp. 391–392.

12 Porter, *FANY*, part I, p. 1, PRO HS 7/169.

13 Mackenzie, *SOE*, p. 405.

14 R. Harris Smith, *OSS: The Secret History of America's First Intelligence Agency* (New York, 1972), p. 242.

15 Bickham Sweet-Escott, *Baker Street Irregular* (London, 1965), pp. 138–139.

16 Thomas Troy, *Wild Bill and Intrepid: Donovan, Stephenson and the Origin of CIA* (London, 1996), pp. 62–132.

17 Jakub, *Spies and Saboteurs*, pp. 74–79.

18 Cipher telegram from New York to London, G [Stephenson] to CD [Hambro], 10 Nov. 1942, PRO HS 3/56.

19 Cipher telegram from Washington to London, GM [Pleydell-Bouverie] to CD [Hambro], 10 Nov. 1942, PRO HS 3/56.

20 Sweet-Escott, *Baker Street Irregular*, pp. 139–140.

21 Cipher telegram from London to New York, CD [Hambro] to G [Stephenson], 11 Nov. 1942, PRO HS 3/56.

22 Ibid.

23 Cipher telegram from London to New York, CD [Hambro] to G [Stephenson], 14 Nov. 1942, PRO HS 3/56.

24 Letter from D/CD(O) [Gubbins] to CD [Hambro], 23 Nov. 1942, PRO HS 3/56.

25 Jakub, *Spies and Saboteurs*, p. 79.

26 Letter from AM [unidentified] to D/CD(O) [Gubbins], circa 23 Nov. 1942, PRO HS 3/56.

27 Julian Jackson, *France: The Dark Years, 1940–1944* (Oxford, 2001), pp. 178–180; Robert Murphy, *Diplomat Among Warriors* (New York, 1964), p. 128.

28 Jackson, *Dark Years*, pp. 224–225.

29 Arthur Layton Funk, *The Politics of TORCH: The Algiers Landings and the Allied Putsch, 1942* (New York, 1969), pp. 246–248.

30 Porter, *FANY*, Part I, p. 2, PRO HS 7/169.

31 Ibid., p. 6.

32 Douglas Dodds-Parker, *Political Eunuch* (London, 1986), p. xiv.

33 Ibid., pp. 25 and 33.

34 Interview with the author, 7 Jan. 2002.

35 Sweet-Escott, *Baker Street Irregular*, pp. 138–140.

36 Porter, *FANY*, Part I, p. 6, PRO HS 7/169. Cap Matifou continued to serve as an administrative centre until all SOE facilities were moved to the Club des Pins on 17 February 1943.

37 Ibid., Part I, p. 4.

38 JCS 170 and JCS 155/4/D, PRO HS 3/56.

39 Sir Brooks Richards, Reel 9, SOE Oral History Collection, IWMOH.

40 F. Brooks Richards, *Secret Flotillas: The Clandestine Sea Lines to France and French North Africa 1940–1944* (London, 1996) pp. 598–607; Arthur Layton Funk, 'The OSS in Algiers', in George C. Chalou (ed.), *The Secrets War: The Office of Strategic Services in World War II* (Washington, DC, 1992), pp. 168–169.

41 Lord Selborne, quoted in Arthur Layton Funk, 'American Contacts with the Resistance in France, 1940–1943', *Military Affairs* 34/1 (February 1970): 18.

42 David Stafford, *Churchill and Secret Service* (London, 2000), p. 292.

43 Ibid.

44 Jackson, *Dark Years*, 448; Porter, *FANY*, Part III, p. 1, PRO HS 7/169.

45 Harris Smith, *OSS*, p. 64.

46 Jakub, *Spies and Saboteurs*, pp. 78–79.

47 Quoted in ibid., p. 79.

48 Douglas Dodds-Parker, *Setting Europe Ablaze: An Account of Some Ungentlemanly Warfare* (London, 1984), p. 124.

49 Troy, *Donovan*, pp. 196–199.

50 Ibid.

51 Robert Dallek, *Franklin D. Roosevelt and American Foreign Policy, 1932–1945* (Oxford, 1995), p. 377.

52 Harold Macmillan, *The Blast of War 1939–1945* (London, 1967), p. 248.

53 Dallek, *Roosevelt*, p. 377.

54 Ibid., p. 378.

55 Maurice Agulhon, *The French Republic 1879–1992* (Oxford, 1990), p. 287.

56 Jackson, *Dark Years*, pp. 442–446.

57 Agulhon, *French Republic*, p. 259.

58 Ibid., pp. 455–456.

59 Ibid.; Peter Wilkinson and Joan Bright Astley, *Gubbins and SOE* (London, 1999), p. 96; Dodds-Parker, Reel 2, SOE Oral History Collection, IWMOH.

60 Porter, *FANY*, Part VI, p. 3, PRO HS 7/169.

61 Dodds-Parker, Reel 2, SOE Oral History Collection, IWMOH.

62 Major Peter Murray Lee, Reel 6, SOE Oral History Collection, IWMOH.

63 Ibid., Reel 7.

64 Ibid.

65 Max Corvo, *The OSS in Italy, 1942–1945: A Personal Memoir* (New York, 1990), pp. 18, 39, 49.

66 Timothy Pickering, Reel 2, SOE Oral History Collection, IWMOH; Lee, Reel 7, SOE Oral History Collection, IWMOH.

67 Harry Hargreaves, Reel 2, SOE Oral History Collection, IWMOH.

68 Ibid.

69 Ibid.; Lee, Reel 7, SOE Oral History Collection, IWMOH.

70 Richards, *Secret Flotillas*, pp. 629–630.

71 Ibid.

72 Ibid.; Richards (note 39), Reel 9; Dodds-Parker *Setting Europe Ablaze*, pp. 152–155.

73 Richards, Reel 9, Oral History Collection, IWMOH.

74 Funk, 'OSS in Algiers', p. 169; Richards, Reel 9, Oral History Collection, IWMOH.

75 Porter, *FANY*, Part VI, pp. 3–4, PRO HS 7/169; Hargreaves, Reel 2, SOE Oral History Collection, IWMOH.

76 Training Report on Tenth Parachute Course [to Eddy and Dodds-Parker] 28 May 1943, National Archive and Records Administration, College Park, Maryland (hereafter NARA) RG 226, Entry 210, Box 128, Folder 1.

77 During the summer Rucker requested an official 'parachute school' syllabus from the US Army and formalized the process. By the end of 1943, he was instructing up to three groups of 20 men *per week*. Syllabus of Parachute School for The Director, Office of Strategic Services, Washington, DC [for Algiers] 28 July 1943; Subject: Aircraft for Operations, from Rucker to Eddy, 4 Aug. 1943, NARA RG 226, Entry 190, Box 90, Folder 26.

78 Night Exercise, Thursday, 18 Mar. [1943], NARA RG 226, Entry 190, Box 90, Folder 26.

79 Report on Boat Training Carried out on Behalf of OSS [by Captain Andrew Croft] 18 Aug. 1943, NARA RG 226, Entry 97, Box 12, Folder 221.

80 OSS Weapons Manual 1943, NARA RG 226, Entry 97, Box 12, Folder 211; Porter, *FANY*, Part VI, pp. 1–2, PRO HS 7/169.

81 Ibid., p. 2.

82 SOE and OSS used a 'one-time pad' cipher system. See David Stafford, *Camp X: Canada's School for Secret Agents, 1941–45* (London, 1986).

83 Dodds-Parker, Reel 2, SOE Oral History Collection, IWMOH.

84 Porter, *FANY*, Part VI, pp. 5–6, PRO HS 7/169; Margaret Harvey-Cope (Peggy Widgery), Reel 2, SOE Oral History Collection, IWMOH.

85 Lee, Reel 7, Oral History Collection, IWMOH.

86 Audrey Rothwell, Reel 1, SOE Oral History Collection, IWMOH.

87 Huntington to Director: Handling of Agents in the Field, William Donovan, Director's Files, Box 13, Reel 97, Churchill Archives Centre, Churchill College, Cambridge (hereafter CCAC).

88 Donovan to Huntington: Interoffice Memo, 7 May 1943, CCAC, Director's Files, Box 13, Reel 97.

89 Troy, *Donovan*, pp. 207–208.

90 Jackson, *Dark Years*, p. 458.

91 Bradley F. Smith, *The Ultra-Magic Deals: And the Most Secret Special Relationship, 1940–1946* (New York, 1993), pp. 46–47; Stafford, *Churchill and Secret Service*, p. 234.

92 Thomas, 'Massingham Mission', p. 708.

93 Porter, *FANY*, Parts I–V.

4   Communist in SOE

Explaining James Klugmann's recruitment and retention

Roderick Bailey

James Klugmann worked on the headquarters staff of the Yugoslav Section of the Special Operations Executive (SOE) from February 1942 until August 1944, rising from private to major and becoming the Section's second-in-command.[1] Former colleagues recall Klugmann's 'owl-like appearance' and 'first-class mind', his 'warm smile' and 'gentle manner' and that 'he inspired great affection and had an encyclopedic knowledge of almost every subject'.[2] He was also a passionate and proactive British communist, who, allege many critics of British policy towards Yugoslavia, exploited his position to trick policy-makers into backing Tito, the communist leader of the Yugoslav 'Partisans', at the expense of Draža Mihailovic's royalist 'Chetnik' guerillas. As the factors at work on that policy have become clearer in recent years, those allegations have lost much of their force. Declassified decrypts of intercepted German signals, for example, confirm that key policy-makers possessed, and based their decisions upon, a picture of events in the field that was significantly more accurate than has long been supposed.[3] The debate over what Klugmann, while in SOE, may or may not have done for the communist cause still appears periodically in the British press.[4] Today, however, that debate seems more a storm in a teacup than a *cause célèbre*.

But important questions about Klugmann remain. How and why, for example, did SOE come to recruit and for so long retain 'one of Britain's most active young Communists'?[5] With reference to SOE and MI5 records, this study disputes theories that MI5 files on him had been destroyed during the Blitz and that SOE and MI5 were unaware of his record of pre-war activism.[6] It is shown here that Klugmann's intellect, skills and experience clearly impressed those who recruited and worked alongside him. But Klugman's ability to disarm suspicion by the quality of his contribution to the Axis defeat was matched by the failure of senior SOE and MI5 officers to see quite how loyal to their own cause British communists like him could be. To underline how serious was Klugmann's communism, the article begins by revisiting, partially in the light of recently declassified records, some of the more serious charges of espionage and subversion that have been levelled against him since the war.

Norman John (James) Klugmann was born in Hampstead, London, on 27 February 1912, the son of German-Jewish parents. His conversion to communism began in his teens. In 1931, after preparatory school in Hampstead and Gresham's

School in Norfolk, he went up with a modern languages scholarship to Trinity College, Cambridge. Very soon he became prominent on the Cambridge far left. Close comrades included David Haden Guest and John Cornford, powerful young forces in Cambridge communist circles. Both would die fighting in Spain. Others were Maurice Cornforth, who married Klugmann's sister, Donald Maclean and Anthony Blunt. Maclean had known Klugmann since schooldays. In 1933, Klugmann joined the Communist Party of Great Britain (CPGB). He remained a loyal and active member until his death in 1977, working full-time for the Party for the last thirty years of his life. During that time he wrote two volumes of the Party's history, edited its monthly publication *Marxism Today* for fifteen years and wrote and edited other works on Christian-Marxist dialogue, Yugoslav communism and related subjects. He became head of the Party's Propaganda and Education Department and a member of its political committee (effectively its Politburo).[7]

Accounts of pre-war communism at Cambridge and the recollections of contemporaries commonly highlight Klugmann's passion and intelligence and influence over others.[8] He had a talent, writes Miranda Carter, Anthony Blunt's recent biographer, for 'preaching a moderate, literate, rather comforting-sounding Communism'.[9] As Haden Guest's 'recruiting sergeant', the 'amiable, assiduous, and gently persuasive' Klugmann played a central role in the expansion of cells both at Cambridge and other universities.[10] He has been credited with becoming a dominant force with Cornford in the Cambridge University Socialist Society, a body some writers describe as the university Communist Party.[11] Blunt considered Klugmann 'an extremely good political theorist' who 'ran the administration of the [Cambridge] Party with great skill and energy . . . It was primarily he who decided what organizations and societies in Cambridge were worth penetrating.' Blunt's own evolving communism was influenced by Klugmann, as apparently was Maclean's.[12] 'My commitment to the cause was for life', Klugmann recalled forty years later; 'it was an exhilarating moment to be alive and young. We simply knew . . . that the revolution was at hand. If anyone had suggested that it wouldn't happen in Britain, for say thirty years, I'd have laughed myself sick.'[13]

That commitment became more focused after Klugmann completed his degree in 1934. After another year pursuing postgraduate research, he moved to Paris for further study and to work for *Le Rassemblement Mondial des Etudiants* (the World Student Assembly), an international body with thousands of members and strong links to the Comintern. In 1936, the Assembly was renamed the World Student Association for Peace, Freedom and Culture and the following year Klugmann was elected Secretary. He worked full-time in that post until 1939. In the course of his duties he attended a series of World Congresses and conferences and visited the Balkans, the Middle East and Asia. In 1938, he headed a delegation to China that met Mao Tse Tung.[14]

Recently evidence has come to light that confirms Klugmann worked more covertly for the Soviet Union: a charge long levelled against him. Weighing Klugmann's pre-war activism against his alleged wartime subversion, one author suggested in 1990 that Klugmann might even have been the so-called 'Fifth Man'.[15]

Soviet records now identify John Cairncross, a young Cambridge graduate and Foreign Office official, as the real Fifth Man.[16] But they also show that Klugmann agreed to assist the Soviets in Cairncross' recruitment.[17] In a Paris park in May 1937, Klugmann introduced him to Arnold Deutsch, the Soviet Union's London-based recruiter.[18] It is possible that Cairncross, who went on to disclose top-secret intercepts and details of atomic research to his Soviet handlers during the war, also passed on Foreign Office policy papers through Klugmann at the time of the Munich crisis.[19]

That Klugmann continued to work for the cause during his SOE career has also been alleged many times in the past. Frequently it is done to explain why British policy in wartime Yugoslavia developed as it did. When the first SOE mission to Yugoslavia landed on the Montenegrin coast in September 1941, the plan had been to cultivate Mihailovic. But from early 1943 that policy changed dramatically. In April, the British Chiefs of Staff authorised SOE to contact Tito's Partisans, with whom the Chetniks were in open conflict. By May, Britain was supporting Mihailovic and Tito in tandem, with SOE missions attached to both. By the end of the year, Churchill had resolved to support only Tito. In February 1944, the British formally abandoned the Chetniks in favour of all-out support for the Partisans. And to explain these policy changes it is claimed that staff officers in SOE's Cairo headquarters (SOE Cairo), from where its Balkan operations were launched and directed until early 1944, conducted a campaign of subterfuge that saw Mihailovic unfairly denied the help, recognition and respect he deserved. By supposedly massaging reports and starving the Chetniks of supplies and favourable publicity, SOE Cairo is held to have sabotaged their cause and helped secure Tito exclusive British backing and post-war power. Klugmann is accused of playing a central part in that campaign.[20]

Thus far, none of Klugmann's critics has succeeded in producing a concrete case that confirms he manipulated policy. Even David Martin, Klugmann's foremost critic, concedes that 'the proof of this is admittedly circumstantial'.[21] Instead, Martin and others point to strong evidence that suggests SOE Cairo was not always impartial in its policy proposals and handling of reports from the field. They highlight the fact that a leading British communist had worked in SOE's Cairo headquarters when all key decisions over Yugoslavia were taken. They point to the posts Klugmann filled, to imply that he had the opportunity to influence signals to and from SOE's missions in the field. They also underline colleagues' recollections that testify to Klugmann's open communism, his popularity and intellect and the long hours he put in, to emphasise his dedication and prominence on the staff and suggest his motivation for wishing Britain to back the Partisans.[22]

Many authors latch on particularly to the memoirs of Basil Davidson, Head of SOE's Yugoslav Section from late 1942 until mid-1943. In *Special Operations Europe*, Davidson writes openly of the pro-Partisan sympathies of officers in SOE Cairo. He also describes how he and his staff, including Klugmann, had embarked on a campaign from the autumn of 1942 to persuade higher authority to lend the Partisans British backing. They felt frustrated by 'high policy' that determined that only the Chetniks could be supported. They were impressed by what they had heard of the Partisans and convinced they merited Allied help. They also felt that the Chetniks, these agents of 'kings and governments-in-exile' with whom Britain naturally sympathised, would never inflict as much damage on the Germans as left-wing resistance movements focused on 'national liberation'. But some staff officers also shared strong ideological sympathy for the Partisan cause. 'You've got to see that this war has become more than a war *against* something, against Fascism', Davidson recalls Klugmann arguing. 'It's become a war *for* something, for something much bigger. For national liberation, people's liberation, colonial liberation.' Davidson's eulogy of his friend's ideals and intellect is often held to confirm Klugmann's prominence and influence on minds in SOE Cairo.[23]

With the recent release of SOE's Yugoslav files, reports by SOE Cairo to higher authority that were directly at variance with reports from Yugoslavia can now be traced directly to Klugmann's pen. A striking example is a four-page paper of December 1943 concerning the withdrawal of SOE missions from the Chetniks. This document presents a record of Chetnik achievement against the Axis that bears only partial resemblance to that reported to Cairo by missions in the field. Listing recent bridge demolitions, Klugmann omitted any reference to that at Višegrad in October 1943.[24] This omission seems especially suspicious because, shortly after the Višegrad action, SOE personnel with the Chetniks were so shocked to hear BBC broadcasts attribute it to the Partisans that they transmitted strong protests to SOE Cairo urging the BBC to get its facts right.[25]

More revealing are some of MI5's files. One recently released document is a 37-page verbatim report of a conversation Klugmann had, while on leave in London in August 1945, with Bob Stewart, a senior member of the CPGB's executive committee and controls commission. The source of the report was described by MI5 as 'very sure' but considered of 'extreme delicacy' and unspecified.[26] But Soviet records reveal that Anthony Blunt, after leaving MI5 in October 1945, warned Moscow that MI5 listening devices in the CPGB's London headquarters had recorded a conversation in which Klugmann 'boasted of secretly passing classified information to the Yugoslav Communists'.[27] If this was the same conversation for which a transcript is now available, it is clear Klugmann had boasted of much more than that.

The conversation consisted principally of details given by Klugmann of his SOE career and subsequent work in Yugoslavia with the United Nations Relief and Rehabilitation Agency (UNRRA). Of his time in SOE, he spoke at length about how, from the autumn of 1942, he had conducted 'two years' of concerted 'political work' to secure support and recognition for Tito's Partisans at the expense of the Chetniks. That work could be divided into six periods, he explained, each of which achieved a specific aim:

> The first political aim was to get permission for our Yugoslav section to learn from Intelligence sources about Partisans, to show that there were Partisans as well as Chetniks. That took about three months – a fight with the Foreign Office and War Office, and GHQ Middle East.

The second step was to get permission to send certain agents not only to the Chetniks but to the Partisans . . . that was another three months, fighting, persuading, documents organising, every type of work.

The next three months was to get permission to send arms to the people that were Partisans as well as arms to the Chetniks.

The next three months, four months about, was to get permission to send people to support the Partisans in Serbia, which was the area where Mihailovitch [*sic*] was strongest. Previously we'd only been allowed to send them to other areas.

The next stage – again for four or five months – was . . . skewing [and] building up reports we were getting from the Chetniks and . . . from the Partisans – [to show there was] no activity against the enemy on the Chetnik side, [but] first-class activity on the Partisan side – [in order] to recall the missions from the Chetniks, and to give all support to the Partisans.

And the last stage . . . was to fight inside the organisation [for] . . . political recognition of the Partisans.

He then expanded on the methods employed to promote the Partisans' interests. To begin with, in Cairo,

to allow us to even find out Intelligence about the Partisans, and then to allow us to send people there . . . I contacted 30 Intelligence Officers and various Yugoslav experts, and formed a group, not [of] . . . Party sympathisers but pro-Partisan people as distinct from the pro-Chetnik.

But Klugmann also claimed to have behaved more covertly, and went on to describe how he had sought to control and manipulate the intelligence gathered and reported by SOE missions in the field.[28]

This, he told Stewart, he had done in three ways. First, he was able to influence the selection and destination of British personnel, being careful to ensure the best ones went to Tito and that 'certain Fascist and really bad elements' were 'always sent to the Chetniks'. Second, once he was appointed 'Captain Regional Officer', he was able to brief agents before they left for the field. '[T]hat was particularly useful because everybody who went to the field had to go through me and I had to tell him what he would find, and you know that people often find what they expect.' Third, he sought to filter the intelligence coming back to help ensure that an overall picture emerged that was favourable to the Yugoslav Partisans. In Bari, to where SOE's Yugoslav Section had started to relocate by the end of 1943, he organised other 'pro-Partisan people' in SOE and its sister agencies 'to act as a sieve . . . to see that what got back was satisfactory . . . to bring propaganda to aid arms; intelligence to aid propaganda'. Klugmann also admitted to passing information to the Partisans 'as guidance on general tactics *vis-à-vis* the British'. He had helped, too, a representative of Soviet intelligence who had, it seems, approached him in Cairo 'and said that he had my name from before the war and could I do certain things for him'. Klugmann did not describe the form that help had taken. Had SOE sent him later to China, he added finally, he would have sought to do again 'what we had been trying to do in Yugoslavia' and 'switch official support from Chiang to the special areas'.[29]

To MI5, everything Klugmann had told Stewart seemed as significant as it did authentic. On 29 August 1945, Sir David Petrie, MI5's Director, informed SOE, the Secret Intelligence Service (SIS), the Political Warfare Executive and the War and Foreign Offices about the transcript's existence. He highlighted Klugmann's 'betrayal of information' and 'most unforgivable offence . . . his efforts to secure that only Intelligence was obtained from the field which supported his policy of recognition for the Partisans and the discrediting of the Chetniks'. As for the 'sieve' Klugmann claimed to have organised in Bari, this was 'very nearly a Party cell established on the traditional basis, and engaged on a Party task'.[30]

Klugmann's claims also fit the campaigns in 1942–1943 that SOE Cairo is held to have waged and several of the specific charges of manipulation that have been levelled at him since. Indeed, given the certainty with which several writers have made those allegations, it seems possible that the existence and something of the content of the MI5 transcript might have leaked into certain circles since 1945.[31]

Yet care must be taken not to exaggerate the influence of Klugmann's apparently meticulous effort to promote the Partisan cause. That writers like Chapman Pincher elevate him to the status of highly effective 'agent of influence' is a mark of the confusion that has long existed over the factors at work on British policy in war-time Yugoslavia.[32] Since the release of Foreign and War Office files in the 1970s, it has become increasingly evident that the key decisions in favour of Tito were taken well above the heads of SOE, reflected an accurate appreciation of who was putting up the most serious resistance in Yugoslavia, sought to take into account the potential strategic and diplomatic gains that Britain might accrue by support-ing the Partisans only, and drew significantly on important intelligence to which SOE staff officers had little or no access.[33] Decryption of enemy radio traffic meant that British policy-makers were well aware of Chetnik passivity and collaboration and the superiority of the Partisan war effort.[34] As Archie Boyle, SOE's Vice Chief, commented on learning of Klugmann's admissions: 'Petrie's letter of course is rather one sided and one would think if one did not know the facts that Klugmann has been responsible for the futility of Mihailovitch [*sic*] and, against the better interests of the Allies, had brought Tito into power.' Still, Klugmann's talk of sieves and groups and other activity does suggest that he had at least tried, in ways that were not always above-board, to exploit operations and influence policy in favour of the Partisans. And what more might he have done, or been made to do, for Soviet intelligence had its officers become more pressing? 'It seems from the evidence that he is a poor type', Boyle concluded.[35]

How, then, had that 'poor type' found himself in SOE and then remained inside it for two and a half years? This question occurred at the time to some of Klugmann's colleagues who believed SOE sought to avoid recruiting men whose political allegiances might jeopardise its security and agents' lives. Peter Kemp had been at Trinity with Klugmann before the war. In the summer of 1943, en route for SOE operations in Albania, he passed through Cairo and met him again, working as the

Yugoslav Section's intelligence officer. 'I was surprised to find Klugmann occupying such a confidential position', Kemp recalled in 1958, 'because when I had last seen him, in 1936, he had been the secretary and inspiration of the Cambridge University Communists. I had innocently supposed that Communists were strictly excluded from SOE, for I myself had been required to sign a declaration that I belonged to no Communist or Fascist party before I was enrolled in the organization.' Kemp assumed that Klugmann must have left the Party in 1939 at the time of the Nazi–Soviet pact. 'I was wrong: like his contemporary, Guy Burgess, he was one of the hard core.'[36]

Several theories have been put forward to explain how Klugmann joined SOE. Each assumes that the authorities must have known of his politics at some stage, given his pre-war profile. Perhaps the most widely known theory is that which appears in M. R. D. Foot's *SOE*, a popular history published in 1984. Foot employs Klugmann's case to illustrate the potential pitfalls of the old boy network so often used by SOE to bring in new recruits. He suggests, too, that the explosion of a German incendiary bomb may also have helped carry Klugmann into SOE. Brigadier Terence Airey, Foot writes, was 'an ambitious regular officer' on the SOE Cairo staff.

> One day in his office he was brought a cup of tea by an NCO whom he recognised as the cleverest boy who had ever been (after his time) at his school – Gresham's at Holt in Norfolk . . . He soon had the NCO promoted major, to assist operations into the Balkans. A routine reference to MI5 – on which the local security staff, more alert than the brigadier, insisted – produced the routine reply that nothing was recorded against him. A chance incendiary bomb at Wormwood Scrubs had burnt the file which recorded the ex-NCO's affiliations; this was how the brilliant and devious James Klugmann, secretary of the Cambridge University Communist Party in the mid-1930s, acquired a post from which he could exert leverage . . .
>
> Presumably like all other recruits into SOE he had been handed a form to sign, which said that he was neither a communist nor a fascist, but as a good communist he knew his duty to tell a lie.[37]

This explanation is reproduced in several studies that claim Klugmann had a critical influence on British policy in the Balkans.[38] It has also found its way into more sober accounts, like *Beacons in the Night*, Franklin Lindsay's acclaimed memoir of his time in wartime Yugoslavia with the American Office of Strategic Services (OSS). Lindsay assumes, too, that Klugmann, like many British communists before the Soviet Union entered the war in 1941, refused to enlist and had to be conscripted. He points to Klugmann's initial presence in the ranks of the Pioneer Corps, a unit into which the British Army shoved many of its troublemakers and generally unwanted, as evidence that the authorities viewed him with suspicion. Klugmann's past, Lindsay writes, 'would have been regarded as more serious than just a radical phase through which many university students passed in the Depression years of the 1930s'.[39]

Another theory has gone the rounds less publicly since the war. This holds that Klugmann was deliberately taken on by SOE *because* he was a communist. A version of it can be found in Richard Deacon's *The British Connection*, published in 1979. Deacon writes that John Baker White, who had worked during the war for the Political Warfare Executive and before it for MI5, told him that SOE 'enrolled' Klugmann 'because as a Communist Party member he was acceptable to the Yugoslavs'. Deacon adds that Klugmann's 'brilliant talent for languages', the 'contacts in many countries' he had made before the war and his 'appointment as an NKVD agent to be groomed for a key post in the Balkan sphere of operations' also played a part. Klugmann was 'undoubtedly' able 'to pull a few strings' to get himself posted to Cairo, Deacon writes. 'Once there his linguistic abilities made him a natural choice for attachment to the [SOE] Yugoslav desk.' Deacon, like Foot, provides no firm evidence to support his claims.[40]

Today, declassified records shed a good deal of new light on how Klugmann managed to join SOE. In 1939, MI5 did move its Registry and record-keeping staff into Wormwood Scrubs. And in September 1940 some of its records do appear to have been destroyed by German bombing.[41] Klugmann's file, however, was not among them. Released in four parts at the Public Record Office in May 2002, it contains a register that records every minute, document and development on file and confirms it remained active from the moment it was opened in 1934 until well after the war. Nothing appears to have been damaged or destroyed, although the Security Service has seen fit to retain everything from 1951 onwards and one or two earlier documents it still considers too sensitive to release. Enough remains to show that MI5 had identified Klugmann as someone to keep an eye on well before his recruitment by SOE. But the file also reveals how both SOE and MI5 found themselves lulled into believing that he did not pose a serious enough threat to be barred from sensitive and secret war work.

The earliest item on Klugmann's file dates from October 1934: a cross-reference to a letter from Klugmann, then still at Cambridge, to the Federation of Students' Societies asking for a speaker on Spain.[42] Three months later SIS forwarded a copy of a report from the Belgian Sûreté recording Klugmann's attendance in Brussels at the recent World Congress of Students against War and Fascism.[43] The earliest entries on his file are mostly of this type: occasional rather than regular or systematic, suggesting that MI5 was merely going through the motions of noting what it heard from time to time of a young left-wing activist.

By 1938, MI5 was taking more of an interest. It knew that Klugmann was connected with the World Student Association for Peace, Freedom and Culture. It also knew that he had been elected Secretary in 1937. In May 1938, Sir Vernon Kell, then head of MI5, informed the Defence Security Officers in Hong Kong, Singapore and Colombo that Klugmann was among a 97-strong delegation from the Association that had recently sailed for India, en route to China. Klugmann was one of two delegates known to MI5. The other was the young Bernard Floud, the future Labour MP, whom MI5 had on record as a one-time Secretary of Oxford University's 'communist October Club' and 'co-worker' of Klugmann's 'in the affairs of the World Students' Association'. Kell noted that the Association had a membership of 1,500,000 and that its 'policy' was 'controlled by the communists'.[44]

In 1940, MI5 placed Klugmann under nominal observation. Early that year it was known he had returned from Paris to Cambridge where he was 'connected' with the Socialist Club and 'awaiting call-up'.[45] In July, Scotland Yard's Special Branch was asked to ascertain his unit and destination.[46] Special Branch replied the following month agreeing to do so and confirming that Klugmann, whom it knew to be Secretary of the World Student Association, had registered himself for military service but not yet been called up.[47] In December, Special Branch reported that Klugmann had arrived at Aldershot on 7 November for duty with a training battalion of the Royal Army Service Corps (RASC).[48] At the end of December, MI5 informed the Aldershot Command that Klugmann 'will have to be placed under observation in his unit, in order to see whether he attempts to carry on anti-war or other undesirable propaganda among his fellow soldiers'.[49]

Given the interest he sensed the authorities were taking in him in 1940, even Klugmann may have been surprised by how he managed to join SOE. In his conversation with Bob Stewart in 1945, Klugmann began with a brief account of his time in Paris and early soldiering and explained that he had become certain early in the war that the authorities were watching him. Two days before the outbreak of war he had left Paris for Britain, where he promptly volunteered to join the Army through the Cambridge University Recruiting Board. But he then waited a year to be enlisted, even though his academic record and languages saw him recommended for 'Intelligence and Liaison and God knows what'. Eventually, 'in spite of all these recommendations and various interviews with every sort of branch in MI', he was called up into the RASC in which he was to remain for months as a private despite being recommended for a commission in 'various things . . . [like] education'. He felt it 'pretty obvious' that obstacles were being placed deliberately in his way.[50]

But as MI5 records now reveal, events began to conspire to allow Klugmann to escape from observation for a crucial twelve months. When informing Aldershot to keep an eye on him in December 1940, MI5 had requested a report 'in a month's time'.[51] Ten months passed. No report was received. In October 1941, MI5 sent a routine letter to Western Command at Chester, under whom it thought Klugmann was then serving, asking for observation to be maintained.[52] Western Command replied that it had no record of a Private Klugmann, but after inquiring with the RASC had learnt that he had left five months earlier in a draft for the Middle East.[53] While there is nothing on Klugmann's MI5 file to confirm that he had been deliberately prevented from obtaining a commission or a job in intelligence work, it is clear that MI5 had reservations about his serving abroad. A letter was quickly dispatched to Cairo and the head of Security Intelligence Middle East (SIME), Lieutenant Colonel Raymund Maunsell.[54] SIME was a special section 'responsible on behalf of the three Services for counter-espionage, counter-sabotage, vetting and the control of travel permits and passes throughout the Middle East'.[55] Maunsell, a regular army officer and former Defence Security Officer in Cairo, had run it since its creation in late 1939.[56] He was now instructed to keep under observation the peacetime Secretary of the 'Communist-inspired' World Student Association, who had 'unintentionally been allowed to proceed overseas'.[57]

That letter never arrived, which further eased Klugmann's entry into SOE by ensuring MI5 in London remained out of step with events for another two months. The next London learnt of Klugmann was in a telegram from Maunsell of 22 January 1942 asking whether it had 'any record against No. 230621 Private Norman John Klugmann, RASC. Formerly General Secretary of International Student Association . . . He is required for most secret work.'[58] SIME's responsibilities included the routine screening of personnel recruited locally by SOE and similar organisations, and records now confirm that Maunsell's January telegram marked the initiation of Klugmann's vetting for SOE. A hand-written scribble on Klugmann's 'Applicant's Particulars' form records that John Bennett of SOE's Cairo headquarters had interviewed him on 7 January.[59]

First, Klugmann had been sent out to the Middle East by mistake; then SOE had taken a look at him before MI5 could warn them off. And at the time, though apparently oblivious to the fact that MI5 remained anxious to control his movements, Klugmann was not unaware that he had come to SOE's attention in Cairo more by luck than design. In 1945, he recalled how, in June 1941, still a private and after training as a clerk, he was 'stuck on a boat' with an RASC draft bound for the Middle East. After a few weeks in a grim 'training depot' on the Suez Canal he found himself posted to Cairo to work as a clerk at GHQ Middle East. He worked there for the next six months and in spare moments 'spent a lot of time studying colloquial Arabic', in which he passed an Army exam. Then Klugmann's brigadier, on discovering he had under him 'a private with a double first at Cambridge, and [who] had passed the Arabic exam', began recommending him around for intelligence work. Eventually the brigadier brought him to the attention of 'a friend of his, a Colonel in an Intelligence organisation'. Klugmann was called for an interview:

I had no idea what it was but I went there . . . and it turned out that this Colonel had been to the school I had been to . . . I knew by that time that the dossier would keep me out of what I'd call the things that I would normally have gone into. I was looking for new work and I thought through Arabic I would perhaps get into something to do with Arab tribes or something, which would at least be interesting. But meanwhile they introduced me to this man, and my record on the face of it is [*sic*] very good. I'd been to his school, which counts a lot in these matters . . . and they asked me if I'd volunteer for special work; I said, 'Yes, of course, I'd love to' – and a fortnight later a civilian major called on me . . . and went through the usual rigmarole that they have for recruiting for special organisations; would you jump out of an aeroplane with a parachute? Go in a submarine? Sign a blank cheque? . . . and I said yes to all the questions; I've got more language and travel qualifications than most people, so that seemed very good to them. And without any check of dossier as far as I could plainly see, I was posted as a private to this Intelligence Organisation. I think that's how I got into it, through this personal contact.[60]

SOE records confirm that Klugmann's superiors in GHQ Middle East, a Brigadier Clowes and a Major Brown, had recommended him to SOE.[61] Klugmann's first interviewer was almost certainly Terence Airey, SOE Cairo's Director of Special Operations, and his second very probably John Bennett.

There is no indication on either Klugmann's MI5 or SOE file that his political views and affiliations were discussed at the interview stage. However, the fact that SIME had noted his pre-war work in Paris does suggest that something in Cairo might have been known of his politics. Indeed, to judge by his completed 'Applicant's Particulars' form, Klugmann may well have decided that his best policy was to present a circumspect version of the truth. He listed his schooling from the age of 7: The Hall Preparatory School in Hampstead, then Gresham's (where, he added, he had spent three and half years in the Officer Training Corps). He put down his double first in modern and medieval languages (French and German) and that he had remained at Trinity as a research student until 1935. He stated clearly that he had then spent four and a half years in Paris, not only as a 'research student in French and German literature' but also gaining 'considerable experience in organizing and lecturing . . . when acting as Secretary of [the] International Student Association'. He listed his pre-war visits to the Balkans, the Middle East and India and his three and a half months in China in 1938 as 'leader of [a] student delegation'. He also listed his languages: fluent French, good German, some Spanish and Italian and a little less of Arabic and Russian. And under 'special remarks', the final section of his application, he added:

> Considerable experience of work with foreign students of all nationalities – experience of lecturing at student, academic and public meetings in English and French both in European and Eastern Universities – including large meetings of 15–20,000 in China. Experience of methods of German, Italian and Japanese propaganda, espionage and infiltration of University and intellectual circles, 1936–1939, and of combating this.

Klugmann did not point out that his work in Paris had been for the Comintern. Nor did he disclose his pre-war contact with Soviet intelligence. But the fact that he had admitted to having been 'General Secretary' of the 'International Student Association' does suggest that he was taking care in Cairo to be relatively open about his politics.[62]

That openness may have worked in his favour. It is now apparent that SOE Cairo proved less concerned than MI5 about Klugmann's political views, to the extent that it recruited him before his vetting was complete and continued to employ him in spite of further warnings from MI5. For contrary to what Klugmann may have believed, there had been a check on his dossier. And contrary to what Foot assumes, it had turned something up. Indeed, had SOE heeded MI5's initial advice, the security screening procedures in place might have seen Klugmann excluded from SOE work.

The ease with which communists and moles assumed positions of influence in Britain's diplomatic and intelligence community is often attributed, at least in part, to the limits of that wartime vetting system.[63] As the intelligence historian Larry Hannant writes, this would be described today as 'a passive system, also known as "negative vetting" . . . MI5 initiated no systematic background inquiry with an applicant's referees and acquaintances . . . In this way it differed from the "positive vetting" set in motion after the Second World War.' In the 'passive' system, names were submitted and simply checked against the records in MI5's Registry.[64] But in Klugmann's case, this procedure worked perfectly. On 22 January, Raymund Maunsell had asked MI5 in London to see if anything was recorded against him. On 31 January, well aware of what it had on Klugmann, London showed no hesitation in advising that he should not be allowed to undertake secret work. It also referred Maunsell to its previous letter in November that detailed Klugmann's background and instructed that he be kept under observation.[65] Maunsell replied on 11 February saying he had never received any November letter.[66] London dispatched another copy and telegraphed again that 'Klugmann should not be employed on Intelligence duties'.[67] A Major Johnstone minuted on Klugmann's file on 15 February: 'It would seem inadvisable that Klugmann should be employed in the manner suggested, at any rate until such a time as our enquiries are completed.'[68]

Hannant adds that while the 'passive' system did enable MI5 'to exclude known Communists, of which MI5 had an extensive list', 'unacknowledged Communists' could still slip through.[69] But in 1942 it was not MI5's place to decide whether men like Klugmann should be barred from secret work. That was left to the judgement of the organisation concerned. In this case it was SOE Cairo which proved itself sufficiently impressed by Klugmann not to wait for the outcome of the security check: he officially joined its strength on 9 February.[70] Indeed, it remains possible that SOE Cairo was both aware of Klugmann's political sympathies and believed that they could be put to constructive use. SOE had yet to identify Tito; but reports of communist resistance were growing and, at exactly that time, both SOE and SIS were liaising with the Canadian Communist Party to find Yugoslav émigré and exiled anti-fascists willing to return to the Balkans to fight. Not long afterwards, SOE Cairo parachuted in its first Yugoslav communist; the first Canadian Yugoslavs were dropped to the Partisans the following spring.[71]

Klugmann was to remain in SOE for the next two and a half years, achieving rapid promotion along the way and even being cleared officially for secret work. And his survival in SOE certainly owed much to his ability to impress others by his dedication and aptitude for the important tasks at hand. In March 1942, for example, Raymund Maunsell informed SOE Cairo that Klugmann was suspected of having once spread communist propaganda among his fellow soldiers. SOE Cairo was asked to check whether Klugmann was still doing so and to ensure that he was kept under observation. In June, SOE Cairo reported to Maunsell that 'Private Klugmann's conduct has been exemplary. There has been no sign of the activities you mentioned. He has since been recommended for, and granted, a commission.'[72]

Klugmann himself told Bob Stewart in 1945 that after joining SOE he had soon proved he 'was able to do more than they'd expect as a private'. He was quickly promoted to local corporal, then granted an emergency commission 'without any attention to London fortunately'. He also became 'sort of identified as a Partisan protagonist' in SOE Cairo; but after 'we sent people to the Partisans, and had tremendous results fighting against the Germans, it naturally raised my prestige . . . So they promoted me first of all to full Lieutenant, then to Captain, and later to Major.'[73]

Yet Klugmann's ability to impress senior officers with the quality of his work was matched by their own complacency where British communism was concerned. This is illustrated by the ease with which Klugmann secured his position by winning the powerful patronage of the formidable Brigadier 'Bolo' Keble, SOE Cairo's chief of staff. A regular officer with twenty years service, Keble was no communist. But he was a forceful personality who believed strongly in bringing the fight to the enemy and, until late 1943, possessed considerable liberty to do with SOE Cairo what he liked. 'A professional staff-trained officer . . . of immense energy and activity', recalled SOE staff officer Bickham Sweet-Escott, 'it was largely due to the tremendous drive he generated that by October 1943, SOE had something like eighty separate missions in the Balkans.' Keble was also 'something of a bully', Sweet-Escott adds, with 'an ugly temper and a sharp tongue'. Nevertheless, 'once he had given a man his confidence, he would back him all the way'.[74] This would seem to have been especially true in Klugmann's case. Indeed, it has been suggested before that Keble valued his qualities so highly that he had sought to ensure Klugmann remained in SOE. Basil Davidson describes one occasion when Keble bundled Klugmann into a lavatory cubicle to protect him from 'Security'.[75]

To judge by his own account, Klugmann himself considered Keble to have been a valuable ally. Klugmann told Stewart that, when SOE London learnt of his commission, 'a routine security check with MI5' had at last turned up his 'dossier'.

> [A]s far as I can gather, the dossier wasn't very full. It said relations with the Communist Party, but whether it said 'membership' I don't know. It said . . . a certain amount about [the] International Student Movement in Germany, Spain, China . . . Well, it didn't seem too bad . . .
>
> [A]ny how, my brigadier . . . called me and said he [had] received a telegram that I was a Communist in relations to the student movement. He was very content with my work, and what about it?
>
> I gave him the correct reply, which [was that] I had done all these things . . . [and that t]he fact that I'd been mixed up with the Spanish and Chinese students ought to have meant that I wanted to win the war probably as much or more than he did; and the fact of this experience probably made me – was really what made me – so useful in . . . helping people behind the lines fight against German occupation . . . [I also said that] since the war, since I was abroad, I had [had] no contact organisationally with [the CPGB] . . . [and that I] thought he ought to trust me, and as he'd promoted me on merit without knowing about it, he ought to let me carry on, but it was his decision . . .

[He] said OK . . . and sent a wire back to London saying that he wanted to keep me on.[76]

In fact, contemporary records show that MI5, not SOE, in London had precipitated this inquiry, after finally hearing of Klugmann's commission from the RASC in November.[77] But MI5's files do suggest that Klugmann's account of the part Keble played in dispelling doubts about him rings true.

Those files reveal that SIME had, on behalf of MI5 in London, approached Keble at the end of December 1942 to ask for the latest on Klugmann.[78] Keble replied a fortnight later:

Whatever suspicion Klugmann may have been under whilst in the UK for spreading Communist Propaganda among his comrades, we have no suspicion whatsoever that he has been continuing any such activity whilst employed by us.

We should be grateful for any information or concrete reason as to why Klugmann should not be employed on Intelligence duties. We have employed him continuously and successfully as a Conducting Officer over Most Secret matters. We consider him to be thoroughly reliable, most painstaking, hard working, absolutely trustworthy, loyal and secure. I can say little more.

We are not really interested in Klugmann's politics which concern this organization but little, and any Communist tendencies he may have had, he would appear to have grown out of as do so many German Jews as they mature. In any case, are we to stamp on Communism when probably our largest ally is a nation composed of nothing but Communists?

I note with satisfaction, however, that there is nothing worse against Klugmann than a suspicion of spreading Communist propaganda. He certainly is not a Pacifist, as his untold energy in completing his small contribution towards the defeat of the enemy proves . . .

I would be very sorry indeed if I ever had to lose Klugmann, as he would be hard to replace. Furthermore, I should be extraordinarily surprised if I ever had to eat any of the above words.[79]

Keble's conviction evidently won over Maunsell, who replied underlining the importance of Internal Security but also acknowledging the high regard in which Klugmann was evidently held. 'As long as the Comintern includes on its programme the subversion of the Armed Forces of non-Communist nations, so long must we continue to keep Communists in the Armed Forces under observation', Maunsell wrote. But with regard to Klugmann, the Security Service was 'not in possession of that close personal knowledge of him that you have now been able to give'. Keble could now 'rest assured that the Security Service will not only clear him from the point of view of suspicion, but will waive any further [objection] to his employment on Intelligence work'.[80] Maunsell passed Keble's report back to MI5 in London. 'It appears from this that Klugmann has been doing extremely good work' he wrote in a covering note. 'The somewhat forceable [*sic*] tone of the letter [from Keble] indicates that they are more than satisfied with his services, and I therefore propose that he should be cleared of suspicion.'[81]

Some MI5 officers in London were less impressed by Keble's assessment.[82] But, crucially, more senior officers did not share their reservations. Lieutenant Colonel W. A. Alexander of MI5's F Division, tasked with monitoring the security of Britain's Armed Forces, minuted on 8 February that

> although it is somewhat unusual to 'clear' the subject of an Internal Security enquiry on a single report, in view of the very favourable one [by Keble] . . . and also because Maunsell has committed me so largely, I would be prepared to authorise him to write off Klugmann's case as cleared from the Internal Security point of view.

He noted that 'we do not know him as an actual member of the CPGB, but *only* [*sic*] as having been connected with various Students' Associations of a Communist type'.[83] On 14 February, Lieutenant Colonel Herbert Bacon, Assistant Director of C Division, responsible for security screening, minuted his verdict: 'No objection to his employment on Intelligence'.[84] Alexander telegraphed Maunsell the following day: 'case cleared'.[85] Maunsell informed SOE Cairo.[86]

In recent critiques of state surveillance in wartime Britain, the historian Richard Thurlow has highlighted the 'tunnel vision' of politicians and MI5 officers 'obsessed with the revolutionary ideology of the CPGB'. Believing the party was 'the main source of Soviet espionage by British citizens' and thrown by the general 'proletarian nature of the phenomenon', they failed to see the 'far more potent threat' posed by 'middle-class communists . . . behind the scenes'. Thurlow points to the activities of the 'magnificent five' as evidence of the establishment's 'prejudices and preconceptions about communism'.[87] The main thrust of Thurlow's argument is hard to fault, but may be qualified a little by reference to Klugmann's case. While allowing for MI5's legitimate concerns about resources and democratic processes, Thurlow writes that 'the real failure of anti-communist counter-espionage during the war' was that of the state in giving 'positive vetting of potential communists a low priority'.[88] It was true, as the intelligence historian Richard Aldrich writes, that 'MI5, overworked but unloved, could not keep up with its routine duties and had little incentive to carry through innovative searches for high-level Soviet penetration in the inner circles of the British establishment'.[89] It was true, too, that MI5 officers monitoring British communism chose to focus most of their attention on the CPGB. But while it was also the case that MI5 did not know until after his clearance that Klugmann was in fact a Party member, here, nevertheless, was a man whom it had flagged as a prominent communist in 1938 and placed under observation in 1940. In the opinion of some MI5 officers at the time, that background was sufficiently documented on file that it should have been enough to bar Klugmann from secret work long before confirmation emerged of his Party affiliations. As one F Division officer minuted in September 1943, 'we should certainly have desired to uphold the objection to his employment on secret duties'.[90]

Klugmann's wartime post was reviewed and, in spite of what was on file, sanctioned again in 1944. In the summer of 1943, SOE finally awoke to some of the risks posed by homegrown communist sympathisers when Captain Ormond Uren, a young officer on the staff of SOE London, was caught passing secret information to Douglas Springhall, the CPGB's National Organiser. In October, Uren was court-martialled, cashiered and sentenced to seven years in prison.[91] The same month, MI5 counted fifty-seven communists known to have access to secret information, eighteen of them in the Army. To the Security Executive, a committee that reported to Churchill, MI5 urged that all fifty-seven should be transferred away from secret work.[92] Whether Klugmann was among those fifty-seven may remain unclear until the day their names are declassified. But in September his MI5 file had arrived on the London desk of F Division officer J. B. Milne, who was at that moment 'looking for members of the Communist Party engaged on secret work in the Forces'. Noting recent additions to the file that showed 'without question' that Klugmann was a member of the CPGB, Milne minuted that 'the circumstances of his employment by SOE against our advice should be investigated and Klugman [*sic*] should be removed from most secret duties without delay'.[93]

Klugmann's case was duly referred to Roger Hollis, Assistant Director of F Division. On 11 October, Hollis wrote to Major the Hon. Thomas Roche, SOE's Assistant Director of Security, informing him of MI5's fresh information on Klugmann's Party links. Hollis underlined its relevance in the light of the Uren affair:

> I cannot say whether he [Klugmann] is at present taking any active part in the affairs of the Communist Party, nor should I be prepared to guarantee that local enquiries in Cairo would afford a positive answer to this question. His Commanding Officer, Colonel Keble, speaks in the highest terms of Klugmann's work, but this unfortunately is not inconsistent with the type of disloyalty we have recently come up against in the case of Uren.[94]

On 13 October, Roche spoke to Lord Selborne, SOE's Minister, about the Uren case. Selborne asked Roche if there were any other weak links in SOE and Roche told him about the letter he had just received from Hollis. Selborne instructed that Roche brief Major-General Colin Gubbins, Head of SOE, who was about to leave London on a visit to SOE's Cairo Headquarters. This was done and it was agreed that Gubbins would discuss the case with SOE Cairo. On 8 November, Gubbins, then in Cairo, wrote to the Military Secretary at GHQ Middle East asking him to transfer Klugmann to a post where his political connections did not potentially jeopardise security.[95]

That action was never taken, possibly because of further local objections from Klugmann's superiors whom he was evidently continuing to impress. 'This officer has borne the burden of the Section dealing with Yugoslavia for many months', wrote Lieutenant Colonel Bill Deakin, then head of SOE's Yugoslav Section, in a confidential report on Klugmann of 10 December. 'He is indispensable to the work, regarding which he possesses great knowledge. He works all hours and has done invaluable service by personal effort with operational personnel.' Instead of being reassigned, Klugmann was recommended for promotion to the post of GII (Coordination). 'A very capable and conscientious officer', observed Major-General Billy Stawell, Commander of SOE Cairo, countersigning. 'A clear thinker and lucid in explanation'.[96]

At a meeting in Cairo on 16 March 1944, Commander John Senter, Head of SOE's Security section, agreed with Gubbins and Stawell that Klugmann 'probably presented no real danger in his present employment'.[97] But it was also felt that Senter, a barrister in peacetime, should interview Klugmann to form his own impression. Senter saw Klugmann that day and reported:

> I explained that he was thought to have left-wing political sympathies and that the Uren case had made the organization review carefully all cases where an officer's political sympathies might be so extreme as to create a situation of divided loyalty. I invited Klugmann to tell me how he stood in that regard.

As before, Klugmann was not coy about his pre-war activities. But he assured Senter that, while 'he had been a member of the Communist Party when he was at Cambridge . . . he had allowed his membership and contacts to lapse when he went to Paris in 1935' and 'that since he had joined the Army he had taken part in no political activities and had not had political contacts. He found no difficulty in deciding to put his politics in cold storage until the end of the War.'

Senter concluded that MI5 should be invited to put forward any evidence they might have inconsistent with Klugmann's story.[98] On returning to London, he also sent Roger Hollis an account of the interview and added:

> Klugman [sic] made a good impression on me and in particular an impression of candour. I find from informal enquiries I was able to make among his colleagues that he had given the impression of single-minded devotion to his work. It is also material to note that much of his work in connection with Jugoslavia was done at a time when the official policy of HMG was to support Mihailovic: this did not appear to any of our officers to bring about any situation of divided loyalty so far as Klugman was concerned. Now that the policy of HMG is to support Tito, naturally no possible question of divided loyalty would arise, and it is not without interest to note that Klugman has found some of his old Left Wing associations in Belgrade to be of value in connection with his work.

Senter remained a little concerned about the 'discrepancy' between Klugmann's 'account of his political past' and MI5's information about his CPGB membership.[99] By the end of April, however, he and Hollis agreed that Klugmann had 'no current political contacts' and did 'not require any special observation'.[100]

Klugmann has left his own account of what he called this second 'Security scare'. He told Stewart that after Uren's trial 'there was a witch hunt, and . . . they went again combing with thin combs through all . . . [the] people who were suspected of radicalism'. Consequently he found himself 'put . . . through it for about four hours'.

> I spoke pretty frankly on just the same line as before, that I had been in the student movement, [that] I wasn't – I was – very proud of it, that I was in the war because I wanted to win the war . . . that I probably had a better record before the war than most of the other people as regards supporting . . . the Partisans, that the work that was given to me by the Army was to send arms to the Partisans, and that they would be ridiculous to have any suspicions. I mean they knew themselves that the thing I always wanted to do was to send arms to the Partisans. [I told them t]hat I didn't approve of contact with outside bodies, [that] I knew you had to observe Army discipline, and that I would observe Army discipline and I'd do what I was told to do . . . and I wouldn't have a political life outside the Army until the war was ended
> . . .
>
> [It was a] long, long, long discussion . . . the line of attack . . . was [the issue of] . . . double loyalty, dual loyalty . . .
>
> They were trying to catch you. If you were a Pacifist, the Judge says 'What would you do if you saw a German raping your sister?' The question they try and put to you is 'what would you do if your loyalty to Russia and your loyalty to your British citizenship conflicts?'. Well, it was easy to answer. I said ['I]t is ridiculous. It's one war, we're three powers together. We're supporting the Partisans and the Russians, and there is no question of divided loyalties, and anyhow I joined the Army and understood their discipline, and would accept it, and I can't do any more than tell them that. You either take it or leave it.['] Well, there again I think it was possible that my Army record was very good to them.

But what had really stood in his favour, Klugmann thought, was that 'they couldn't have got anyone else to do the work – that was the main factor'.[101]

When the war in Europe ended, MI5 still did not suspect him of having indulged in the kind of activity he described later to Bob Stewart. In the spring of 1944, MI5's 'designate' for Yugoslavia in Bari was sent a short précis of Klugmann's case and told to 'keep an eye' on him. 'I have never noticed anything suspicious' the officer reported six months later. 'His appreciation of military situations in Jugoslavia has always been a sober and factual one . . . and [he] has always been, at least in conversations with me, moderate in outlook.'[102]

In January 1945, confirmation came to light that Klugmann had been active in Cairo in the CPGB's Forces Organisation.[103] By then he had left SOE and the news did not cause much of a stir. In July, Roger Hollis sent a brief note to SIS saying simply that they should perhaps have Klugmann, who had since joined UNRRA, on record. 'His case,' Hollis wrote, 'has been considered closely by SOE, who decided that there was no indication that it had been influenced by his Communist views.'[104] Only in August, on overhearing his conversation with Bob Stewart, did MI5 suspect finally that there was more to Klugmann than had earlier met the eye.

The significance of that conversation should not be overstated. Klugmann may have sought, sometimes by unscrupulous means, to ensure that British policy benefited the Yugoslav Partisans. But his efforts had little impact on policy-makers, who, while not sharing Klugmann's passionate commitment to the communist cause, could see clearly a Partisan case for extensive and increasingly exclusive support. Care must be taken, too, not to overlook Klugmann's dedicated anti-fascism and his valued contribution to the defeat of Nazi Germany. Indeed, aside from the tributes to him found in SOE's files, the fact that he managed to join and stay for so long inside it reflects well on his compatibility with SOE's needs and unique line of work. The old boy network, together with breaks in communication between various military and security bodies, had proved important but SOE was always more interested in killing the common enemy than weeding its own ranks of communists, as illustrated by 'Bolo' Keble's defence of Klugmann in 1943. As J. H. Curry, MI5's in-house historian, writes: 'the natural reaction of a C.O. to representations on the subject of Communists under his command was that he was concerned with the present rather than the future'. MI5, 'on the other hand, was unable to overlook the long-term problem which might arise if Communists attained high positions in the Armed Forces'.[105] Yet the ease with which a man with Klugmann's known record of political activism survived in SOE remains striking. The preparedness of MI5 and SOE to clear him for secret work, even when confirmation of his CPGB membership and activities came to raise doubts over his honesty, underlines their lack of concern about the theoretical threat to SOE's integrity that dedicated communists like Klugmann could pose.

Notes

1   In August 1944, Klugmann joined the base headquarters of Brigadier Fitzroy Maclean's mission to Tito. In April 1945, he was released from military service to join UNRRA. Information provided by Duncan Stuart, the SOE Adviser to the Foreign and Commonwealth Office, to whom I am grateful for allowing me access to several SOE documents prior to their release in 2003. I am grateful, too, to Professor Rhodri Jeffreys-Jones, Dr David Stafford and Jon Naar, the intelligence officer of SOE's Albanian Section in Cairo and Bari between 1943 and 1945, for their advice and comments on drafts of this chapter.

2   P. Howarth, *Undercover: The Men and Women of the Special Operations Executive* (London, 1980), p. 89; M. Lees, *The Rape of Serbia: The British Role in Tito's Grab for Power* (New York, 1990), pp. 17–18.

3   See, for example, J. Cripps, 'Mihailovic or Tito?' in R. Erskine and M. Smith (eds), *Action This Day* (London, 2001), pp. 237–263; R. Bennett, *Behind the Battle: Intelligence in the War with Germany 1939–1945* (London, 1999), pp. 222–229, and *Ultra and Mediterranean Strategy, 1941–1945* (London, 1989), pp. 334–347.

4   See, for example, 'How a Soviet Mole United Tito and Churchill', *The Independent*, 28 June 1997; letters, *The Spectator*, 14, 21 and 28 Aug., 4 and 11 Sept. 1999.

5   C. Andrew and V. Mitrokhin, *The Sword and the Shield: The Mitrokhin Archive and the Secret History of the KGB* (New York, 1999), p. 63.

6   M. R. D. Foot, *SOE: An Outline History of the Special Operations Executive 1940–46* (London, 1984), p. 46.

7   T. E. B. Howarth, 'Klugmann, Norman John ("James")', in *Dictionary of National Biography 1971–80* (Oxford, 1986), pp. 470–471; J. Klugmann, 'The Crisis of the

Thirties: A View from the Left', in J. Clark *et al.* (eds), *Culture and Crisis in Britain in the Thirties* (London, 1979), p. 28; *The Times*, 26 Sept. 1977.

8   See, for example, A. Boyle, *The Climate of Treason: Five Who Spied for Russia* (London, 1979), pp. 61–76.

9   M. Carter, *Anthony Blunt: His Lives* (London, 2001), p. 122.

10 Howarth, 'Klugmann, Norman John ("James")', p. 471.

11 M. Worley, *Class against Class: The Communist Party in Britain Between the Wars* (London, 2002), p. 277; E. Hobsbawm, *Interesting Times: A Twentieth Century Life* (London, 2002), p. 111.

12 Andrew and Mitrokhin, *Sword and the Shield*, p. 63; M. Carter, *Anthony Blunt*, p. 124.

13 Boyle, *Climate of Treason*, p. 72.

14 Howarth, 'Klugmann, Norman John ("James")', p. 471.

15 D. Martin, 'James Klugmann, SOE-Cairo and the Mihailovich Deception', in D. Charters and M. Tugwell, *Deception Operations: Studies in the East-West Context* (Oxford, 1990), p. 80.

16 C. Andrew and O. Gordievsky, *KGB: The Inside Story of its Foreign Operations from Lenin to Gorbachev* (London, 1990), pp. 171–172.

17 Andrew and Mitrokhin, *Sword and the Shield*, pp. 63–64; N. West and O. Tsarev, *The Crown Jewels: The British Secrets at the Heart of the KGB Archives* (London, 1998), p. 206.

18 J. Cairncross, *The Enigma Spy: The Story of the Man Who Changed the Course of World War Two* (London, 1997), p. 61.

19 Andrew and Gordievsky, *KGB*, p. 321; West and Tsarev, *The Crown Jewels*, pp. 208–209, 228.

20 See, for example, D. Martin, Introductory Essay, in *Patriot or Traitor: The Case of General Mihailovich: Proceedings and Report of the Commission of Inquiry of the Committee for a Fair Trial of Draja Mihailovich* (Stanford, CA, 1979), pp. 117–119; D. Martin, *The Web of Disinformation: Churchill's Yugoslav Blunder* (New York, 1990) Chapter 1, passim, pp. 94–110; D. Martin, 'James Klugmann, SOE-Cairo and the Mihailovich Deception', pp. 53–84; Lees, *Rape of Serbia, Chapter 1, passim, pp. 206–207, 230–236;* C. Pincher, Too Secret Too Long: The Great Betrayal of Britain's Crucial Secrets and the Cover-up (London, 1984), pp. 397–401; R. Deacon, *The British Connection: Russia's Manipulation of British Individuals and Institutions* (London, 1979), pp. 162–170; R. Lamb, *Churchill as War Leader – Right or Wrong?* (London, 1991), pp. 253–265.

21 Martin, *Web of Disinformation*, p. 9.

22 See, for example, Martin, Introductory Essay, in *Patriot or Traitor*, pp. 117–159; Martin, *Web of Disinformation*; Martin, 'James Klugmann, SOE-Cairo and the Mihailovich Deception'; Lees, *Rape of Serbia* Chapter 1, passim; N. Beloff, *Tito's Flawed Legacy: Yugoslavia and the West, 1939–84* (London, 1985), pp. 87–95. See also J. Jakub, *Spies and Saboteurs: Anglo-American Collaboration and Rivalry in Human Intelligence Collection and Special Operations, 1940–45* (London, 1999) Chapter 5, passim.

23 B. Davidson, *Special Operations Europe: Scenes from the Anti-Nazi War* (London, 1980) pp. 79–136 passim. Davidson's first-hand account of life inside SOE Cairo ends in the summer of 1943 with his departure on operations.

24 'Note on Evacuation of British Missions from Mihailovic Areas', memorandum, Capt. J. Klugmann to Lt.-Col. Deakin, 21 Dec. 1943, National Archive, United Kingdom, Public Record Office (hereafter PRO) HS5/901.

25 Cipher telegram, Brig. C. Armstrong to SOE Cairo, 18 Nov. 1943, PRO WO 202/140, quoted in D. Martin, *The Web of Disinformation*, p. 157. A memorandum, 'Cetnik Collaboration with the Axis in Serbia', drafted by Klugmann and signed off by his then superior, Lt.-Col. Vivian Street, on 1 August 1944, was attached to Klugmann's

SOE Personal File as a further example of slanted reporting. Information provided by the SOE Adviser to the Foreign and Commonwealth Office.

26   Sir David Petrie to Maj.-Gen. Sir Stewart Menzies, 29 Aug. 1945, PRO KV2/791.

27   Carter, *Anthony Blunt*, pp. 318–319; Andrew and Mitrokhin, *Sword and the Shield*, p. 127.

28   Untitled transcript of conversation between James Klugmann and Bob Stewart, 8 Aug. 1945, PRO KV2/791.

29   Ibid.

30   Sir David Petrie to Maj.-Gen. Sir Stewart Menzies, 29 Aug. 1945, PRO KV2/791.

31   There are also intriguing similarities between the transcript and the account apparently rendered many years later by Kim Philby to Genrikh Borovik, a Moscow journalist, of Klugmann's links to Soviet intelligence and wartime work with SOE. See G. Borovik, *The Philby Files: The Secret Life of the Master Spy – KGB Archives Revealed* (London, 1994), p. 300.

32   C. Pincher, *Traitors: The Labyrinths of Treason* (London, 1987), pp. 50, 85. See note 22.

33   See, for example, E. Barker, *British Policy in South-East Europe in the Second World War* (London, 1976), pp. 157–167, 170–172, and D. Stafford, *Britain and European Resistance 1940–1945: A Survey of the Special Operations Executive with Documents* (Toronto, 1983), pp. 119–122, 126–127, 167–170.

34   See note 2.

35   Air Commodore A. Boyle to Lt.-Col. T. Roche, 31 Aug. 1945, PRO HS9/1645.

36   P. Kemp, *No Colours or Crest* (London, 1960), p. 77.

37   Foot, *SOE*, pp. 46–47.

38   Martin, *The Web of Disinformation*, pp. 95–96; Martin, 'James Klugmann, SOE-Cairo and the Mihailovich Deception', p. 60; M. Lees, *Rape of Serbia*, p. 33.

39   F. Lindsay, *Beacons in the Night: With the OSS and Tito's Partisans in Wartime Yugoslavia* (Stanford, CA, 1993), pp. 341–342. See also J. Ridley, *Tito: A Biography* (London, 1994), pp. 196–197, A. Cooper, *Cairo in the War* (London, 1989), p. 265, and G. Elliot, *I Spy: The Secret Life of a British Agent* (London, 1998), p. 79. Lindsay, Cooper and Elliott all suggest that Airey and Klugmann had been at Gresham's together. But Airey, born in July 1900, was almost twelve years older than Klugmann and had left Gresham's in 1916. Klugmann started at the school in 1926 and left in 1931. *Gresham's School: History and Register 1555–1954* (1955), pp. 160, 202. The archives of Gresham's School also provide grounds on which to challenge Richard Deacon's charge that 'Klugmann was no more than an average pupil'. Contemporary issues of the school magazine, *The Gresham*, confirm that Klugmann did very well academically. He won prizes for English and French. He played an active part in the school debating society: minutes of its meetings confirm the high quality of the debates and the high-mindedness of the participants. In 1931 his achievements were crowned with a Modern Languages Exhibition to Cambridge (Donald Maclean was similarly honoured that year). Deacon's source, Harry Hodson, who went on to become editor of *The Sunday Times*, attended Gresham's between 1920 and 1925 and left the year before Klugmann arrived. Quite possibly he confuses Klugmann with one of the latter's relatives. Frank Norman Klugmann (born 1904) attended Gresham's between 1918 and 1922. John Donald Klugmann (born 1907) was an exact contemporary of Hodson's. *Gresham's School*, pp. 177, 185. I am grateful to Mr John Rayner of Holt, Norfolk, for confirming these details.

40   Deacon, *The British Connection*, p. 164.

41   According to the official history of British wartime intelligence, 'on 24–25 September 1940 the central index and some of the records were damaged in an air raid'. F. H. Hinsley and C. Simkins, *British Intelligence in the Second World War. vol. IV:* Security and Counter-Intelligence (London, 1990), p. 67. MI5's in-house history dates the raid to 29 September, when 'an oil bomb fell on the Registry and destroyed nearly all

the card index and some files'. J. Curry, *The Security Service 1908–1945: The Official History* (London, 1999), pp. 378, 176. Klugmann's file may have been lucky to survive. During the 1960s, MI5 officer Peter Wright was put to work examining the pre-war files of British communists. 'It was a difficult process, prizing apart the charred pages with tweezers and wooden spatulas'. P. Wright, *Spycatcher: The Candid Autobiography of a Senior Intelligence Officer* (New York, 1987), p. 37.

42   J. Klugmann to J. Gillett, 12 Oct. 1934, PRO KV2/788.

43   SIS to MI5, 18 Jan. 1935, PRO KV2/788.

44   Sir Vernon Kell to Lt.-Col. H. Holt, Hong Kong (with copies to Singapore and Colombo), 2 May 1938, PRO KV2/788. Bernard Floud was another 'Old Greshamian'. Three years younger than Klugmann, he left the school in 1932. *Gresham's School*, p. 202.

45   'Lt Norman John Klugman [*sic*] (James)', memorandum by J. Milne, 16 Jan. 1944, PRO KV2/788.

46   MI5 to Chief Constable, Special Branch, 28 July 1940, PRO KV2/788.

47   Special Branch to MI5, 27 Aug. 1940, PRO KV2/788.

48   Special Branch to MI5, 6 Dec. 1940, PRO KV2/788.

49   Maj. W. Alexander to Maj. J. Avison, 30 Dec. 1940, PRO KV2/788.

50   Untitled transcript, 8 Aug. 1945, PRO KV2/791. Klugmann told Stewart that he came home to enlist 'with the agreement of the Comintern'. He did not indicate his reaction to the CPGB's policy of 'revolutionary defeatism' adopted, under pressure from Moscow, in October 1939 in support of Soviet neutrality. It is possible that Klugmann volunteered with the intention of penetrating the British Army and subverting it from within. But it is also possible that he found himself wrong-footed by the CPGB, or that his hatred of fascism had overridden his loyalty to the Soviet Union. Many British communists who had enlisted on the outbreak of war were shocked and disgusted by the CPGB's subsequent 'about-turn'. See, for example, J. Attfield and S. Williams, *1939: The Communist Party of Great Britain and the War* (London, 1984), pp. 49–78, 115–116, 125, 128–129. Harry Pollitt, the Party's General Secretary, was compelled to resign over his support for the war. A. Thorpe, *The British Communist Party and Moscow, 1920–43* (Manchester, 2000), pp. 256–261. The 'traumatic effect' on Guy Burgess of news of the Nazi-Soviet pact is also well documented. See, for example, Boyle, *Climate of Treason*, pp. 177, 181–182. But whatever Klugmann's reasons for volunteering to join the Army, the fact that he did so before the Soviet Union entered the war may well have helped dispel others' doubts about his commitment to Britain's war effort.

51   Maj. W. Alexander to Maj. J. Avison, 30 Dec. 1940, PRO KV2/788.

52   Capt. N. Watson to Capt. L. Rutherford, 30 Oct. 1941, PRO KV2/788.

53   Capt. L. Rutherford to Capt. N. Watson, 5 Nov. 1941, PRO KV2/788.

54   Capt. M. Johnstone to Lt.-Col. R. Maunsell, 11 Nov. 1941, PRO KV2/788.

55   Hinsley and Simkins, *British Intelligence in the Second World War*. Vol. IV, p. 153.

56   R. Aldrich, 'Soviet Intelligence, British Security and the End of the Red Orchestra: The Fate of Alexander Rado', *Intelligence and National Security* 6/1 (1991): 200; H. Dovey, 'Maunsell and Mure', *Intelligence and National Security* 8/1 (1993): 60.

57   Capt. M. Johnstone, MI5, to Lt.-Col. R. Maunsell, 11 Nov. 1941, PRO KV2/788.

58   Cipher telegram, Lt.-Col. R. Maunsell to MI5 London, 22 Jan. 1942, PRO KV2/788.

59   Applicant's Particulars, PRO HS9/1645.

60   Untitled transcript, 8 Aug. 1945, PRO KV2/791. That Klugmann became aware of his good fortune is supported by a post-war study of CPGB members' wartime experiences by Richard Kisch, a former international brigader. 'Officially he was classified as a dangerous red, to be kept continuously under observation, and on no account to be posted out of the country', Kisch writes of Klugmann. 'Somehow, it did not work out that way. Although everywhere Klugmann went, his papers, like Mary's little lamb, followed after, "almost invariably they arrived after someone had

conveniently posted me elsewhere", he would explain, almost apologetically, with a grin'. R. Kisch, *The Days of the Good Soldiers: Communists in the Armed Forces, World War II* (London, 1985), p. 42.

61   'Capt. N.J. Klugmann', note, 5 Nov. 1943, PRO HS9/1645. Terence Airey was then a colonel, not a brigadier as Foot suggests. W. Mackenzie, *The Secret History of SOE: The Special Operations Executive 1940–1945* (London, 2000), p. 182.

62   Applicant's Particulars form, PRO HS9/1645.

63   A. Glees, *The Secrets of the Service: British Intelligence and Communist Subversion 1939–51* (London, 1987), pp. 337–338.

64   L. Hannant, 'Inter-war Security Screening in Britain, the United States and Canada', *Intelligence & National Security* 6/4 (1991): 713.

65   Cipher telegram, MI5 London to Lt.-Col. R. Maunsell, 31 Jan. 1942, PRO KV2/788.

66   Cipher telegram, Lt.-Col. R. Maunsell to MI5 London, 11 Feb. 1942, PRO KV2/788.

67   Maj. M. Johnstone to Lt.-Col. R. Maunsell, 21 Feb. 1942, PRO KV2/788; cipher telegram, MI5 London to Lt.-Col. R. Maunsell, 18 Feb. 1942, PRO KV2/788.

68   Minute, Maj. M. Johnstone, 15 Feb. 1942, PRO KV2/788.

69   Hannant, 'Inter-war Security Screening', 713–714.

70   'SOE Record of Service: Major. N.J. Klugmann, Gen List', PRO HS9/1645.

71   R. Maclean, *Canadians Behind Enemy Lines, 1939–1945* (Vancouver, 1981), pp. 133–139.

72   SOE Cairo to Lt.-Col. R. Maunsell, 27 June 1942, PRO HS9/1645.

73   Untitled transcript, 8 Aug. 1945, PRO KV2/791. M. R. D. Foot holds that Terence Airey had Klugmann promoted major. This seems unlikely, since Airey moved on from his post as SOE Cairo's Director of Special Operations in the spring of 1942 and Klugmann was only promoted captain in 1943. Mackenzie, *Secret History of SOE*, p. 188. Indeed, it remains only possible that Airey had a hand in Klugmann's earlier promotion. Kenneth Greenlees was Head of SOE's Yugoslav Section in Cairo in the early summer of 1942 before being dropped into Yugoslavia to work with the Chetniks. Thirty-five years later, Greenlees wrote Klugmann's obituary for the newsletter of Britain's Special Forces Club. He recalled that he had first met Klugmann in 1942 when the latter was posted to him in Cairo. 'I soon realised his sterling qualities – conscientious, a glutton for work, much travelled; speaking several languages, a double first in modern languages from Cambridge; of an intellect way ahead of myself and many of those around me. I recommended him for Sergeant and, before I left for Yugoslavia, for a Commission.' Martin, *The Web of Disinformation*, p. 7.

74   B. Sweet-Escott, *Baker Street Irregular* (London, 1965), p. 170.

75   Davidson, *Special Operations Europe*, pp. 122–123.

76   Untitled transcript, 8 Aug. 1945, PRO KV2/791.

77   RASC Records to MI5 London, 19 Nov. 1942, PRO KV2/788; Maj. M. Johnstone to Lt.-Col. R. Maunsell, 19 Dec. 1942, PRO KV2/788.

78   SIME to Col. C. Keble, 30 Dec. 1942, quoted in first 'Note on K' by Commander J. Senter, 17 Mar. 1944, PRO HS9/1645.

79   Col. C. Keble to Lt.-Col. R. Maunsell, 12 Jan. 1943, PRO KV2/788.

80   Lt.-Col. R. Maunsell to Col. C. Keble, 14 Jan. 1943, PRO KV2/788.

81   Lt.-Col. R. Maunsell to Lt.-Col. W. Alexander, 14 Jan. 1943, PRO KV2/788.

82   'You will see that this officer's C.O. rather resents the application of the Internal Security system' minuted S. A. Minto of F Division to Lt.-Col. W. A. Alexander on 8 Feb. 1943. 'You will [also] note that [Maunsell] . . . requests you to cable if you agree to Lieut. Klugmann's clearance but I do not think that you will be inclined to do so.' Minute, S. Minto, 8 Feb. 1943, PRO KV2/788.

83   Minute, Lt.-Col. W. Alexander, 8 Feb. 1943, PRO KV2/788.

84   Minute, Lt.-Col. H. Bacon, 14 Feb. 1943, PRO KV2/788.

85 Cipher telegram, Lt.-Col. W. Alexander to Lt.-Col. R. Maunsell, 15 Feb. 1943, PRO KV2/788.
86 SIME to Col. C. Keble, 17 Feb. 1943, quoted in first 'Note on K' by Commander J. Senter, 17 Mar. 1944, PRO HS9/1645.
87 R. Thurlow, '"A Very Clever Capitalist Class": British Communism and State Surveillance, 1939–45', *Intelligence & National Security 12/2 (1997): 3–4, 19–20; R. Thurlow,* The Secret State: British Internal Security in the Twentieth Century (Oxford, 1994), pp. 263–264.
88 Thurlow, '"A Very Clever Capitalist Class"' p. 19.
89 R. Aldrich, *The Hidden Hand: Britain, America and Cold War Secret Intelligence* (London, 2001), p. 92.
90 Minute by J. Milne, 25 Sept. 1943, PRO KV2/788.
91 *The Times*, 8 Nov. 1943.
92 Hinsley and Simkins, *British Intelligence in the Second World War*. Vol. IV, p. 287.
93 Minute by J. Milne, 25 Sept. 1943, PRO KV2/788.
94 R. Hollis to Maj. The Hon. T. Roche, 11 Oct. 1943, PRO KV2/788.
95 Maj.-Gen. C. Gubbins to Military Secretary, GHQ Middle East, 8 Nov. 1943, PRO HS9/1645.
96 Confidential Report, PRO HS9/1645.
97 First 'Note on K' by Commander J. Senter, 17 Mar. 1944, PRO HS9/1645.
98 Second 'Note on K' by Commander J. Senter, 17 Mar. 1944, PRO HS9/1645.
99 Commander J. Senter to R. Hollis, 29 Apr. 1944, PRO KV2/788.
100 Commander J. Senter to Massingham, 29 Apr. 1944, PRO HS9/1645.
101 Untitled transcript, 8 Aug. 1945, PRO KV2/791.
102 Quoted in G. Eyres-Monsell to Lt-Col. J. Baskervyle-Glegg, 2 Nov. 1944, PRO KV2/788.
103 Sir David Petrie to Maj.-Gen. Sir Stewart Menzies, 29 Aug. 1945, PRO KV2/791.
104 R. Hollis to Col. V. Vivian, 5 July 1945, PRO KV2/788.
105 Curry, *Security Service*, p. 351.

5 'Kipling and all that'

American perceptions of SOE and British imperial intrigue in the Balkans, 1943–1945

Matthew Jones

Accounts of the Allied campaigns in the Mediterranean theatre during the Second World War, from the landings in French North Africa in late 1942 onwards, are often littered with the tensions and disagreements that marred the record of cautious Anglo-American cooperation that was established at General Dwight D. Eisenhower's Allied Force Headquarters (AFHQ).[1] Rivalry and distrust frequently flared up between different British and American commanders over the conduct of operations in Tunisia, Sicily and Italy, the former usually decrying their newly arrived allies as inexperienced, over-zealous and hopelessly amateur in their approach to war, while the latter were stung by British condescension and frustrated by the innate conservatism of British generalship.[2] This in-theatre discord had its higher-level parallel with some of the serious disputes between the US Joint Chiefs of Staff (JCS) and their British counterparts over grand strategy, where the Americans saw the Mediterranean operations instigated by the decision in July 1942 to mount Operation TORCH, and followed up with a commitment to invade Sicily made at the Casablanca Conference of January 1943, as sideshows which distracted from the major Allied task of mounting a decisive cross-Channel attack.[3]

A common thread running through American perceptions was that British military and political policy was tied together in a seamless mesh, with everything lying subordinate to the promotion of post-war British imperial interests; a natural corollary to this was that US manpower and resources were being hijacked and harnessed to the goals of maintaining Britain's global position, irrespective of the new age of democracy and self-determination that the Allied war effort was supposed to herald.[4] The utter conviction with which Churchill and the British Chiefs of Staff (COS) argued for the extension and prolongation of military operations ever deeper into the Mediterranean, as opposed to what American strategists viewed as the logic of a concentration of force against the heart of German military power in North-west Europe, was interpreted by many in Washington as a preoccupation with preserving political interests in the Balkans, where indigenous resistance movements and (later) Russian ambitions could upset the British Foreign Office's plans to re-install friendly governments. The JCS were told by President Franklin D. Roosevelt at a White House meeting in August 1943: 'the British Foreign Office does not want the Balkans to come under Russian influence. Britain wants to get to the Balkans first'.[5] Churchill's ill-fated backing for Operation ACCOLADE, a disastrous British attempt to establish a foothold in the Dodecanese islands of the Aegean Sea in the autumn of 1943 only reinforced the strong American impression that British strategy was focused less on the urgent need to defeat the enemy than on preserving vital imperial lines of communication extending through the eastern Mediterranean towards the Middle East and Indian Ocean.[6]

The efforts of General William J. Donovan's Office of Strategic Services (OSS) to develop its own special operations (SO) and intelligence gathering (SI) capabilities in the Balkans as the Allied campaigns in the central Mediterranean drew attention ever further eastward in 1943 provide further evidence of how much resentment could be bred by apparent British attempts to 'control' their American partners and uphold imperial interests in the clandestine sphere. This situation has echoes of the kinds of rancour that featured in Anglo-American relations in the Far East. Here, OSS clashed with the various British covert services operating in India, Indochina, Thailand and China, and the Americans detected British imperial machinations to be at work once more.[7] Despite the many positive contacts with British service personnel and officials, and the lasting friendships that could result, for some Americans it was difficult to overcome the ingrained belief that the British were inveterate 'empire-builders', where an instinctive regard for imperial interests suffused their behaviour. In the Balkan context, American officers felt their British opposite numbers were trying to deny them any role at all, or when invited to 'cooperate', were too often expected to show subservience. The result was an increasing determination to establish an independent OSS set-up and approach in the region sometimes at odds with official British policy toward the local forces of resistance.[8]

The basis for world-wide cooperation between OSS and SOE was initially laid down by a June 1942 agreement reached in London between Donovan and Sir Charles Hambro, the then head of SOE. The Americans approached the negotiations knowing that they held a weak hand: OSS was just in the process of being formed and for some time to come would be reliant on the British for their experience, contacts, information, training facilities, logistical support and communications. Indeed, both SOE and the Secret Intelligence Service (SIS) expected that they would control the activities of Donovan's fledgling organisation.[9] Nevertheless, Donovan was determined not to be overawed, and he was already ruffling British feathers with ideas to set up an American mission in Cairo, and run agents into the Lebanon, even though the British considered the Middle East as beyond US purview.[10] The June agreement stipulated that primary responsibility for India, West and East Africa, the Balkans and Middle East be given to SOE, while OSS was granted China, Korea, the South Pacific and Finland, allowing them only, as Bradley F. Smith remarks, 'slim wedges of the world for independent operations'. Western Europe was to be equally shared; indeed, it was assumed that joint missions would eventually be created for France and the Low Countries. Hambro reported to the COS that there had been 'considerable disagreement' over the position of French North Africa, and that an eventual settlement was reached which gave the Americans the lead, but with general policy to be coordinated between London and

Washington beforehand. The compromise formula arrived at would give 'general direction and control' to OSS, while SOE could still run their own missions in the area; secret intelligence activities were not covered by the talks.[11]

OSS had reason to be pleased with the negotiations, for they had resisted London's ideas for a single Allied organisation (which would at this stage of the war be a British-dominated body), and the decision to mount an invasion of French North Africa taken the following month meant that they could contribute an important role in the first major Anglo-American offensive in the war. However, the relationship between SOE and OSS was not always easy in the lead-up to Operation TORCH, while some confusion arose over arrangements for the post-invasion phase where Donovan was aggrieved he had not been informed of a private agreement between Eisenhower and SOE that it be allowed to deploy its own MASSINGHAM mission to Algiers, which would take charge of all future SO work into occupied Europe from the western Mediterranean.[12] Nevertheless, following TORCH, cooperation in the field did develop, helped by the formation of a joint controlling committee in February 1943 to arbitrate in cases of SOE–OSS disagreement, and also through the high example set by Eisenhower in the theatre.[13]

Yet to increasing SOE disquiet, OSS ambitions were set to expand during 1943, as their resources and geographical reach grew in line with a burgeoning US global war effort generally. Furthermore, OSS officers, with Donovan to the fore, had begun to chafe under the restrictions of the 1942 agreement, and were convinced that OSS operations should wherever possible be free from British control, not least as it was becoming apparent that association with the stigma of British imperialism could be a serious handicap in the search for collaborators against the Axis powers.[14] Lieutenant Colonel Ellery C. Huntington, the head of OSS's SO section, wrote with scorn of British attitudes to Donovan in November 1943,

> It is agreeable that British political aims preclude the consideration of independent American Military action except in the Pacific Theatre, and that our work, everywhere, will be affected [*sic*] by this philosophy. This may be an overstatement but . . . it is becoming increasingly clear that the British do not welcome any secret intelligence organisation in Europe which is not managed, if not controlled by them.[15]

It is noticeable that Huntington's concerns were related here to the field of secret intelligence work, and OSS were always most sensitive that its SI functions should be kept separate from British organisations and British scrutiny. Collaboration with the British on the SO side might be accepted, even welcomed, particularly in an area where the British were already well established (such as the Balkans), but this was combined with a conviction that British information and reporting were inherently biased, essentially so that it conformed with the main lines of political policy, or did not offend American sensibilities. 'We must strive to pull up abreast of the British in this intelligence work,' Colonel C. B. Guenther, the first head of OSS Cairo was writing to Donovan as early as April 1943:

They are coloured in their views to a point that their field groups are no longer free to present unbiased intelligence. We would be making a great mistake to accept blindly the well moulded statements which obviously are issued to us with definite intent to retain us within their orbits in certain very important fields.[16]

Throughout the war, the American self-image was that they were fighting the Axis powers in an 'apolitical' fashion, where calculations of post-war interests were not allowed to infringe on the cold logic with which strategic and military decisions were taken and executed. Revisionist scholarship offers a far different picture, however, where the search for commercial opportunities and the establishment of American primacy often featured in the conduct of US wartime policy.[17] Nevertheless, Americans entertained exaggerated fears that the cunning and manipulative British would exploit their relative innocence and lure OSS into entanglements where, as Axis power receded, they would find themselves supporting the restoration of British control and influence against popular will, allowing high-minded statements of Anglo-American policy such as the Atlantic Charter to fall by the wayside. In March 1943, Hugh Dalton was told by Averell Harriman that:

most Americans believe that we are so damned clever that we have already got all our post-war plans worked out to the last dot, and intend to inveigle the Americans into accepting them to their own great disadvantage. In view of our chronic indecisions, this is really frightfully funny.[18]

Donovan was always alive to the dangers of manipulation by the British, and was determined to maintain the independence of OSS missions wherever possible. One formal product of his unremitting efforts in this area was an instruction sent in March 1944 from the JCS to General Jacob L. Devers, the senior US officer in the Mediterranean theatre (and the Deputy Supreme Allied Commander), and Major-General Ralph Royce, commander of US forces in the Middle East, that, 'Nothing is to operate in the organisation and conduct of OSS–BRITISH combined activities to jeopardise the independence of American Secret Intelligence (SI) or morale subversion (MO) [operations].'[19] Thus, for example, when the (British) Supreme Allied Commander in the Mediterranean, General Sir Henry Maitland Wilson, made the decision to place all special operations activities in the theatre responsible to him under one coordinating body, headed by Major-General W.A. Stawell, OSS in Italy proved unwilling in practice to amalgamate with SOE in the new Special Operations Mediterranean (SOM) HQ that was formed in April 1944.[20] In a further sign of independence, by July 1944, and in a parallel with British concerns over the GUARD procedure for signal communications, OSS Cairo was warning other stations about the careful handling of intelligence reports that it was undesirable for 'non-Americans' to see, and that such reports would henceforth be stamped CONTROL.[21]

The many problems that would surface in the relationship between OSS and the British in South-east Europe need to be considered within the overall context of contrasting British and American attitudes towards involvement in the region. To the majority of Americans the Balkans were the archetypal setting for the un-principled intrigues of European power politics. As Richard Leighton once observed: 'The area to the east of the Adriatic was regarded by American strategists with something akin to the superstitious dread with which medieval mariners once contemplated the unknown monster-infested reaches of the Western Ocean.'[22] Certainly the JCS consistently refused to allow the deployment of US troops in that part of the world, and they did not accord it any major role in their plans.[23] However, British interest in the area was pronounced, and as London's policy evolved, the State Department became alive to its implications, in terms of relations both with the Soviet Union (possible clashes with Britain in the Balkans could wreck US ideas of post-war Great Power cooperation) and with the Balkan peoples themselves. Moreover, commitments had been made toward post-war relief and rehabilitation in the area, and the growth in indigenous resistance movements demanded some response. Diplomatic interest was shown by the decision of September 1943 to appoint Lincoln MacVeagh as US Ambassador to the Greek and Yugoslav governments-in-exile at Cairo, primarily to keep a watch on British activities in the Balkans and to pursue a distinctly American approach to the problems of the area. MacVeagh proved a lucid and critical observer, reporting to Roosevelt in February 1944:

> British policy . . . is essentially today what it has always been . . . It is directed primarily at the preservation of the Empire connections and sea route to India . . . it all shapes up to finding where Britain can secure the firmest vantage ground for the preservation of a stake in the Balkans – obviating total control of Southeastern Europe by any other great power. It is very far from a policy aimed at the reconstruction of the occupied countries as free and independent states.[24]

Yet as senior State Department officials such as Adolf Berle privately acknow-ledged, and as MacVeagh would frustratingly come to discover, the United States itself had no clear line of policy to follow in response.[25] War Department opposition to anything resembling an active Balkan policy coupled with the characteristic vacillations of the President resulted in something very close to inertia, allowing the British to keep the initiative; Roosevelt's casual approach to such issues was summed up by his flippant aside in December 1943 that 'the best way to handle Yugoslavia and Greece would be to put walls round them and let those inside fight it out, and report when all was over who was top dog'.[26] Almost by default then, overall American policy could be summarised only in negative terms as a desire not to be drawn into support for British-held political positions, or to becoming a potential arbiter in any Anglo-Soviet confrontation.

To Donovan, by 1943 the Balkans had become an attractive area for an expansion of OSS activities: the area seemed to offer a good environment to hold down and harass Axis occupation forces at relatively little cost, and could provide an ideal testing ground to assess the effectiveness of SO methods. American personnel might even possess the advantage with local populations that they were not identified with the 'imperialistic' attitude of British officers.[27] However, the existence of the June 1942 agreement with SOE, stipulating that the British would oversee all special operations work in the region, was likely to complicate Donovan's ambitions. Already during the autumn of 1942 there had been tensions as OSS felt that opportunities were being missed by SOE Cairo to promote resistance activities in Yugoslavia, and as American SO personnel began to arrive in Egypt only to find that the British expected to absorb them into their existing organisation.[28] In practice, the Americans found that any efforts to build up their own capabilities were frustrated by their allies; as the OSS/SO Cairo Internal History put it, '[the] unspoken objection . . . was against participation by Americans in military operations in a section of Europe which the British regarded as their sphere of influence'.[29]

In early 1943, the SO section of OSS began preparations to set up a full mission in Cairo from where American agents could be sent to the resistance forces in Yugoslavia and Greece. After a conference held at Cairo in mid-February on co-operative arrangements, Huntington felt compelled to protest to the head of SOE Cairo, Lord Glenconner, at the limitations placed on the prospective mission.[30] With SOE having the advantage of agents and transmitters already in place, OSS/SO had little choice initially but to work through SOE networks, use British transport facilities, and thus be under general SOE direction. By March 1943, OSS had established their Cairo office, with Major Louis Huot as chief of the SO section, but it was still to be some time before American agents would be dispatched, due both to the chronic shortage of aircraft available for special operations work, and the hesitancy of the British authorities towards US involvement. This hesitancy was partly explained by the ongoing internal British debates over which guerrilla groups to back in Yugoslavia; in April 1943, the decision was finally taken to send an SOE mission to Tito and his Partisans, while the existing SOE officers with Mihailovic's Chetniks would use their control over supplies to persuade Mihailovic to drop his periodic collaboration with the Italians and turn more vigorously against the Germans.[31]

In view of the ongoing problems of persuading SOE Cairo that the 1942 agreement should not be interpreted as excluding OSS altogether from Balkan operations, in July 1943 Donovan visited London and reached a new understanding with Hambro covering OSS–SOE collaboration in South-east Europe.[32] The Americans would now be given greater opportunities to send their agents into the Balkans, but it was stipulated that American SO activities in Yugoslavia, Greece and Albania were to be coordinated by SOE Cairo and OSS personnel would have to rely on British communications and codes to send their messages back to OSS Cairo; Donovan also agreed to try to secure more transport aircraft from US sources for use in Balkan operations. In addition, OSS were urged to take the lead in setting up networks in Bulgaria and Romania, and indeed Donovan would use this discretion to transfer the base for OSS operations into these countries from Cairo to Turkey.[33] As far as the latter arrangement was concerned, the Jadwin mission affair at the end of 1943 (where Bulgarian emissaries were contacted in Istanbul without British knowledge), helped to convince SOE that such encouragement of independent OSS operations was an unfortunate development.[34]

Following Donovan's talks in London, OSS at last established an active presence in the Balkans, when in mid-August 1943 Captain Walter R. Mansfield and Captain Melvin O. Benson were dispatched to Yugoslavia as American liaison officers, the former to Mihailovic and the latter to Tito, with others soon to follow. As already noted, the Americans were reliant on British communications facilities (until the spring of 1944), and were assigned to act with the in-place British missions, initially Colonel S. W. Bailey's with the Chetniks and Colonel F. W. Deakin's with the Partisans.[35] Although relations between the liaison officers began amicably, difficulties did begin to develop, with Mansfield, in particular, criticizing Bailey's increasingly negative view of Mihailovic.[36] Matters did not improve when the British missions were upgraded in the autumn of 1943, Brigadier Fitzroy Maclean arriving with Major Linn M. Parish of OSS to join Tito, and Brigadier C. D. Armstrong joining with Mihailovic, accompanied by another OSS man, Lieutenant Colonel Albert C. Seitz.[37] The Americans had to seek the approval of Maclean or Armstrong before gaining access to the Yugoslav guerrilla leaders, while Seitz's messages to OSS Cairo, much to his resentment, were subject to Armstrong's vetting and sometimes censorship.[38] Armstrong was felt to be anti-American by Seitz and the latter considered the only function of the American presence was to present 'an Allied illusion' to Mihailovic.[39] Matters reached a low point in October–November 1943 when, as the historian Jay Jakub has detailed, SOE Cairo probably acted to block a crucial report on conditions in Yugoslavia that Seitz had submitted to his OSS superiors in Washington.[40]

By the end of 1943, there was considerable disillusionment within OSS at the high-handedness shown by the British authorities in Cairo and elsewhere. Although individual relationships could be cordial, the overall pattern was disquieting. 'During the writer's entire stay in Cairo [during October 1943],' Commander R. David Halliwell observed in a report of January 1944:

> it became more and more evident from the examination of documents passing back and forth between OSS and SOE, from the general atmosphere, and from the trend of conversations, that it was the desire of the SOE people to dominate in so far as practicable our operations in the Balkans.[41]

Donovan had already decided to replace Huot with Lieutenant Colonel Paul West as SO chief in Cairo, believing the former had not done enough to protect American interests.[42] The head of OSS also tried to use his personal influence with Roosevelt to press for more radical change, and in late October 1943 the President suggested to Churchill that Donovan should be sent to Cairo in an effort to unite the rival guerrilla factions in Greece and Yugoslavia and that he should take over the direction of all the Allied agencies working into the Balkans. Churchill quickly rejected the alarming proposal, asserting, 'I have great admiration for Donovan, but

I do not see any centre in the Balkans from which he could grip the situation.'[43] The Foreign Office, in the form of Sir Orme Sargent, the Deputy Under Secretary (and contrary to the instructions of the Prime Minister), passed on the substance of this exchange to the British ambassadors to the Yugoslav and Greek governments-in-exile, perhaps as a warning to Cairo as to what trouble might lie ahead.[44]

British SOE and military authorities were made even more nervous by Donovan's visit to Cairo in November 1943, where he argued vigorously that SOE should not obstruct his independent SI operations in the Balkans, while SOE were forced to concede that more American personnel would be allowed to join the missions with Tito and Mihailovic.[45] Following these meetings, the head of SOE, Major General Sir Colin Gubbins, wrote to the Chief of Staff at GHQ Middle East Cairo that although previous agreements had made SOE the senior and predominating partner in Balkan operations, things now appeared to be changing. It had become clear that Donovan would only accept light SOE control and would disregard Baker Street when it suited him: at one stage he even talked of OSS becoming an equal partner. Gubbins felt that some form of Foreign Office–State Department agreement was required to reduce the risk of possible future conflicts, for although SOE could limit the number of OSS personnel in the Balkans in the short term, it could clearly not hope to hold the line indefinitely.[46] At the end of 1943, Sir Ronald Campbell, the British Minister at the Washington Embassy reported to the Foreign Office a 'distressing' conversation he had had with a representative of OSS, complaining of British efforts to obstruct OSS work in the Balkans. Campbell was forced to conclude that the 'regrettable impression' he had received was that, 'the Americans just have born in them a thorough dislike and distrust of the British and that their spontaneous reaction to our presence or to anything we say is one of dislike and distrust'. He none too optimistically continued:

> I now feel sure that general and seemingly irrevocable and innate amongst Americans is a revulsion from the English and that all we can do for tolerable relations is to insist on community of interest to try to force respect by our actions and to eschew any attempt to get ourselves loved or any reference to Anglo-American relations.[47]

In an ironic twist, given the long history of frosty Foreign Office–SOE relations, one of the most serious American complaints against the British covert apparatus at Cairo during this period was that they were completely subject to Foreign Office control (and also ironic as the evidence suggests that Foreign Office–SOE tensions persisted into 1944, for example, over the final break with Mihailovic).[48] An added complication to the situation was the status of someone like Maclean, who although operating under SOE auspices when sent into Yugoslavia in September 1943, was actually Churchill's personal representative; indeed, SOE had gone to remarkable lengths to block his appointment and Maclean obviously had no liking for the organisation.[49] These nuances, along with the reorganisation of SOE Cairo in autumn 1943, may have coloured OSS perceptions of the nature of Britain's game in the Balkans. In November 1943, Donovan was telling the JCS after his trip to Cairo:

The course of action in the Balkans has been directed by the Foreign Office and, in some cases by Foreign Office representatives in uniform and ostensibly under SOE orders but in reality (as we have actually experienced) responsive not to SOE but only to the Foreign Office. The policy of dealing with the situation has been dictated by the considered long-range political necessity of the British in the Balkans rather than the immediate and vital military problem here or its relation to overall Allied operations.[50]

In a similar vein, MacVeagh observed to Roosevelt in a letter of February 1944:

[W]hile our OSS remains strictly under military and not State Department control, and is operating for purely military ends, the Foreign Office has taken over the guidance of British agents and has immersed them deeply in political manoeuvres. This throws our agents, 'by association', into a similar position, and despite . . . our carefully disinterested attitude toward internal political matters . . . involves our government . . . in responsibility for all the British schemes.[51]

A particular problem for the British was the innate suspicion many Americans held for any of their organisations based in Cairo, given the city's reputation as the nerve-centre of British imperialism in the Middle East, and the home for the Yugoslav and Greek governments-in-exile. Regarding Greece, as the British in Cairo became ever more determined that the Communist-dominated EAM/ELAS should not emerge as the controlling voice in post-war Greek affairs and use SOE's supply of arms to position itself to eliminate its domestic political rivals, the Americans were convinced that military considerations were taking a back seat as policy toward support for resistance forces was politicised. Expressing his doubts, Captain Charles Edson, working for OSS/SI in Cairo, wrote to Robert Wolff of the Research and Analysis branch's Balkan section at OSS Washington in December 1943:

One thing I regard as established and in this every person of any information agrees; the British have tragically mismanaged the Greek situation . . . As a type I have the strong impression that the Englishmen here in this theatre are Empire-builders. They are brave and honourable men devoted to the Empire and to what they conceive to be the Empire's interests . . . The British believe that it is essential for British interests in the M[iddle] E[ast] that Greece after the war be under effective British control . . . Nothing I have seen or learned of the British since I have been here causes me to believe that we would be wise, or that it would be to our interest, to follow blindly their South-East Europe policy . . . For us to give them a blank check means that sooner or later . . . we are going to have to accept responsibility for their policy, and one cannot anticipate how large and how serious that responsibility may be.[52]

It was to allay such suspicions of Cairo's handling of Balkan affairs that when the command structure in the Mediterranean theatre was unified after the SEXTANT

Conference of December 1943 under AFHQ, the British Resident Minister, Harold Macmillan, hoped that responsibility for all special operations activities in the Balkans could be transferred to that same headquarters at Algiers. In fact, the first eight months of 1944 witnessed a quiet battle for control of Balkan affairs between Cairo and AFHQ, with the former (with backing from Eden and the Foreign Office) reluctant to cede oversight and control to an integrated Anglo-American head-quarters.[53] Macmillan summed up the perspective of the British contingent at AFHQ when he noted in his diary in June 1944 his feeling

> that we should try to bring the Americans into Balkan affairs. And I feel equally sure that the way to do it is through AFHQ (which was started by Americans and has a genuine Allied tradition) rather than through Middle East. Cairo is suspect – it is somehow connected in their minds with imperialism, Kipling and all that.[54]

General Wilson, who had taken over from Eisenhower at AFHQ as the newly-designated Supreme Allied Commander in the Mediterranean, met Donovan alongside Macmillan at Algiers in January 1944 to propose that OSS assign officers to act as a full part of Maclean's mission in Yugoslavia. However, Donovan rejected the idea, considering it another means by which the United States would be made to share responsibility while remaining a junior partner and lacking the power of independent action.[55] Worried by the trend of Anglo-American relations since Eisenhower's departure from the theatre, Wilson was keen to remove any such sources of irritation. He wrote to Field Marshal Sir Alan Brooke, the Chief of the Imperial General Staff, at the end of January, extolling the idea of a joint mission of full partnership, with lines of communication back to AFHQ at Algiers, not to the hot-bed of political intrigue at Cairo:

> The Americans are restive over the Maclean Mission to Tito having become a political one which reports to the PM or FO . . . If a joint Anglo-American Mission with Tito reported back here to be dealt with by Macmillan, [Robert] Murphy [US political adviser at AFHQ] and myself, the Americans would be happy. Unfortunately, this idea does not coincide with the PM's ideas.[56]

A few days later, Macmillan reported to Churchill that Wilson was receiving no reports at AFHQ from the Maclean mission, that Devers and Rooks (the American Deputy Supreme Allied Commander and Deputy Chief of Staff) were not clear about the status of the OSS personnel with Maclean, and that Donovan did not want them under Macmillan's orders. It was added that Wilson's scheme for a joint Anglo-American mission had the support of Devers.[57]

The Prime Minister, as Wilson had predicted, was unmoved. Churchill informed Eden that he was not prepared to put the mission under Wilson and did not mind if it had no American members. Placing the mission under Wilson would pass it to Combined Chiefs of Staff (CCS) oversight, and it was contended that the CCS was a body for dealing solely with military matters, not political. Insisting on the right of direct correspondence with Maclean, the Prime Minister saw Maclean's role as helping Britain to develop her political policy in Yugoslavia.[58] It was a view with which Eden concurred. Eden pointed out that signals from Maclean would have to come through Cairo anyway for technical reasons before reaching London or Algiers, and he could see no good reasons to transfer the handling of Yugoslav affairs from Cairo to AFHQ.[59]

While the British were discussing the merits or otherwise of various command structures, the Americans were moving to establish their own separate missions in the Balkans. American representatives had been admitted onto the Special Operations Committee at GHQ Middle East in early 1944, but they were unimpressed with its proceedings. The presence of the British ambassadors to the Greek and Yugoslav governments-in-exile, along with Christopher Steel (Foreign Office adviser to SOE Cairo) and Eric Waterhouse (Foreign Office adviser on Greek affairs), created the strong impression that the Committee was just another vehicle for the implementation of British political policy. As the OSS/SO Cairo History explained:

> Times without number the OSS members . . . were secretly amused at the polite but positive manner by which these diplomats directed the Military in whatever channels seemed politic at the time. A familiar expression emanating from these civilians ran generally in the vein – 'of course we have no disposition to tell the British Army what it shall do, but I feel the Foreign Office would take an extremely dim view of the operation proposed by Brigadier Blank. There are political factors involved in his proposition which are perhaps not known to you, and we should suggest that the matter be held in abeyance until London has had an opportunity to consider it.' Thus down the drain went another military plan. This illustrated perfectly to the OSS personnel the dominance of the British Foreign Office and as often as it was manifested, just that often did the Americans thank their lucky stars that they were under no such curbs from Washington.[60]

It was precisely because OSS were under 'no such curbs' from the State Department that the British in Cairo wanted to secure coordination in special operations and intelligence activities to avoid damaging divergences of policy. However, by this stage, OSS were not prepared to accept a collaboration that was to be largely on British terms and that involved them in London's interference in Balkan politics.

Those Balkan politics were becoming increasingly tangled. British policy towards Mihailovic had undergone a major re-evaluation at the end of 1943, as his military effectiveness dwindled and evidence of Chetnik contacts with the Axis accumulated. In February 1944, with Churchill's endorsement, SOE Cairo moved to sever all links with Mihailovic and withdraw its missions.[61] The Americans, nonetheless, remained unconvinced, and were determined not to be rushed into following the British lead. According to the OSS/SO Cairo History, Force 133 (the operational arm of SOE Cairo) put 'charming pressure' on the OSS to end its own contact with Mihailovic.[62] However, led by Donovan, the OSS resisted and tried to preserve a presence in the Serbian mountains with the Chetniks. Even if SOE and OSS/SO were prepared to forsake their operational and liaison tasks, the SI branch of OSS wanted intelligence-gathering functions with the Chetniks to continue.[63] Virtually all the OSS men with Mihailovic had left Yugoslavia by March, but Donovan suggested to the JCS and the State Department that a purely SI mission should remain. After approval from Roosevelt, preparations were begun to send an enlarged intelligence team back to Chetnik territory.[64] In early April 1944, Churchill learnt of the OSS plan and voiced his objections in a message to the President, mentioning that, 'it will show throughout the Balkans a complete contrariety of action between Britain and the United States'. Roosevelt agreed not to send the mission, but pointed out that it was purely for intelligence and 'had no political function whatever'.[65] Thwarted in the short term, OSS still went ahead with preparations for a reduced mission to Mihailovic's HQ, headed by Lieutenant Colonel Robert McDowell; they also used the pretext of air crew rescue to re-insert OSS personnel into Chetnik territory during the summer of 1944.[66]

Meanwhile, in May 1944, the State Department and JCS acceded to Donovan's request that a full US military mission be sent to Tito. By the time Colonel Huntington and his official team joined Partisan headquarters in August, there were already ten independent OSS teams in Yugoslavia. With British support for Tito's communist Partisans having become total, efforts were being made to reach some form of accommodation for the post-war situation between the Yugoslav government-in-exile, the exiled king, and Tito himself. It was especially annoying to Churchill, then, to learn of McDowell's arrival in Yugoslavia in August 1944. 'We are endeavouring to give Tito the support and . . . if the United States backed Mihailovic complete chaos will ensue', an understandably irate Churchill signalled to Roosevelt, 'if we each back different sides we lay the scene for a fine civil war. General Donovan is running a strong Mihailovic lobby, just when we have persuaded King Peter to break decisively with him.' The President admitted his error at failing to check that his instructions had been carried out, and advised Donovan to withdraw his mission.[67] Confused local conditions, and the obvious reluctance of OSS to comply with British wishes, meant that McDowell did not leave Yugoslavia until the beginning of November 1944.[68]

Just as in Yugoslavia, over support for the resistance forces in Greece, OSS personnel felt that calculations of post-war political interests were the controlling factor in British policies. Moreover, the imperial and class-conditioned mentality possessed of most British officers, so the Americans tended to believe, gave them an inherent bias against the left-wing guerrillas of ELAS, and led them to portray its parent organisation, EAM, as dominated by a Greek Communist Party whose primary method of gaining popular backing was through coercion and violence. Greek-American members of OSS were said to be particularly animated against British policy which under Churchill's influence favoured the return of the discredited and unpopular monarchy.[69] One typical report, produced in June 1944 by the Research and Analysis branch of OSS, criticised any close relationship with British policies in Greece and pictured EAM as an organisation which commanded genuine popular support; the paramount goal of British policy was to secure the post-war naval and air bases from which they could control the eastern Mediterranean.[70] It was not that Donovan, the OSS or the State Department wanted to embrace EAM; on the contrary, the Americans were very averse to the idea of EAM holding power after the war. However, they felt this eventuality was most likely (and EAM would become even more dominated by the radicals) if moderate republican opinion across Greece and within the organisation was alienated by an archaic attachment to restoring the pre-war king in the face of popular hostility. Even though SOE had moved to cut off all arms supplies to EAM/ELAS by July 1944, individual members of OSS in Greece continued to give them succour, and Donovan refused to accede to British requests in the same month to withdraw OSS personnel from Greece.[71]

Against a background of US press criticism of British policy toward Greece, complaints began to surface in the summer of 1944 about what a Foreign Office Periodical Intelligence Summary described as the 'increasingly mischievous' activities of OSS, including accusations that arms were being furnished to EAM/ELAS by its SI branch, and that in Cairo Americans were spreading 'the most puerile and false political gossip'.[72] Foreign Office officials believed that OSS was 'out of hand', and that Donovan was alleged to have prevented the return of a cooperative OSS officer to Greece (Major Gerald K. Wines), on the grounds that he had been duped into becoming 'a tool of British Imperialism.'[73] At the end of August 1944, Churchill was moved enough to send a personal message to Donovan which talked of the 'campaign of the OSS against the British', and warned of the 'very formidable trouble brewing in the Middle East against OSS'. The Prime Minister asked for Donovan's help to ease tension, hinting that he would take things up with Roosevelt if no improvement resulted.[74]

However, Donovan's criticism of the British role in Greece continued. In September, he sent a memorandum to Roosevelt which talked of the 'resentment' felt by the Greeks in Cairo at British interference in Greek internal affairs:

> This feeling is shared by liberal and conservative elements alike, and it is said to have been caused by British action in arresting individuals in Cairo and Alexandria for security reasons without preparing charges, by severe censorship and distortion of news, and by British control over the Greek Government.[75]

Donovan's concerns over the way the British were directing events and pulling the United States by association into supporting policies with an imperial imprint were also given expression at the State Department by Berle who warned that,

> if care is not taken at once we shall find ourselves made jointly responsible for a situation in Greece which in practice is being determined by the Middle Eastern Command and carried out by British propaganda and intelligence officers; and for policing eventually by troops brought to Greece under British command.[76]

Again one sees an aversion here to 'Cairo', a place linked in the American imagination with the machinations and intrigue of the Arab Bureau and of British clandestine organisations in general.

The EAM/ELAS-led rebellion in Athens and elsewhere in December 1944, following the British entry into Greece in October, greatly exacerbated Anglo-American tensions, as the British aligned with the forces of reaction in the Greek government to suppress the rising. Much to British vexation, the majority of Americans in Greece maintained a studied neutrality in the conflict; Colonel C. M. Woodhouse, who had led the SOE mission in Greece, even talked of 'a benevolent bias in favour of EAM'.[77] Many OSS members remained critical of the premises of British policy after the civil war was temporarily ended by the Varkiza Agreement of February 1945. That same month an OSS Research and Analysis branch summary of British policy was compiled. It asserted that the British had

> consistently supported Greek rightist elements and opposed Greek moderate and leftist elements, apparently in the hope of installing in Greece a 'stable' government upon whose continuous co-operation it could rely. This policy . . . appears to derive from fundamental misconceptions which may be attributed, in considerable part, to faulty intelligence supplied by ill-selected British personnel.[78]

The criticism contained here echoed the field reports of OSS personnel in Greece in 1944. One such report, filed by a Captain W. W. Ehrgot, portrayed Woodhouse as a man incapable of understanding the EAM mentality due to his privileged upbringing, and described the unpopularity of aloof British liaison officers with the Greek guerrillas. 'All of the MO4 [SOE Cairo] officers whom I have seen . . . both in Cairo and in Greece,' it noted, 'appear to be of a class, and with social backgrounds, which do not give them very great understanding of the majority of the people with whom they have to work in occupied countries.'[79] Moreover, according to the Research and Analysis summary mentioned above, EAM was judged to be not more than about 20 per cent communist:

> Contrary to the premises on the basis of which the British government seems to have been operating, EAM appears to represent an actual majority of Greek opinion; it is not predominantly Communist; it is primarily concerned with achieving a liberated and independent Greece, secondarily with internal reforms, and last of all with forcing Greece into an international position hostile to British interests.[80]

By the summer of 1945, the head of OSS/SI in liberated Athens, Captain Charles Edson, was being warned by the head of SIS in Greece, Major Dudley A. C. Bennett, that the American position in the country was 'tenuous'. Edson reflected

> Generally speaking, during and for most of the time after the civil war the British were very 'fed up' with all Americans in Greece, including us [and] I

believe definitely that we were subject to a certain amount of calculated though concealed obstruction . . . It is my present feeling that our field missions are likely to encounter increasing difficulties and possibly actual danger.[81]

At this relatively early stage of US involvement with the problems of post-war Greece, American attitudes were still conditioned more by their innate suspicions of traditional British policy than by belief that the Soviet Union might seek to take advantage of the Greek turmoil to extend the scope of their influence further southward from Romania and Bulgaria. While British and American policy-makers may have shared certain long-term goals, OSS reporting helped to persuade Washington that British attitudes and actions were only serving to polarise political opinion in Greece, making more likely the full-scale civil war that was, in fact, eventually to break out in 1946.

The Balkans never featured in any significant way in US strategic planning during the Second World War, and American forces were never deployed on major operations in the eastern Mediterranean. In the absence of a conventional US military presence, Anglo-American relations at a field level, unlike many other theatres, were mediated by contacts between the clandestine services. Without a clear-cut wartime policy towards Yugoslavia and Greece from the United States, and in a situation of great confusion and complexity, the Americans of OSS found themselves guided by an instinctive desire to assert their independence from British control; this was especially so after OSS lost confidence in British reporting from Yugoslavia in the autumn of 1943. Fundamental distrust concerning the motives of British policy in the Balkans, and doubts over the reliability of British information and judgement, constituted the basis upon which OSS interpreted developments and reached conclusions about the nature of its own role in the area, and the actions it should take. Divergence from the British approach was also likely as OSS wanted to demonstrate what it was capable of achieving away from SOE tutelage.[82] What is also striking is the degree to which the Americans felt that British military and political policy was effortlessly 'joined up', so that SOE would naturally conduct their work with one eye trained on the Axis enemy, and another on the post-war maintenance of empire and British great power prestige. In view of the deep tensions and disagreements that marked the Foreign Office–SOE relationship in 1943–1944, this seems especially ironic.

The SOE man in Washington charged with liaison with OSS was told by Brigadier Vivian Dykes, the first British Secretary of the CCS, that there were two reasons that would militate against the Americans listening to British advice:

the suspicion that the Machiavellian British had so advised because they had some ulterior and probably sinister motive, or the fear that if an American accepted our advice he would be told by the isolationists he had sold out to the Limeys.[83]

The formation of joint or integrated command arrangements might help to improve levels of coordination and collaboration, but could not always escape from the effects of national rivalries and differences (it often needed the exemplary example of individuals such as Eisenhower to keep the machinery working). Examples of effective Anglo-American cooperation in covert warfare in many parts of the Mediterranean need to be set beside the many instances of serious and damaging rivalry, to understand that beneath the surface lay fundamental differences in policy and approach, and the limits to which cooperation was subject by the demands of national autonomy in the fields of intelligence and special operations.

Notes

1 An overall treatment of the Anglo-American relationship in the Mediterranean theatre is offered in Matthew Jones, *Britain, the United States and the Mediterranean War, 1942–44* (London, 1996).

2 See, for example, Dominic Graham and Shelford Bidwell, *Tug of War: The Battle for Italy, 1943–45* (London, 1986), and the works by Carlo D'Este, *Bitter Victory: The Battle for Sicily, 1943* (London, 1988), and *Fatal Decision* (London, 1991).

3 See Michael Howard, *The Mediterranean Strategy in the Second World War* (London, 1968), and *Grand Strategy*, vol. IV (London, 1972); Mark A. Stoler, *The Politics of the Second Front: American Military Planning and Diplomacy in Coalition Warfare, 1941–43* (Westport, CT, 1977).

4 See, for example, Mark A. Stoler, *Allies and Adversaries: The Joint Chiefs of Staff, the Grand Alliance, and US Strategy in World War Two* (Chapel Hill, NC, 2000), pp. 103–104.

5 See record of meeting between President Roosevelt and the JCS, 10 August 1943, *Foreign Relations of the United States, 1943, Conferences at Washington and Quebec* (Washington, DC, 1970), p. 499.

6 See Jones, *Mediterranean War*, pp. 98–103.

7 On French North Africa, see Tom C. Wales' chapter in this collection. On the Far East, see, for example, Richard J. Aldrich, 'Imperial Rivalry: British and American Intelligence in Asia, 1942–46', *Intelligence & National Security* 3/1 (1988): 5–56, and *Intelligence and the War Against Japan: Britain, America and the Politics of Secret Service* (Cambridge, 2000); and most recently, E. Bruce Reynolds, *Thailand's Secret War: OSS, SOE, and the Free Thai Underground during World War Two* (Cambridge, 2005).

8 Several studies have begun to take on the subject of OSS relations with the British in the Balkans, most notably Jay Jakub, *Spies and Saboteurs: Anglo-American Collaboration and Rivalry in Human Intelligence Collection and Special Operations, 1940–45* (London, 1999), Chapter 5. Also of relevance are Heather Williams, *Parachutes, Patriots and Partisans: The Special Operations Executive and Yugoslavia, 1941–1945* (London, 2003), and for the basis of US suspicions, Christina Goulter-Zervoudakis, 'The Politicization of Intelligence: The British Experience in Greece, 1941–44', *Intelligence & National Security* 13/1 (1998): 165–194. W. J. M. Mackenzie's *The Secret History of SOE: The Special Operations Executive, 1940–1945* (London, 2000) does not cover SOE–OSS relations to any great extent. Still indispensible for general background is Bradley F. Smith, *The Shadow Warriors: OSS and the Origins of the CIA* (London, 1983), while an excellent overview is M. R. D. Foot, 'The OSS and SOE: An Equal Partnership?', in George C. Chalou (ed.), *The Secrets War: The Office of Strategic Services in World War Two* (Washington, DC, 1992), pp. 295–300.

9 See F. H. Hinsley, *British Intelligence in the Second World War*, vol. II (London, 1981), p. 52.

10 See Bickham Sweet-Escott, *Baker Street Irregular* (London, 1965), pp. 128–129, 136–137; Mackenzie, *Secret History*, p. 390.

11   See Jakub, *Spies*, pp. 49–53; Smith, *Shadow Warriors*, pp. 146, 170–171; David Stafford, *Britain and European Resistance, 1940–45* (London, 1980), pp. 89–90; note by Sir Charles Hambro, COS(42)327, 30 June 1942, The National Archive, Public Record Office (hereafter PRO) CAB 80/37. In his official history of SOE, Mackenzie eschewed reproduction of the text of the agreement, noting (with some accuracy) that 'the documents involved are very detailed and bore too little relation to later practice to be worth quoting in full', see *Secret History*, pp. 391–392.

12   See Sweet-Escott, *Baker Street*, pp. 137–139, 146; M. R. D. Foot, *Resistance: An Analysis of European Resistance to Nazism, 1940–45* (London, 1976), p. 143; J. G. Beevor, *SOE: Recollections and Reflections, 1940–45* (London, 1981), pp. 84–85.

13   Hinsley, *British Intelligence*, vol. II, p. 54; Jakub, *Spies*, pp. 72–77; Douglas Dodds-Parker, *Setting Europe Ablaze* (Surrey, 1984), pp. 117, 124, 128; Arthur L. Funk, 'The OSS in Algiers', in Chalou, *Secrets War*, pp. 166–182.

14   See Jakub, *Spies*, pp. 81–2.

15   Huntington to Donovan, 17 November 1943, US National Archives and Records Administration (hereafter NARA), RG 226 Entry 99, Box 30, Folder 142, US National Archives.

16   Guenther to Donovan, 29 April 1943. NARA RG 226, Entry 99, Box 43, Folder 212.

17   On the thoroughly political nature of the higher direction of the war in Washington, see, for example, Stoler, *Allies*, pp. 108–109.

18   Ben Pimlott (ed.), *The Second World War Diary of Hugh Dalton, 1940–45* (London, 1986), entry for 3 March 1943.

19   JCS to Devers and Royce, AFHQ 1238, USAFIME 979, 2 March 1944, NARA RG 226, Entry 154, Box 3, Folder 63.

20   See Beevor, *Recollections*, p. 85; F. H. Hinsley (ed.), *British Intelligence in the Second World War*, vol. 3, Part 1 (London, 1984), p. 463; Mackenzie, *Secret History*, p. 406.

21   Reports Office Cairo to other stations, 21 July 1944. NARA RG 226, Entry 154, Box 12, Folder 153a. British documents marked GUARD, and often dealing with sensitive matters of post-war policy, were supposed to be kept away from American eyes, a procedure which presented problems at an integrated headquarters, see Jones, *Mediterranean War*, pp. 112–117, 194–195, and material in WO204/17.

22   Richard M. Leighton, 'Overlord Revisited: An Interpretation of American Strategy in the European War, 1942–1944', *American Historical Review* 68 (1963): 919–937.

23   See, for example, Stoler, *Allies*, p. 172; Jones, *Mediterranean War*, pp. 101–102, 106, 123–124.

24   See MacVeagh to Roosevelt, 17 February 1944, in J. O. Iatrides (ed.), *Ambassador MacVeagh Reports: Greece, 1933–47* (Princeton, NJ, 1980): 454.

25   See, for example, Berle memorandum for the files, 13 September 1943, Reel 5, F.102. Adolf Berle papers, Sterling Memorial Library, Yale University, CT.

26   See *MacVeagh Reports*, diary entry for 3 December 1943.

27   See Smith, *Shadow Warriors*, p. 183.

28   See Jakub, *Spies*, pp. 59–60, 118–119; Williams, *Parachutes*, pp. 151–152.

29   Cairo History SO-OSS-ME file. NARA RG 226, Entry 99, Box 44, Folder 215.

30   Ibid., and see Jakub, *Spies*, p. 123.

31   See W. R. Roberts, *Tito, Mihailovic and the Allies, 1941–45* (New Jersey, 1973), p. 98; Howard, *Grand Strategy*, p. 485; 'Chronological Summary of Cairo SO Activities Appendix A' (CAIRO-SO-OP-4). NARA RG 226, Entry 99, Box 44, Folder 215.

32   Only a month before, Hambro had advised his senior staff in London that OSS was likely to strive constantly for ever more independence; care had to be taken that no resentment was shown, and also that control was not surrendered over areas where SOE had established primacy, see Foot, 'The OSS and SOE', p. 297. Nevertheless, SOE realised that such was their need for American resources, particularly the transport aircraft that were in such desperately short supply, that the OSS could not be denied a role in the eastern Mediterranean indefinitely.

33 See Jakub, *Spies*, p. 124; and Balkans file, Box 95A. William J. Donovan papers, US Army Military History Institute, Carlisle, PA.
34 See Smith, *Shadow Warriors*, pp. 237–238.
35 Roberts, *Tito*, pp. 138–140.
36 See Jakub, *Spies*, pp. 126–127.
37 Roberts, *Tito*, pp. 141–142.
38 See Williams, *Parachutes*, p. 179.
39 Roberts, *Tito*, p. 143.
40 See Jakub, *Spies*, pp. 129–130.
41 Halliwell report on trip to Middle and Far East, September–December 1943, Doc. 374, Box 68B, Donovan papers.
42 Ibid.
43 See Roosevelt to Churchill, 22 October 1943, and Churchill to Roosevelt, 23 October 1943, Warren F. Kimball (ed.), *Churchill and Roosevelt: The Complete Correspondence*, vol. 2 (Princeton, NJ, 1984), pp. 549, 554.
44 See Sargent minute, 24 October 1943, PRO FO371/37184 R10650/6780/67.
45 See Jakub, *Spies*, p. 131.
46 See Gubbins to CGS, MEF, COS/181/256, 25 November 1943, PRO WO201/1598.
47 Campbell to Scott, 13 December 1943, A33/6/G45, PRO FO371/38504.
48 See, for example, Phyllis Auty and Richard Clogg (eds), *British Policy Towards Wartime Resistance in Yugoslavia and Greece* (London, 1975), p. 46.
49 See ibid., pp. 221–228.
50 Donovan memorandum for JCS, 26 November 1943, NARA RG 226, Entry 99, Box 43, Folder 211.
51 MacVeagh letter to Roosevelt, 17 February 1944, *MacVeagh Reports*, pp. 453–454.
52 Edson to Wolff, 11 December 1943, NARA RG 226, Entry 145, Box 4, Folder 45.
53 See Matthew Jones, 'Macmillan, Eden, the War in the Mediterranean and Anglo-American Relations', *Twentieth Century British History*, 8/1 (1997): 27–48.
54 Harold Macmillan, *War Diaries: Politics and War in the Mediterranean, January 1943–May 1945* (London, 1984), entry for 5 June 1944, p. 456.
55 See Roberts, *Tito*, pp. 199–200; Smith, *Shadow Warriors*, p. 239; also COS(44)66(O), 23 January 1944, PRO CAB80/78.
56 Wilson to Brooke, 31 January 1944, Alanbrooke papers, personal files, 14/44, Liddell Hart Centre for Military Archives.
57 Macmillan to Churchill, No. 192, 4 February 1944, PRO FO371/43633 R2142/43/67.
58 Churchill minute for Eden, M.71/4, 5 February 1944, ibid.
59 Eden to Churchill, P17/44/56, 10 February 1944, ibid.
60 Cairo History SO-OSS-ME file, NARA RG 226, Entry 99, Box 44, Folder 215.
61 There are many accounts of this crucial shift in British policy; see, for example, Stafford, *Britain*, pp. 168–169; Mackenzie, *Secret History*, pp. 432–442; Jakub, *Spies*, pp. 135–139.
62 Cairo History SO-OSS-ME file, NARA RG 226, Entry 99, Box 44, Folder 215.
63 Roberts, *Tito*, p. 198.
64 Ibid., pp. 255–256.
65 Warren F. Kimball (ed.), *Churchill and Roosevelt: The Complete Correspondence*, vol. 3 (Princeton, NJ, 1984), Churchill to Roosevelt, 6 April 1944, Roosevelt to Churchill, 8 April 1944, pp. 80, 82. See also Smith, *Shadow Warriors*, p. 240; Jakub, *Spies*, p. 140.
66 See ibid., p. 142.
67 Kimball, *Churchill and Roosevelt*, vol. 3, Churchill to Roosevelt, 1 September 1944, Roosevelt to Churchill, 3 September 1944, pp. 306, 308–309.
68 See Smith, *Shadow Warriors*, pp. 282–283, and Dusan Biber, 'Failure of a Mission: Robert McDowell in Yugoslavia', in Chalou, *The Secrets War*, pp. 194–217.

69 See Smith, *Shadow Warriors*, p. 281; also the reports in NARA RG 226, Entry 99, Box 45, Folder 217.
70 'The Interests and Policies of the Major Allies in Greece', 2 June 1944, Research and Analysis Report No 2205, NARA RG 59, M1221.
71 See Stafford, *Britain*, p. 166; Lawrence S. Wittner, *American Intervention in Greece, 1943–49* (New York, 1982), p. 16.
72 Periodical Intelligence Summary No. 28, 16 August 1944, in PRO FO371/43691 R13725/9/19.
73 See Warner to FO, 21 August 1944, PRO PREM3/212/2.
74 Churchill to Bedell Smith (for Donovan), T: 1664/4, 24 August 1944, ibid. The British ambassador to the Greek government-in-exile noted of this row that, 'It is the SI and not the SO part of OSS who are making the mischief, the SO part being reasonably under our control. Their misdeeds may be due more to a crusading enthusiasm than to a considered anti-British policy but at times it would be difficult to distinguish between the two,' Leeper to FO, No. 645, 2 September 1944, ibid.
75 Donovan memorandum for Roosevelt, 25 September 1944, Box 67A. Donovan papers.
76 Berle memorandum, 26 September 1944, Beatrice Bishop Berle and Travis Beal Jacobs (eds), *Navigating the Rapids, 1918–1971: From the Papers of Adolf A. Berle* (New York, 1973), p. 465.
77 C. M. Woodhouse, *Apple of Discord* (London, 1948), p. 218.
78 Research and Analysis Report No. 2818, NARA RG 59, M1221.
79 Report by Captain W. W. Ehrgot, NARA RG 226, Entry 154, Box 39, Folder 598.
80 Research and Analysis Report No. 2818, NARA RG 59, M1221.
81 Review of OSS Greek Mission by Captain Edson, 21 June 1945, NARA RG 226, Entry 154, Box 33, Folder 499.
82 See Smith, *Shadow Warriors*, p. 241.
83 Sweet-Escott, *Baker Street*, p. 146.

6   Ungentlemanly warriors or unreliable diplomats?

Special Operations Executive and 'irregular political activities' in Europe

Neville Wylie

The aim of this chapter is to investigate the role played by the Special Operations Executive (SOE) in the conduct of what I will call 'irregular political activities'. SOE's reputation largely rests on its military contribution to the Allied war effort, especially in training, equipping and finally mobilising European resistance movements against German domination during the last years of the war.[1] While this reputation is entirely deserved, SOE's *military* operations have tended to overshadow other less dramatic, or glamorous, aspects of its work. SOE's political activities fall into this category: yet for historians, this part of SOE's war record is important on two counts. First of all, even a cursory study of SOE's own records suggests that the 'political' aspect of SOE's brand of special operations frequently writ large in SOE thinking. While its development was far from uniform, and had as much to do with chance and contingency as it did to the convictions of the SOE leadership or the strategic imperatives of Britain's military position, throughout the war politics was an unavoidable and integral ingredient in SOE's activities. Second, an assessment of SOE's irregular political activities during the war helps in part to explain the role occupied by such activities in Britain's post-war operations, and the absence, in comparison with other national agencies of the time, of an 'activist' tradition in British secret service. The chapter begins with an assessment of SOE's initial approach to political warfare, which reflected the views of SOE's first Minister, Hugh Dalton. It then traces the emergence of 'irregular political activities' over the war, a concept that foreshadowed the various forms of 'covert operations' (typically political subversion, disruption and regime-destabilisation) that became such an integral part of the Cold War, and remain with us today in the shape of 'regime change'.

Hugh Dalton and 'political warfare'

The explicitly 'political' nature SOE's work was part of the organisation's birthright. The handful of mavericks who championed a doctrine of 'irregular warfare' before the war, most notably Col. Lawrence Grand, Head of Section D of the Secret Intelligence Service (SIS), all in one way or another acknowledged that politics was integral to their new form of warfare. All the precedents upon which their observations were based, were driven to a greater or lesser extent by political motives, from the Arab 'revolt' in the First World War, to the activities of the IRA in Ireland and the Red Army in Russia. In each case, the existence of a common, clearly defined set of political goals was central to the strategic success of the 'revolt'. This alone provided the guerrilla bands with the necessary cohesion, and bestowed their acts with the necessary 'legitimacy' in the eyes of the local population, to assure them of military success and popular support. It is important to realise that politics did not simply give irregular warfare its distinctive complexion: in a very real sense, it gave it its irresistible force. As a result, irregular warfare enthusiasts such as Grand could see no limit to the damage Britain could inflict on its continental foes. In his seminal March 1939 paper on the prospects of subversion in a coming war, in which he set out the case for embracing a doctrine of irregular warfare, Grand confidently predicted that a 'combination of guerrilla and IRA tactics' could have Romania ripe for collapse in a mere three weeks, while 'simultaneous disturbances throughout German occupied areas' could be triggered in a matter of three or four months![2]

Historians have rightly been sceptical about the extent to which this pre-war thinking on irregular warfare permeated SOE's institutional consciousness.[3] The subject was, for instance, notably absent from the Staff College curriculum between the wars, and such discussion as there was, failed to percolate up to the higher military decision-making authorities.[4] SOE's last Director-General, Major-General Sir Colin Gubbins, freely admitted his ignorance of any pre-war studies distilling the lessons learnt from the conduct of irregular operations in Ireland, Palestine or Spain when he joined SOE in 1940, even though he had himself seen at first hand the effectiveness of Bolshevik and IRA tactics in the 1920s.[5] The early files kept by SOE certainly bear out Gubbins' recollections. When Hugh Dalton, SOE's first minister, asked his colleagues in October 1940 whether there had been 'any real study been made of the theory and technique of Revolutions' or if 'there any books on the subject worth reading?' his inquiries met with a deafening silence.[6]

Yet irrespective of whether pre-war debates fed into SOE's strategic thinking, the distinctive political complexion of the new brand of warfare proposed in July 1940 was obvious. Indeed, it was precisely this aspect of the project that made SOE so appealing to the Labour members of Churchill's new administration. Clement Attlee, the Deputy Prime Minister, and Hugh Dalton, the Minister of Economic Warfare, were both fired by the belief that 'special operations' was essentially a form of political warfare, best waged, in Dalton's opinion, by the sort of people found in his own constituency – the Durham miners. In his bid to win control of the new organisation, Dalton made no secret of the direction he thought SOE should go. In a letter to Lord Halifax, the Foreign Secretary, on 2 July 1940, he spoke of the creation of a 'democratic international', capable of employing 'many different methods, including industrial and military sabotage, labour agitation and strikes, continuous propaganda, terrorist acts against traitors and German leaders, boycotts and riots'.[7] This was not simple special pleading. In private, the distinction drawn between 'special operations' – political warfare – and 'normal' or regular warfare, was even more explicit. The evening before sending his letter to Halifax, Dalton wrote in his diary, 'what we have in mind . . . concerns Trade Unions, Socialists etc; the making of chaos and revolution – no more suitable for soldiers than fouling at football, or throwing when bowling at cricket'.[8] For Dalton, SOE's military objectives were inseparable from its political message. Special operations were at heart a form of political warfare.

It is by no means clear how long Dalton clung to the conviction that Nazi rule could be overthrown by fomenting popular revolutions across Europe. As late as January 1942, little more than a month before his 'promotion' to the Board of Trade, he can be found exalting the virtues of proletarian activism.[9] It would appear, however, that while Dalton's confidence in working-class activism remained undiminished, the naïve hopes he entertained of their revolutionary potential in the face of a determined occupation regime – a belief which had figured so prominently in his 'pitch' to Halifax in mid-1940 – did not long outlive the summer. After the brief flurry of excitement in July and August 1940, when Dalton tried to inculcate SOE's senior staff into his politico-military ideas, the organisation seems to have turned its back on its leader's dogmatic political beliefs, as well as some of his more outlandish ideas.[10] As Gladwyn Jebb, one of the organisation's most enthusiastic, and thoughtful, advocates of 'subversion', pointed out in early October, 'there is surely no objection to our employing any particular slogan at any time and in any place which may seem desirable. We may even find it necessary in certain countries, to encourage the Right and the Left simultaneously.'[11] Indeed, already by mid-October 1940, Dalton seems to have abandoned his earlier optimism and replaced it with a rather more sober outlook. He was, he admitted to senior officials, 'by no means certain that this time, Revolutions in Europe would take an ideological form'. The 'moral delinquency' that had so tragically sapped French strength before the summer seemed to have infected the rest of occupied Europe. Only in Poland was there any semblance of real resistance; elsewhere it looked like SOE would have to rely on its own resources.[12] Dalton's sobriety was reflected in the first strategic directive for SOE, completed at the end of November 1940 from the Chiefs of Staff (COS). Tellingly, the document said little about any explicitly political function for the new organisation.[13] The fact that the directive bore the mark of SOE's headquarters staff suggests that Dalton's enthusiastic ideas on revolutionary warfare had palpably failed to strike a chord among his lieutenants.[14]

The waning of confidence in Dalton's initial exotic ideas about dragooning Europe's subjugated proletariat into a political crusade against Nazism was to some extent a logical consequence of changes to SOE's institutional structure. For reasons that need not concern us here, the two components of Dalton's concept of political warfare – subversive propaganda and special operations – were hived off into different departments, SO1 and SO2 respectively. While there might have been some merit on political and organisational grounds for this arrangement, the splitting of the two wings, in particular, the physical removal of SO1 to the Duke of Bedford's leafy estate at Woburn, forty miles from London, inevitably impeded the all-important symbiosis that was essential if Dalton's vision was ever to see the light of day. In the words of Gladwyn Jebb, the Foreign Office mandarin who occupied the nebulous position of Chief Executive Officer in SOE until May

1942, on strategic grounds, the division of the two competencies was a 'cardinal error'. Before long, Jebb remarked in his valedictory report on 'The Technique of Subversion':

> subversive propaganda was conceived of as something apart from subversive action; separate loyalties followed and whereas SO1 tended to regard their colleagues as rather bungling assassins, SO2 equally unjustly began to think of SO1 as half-baked theorists, who were not to be trusted for reasons of security.[15]

The process of disintegration reached its conclusion in August 1941 when SO1 was dismantled and submerged into the Political Warfare Executive. But before this time, SOE had failed to make up for the paucity of pre-war studies on special operations to develop any cogent doctrines on political warfare or put flesh on the bones of Dalton's rickety ideas on popular revolts.[16]

Although SOE's organisational structure certainly compounded Dalton's difficulties, the main reason for the demise of Dalton's conception of political warfare had more practical roots. As David Stafford argued in a seminal article in 1975, it was ultimately events in Europe that forced Dalton to abandon any hope of mobilising large-scale popular resistance against Nazi rule. Europe was simply not the smouldering hotbed of resistance that Dalton had hoped for; there was nothing like a genuine 'revolutionary' situation among Europe's working class. In the months following the collapse of France, with Britain under constant bombardment by the *Luftwaffe*, Churchill was barely capable of lighting a cigar, let alone 'setting Europe ablaze', as he had confidently predicted earlier that summer. SOE's painful education of the harsh realities of fomenting resistance on the Continent was, moreover, viewed with not a little *Schadenfreude* by its critics in Whitehall – especially the Chiefs of Staff and the Foreign Office – for whom Dalton's fanciful ideas of a 'democratic international' were distinctly unappealing. The overtly political character of Dalton's 'detonator concept', triggering a spontaneous revolt across Europe by means of political agitation, was therefore demoted in favour of a more 'military' approach to the task in hand. Henceforth, SOE's strategic doctrine came increasingly to resemble the ideas and military outlook of the organisation's first Director of Operations, Colin Gubbins, which emphasised the importance of sabotage operations alongside the careful nurturing of 'secret armies' across occupied Europe.[17] By early 1942, while hopes that Germany might miraculously crumble from within still lingered on in some quarters, special operations had been pushed to the margins of Britain's grand strategy.[18]

The apparent 'de-politicisation' of SOE's strategy did not, however, end SOE's involvement in political affairs. The very nature of special operations made SOE a staple ingredient in the cauldron of wartime politics. SOE's war record is punctuated with bitter political disputes – with other Whitehall departments, with the armed services or with the governments-in-exile. The latter in particular were obviously going to take a dim view of SOE striking deals with individuals or underground groups on the Continent, whose ideas and political sentiments differed from their own. With Dalton's hand at the helm, SOE was always likely to have a hard time convincing others of the purity of its political intentions. Gladwyn Jebb tellingly warned Dalton's successor, the Earl of Selborne, in April 1942 that 'our job is, somehow or other, to allay the suspicion of the older generation'.[19] Yet in retrospect, it is questionable whether the accusations levelled against SOE's supposed political bias were entirely justified. Dalton himself dismissed such ideas by calmly pointing out that SOE's council comprised of 'a Foreign Office official, a Conservative M.P., a member of the Bank of England Board who is also Chairman of the G[reat] W[estern] R[ailway], a regular soldier, an ex-Director of Air Intelligence, a Director of Courtaulds . . .'.[20] William Mackenzie, SOE's first historian, could find no instance in which Dalton's interpretation of SOE's remit on the Continent ever seriously affected its operational decisions, or its choice of friend or foe.[21] The fact of the matter was that, for SOE, stepping on foreigners' toes was an occupational hazard:

> With rare exceptions (Norway and Denmark the strongest cases), every saboteur and guerrilla was a politician: not every politician was a saboteur, but every politician's career depended on harnessing the potential saboteurs to his own purposes. Nothing could be done by SOE which did not have political implication.[22]

Mackenzie's point is a fair one. SOE's difficulties with the exiled governments were an inevitable by-product of its primary task of building up secret armies, saboteurs and agents in the parts of Europe where their activities would be of greatest value to Britain's military effort. Politics encroached on SOE's activities: it was not an end point in itself.

From irregular warriors to irregular diplomats

There was, however, another line of political action, distinct from Dalton's ideas of 'political warfare' and the day-to-day friction mentioned by Mackenzie, that characterised SOE's operations in Europe after the winter of 1940. Even though SOE's operational profile became increasingly 'military' at this time, the organisation showed much greater reluctance to abandon its political ambitions than is generally assumed. The political aspect of SOE's operational role did not, however, boil down to Dalton's mischievous habit of 'lighting fires and letting the Foreign Office extinguish them if they must'.[23] Instead SOE's political activities from early 1941 were ostensibly designed with the interests of the Foreign Office in mind. In a nutshell, it entailed using SOE's agents to forge contacts with dissident political circles in Europe and thereby harness these forces for the benefit of Britain's diplomacy on the Continent.

The genesis of this role is not easily identifiable. It is probable that SOE's planning staff became increasingly attracted to the idea of reinforcing the organisation's political and subversive activities over the winter of 1940, in the light of the mounting evidence that revealed the extent of Italy's political and social disintegration. Attacking Italian morale had been given highest priority in the Chiefs of Staff's directive the previous November. The onset of a chilly winter, coupled with Italy's humiliating military setbacks at the hands of the Greeks, inevitably encouraged SOE to consider what measures could be taken to fan domestic opposition to Mussolini's regime.

It was not, however, in Italy, or any of the other states that Britain found itself formally at war with, that SOE's political ambitions bore fruit in the short term. Instead, it was those states still clinging to a semblance of neutrality that SOE's budding irregular diplomatists sought to ply their trade. Ever since the start of the war, SOE's predecessors, SIS's Section D and the War Office's MI(R), had been particularly active in the Balkans and South-east Europe. While their work had focused primarily on preparing industrial sites and communications facilities for demolition, officers of the two services had taken a lead in promoting British interests among the local political and business elites. This process did not come to an end in the summer of 1940, when most of the officers involved were absorbed directly into SOE.[24] Instead the work was given an added sense of urgency over the autumn and winter months as Germany's aggressive intentions towards the Balkan states became increasingly obvious. By the early spring of 1941, the political functions of SOE's station in Belgrade had taken on a discrete form, quite distinct from the various military and sabotage arrangements it was carrying out in preparation for a German invasion. The objective of this activity went beyond merely encouraging pro-British sentiment in the region, but explicitly aimed at courting members of the political opposition to the government of the Regent, Prince Paul, and making these contacts available to the diplomatic mission. The 'rules of engagement' governing such activity were set out in a memorandum written by the station's senior staff in June 1941:

> It is obvious that for the proper functioning of SO2 on these lines (indirect political activities on behalf of H.M.G. diplomats) the strictest cooperation between that organisation and the Diplomatic mission is essential. There must be only one policy for H.M.G. being pursued in part by the regular mission, in part by SO2. Inevitably since the policy of H.M.G. is indicated to the Diplomatic Mission by the Foreign Office, SO2 must work under the general direction of the former. At the same time it is equally important that the Diplomatic Mission not only keep SO2 fully informed but also take every opportunity of making use of the irregular organisation which is thus placed at its disposal.[25]

So far as SOE's Belgrade station was concerned, this 'ideal arrangement . . . worked about as perfectly as could be expected' in late March 1941. While historians disagree over the precise role played by SOE in toppling Prince Paul on 27 March,[26] there can be little doubt that this foray into the world of secret diplomacy was recognised as a new and potentially rewarding departure for Dalton's 'Baker Street Irregulars'. The successful *coup* generated a great deal of pride and excitement in Baker Street, all the more since SOE's efforts to ignite armed revolt elsewhere on the Continent by this date had met with resounding failure.[27] While Dalton extracted rather more credit for the Belgrade *coup* than was altogether his due, the publicity campaign in London was not without effect and created something of an expectation that similar rich rewards might come SOE's way in the future. Praise for SOE's 'careful and patient work' could be heard in most corners of Whitehall.[28] If the *coup* had shown that 'Yugoslavia had found its soul', as Churchill jubilantly announced to the House of Commons, it might equally be said that the *coup* had enabled SOE to 'find its role'. It only remained to be seen whether the organisation could capitalise on its success and export its tactics to other parts of the neutral world.

Before assessing SOE's record in this area, it is worth pausing to consider the position that neutral Europe occupied in SOE's strategic outlook at the time. This is all the more necessary given that, as a group, they have tended to be overlooked by historians of both SOE and the war more generally.[29] The importance of the neutrals to SOE is perhaps best seen in their prominence in the COS' directive in November 1940. While Dalton and his lieutenants were only too happy to talk up the prospects of widespread resistance in occupied Europe, it was ultimately only in the neutrals that SOE had any immediate chance of testing out its emerging theories of irregular warfare. Six out of the nine targets given 'first priority' by the COS entailed SOE operations in neutral countries; from interdicting Swiss railway traffic to preparing guerrilla units for activation in the event of a German invasion of Spain and Portugal. Sadly the comparatively benign operational conditions in these countries did not crown SOE's endeavours with immediate success. It was not until the spring of 1941 that country stations could be established in Spain, Portugal and Switzerland, and a succession of operational obstacles and poor planning stymied its efforts at sabotaging Romanian oil installations, river transport on the Danube and other communications facilities in Yugoslavia and Bulgaria before the arrival of German troops. These setbacks were unfortunate, but they paled into insignificance in comparison with the problems SOE faced in enemy and enemy-occupied Europe, where all efforts to establish effective operational networks on the ground were stillborn until the final months of 1941. SOE's expansion of its non-operational activities was therefore a deliberate policy, and aimed at developing a political string for what was, at this stage of the war, a distinctly threadbare bow. SOE's work in neutral Europe in 1941 may have seemed marginal to the central task of undermining German power on the continent; it might also have failed to deliver the range of easy pickings many in SOE had initially hoped for, but it was far from a side-show for Britain's fledgling irregular warriors.

From early 1941, in the wake of the successful Belgrade *coup*, Baker Street deliberately sought to expand what it termed its 'irregular political activities' and encourage its stations in neutral Europe and elsewhere to cultivate contacts from across the political spectrum.[30] These initiatives inevitably dovetailed with SOE's military objectives. It was frequently those people who lay outside the political mainstream who proved the most willing recruits for SOE's embryonic guerrilla bands and sabotage units.[31] But the principal aim of these activities was political and boiled down to establishing relations with figures who were capable of mounting a credible opposition to the incumbent regime, should the need arise. As in Yugoslavia, the advantage of having SOE take responsibility for cultivating contacts with 'the political underworld and the murkier side of local politics', as Jebb put it, lay in the fact that it broadened the embassy's network of political influence without endangering its relations with the host government.[32] There were few neutral countries where, in SOE's eyes, such unofficial – and therefore un-attributable – services were not of intrinsic value to British diplomacy. In the authoritarian regimes in Spain, Portugal and Turkey, the benefits were self-evident; so too in Syria, Palestine, Trans-Jordan, Persia, Iraq and Egypt.[33] Yet, even in pluralistic societies such as Switzerland, there was much to be gained from operating along the lines SOE proposed. According to Britain's minister in Berne, the Swiss socialists, the largest party in the lower house, were 'so hated in Government and business circles' that it was only though the informal contacts of his assistant press attaché, the journalist and historian Elizabeth Wiskemann, that he was able to ' "get away with it" without compromising the Legation'.[34]

Local conditions and the existence of other, competing priorities ensured that SOE was never able to develop its political work in quite the way it had intended. In Switzerland, SOE's function was ably fulfilled by Elizabeth Wiskemann, and while SOE's station chief, Jock McCaffrey, drew on the assistance of socialist politicians, the actual scope for manipulating internal Swiss politics to Britain's advantage was negligible.[35] SOE's political activities in Stockholm appear to have been more extensive than in Berne, but again there was little real opportunity to effect significant – even if subtle – changes in Swedish politics.[36] In Spain, SOE was confronted with problems of a different order. The delicacy of Britain's relations with the Franco regime after the summer of 1940 prompted the ambassador, Sir Samuel Hoare, to embargo all covert activities in the country. When he finally relented and agreed to SOE opening a base in February 1941, he insisted that all operations were vetted by his trusted Naval Attaché, Alain Hillgarth, and maintained the prohibition against any activities which involved collaborating with the Republican opposition within Spain.[37] Consequently, although SOE trained bands of Spanish Republican volunteers in Scotland, it was not able to establish any explicit political role for its station in Madrid. The infamous bribing of Franco's generals, so as to convince them of the merits of non-belligerency, was handled by Hillgarth with little SOE involvement.[38]

Rather more intriguing was the experience of Jack Beevor in Lisbon. Besides the need to prepare demolition sites and guerrilla bands for activation in the event of a German invasion, Beevor was specifically directed to, in his words, 'ascertain the basic attitude of the Portuguese government, with a view to subverting it if pro-German, stimulating it if wavering, and rallying internal support for it if basically pro-Allied'.[39] This was no easy task, for while pro-British sentiment in Portugal was widespread, the Portuguese dictator, Salazar, had a neurotic aversion towards any hint of opposition to his regime. Beevor therefore had to tread carefully, and it is a measure of his tact and resourcefulness that by the end of 1941 he had knitted together a network of contacts across Portugal's diverse political spectrum, including relations with the leading opponents of Salazar's regime. Some progress had also been made in combating German influence in police circles by following Hillgarth's lead in Spain and judiciously deploying the 'cavalry of Saint-George'.[40]

The sensitivity of Beevor's mission was compounded by the fact that he was being asked to cultivate contacts among opponents of a regime with whom Britain not only enjoyed good relations, but was also bound to by a treaty of alliance that stretched back over five centuries. Britain's alliance with Turkey was of rather newer vintage, dating from October 1939, but London was, for good political and military reasons, more inclined to treat Ankara with the respect and esteem that befitted an ally than it was Lisbon. It was therefore no surprise that Britain's ambassador in Ankara, Sir Hughe Knatchbull-Hugessen, took as jaundiced a view of SOE's political aspirations as his counter-part in Madrid. Political subversion was a delicate matter at the best of times, without being directed at a government whose friendship Britain relied on for the defence of its interests throughout the eastern Mediterranean. Such was the importance placed on maintaining Turkish confidence that when Section D set up a base in Istanbul in May 1940, it did so on the understanding that SIS had the right to brief the Turkish police on its activities whenever it felt necessary. SOE's Istanbul station was limited to mounting operations in the Balkans only; it had no authority to operate inside Turkey, far less indulge in activities directed against the Turkish government. Before Germany's sudden descent into the Balkans in the spring of 1941, there was little reason for SOE to baulk at these restrictions: London had every confidence in the good faith of Inonu's government. But the arrival of German troops at the Turkish-Bulgarian frontier, and Hitler's subsequent invasion of Soviet Russia transformed Turkey's strategic situation, and raised doubts over whether Turkey would be able to maintain its non-belligerency in the future. The conclusion of a German-Turkish pact of friendship in July 1941 and mounting evidence of German involvement in Turkish internal affairs seemed to lend credence to these fears.[41] As one senior planning officer in SOE commented in mid-July, these events called into question the appropriateness of SOE's operational remit in Turkey:

> The original ban on SOE work was based on the fact that Turkey [was] an ally. It is now, I believe, in the opinion of the people in the best position to know, that Turkey must be regarded henceforth as certainly no longer an ally, and possibly a country which is on its way towards acceptance of the German New Order.[42]

Over the second half of 1941, Baker Street made repeated efforts to overturn the veto imposed on its activities in Turkey and secure a foothold in Hugessen's embassy. As with all stations in neutral Europe, the task of the proposed organisation covered preparations for sabotage and demolition activities in the event of an invasion and fostering stay-behind groups and guerrilla bands for operation after a German occupation. Nevertheless, as Jebb explained in a letter to Dalton in early August, 'irregular political activities' held a prominent place in Baker Street's thinking:

> One of the principal reasons for getting a good SO2 organisation going in
> Turkey is the possibility that there may be a real cleavage of opinion in that
> country, giving us the opportunity to swing the balance in our direction by the
> exercise of subversive propaganda, whispers and graft.[43]

This campaign also entailed replicating SOE's tactics elsewhere in the Levant and
distributing 'inducements', totalling over £50,000, among 'certain officials on the
Turkish General Staff and in the ministries of National Defence, Communications
and Interior – all [of whom were] involved in military work at ports and interior
communications'.[44]

SOE's ambitions for its 'irregular political activities' were clearly extensive. The
main focus of this effort was in neutral Europe – Portugal, Turkey and Spain – but
SOE's enthusiasm for meddling in the internal political affairs of other states
extended to the Middle East, Thailand, and possibly even Argentina as well.[45]
In nearly every case, SOE deliberately set out to carve a niche for itself within
British diplomacy and establish itself as a key player in Britain's foreign policy.
Its aspirations in this regard were not motivated by the desire to recapture the heady
optimism and political ambitions found in Dalton's earliest pronouncements
on special operations. In a very real sense, the strategy developed out of an understanding of the neutrals' changing position in the war, and a recognition of their
importance to British belligerency at a time when London had few other means
at its disposal to continue the struggle against German Nazism. SOE's dabbling
in the arcane art of political subversion was not then, a whim, but was, for the best
part of sixteen months, a distinctive and integral element in its brand of 'irregular
warfare'.

There is little doubt that SOE would have achieved greater success had it
conducted its activities with rather more finesse. It should not have surprised SOE
that its effort to muscle in on Britain's political relations would provoke unease
among members of the permanent civil service. This problem was clearly aggravated by the prickly personality and scarcely concealed political ambitions of SOE's
minister. Many mandarins in the Foreign Office were alarmed not only by Dalton's
political aspirations at home but also by his determination to further SOE's political
role abroad, not least since it invariably seemed to involve sponsoring the kinds
of people – trade unionists, socialist politicians, and so forth – whose political views
were so obviously aligned with his own. For British diplomats abroad, Dalton's
political ambitions were made all the more objectionable by the fact that they
appeared to impinge on their own careers. The sudden and frequently unannounced
arrival of Dalton's lieutenants, with ill-defined tasks and commanding hidden
resources, inevitably provoked concern, if not outright hostility, among the regular
diplomatic staff. Although SOE was inclined to exaggerate the problem, there are
a significant number of documented cases in which SOE's work was unnecessarily
hampered by the jealousy and obstruction of senior embassy staff.[46]

The situation would have been eased had SOE taken heed of the advice of its
Belgrade station, and ensured that its activities complemented those of Britain's
regular diplomats and adhered to the general policy line enunciated by the head of

mission. The problem in this regard was not so much SOE's 'political bias' as what Mackenzie calls its 'fanaticism' and its conviction that it alone had the measure of the political situation in any given country.[47] Time and time again, SOE exaggerated the extent of domestic political opposition in neutral countries, and ignored, or mis-read, the broader political and strategic environment, and how this might impinge on Britain's interests. Turkey was perhaps the most prominent case; however, the problem manifested itself, in varying degrees, across the spectrum of neutral states in Europe, the Middle East and Asia.[48] It is noticeable that SOE's myopia afflicted its headquarters staff rather more than its officers abroad. At least one neutral station officer returned to London in late 1941 in an attempt to talk some sense into Baker Street, and alert his superiors to the dangers of their policies.[49] There is more than a suspicion that SOE's penchant for 'irregular political activities' arose as much from its belief in the utility of such operations, as its desire to justify its existence at a time when all attempts to 'set Europe ablaze' were meeting with such a singular lack of success.

Although, as Saul Kelly shows, Rommel's thrust into Egypt in mid-1942 led to an intensification of SOE's political work in the region, which only began to sub-side at the end of the year, Baker Street's hopes of operating as an adjunct to British diplomatic activity in Europe petered out over the first half of the year. The stemming of Germany's assault against Russia that winter, coupled with the entry of the United States into the war, meant that for the first time since June 1940, British diplomats in neutral Europe could approach their hosts from a position of strength. While the war still had another two and a half years to run, from early 1942 neutral governments could no longer treat British interests in quite the same cavalier fashion as they previously had. At the same time, the danger of German invasion, though never entirely disappearing, obviously receded as German armies became bogged down in Russia. In such circumstances the advantages London might have gained from SOE's military preparations in the neutrals, or its political services, naturally diminished. Britain simply did not need the same kind of leverage on neutral governments it had required in the past. SOE's 'irregular political activities' had to a large extent become surplus to requirements.

As if to ram the point home, the danger inherent in indulging SOE's penchant for unofficial diplomacy was graphically underlined in early 1942, when the Portuguese police blew the cover off Beevor's underground networks. The sub-sequent events, which involved Beevor's expulsion from Portugal and the collapse of almost a year's painstakingly work, emphasised the hazards of SOE's work. No government could be expected to put up with the presence of a clandestine foreign agency whose actions strengthened the hands of its domestic opponents and whose mandate appeared to include the aim of fomenting 'chaos and revo-lution'. The 'Lisbon incident' thus illustrated the point, made often enough by Britain's ambassadors, that SOE's brand of diplomacy tended to be rather more trouble than it was worth.[50]

The exposure of Beevor's organisation in Portugal had a major impact on SOE's aspirations in neutral Europe. Anxious lest other stations suffer the same fate as Lisbon, officers across neutral Europe deliberately reined in their activities, and tried to insulate themselves and their work from the danger of contamination from domestic political intrigues. It is noticeable that having as recently as January 1942, endeavoured to persuade the Foreign Office to allow SOE to conduct subversive operations in Turkey, Baker Street appears to have shelved all future plans of this nature. SOE's operational freedom received a more damaging blow in May 1942 when it was forced to accept a new 'Charter' from the Foreign Office governing its activities across Europe. While SOE's political work was not specifically mentioned, it is clear, both in the text governing SOE activities in the neutrals, and in preparatory correspondence, that the Charter aimed at eliminating this kind of operation from SOE's remit. Henceforth the Foreign Office assumed 'full responsibility for deciding whether or not SOE [was] to conduct activities in neutral countries'; SOE could, moreover, only receive directives on such activities from the Foreign Office.[51]

Revival and fall: Italy, 1943, Romania, 1944

The collapse of SOE's effort to endear itself to Britain's diplomats was frustrating and embarrassing, but was not, in the end, detrimental to its military prospects. Whatever SOE's problems, the fact remained that by the time the disgraced Beevor made his way back to London in the summer of 1942, his colleagues in France and the Balkans had begun to open up new battle-fronts against German power on the Continent, in areas, moreover, where their actions were likely to have a direct, rather than merely indirect, impact on Germany's war effort. With Allied forces likely to return to the European mainland in the near future, SOE could rightly claim that its fledgling network of agents and sympathisers across occupied Europe were a valuable *military* resource, whose presence Allied planners ought to take into consideration. The upsurge of interest in SOE's likely military contribution to future Allied land operations gave SOE more than enough to think about, without having to mull over the demise of its activities in neutral Europe. SOE officials accepted the Foreign Office's ruling with equanimity, and set about building up their neutral stations as support bases for future military operations inside enemy and enemy-occupied territory.

'Irregular political activities' thus dropped off SOE's agenda over the second half of 1942, with little fanfare and few regrets. Precious little attention was given to the subject after this time, and nobody appears to have conducted a post-mortem on SOE's experience in neutral Europe. The re-emergence of irregular political activities in SOE thinking a year later, in the summer of 1943, was therefore largely unplanned and unexpected. It was not an organic development, nor, from what one can tell, was there much conscious thought given to what might be learnt from earlier events. Indeed, there is some doubt as to whether Baker Street would ever have considered returning to this area of activity, had the job of acting as a intermediary in Italy not fortuitously fallen into its lap. The SOE officer, Dick Mallaby, who was dropped into Lake Como on the night of Friday, 13 August, was directed simply to set himself up in a safe house and give SOE its first regular wireless operator in Northern Italy. He was not briefed to provide a future royal government with a secure radio set and codes to transmit its armistice terms to Eisenhower's headquarters. That this was ultimately what occurred – Mallaby exchanged over seventy messages in the week following his release on 30 August – can be put down to extraordinary good fortune, and SOE's ability, in the words of one official historian, to 'act decisively and by flexibility exploit a failure to their advantage'.[52]

Just as with SOE's earlier chance windfall – the Belgrade *coup* in March 1941 – the unexpected triumph in Italy provided the blueprint for the organisation's subsequent activities in political affairs. Mallaby's experience had demonstrated the supreme advantage of having someone on the ground, and on hand, at the decisive moment. His presence had probably not been decisive, but it had helped SOE meet the urgent need to provide a clandestine channel of communications with the Italian General Staff and thereby enable the Allies to capitalise on Italy's secret approach for surrender terms in mid-August. Though SOE did its best to extract maximum benefit from its apparent clairvoyance, those inside the organisation were well aware of how fortunate they had been. Italy had stubbornly refused to live up to its billing as a soft target for special operations, and Mallaby's incarceration in Rome had saved SOE from having to cobble together a set and operator team at a moment's notice. In the aftermath of the Italian armistice negotiations therefore, and with the prospect of other Axis states queuing up to exit the war, SOE made a concerted effort to prepare the ground for similar operations in the future. Wireless sets were readied in neutral capitals in case armistice negotiations started without warning, and SOE's staff in both London and Cairo began paying greater attention to the avenues open to influencing political developments across occupied Europe.[53]

The state that appeared to offer the greatest opportunity for SOE repeating its Italian success was Romania. In many respects, Romania had epitomised the difficulties that had confounded SOE's 'irregular political activities' earlier in the war. Ever since 1938, British officials had been captivated by the enormous rewards that could be gained by sabotaging Romania's oil-fields and the important traffic that ploughed up and down the River Danube. It is probable that fixation with these economic targets held back serious discussion over the merits of political subversion in Romania, for it was only after the chance of mounting large-scale sabotage operations in the country had receded in early 1941 that SOE's station in Bucharest pressed for, and finally received, official sanction to build up clandestine links with opposition figures. Until that time, London's confidence in King Carol's ability to keep Germany at arm's length had effectively enabled the ambassador, Sir Reginald Hoare, to veto any SOE talks with opposition politicians. Notwithstanding these setbacks, Romania was in many respects an ideal environment for SOE's irregular diplomats. The principal opponent of Antonescu's regime, M. Iuliu Maniu, not only kept his political power base, the National Peasants' Party, intact throughout the war, but his standing among the Romanian population to all intents and purposes put him beyond the reach of Antonescu's security forces. Opposition there was aplenty; SOE's difficulty lay in hammering it into a force capable of contesting German influence. It endeavours in this direction met with only partial success. In August 1941, SOE's principal agents inside Romania were arrested and thrown into jail: SOE was able to pass funds into the country to keep those arrested away from trial, but its radio set in Romania had been lost, and all future communications with Maniu and other opposition figures had to be directed through American diplomatic couriers, neutral diplomats and the few reliable Romanians able to travel overseas.[54] Stirring Maniu into action in these circumstances was never going to be easy, and despite promising noises, Maniu steadfastly refused to take the plunge. By mid-1943, it became clear that only through direct contact could Maniu ever be persuaded to commit himself to the Allies' cause. A team was infiltrated into the country in late August, but the British commander, Captain David Russell, was killed in strange circumstances shortly afterwards. Another mission, led by Lt.-Col. Gardyne de Chastelain, SOE's former head of station in Turkey, was parachuted in, four months later, but had equally bad luck, and was picked up and arrested within a day of its arrival.[55]

Despite the inauspicious start, de Chastelain's party ultimately replicated Mallaby's success in Rome. Instead of a week's incarceration, however, de Chastelain had to while away nearly eight months in prison before Antonescu was finally removed from power on 23 August and the young King Michael called upon his British prisoners to act as go-betweens with the Allied authorities. SOE's role in the *coup* was a significant one. As SOE's Director General, Colin Gubbins, triumphantly reminded the Foreign Secretary, Anthony Eden, in mid-September, 'the only Englishmen to whom King Michael and the new Romanian prime minister have spoken to in this crisis are SOE officers'.[56] De Chastelain's *physical* presence in Bucharest was also important. The Romanian opposition, in collaboration with SOE, had planned to overthrow Antonescu on 26 August: King Michael's abrupt dispatch of Antonescu had caught the plotters by surprise and de Chastelain's work in Bucharest, and subsequent trip to Istanbul, were important in easing Romania's departure from the Axis camp. The SOE party remained in Bucharest, liaising with the Romanian government, until the arrival of the British control commission in September. SOE's machinations might well have been crowned with success as early as April 1944. On the day of his release, de Chastelain was informed by the head of Antonescu's security service, General Tobescu, that had his party avoided arrest in December 1943, 'Romania would have been out of the war six months earlier.' Romania stood on the brink of exiting the war in early April. De Chastelain had persuaded Antonescu to dispatch an emissary to Cairo the previous month, and while Antonescu's demands were probably unacceptable in Allied eyes, de Chastelain himself put down Maniu's failure to capitalise on the situation in April to the unexpected American air raid on Bucharest on the 4th, which worked against creating an atmosphere suitable for a successful *coup*.[57]

Whether or not de Chastelain could have precipitated Romania's departure from the war before mid-August 1944, the fact remains that, as in Italy a year earlier, SOE had demonstrated its ability to influence political developments within enemy territory by having its men on the ground. This was new. Before Mallaby's happy resurrection, SOE had largely conceived of its irregular diplomacy as an activity that took place within states that were still at peace. Eisenhower's urgent appeal for a secure channel of communication to the Italian General Staff in August 1943 had not therefore simply breathed new life into an area of activity that had been dormant for the best part of a year; it had ushered in an entirely new phase in SOE's political work.[58] The revival of SOE's fortunes in this area was particularly welcome in SOE. To many senior staff, it was precisely these nebulous political functions that seemed to offer the most promising avenue for expanding SOE's activities after the return of peace. They can be seen, for instance, in Gubbins' estimation of SOE's role in Germany in the final months of the war, where his men would not only fulfil immediate wartime needs, but also build up inside Germany 'a suitable organisation to use during the post-armistice period and perhaps to lead to future clandestine and subversive work by whatever agency is charged by H.M.G. with these functions in peacetime'.[59] The prominence given to irregular political activities in Gubbins' thinking is no better expressed than in his memorandum, 'Tasks for SOE in Peace and War', composed in September 1945, in which 'operations of a political or general nature' were placed alongside sabotage and anti-scorched earth operations, as SOE's principal contributions to the Allied war effort.[60] In effect, SOE's irregular political activities had been elevated from a marginal sideshow to one of the principal rationale justifying the organisation's continued independent existence after the war had come to an end.

The problem facing Gubbins and his colleagues in late 1945 was that the task of winning sceptics in Whitehall over to SOE's side was no easier than it had been four years earlier. Suspicions of SOE remained deeply engrained in the SIS and the Foreign Office, and neither department was willing to see an agency, established at a time of national emergency in July 1940, extending its life indefinitely into the post-war world. Despite its undoubted contribution to British diplomacy in Belgrade (March 1941), Rome (August 1943) and Bucharest (August 1944), SOE had manifestly failed to allay the anxieties of its critics and claim a place as of right in the conduct of British foreign policy. Richard Aldrich has recently suggested that by late 1944, the Foreign Secretary, Anthony Eden, had come to appreciate the benefit SOE's political activities could bring to British diplomacy. On 23 November, in a letter to the Prime Minister, Eden argued in favour of maintaining 'the machinery for "special operations", even when the war is over'. 'In liberated territories and in neutral countries', he wrote, 'there may from time to time be useful scope for a covert organisation to further [British] policy.' It is of course tempting to see in this letter a foretaste of Eden's penchant for irregular methods that was to reappear twelve years later during the Suez Crisis, but Eden's apparent belief in the utility of SOE's brand of diplomacy should be taken with a pinch of salt. In reality, Eden's 'conversion' was little more than a ploy to align himself as the natural heir to SOE at a time when SOE's minister, Lord Selborne, was known to be contemplating resignation.[61] In practice, there is little to suggest that Eden was the slightest bit persuaded by SOE's claims. Indeed, in a letter to Selborne in early September, little more than three months after de Chastelain's dramatic *coup de main* in Romania, Eden's suspicions of the organisation's political activities were clearly unabated. The whole thrust of Eden's letter aimed at keeping

SOE's irregular diplomats away from anywhere, where they were likely to cause mischief. Contrary to his letter to Churchill, Eden insisted that in liberated areas SOE restrict itself to assisting operations against the remnants of German armed forces and, if the need arose, aiding those political forces favoured by the British government against insurgents or civil strife. 'Until such a situation of chaos [and civil war] does arise', Eden wrote in conclusion, 'I am strongly of the opinion that it would be better for SOE not to operate in armistice countries where there are no military operations in force under British command.'[62] Notwithstanding SOE's unique experience in Romania and Bulgaria, Eden was unwilling to sanction SOE missions in these, or, it seemed, any other countries, for fear of exciting Moscow's suspicions and undermining British efforts to retain a foothold in countries inside the Soviet orbit.[63] It is difficult to avoid the conclusion that such thinking continued to colour Foreign Office attitudes towards SOE's post-war role until the fate of the organisation had been sealed in the late summer of 1945.[64]

SOE's foray into the field of political warfare or irregular diplomacy during the Second World War can scarcely be held up as a success. Dalton's dabbling with revolutionary or political warfare soon fizzled out. Although the Belgrade *coup* had revealed the potential value of SOE involvement in British diplomacy, in subsequent months SOE failed to substantiate the claim that its 'irregular political activities' were in any way vital for the maintenance, or furtherance, of Britain's political and strategic interests. On the contrary, SOE's efforts to sustain an active political role for itself were either mishandled, as in the case of Portugal, or based on assumptions that bore little resemblance to the political realities of the countries concerned. The collapse of SOE's political activities in neutral Europe over 1942 did not, of course, end the organisation's work in this area. Outside Europe, where regional circumstances worked more in its favour, SOE's brand of irregular diplomacy could strike a chord among Britain's regular diplomats. Even inside Europe, as events in Italy and Romania showed, SOE could still pull off operations that other agencies could not hope to emulate. But SOE's experience in political activities over the course of the war lacked consistency and coherence. It had neither allayed the suspicions of those in Whitehall, who wrote off its personnel as 'nasty people who run around with explosives', nor had it won the case for maintaining a *dedicated* sabotage and subversion organisation in the post-war world.[65] Perhaps most worrying of all, after four years in business, it had failed to overturn the 'tendency for officials, and even Ministers, to say that Britain has never interfered in the internal affairs of other countries, and never will do so', despite the fact that, as Gubbins' deputy, Harry Sporborg, put it, governments had indulged in this dark art 'since the days of Queen Elizabeth'.[66] The government's refusal to maintain SOE in business after the war was symptomatic of its reluctance to accept that 'irregular political activities' had a place in British peacetime foreign relations in the middle of the twentieth century.

The Second World War was then, in many respects a missed opportunity. Bad luck, bad planning and official obstructionism ensured that by the time the war ended, thinking about covert operations or subversion had advanced little beyond the debates that had taken place four years before. While tentative efforts had been made to learn from experience and carry the examples of Belgrade and Rome forward into future operations, in reality, SOE found itself reacting to political opportunities rather than engineering them for its own ends. SOE's claims to proficiency in the murky arts of political warfare thus brought it little credit in the long run, and caused it considerable damage in the short run. Moreover, its chequered experienced in this form of warfare ensured that the doctrinal legacy it bequeathed to Britain's post-war diplomats was probably a thin one. Some of the old SOE hands who agreed to stay on in SIS after the organisation's formal merger with SIS in early 1946, such as David Smiley and Robin Zaehner, went on to play an important part in SIS's faltering efforts at political subversion at the end of the decade.[67] But these operations suffered from many of the difficulties that had blighted SOE's wartime: policy was developed on the hoof, activities and situations were responded to as they arose. It was only after the successful *coup* against Mossadegh in 1953,[68] that a coherent doctrine of 'special political action' emerged and, for a time at least, dominated British policy towards political problems in the Middle East.[69] Baker Street's 'ungentlemanly warriors' might have won their battles in Yugoslavia, Italy and Romania, but they had failed to win the argument at home. So far as the Foreign Office and Diplomatic Service were concerned, SOE's irregular diplomats were distinctly unreliable ones, and as a result they, and their immediate successors, would remain largely unwelcome.

Acknoweldgements

A version of this chapter was given at the British International Studies Association conference in Edinburgh on 18 Dec. 2001. The author would like to thank Sheila Kerr, Eunan O'Halpin, Peter Jackson and Kevin O'Brien for their constructive comments.

Notes

1 See M. R. D. Foot, 'Was SOE Any Good?', *Journal of Contemporary History* 16/1 (1981), pp. 167–181.

2 Paper by Col. L. Grand, 20 March 1939, cited in William Mackenzie, *The Secret History of SOE: The Special Operations Executive, 1940–1945* (London, 2000), p. 9.

3 M. R. D. Foot, 'Special Operations/2', in Michael Elliott-Bateman (ed.), *The Fourth Dimension of Warfare* vol. 1, *Intelligence, Subversion, Resistance* (Manchester, 1970), pp. 35–47.

4 For the inter-war Staff College, see Brian Holden Reid, *War Studies at the Staff College 1890–1930* (Camberley, 1992), esp. pp. 11–23, and pre-war antecedents, Brian Bond, *The Victorian Army and the Staff College, 1854–1914* (London, 1972).

5 Maj.-Gen. Sir Colin Gubbins, 'SOE and the Coordination of Regular and Irregular War', in Michael Elliott-Bateman (ed.), *The Fourth Dimension of Warfare*, vol. 1 *Intelligence, Subversion, Resistance* (Manchester, 1970), pp. 83–103 (p. 86).

6 Minutes of meeting held in SOE on 19 Oct. 1940, the National Archive, United Kingdom, Public Record Office (hereafter PRO) HS8/268. Foot commented, 'I gathered from people in SOE that there was absolutely nothing placed on record that was of any use when, in 1938/39/40 people began to put that organisation together.' Foot, 'Special Operations/2', p. 37.

7 Dalton to Halifax 2 July 1940, cited in Foot, 'Was SOE Any Good?', p. 169.

8 Ben Pimlott (ed.), *The Second World War Diaries of Hugh Dalton* (London, 1986), p. 52 (for 1 July 1940). Dalton expressed similar sentiments in his memoirs: *The Fateful Years: Memoirs, 1931–1945* (London, 1957), p. 367.

9 Dalton told Lord Mountbatten on 9 Jan. 1942 that Britain must put its faith in 'the French industrial working class': David Stafford, *Britain and the European Resistance*, (London, 1980), p. 29.

10 For these developments, see Mackenzie, *Secret History*, pp. 84–93, Ben Pimlott, *Hugh Dalton* (London, 1985), pp. 295–319, esp. p. 318.

11 Memo by G. Jebb, 'Subversion: A Description of the Special Operations Machine and Some Suggestions as to Future Policy', 5 Oct. 1940, cited in Mackenzie, *Secret History*, pp. 86, 91.

12 Minutes of meeting held in SOE on 19 October 1940, PRO HS8/268. For SOE's activities in Poland, see E. D. R. Harrison, 'The British Special Operations Executive and Poland', *Historical Journal* 43/4 (2000), pp. 1071–1092; Josef Garlinski, *Poland, SOE and the Allies* (London, 1969) and a more personal account in Peter Wilkinson, *Foreign Fields: The Story of an SOE Operative* (London, 1997), pp. 122–130.

13 The document, COS(40)27(0), 25 Nov. 1940, is reproduced in David Stafford, *Britain and the European Resistance 1940–1945: A Survey of the Special Operations Executive with Documents* (London, 1980), pp. 219–224.

14 The directive was drafted by SOE's Director-General, Sir Frank Nelson, Jebb, and its Balkan expert, George Taylor. Peter Wilkinson and Joan Bright Astley, *Gubbins & SOE* (London, 1993), p. 79; M. R. D. Foot, *SOE: Special Operations Executive 1940–1946* (London, 1984/1990), p. 250.

15 'The Technique of Subversion', by G. Jebb, May 1942, PRO HS8/251.

16 The same restructuring was carried out in SOE's headquarters in Cairo early the following year. See David Garnett, *The Secret History of PWE: The Political Warfare Executive 1939–1945* (London, 2002), pp. 1–73, esp. pp. 68–73; Michael Balfour, *Propaganda in War, 1939–1945: Organisations, Policies and Publics in Britain and Germany* (London, 1979), pp. 88–93; and Michael Stenton, *Radio London and Resistance in Occupied Europe British Political Warfare, 1940–1943* (Oxford, 2000), pp. 41–49.

17 David Stafford, 'The Detonator Concept: British Strategy, SOE and European Resistance after the Fall of France', *Journal of Contemporary History* 10/2 (1975), pp. 185–217; Wilkinson and Astley, *Gubbins & SOE*, pp. 79–96; Mark Seaman, 'Founding Father? Sir Colin Gubbins and the Origins of SOE', *Intelligence & National Security* 11/2 (1996), pp. 360–363.

18 See David J. Reynolds, 'Churchill the Appeaser? Between Hitler, Roosevelt and Stalin in World War Two', in David Dockrill and Brian McKercher (eds), *Diplomacy and World Power: Studies in British Foreign Policy 1890–1950. Essays for Zara Steiner* (Cambridge, 1996), pp. 197–220.

19 CEO to SO 10 April 1942, PRO HS3/189.

20 Pimlott, *Second World War Diaries of Hugh Dalton*, p. 324 (for 25 Nov. 1941). Dalton's biographer cites evidence suggesting that Dalton's behaviour was not beyond reproach in this matter: Pimlott, *Dalton*, p. 312.

21 Mackenzie tellingly notes that SOE's 'esprit de corps' was more noticeable and intangible than its supposed political bias: *Secret History*, p. 335. For instances of Dalton's politics impinging on the management of SOE, see Pimlott, *Dalton*, p. 312, and Bickham Sweet-Escott, *Baker Street Irregular* (London, 1965), p. 65.

22 Mackenzie, *Secret History of SOE*, p. 346.

23 Pimlott, *Second World War Diaries of Hugh Dalton*, p. 6 (for 16 May 1940). This remark related to Dalton's attitude towards economic warfare, but there is no doubt that it echoed his sentiments about special operations.

24 Mackenzie, *Secret History*, pp. 86–89.

25 'Report on SO from A/D [George Taylor] and D/HY on Certain SO2 Activities in Yugoslavia', 24 June 1941. London School of Economics. Hugh Dalton papers, 7/3 folio 99.

26 F. H. Hinsley *et al.*, *British Intelligence in the Second World War: Its Influence on Strategy and Operations*, vol. 1 (London, 1979), pp. 369–370, Mackenzie, *Secret History*, pp. 104–112, David Stafford, 'SOE and British Involvement in the Belgrade *Coup d'Etat* of March 1941', *Slavic Review* 36, 3 (1977), pp. 399–419; Elizabeth Barker, *British Policy in South-East Europe in the Second World War* (London, 1976), pp. 84–95.

27 The first operation to supply resistance fighters on the Continent – a drop to the Polish 'Home Army' – took place in March 1941, but the event underlined the difficulties of such operations as much as their feasibility.

28 General Ismay (Secretary, War Cabinet) to Dalton, 28 Mar. 1941, cited in Mackenzie *Secret History*, p. 112.

29 For an analysis of SOE's activities in these states, see Neville Wylie, 'SOE and the Neutrals', in Mark Seaman (ed.), *Special Operations Executive: A New Weapon of War* (London, 2005), and neutral Europe's place in the war, Christian Leitz, *Nazi Germany and Neutral Europe during the Second World War* (Manchester, 2001) and Neville Wylie (ed.), *European Neutrals and Non-belligerents during the Second World War* (Cambridge, 2001).

30 Sweet-Escott to Jebb, 13 July 1941, PRO HS3/222.

31 In Portugal, where Anglophile sentiments ran deep, the problem of finding willing recruits was not as acute as elsewhere. See the memoirs of the Lisbon station chief, 1940–1942, J. G. Beevor, *SOE: Recollections and Reflections 1940–1945* (London, 1981).

32 Jebb to Sargent (FO) 14 August 1941, PRO HS3/222.

33 Saul Kelly's chapter in this volume dwells at some length on SOE political activities in the Middle East, and so will only be referred to in passing.

34 Kelly (Berne) to Hopkinson (FO) 16 April 1941, PRO FO898/256. For Elizabeth Wiskemann's own account: *The Europe I Saw* (London, 1968), 141.

35 See J. G. Lomax, *The Diplomatic Smuggler* (London, 1965), pp. 117–121, and Neville Wylie, *Britain and Switzerland during the Second World War* (Oxford, 2003), pp. 51–83.

36 For SOE activities in Sweden, see C. G. McKay, *From Information to Intrigue: Studies in Secret Service Based on the Swedish Experience, 1939–1945* (London, 1993), pp. 64–69; Charles Cruickshank, *SOE in Scandinavia* (London, 1986); and Peter Tennant, *Touchlines of War* (Hull, 1992), pp. 133–152.

37 For British policy towards Spain and the Spanish Republicans: Denis Smyth, *Diplomacy and Strategy for Survival: British Policy and Franco's Spain, 1940–1941* (Cambridge, 1986) and David J. Dunthorn, *Britain and the Spanish Anti-Franco Opposition, 1940–1950* (London, 2000), esp. pp. 28–44.

38 Denis Smyth, 'Les Chevaliers de Saint-George: la Grande-Bretagne et la corruption des généraux espagnols (1940–1942)', *Guerres mondiales et conflits contemporains* 162 (1991): 29–54; David Stafford, *Churchill and Secret Service* (London, 1997), pp. 202–203; Javier Tusell, *Franco, Espanã y la II Guerra mundial: Entre el Eje y la neutralidad* (Madrid, 1995), pp. 178–179, David Messenger's chapter in this volume suggests a larger SOE involvement in internal Spanish politics than I argue for here.

39 Minute by Beevor, 12 Oct. 1942, PRO HS6/991.

40 Neville Wylie, '"An Amateur Learns his Job?" Special Operations Executive in Portugal, 1940–1942', *Journal of Contemporary History* 36/3 (2001), pp. 455–471.

41 In April 1941, evidence emerged suggesting that the German embassy had bribed General Kazim Dirik Pasha, in preparation for a massive effort to suborn the rest of the Turkish establishment. Cadogan (FO) to Knatchbull-Hugessen, 16 April 1941, PRO

HS3/238. See also Sir Hughe Knatchbull-Hugessen, *Diplomat in Peace and War* (London, 1949); Robin Denniston, *Churchill's Secret War: Diplomatic Decrypts, the FO and Turkey, 1942–1944* (Stroud, 1997), pp. 33–66; and Selim Deringil, *Turkish Foreign Policy during the Second World War* (Cambridge, 1989), pp. 117–132.

42 'AD' [G. Taylor] to 'CEO' [Jebb] 13 July 1941, PRO HS3/222.

43 Jebb to Dalton, 7 Aug. 1941, PRO HS3/238.

44 Dalton to Eden, 1 Jan. 1942, PRO HS3/238. For SOE's use of bribery in the Levant, see Chapter 7 by Saul Kelly in this volume.

45 See Saul Kelly's Chapter 7 in this volume for SOE political action in the Middle East. Richard Aldrich explores SOE enthusiasm for coups in Thailand and the Argentine in *The Key to the South: Britain, the United States, and Thailand during the Approach of the Pacific War, 1929–1942* (Kuala Lumpur, 1993), pp. 335–337, 356–7, note 81.

46 See the experience of SOE's Bickham Sweet-Escott on visiting Ankara in 1941 – *Baker Street Irregular*, p. 81, and the comments of SOE's officer in Stockholm, cited in Ian Dear, *Sabotage and Subversion: The SOE and OSS at War* (London, 1996), p. 75.

47 Mackenzie, *Secret History*, p. 335.

48 According to Sargent (FO) to Jebb (SOE), 22 Aug. 1941:

> The conditions which in other countries make SO2 activities possible and desirable do not exist in Turkey, where the government are in effective control of every branch of the country's life and activities and where these exists no element with which SO2 could enter into contact to any purpose. Moreover, any attempt on the part of SO2 to make such contacts would certainly become known to the Turkish Secret police and upset our whole position in Turkey.

See also Hugessen to FO, 18 Aug. 1941, PRO HS3/238.

49 Beevor, *SOE: Recollections and Reflections*, p. 39.

50 For the 'Lisbon incident', see Wylie, '"An Amateur Learns his Job?"', pp. 455–571; Antonio Telo, *Propaganda e Guerra secreta em Portugal 1939–1945* (Lisbon, 1990), pp. 104–107; and Julia Leitão de Barros, 'O Caso Shell: a rede espionagem anglo-portuguesa (1940–1942)', *História XIV*, 147 (1991), pp. 55–83.

51 The full text of this 'Charter' is now available in Mackenzie, *Secret History*, pp. 759–62 (Appendix D). Eden specifically referred to SOE's activities in Turkey and Portugal to justify Foreign Office control over SOE activities in the neutrals. Minute by Eden for Churchill, 7 April 1942, PRO FO954/24, folio 125.

52 Christopher Woods, 'A Tale of Two Armistices', in K. G. Robertson (ed.), *War, Resistance and Intelligence. Essays in Honour of M. R. D. Foot* (Barnsley, 1999), pp. 1–17, quotation on p. 6.

53 'Having learnt our lesson from events preceding Italy's collapse, we had placed such sets in Stockholm, Istanbul and Lisbon on the off chance of armistice negotiations commencing with Romania requiring W/T links to carry heavy traffic.' Draft SOE paper for the War Cabinet, 'Romania', June 1945, PRO HS7/186.

54 See Lt. Col. G. de Chastelain, 'History. SOE Romania', 7 Sept. 1945, PRO HS7/186.

55 Mackenzie, *Secret History*, pp. 497–501; Foot, *SOE*, p. 332; Ivor Porter, *Operation Autonomous: With SOE in Romania* (London, 1989).

56 Minutes of meeting held between Gubbins (SOE), Sporborg (SOE), Eden (FO) and Sargent (FO), 13 Sept. 1944, PRO HS8/281.

57 Lt. Col. de Chastelaine, 'History: SOE Romania', 7 Sept. 1945, PRO HS7/186.

58 It is worth noting that SOE decided in March 1944 to send a mission to Romania to establish direct contacts with Maniu.

59 Memo by Gubbins, 11 Aug. 1944, PRO HS6/632.

60 Memo by Gubbins, 'Tasks for SOE in Peace and War', 22 Sept. 1945, PRO HS8/202.

61 Eden to Churchill, 23 Nov. 1944, cited in Richard J. Aldrich, *The Hidden Hand: Britain,*

America and Cold War Secret Intelligence (London, 2001), p. 74. Wary of Eden's ambitions, Churchill persuaded Selborne to remain until the end of the war.

62 Eden to Selborne, 9 Sept. 1944, PRO HS8/281.

63 The fact that SIS and SOE's American counterpart, the OSS, had stations in Romania, and that the Soviet's NKVD were already running amok in Italy, apparently passed Eden by.

64 See Stephen Dorril, *MI6: Fifty Years of Special Operations* (London, 2000), pp. 18–34; Wilkinson and Astley, *Gubbins and SOE*, pp. 217–237.

65 Minute by Gubbins, 18 Feb. 1942, cited in Mackenzie, *Secret History*, p. 344. Churchill commented in May 1944, 'the part which your naughty deeds in war play, in peace cannot at all be considered at the present time'. Churchill to Selborne, 1 May 1944, cited in Wilkinson and Astley, *Gubbins and SOE*, p. 217.

66 Minutes of SOE–Foreign Office meeting, 13 Sept. 1944, PRO HS8/281. Selborne admitted as much in his final letter to Churchill as Minister for SOE on 22 May 1945: 'It is no doubt my fault that I have been unable to persuade Eden that underground activities would prove useful to the Foreign Office after the war', cited in Wilkinson and Astley, *Gubbins and SOE*, p. 232.

67 For SOE's post-war legacy, see Richard Aldrich, 'Unquiet in Death: The Post-War Survival of the "Special Operations Executive", 1945–1951', in Anthony Gorst, Lewis Johnman and W. Scott Lucas (eds), *Contemporary British History, 1931–1961: Politics and the Limits of Policy* (London, 1991), pp. 193–217; Aldrich, *The Hidden Hand*, pp. 160–162; Philip H. J. Davies, 'From Special Operations to Special Political Action: The "Rump SOE" and SIS Post-War Covert Action Capability, 1945–1977', *Intelligence & National Security* 15/3 (2000): 55–76.

68 See *inter alia* Dorril, *MI6*, pp. 558–99; C. M. Woodhouse, *Something Ventured* (London, 1983), esp. pp. 105–112; Aldrich, *The Hidden Hand*, pp. 464–76.

69 For an insight into the pervasiveness of 'special political action' in British policy towards the Middle East, even after the Suez debacle, see Matthew Jones, 'The "Preferred Plan": The Anglo-American Working Group Report on Covert Action in Syria, 1957', *Intelligence & National Security* 19/3 (2004): 401–415.

7   A succession of crises?

SOE in the Middle East, 1940–1945

Saul Kelly

Introduction

A detailed account of SOE in the Middle East is a prominent omission from the collection of studies on SOE during the Second World War.[1] This is surprising given the importance of the region to Britain and the fact that some records were released, with a helpful guide, in 1994.[2] The most complete account to date is contained in William Mackenzie's in-house history of the SOE, which contains two chapters on SOE in the Middle East.[3] These are concerned mainly with organisational matters but there is some information on operations. Mackenzie was necessarily restricted by space in the amount of detail he could include on SOE in the Middle East, the fact that he wrote the narrative remarkably quickly after the war and that he could not access all SOE material. As far as the Middle East chapters were concerned, he depended on the narratives of the section dealing with the Arab World, certain series and branch files, the demi-official correspondence of Lord Selborne (Minister of Economic Warfare, responsible for SOE from February 1942 to May 1945), those reminiscences published at the time, interviews with SOE staff, and some Cabinet and Chiefs of Staff papers in the Cabinet Office. The papers of other departments, such as the Foreign Office, are referred to only when the originals or copies appeared in the SOE archives. His narrative is written primarily from the point of view of SOE. As Mackenzie pointed out, the SOE section narratives, though primary sources, 'vary enormously in quality and in the number of references they give'.[4] This applies particularly to the 'History of SOE in the Arab World' which, though written by an SOE official in Cairo (AW/100) in September 1945 was 'very disappointing, chiefly no doubt because it was written entirely from memory, as all documents referring to S.O.E. Arab World activities were burned at the time of El Alamein'[5] (a reference to 'the great bonfire' at General Headquarters Middle East in Cairo as Rommel approached El Alamein in June 1942). Also the 'History of SOE in the Arab World' was only concerned with the period up to El Alamein as subsequent activities to the end of hostilities were thought by AW/100 to be of a subversive nature too secret to be embodied in one single document. When AW/100 was asked to include post-Alamein material, he refused on grounds of security and also stated that no detailed records were kept as SOE Field Commanders were instructed to destroy any incriminating documents as soon as was practicable. Therefore, it was doubted whether this 'secret history' of SOE operations in the Middle East, as opposed to the open history which he had produced, could ever be written.[6]

This is an unnecessarily pessimistic conclusion. Despite the destruction of files both during and after the war, whether through fire or weeding, and the continued retention of many relating to Arab countries, 'a good deal of information about these areas can be gleaned from the general files of the Middle East mission', which were released in 1994[7] (including a more authoritative memorandum on 'SOE Activities in Arab Countries, Persia, Egypt and Cyprus', written in 1945 and covering the post-Alamein period).[8] Some, but not all, of these files were used by Mackenzie. This source can also be supplemented by the SOE War Diary (released in 1999), which is a mine of information and does not seem to have been quarried by Mackenzie when writing about the Middle East. Unfortunately the relevant files of the Foreign Office are still retained by that department[9], and those of the Cabinet Office (the Joint Planning Staff, the Joint Intelligence Committee and the Cabinet) contain little useful information. So it is still difficult to chronicle the Foreign Office's side of its often stormy relations with SOE over its activities in the Middle East. But, as I hope to show in this chapter, it is possible to make at least a start in documenting the 'secret history' of SOE operations in the Middle East. When the remaining SOE files relating to Arab countries are released, it should be possible to present a fuller picture.[10] (From what I have divined from available SOE records, I suspect they contain much interesting evidence on how widespread was SOE's use of bribery in the Middle East, usually on behalf of the Foreign Office, in order to win Arab support during the war in the face of the Axis threat.) This would add another dimension to our understanding of the mechanics of British policy in the region at this critical juncture.

A word on the title. I have chosen 'SOE *in* the Middle East' rather than the official designation: 'SOE Middle East', because the latter's responsibilities included the Balkans, as well as the Arab countries, Persia and Turkey. The Balkans have been well dealt with by other authors and I do not intend to cover them in this chapter. Instead I will concentrate on SOE's operations in the geographic region known as the Middle East. And, as I hope to show, they were characterised by a succession of crises. These fall into three periods: (1) the early activities in 1940–1941; (2) the post-occupational planning phase from 1941–1943; and (3) the post-October 1943 period which saw reorganisation, the recession of the German threat, the disbandment of the post-occupational schemes and the desire to re-tool SOE in the Middle East for peacetime/post-war problems.

The early activities: 1940–1941

> Nobody who did not experience it can possibly imagine the atmosphere of jealousy, suspicion, and intrigue which embittered the relations between the various secret and semi-secret departments in Cairo during that summer of 1941, or for that matter for the next two years. It would be quite beyond my powers to describe it.[11]

It seemed, indeed, to be the stuff of fiction, for Bickham Sweet-Escott recommended to his readers two novels[12] by Christopher Sykes, another former SOE officer, which were set in wartime Cairo. '[E]ven if security has compelled him to invent certain episodes, his account of the way people behaved is severely objective.'[13] Sweet-Escott thought that, as 'interlopers', the semi-secret propaganda (SO1) and sabotage (SO2) sections of SOE in the Middle East were easy targets for those within the older secret organisations in the region who either misunderstood the role of SOE or 'who wished to make a reputation for integrity and ruthlessness by exposing them, and for the empire-builders who saw the chance of creating jobs for themselves by denouncing the incompetence and worse of those who for the time being were in charge of them'.[14] There is much truth in this, as we shall see, but Sweet-Escott tended to gloss over, perhaps for reasons of loyalty and security, the fact that it was well known in Cairo in the summer of 1941 'that a bloodthirsty internecine warfare was going on and had been for some little time between two parts of the same entity, viz between SO1 and SO2 who should of course have been S.O.E.'[15] How had this parlous situation come about, only a year after Hugh Dalton, the Minister of Economic Warfare, tasked by the War Cabinet with 'secret action of all kinds against the enemy', had taken over an 'elaborate and ramshackle machine which . . . was now to be known as the Special Operations Executive'?[16]

In part, the crisis in the summer of 1941 in Cairo was due to the failure to streamline this 'elaborate and ramshackle machine' in London and Cairo along the same lines. In London, the various constituent parts had been fully amalgamated by the autumn of 1940, with the Foreign Office's propaganda section, Electra House (EH), becoming SO1, and the sabotage sections of the War Office (Military Intelligence, Research (MI(R)) and the Secret Intelligence Service (Section D) being merged to form SO2. But this administrative rationalisation was not replicated in Cairo. In fact, relations were so bad between MI(R) and Section D in the Middle East (respectively known as GSI(R), or G(R) for short, and D/H), who were both under the direction and control of the C. in C. Middle East through his Deputy Director of Military Intelligence (DDMI), that it was proposed that G(R) should take over D/H. Although Dalton managed to dissuade the C. in C. Middle East, General Sir Archibald Wavell, from taking this course and agreeing to the appointment of a 'highly successful' London lawyer, George Pollock, as head of D/H, it was on the condition that SOE sent out a senior official to broker a general settlement. In the event, this did not occur and matters were allowed to drift until a crisis was reached in the summer of 1941. In the interim D/H (which became, by default, SO2 in the Middle East) and G(R) maintained an uneasy dual responsibility, with their small, separate headquarters, for sabotage operations in the Middle East.[17]

The situation with regard to propaganda had even more potential for conflict, with more than six agencies involved: D/H in Cairo, which distributed propaganda; D/H in Turkey under Donald Mallett; D/K under Colonel Longrigg which dealt with Abyssinia and was responsible for subversive propaganda in the whole of the Middle East, with the exception of propaganda to Italy and Free French propaganda in Syria; Colonel Thornhill, who represented SO1 and who handled all propaganda for Italy and its distribution there and in Africa; the Ministry of Information and '[c]ertain independent agencies operated directly by the DDMI, Brigadier Clayton'.[18] Pollock made a bid in the winter of 1940–1941, with the backing of Dalton and SO2 in London, to bring all these organisations under his control so as to coordinate more effectively political subversion, covert propaganda and sabotage and fifth column work, thus countering increased Axis and pro-Axis activity in the Middle East.[19] Pollock was thwarted, however, by Thornhill's refusal not only to work under him but even to coordinate propaganda. Consequently, what emerged were 'two completely separate bodies, SO1 and SO2, with parallel communications to their headquarters in London which were in a state of absolute warfare' with each other over the control of propaganda.[20] This seems to have soon become common knowledge in Cairo but not in London, until August 1941. Wavell's concern to counter enemy subversion in the Arab world, especially in Iraq and Syria, led him to take action in June 1941, without even consulting Pollock, to improve British propaganda in the region. Although SOE in London managed to thwart Wavell's proposal to appoint a Ministry of Information Coordinator for all propaganda based on the Middle East (including the Balkans), they felt constrained to accede to his request to coordinate all propaganda within the area of Middle East Command under a new body, the Jerusalem Bureau, which would control all SO1 and Ministry of Information activities. The problem of the higher coordination of propaganda and subversive warfare was seemingly solved by the appointment on 1 July 1941 of Oliver Lyttleton as Minister of State in the Middle East, with Cabinet rank, to arbitrate between the warring Ministries and their agents in Cairo.[21]

Unaware of the 'state of absolute warfare' prevailing between SO1 and SO2 in Cairo, Dalton in June 1941 expressed himself 'entirely satisfied' with SO1's work within its own sphere.[22] In recognition of this he was prepared to promote Thornhill to Brigadier. In contrast, both Dalton and Wavell had serious concerns about Pollock's running of SO2. Apart from his failure to keep London adequately informed of his operations, there were allegations, much exaggerated by the rumour mill in Cairo, of financial extravagance and improper expenditure, of unsuitability of personnel and lapses in security. Above all, there was a feeling in London and Cairo that Pollock's control of this large, expensive and ill-coordinated organisation was 'lax and ineffective', that it had 'failed to produce results' in the Balkans, Iraq and Syria and that it would be best if he were dismissed.[23] This is not entirely fair since SO2 had fought reasonably well, and with some real results, in the Balkans, but its record in the Middle East was unimpressive. Pollock's ignorance of Iraq had meant that he had failed in the winter of 1940–1941 to make full use of well-placed Britons and Iraqis to counter the growing Axis influence in that country. However, he was not helped by the obstructiveness of the Ambassador, Sir Basil Newton, who 'refused absolutely' to allow SO2 operatives to join his staff to conduct covert propaganda and political subversion. By the time his more dynamic successor (and former director of the Arab Bureau), Sir Kinahan Cornwallis, arrived in the Spring, it was too late to do anything before the Rashid Ali revolt. In fact, Pollock and the newly-appointed SO2 representative in Baghdad, the British

Consul, Hope-Gill, spent the first fortnight of the revolt besieged in the British Embassy together (shortly afterwards Hope-Gill was posted to Addis Ababa). SO2 proved unable to carry out a mission to destroy an aviation spirit dump in Baghdad and so handed the task to G(R). But the latter's planned use of 'Jewish toughs', from the Irgun, failed, when their leader, David Raziel, was killed. Apparently, they spent the remainder of their time in Iraq 'lamenting their dead leader and complaining that SOE had not fitted them out to adopt the role of Iraqi Arabs'. An SOE officer later commented that: 'The whole of this undertaking was most dangerous and ill-conceived, and it is lucky that the Iraqis have never discovered that we employed Palestinian Jews against them during their revolt.'[24] But G(R)'s sabotage of sixteen new US-supplied Northrop aeroplanes, the only modern aircraft the Iraqi Air Force had, proved to be one of the main reasons for the failure of the revolt, according to the German Minister to Iraq, Dr Fritz Grobba.[25]

SO2 were 'greatly hampered' in their attempt to set up an organisation in Syria and the Lebanon by the 'unshakeable decision' of Wavell and Clayton in Cairo and the Morton Committee in London to allow no activity which might undermine the position of the Vichy French High Commissioner, Dentz, in the hope that he might defect to the British or at least oppose any German attempt to infiltrate or occupy the Levant states. In an attempt to win over Dentz, SO2 was banned in March 1941 from using Palestinian Arab and Jewish agents to smuggle Arabic and Free French propaganda into Vichy territory. Wavell also had severe reservations about allowing SO2 to train Palestinian Jews as saboteurs (they were known as 'The Friends', since they were thought to be Britain's only reliable allies in the Middle East) and this was banned after the 'Patria' incident.[26] 'A certain "neglect" of these instructions' meant that Pollock had some men and supplies in place in Syria, and others trained for para-naval work, when GHQ Middle East suddenly lifted the ban and demanded action, following the Greek debacle and the rapid deterioration of the situation in Iraq and Syria.[27] SO2 units seized key pumping stations along the trans-desert oil pipelines (near the bifurcation point at Haditha en route to Haifa and Tripoli) and an important road junction at Iskanderoun, but Operation SEALION, the attempt by a Palestinian Jewish commando unit led by Major Sir Anthony Palmer to attack the Tripoli oil refinery, failed.[28] Although it was later well established that some of the claims of sabotage of Vichy installations in Syria were false, there is no doubt that Palestinian Jews and Arabs conducted reconnaissance missions, cut communications and disseminated propaganda and proclamations in the run-up to the Anglo-Free French invasion in June 1941.[29]

SO2 had no real organisation to speak of in Turkey and Iran, because of the obstruction or lack of confidence respectively of Britain's diplomatic representatives Sir Hughe Knatchbull-Hugesson and Sir Reader Bullard.[30] This hampered attempts by SO2, on the orders of the 'highest authorities' in London, to use Jewish agents to assassinate German and Italian agents (von Hentig, Rosen, von Oppenheimer and Gabriella) and Arab and Indian nationalist leaders (the Mufti, Rashid Ali and Subhas Chandra Bose) as they fled Iraq, Syria, Iran and Afghanistan to Turkey and Berlin[31]. However, the head of the SO2 office in Istanbul (for work into the Balkans), Gardyn de Chastelain, managed to bribe Turkish railway officials and staff officers to hold up the shipment of German armaments through the ports of Samsun and Trebizond to Iraq and Iran in May 1941.[32]

SO2 had not bothered to set up organisations in Palestine or Egypt because their defence and pre-occupational demolition or post-occupational subversion were held to be the responsibility of the military. SO2's plans for using Libyan exiles in Egypt and Free French operatives in Tunisia to raise tribal revolts in Libya came to nothing, as did their original intention to use the Galla tribes in south-western Ethiopia to undermine Italian rule. In the event, it was G(R) that success-fully raised a revolt in Ethiopia under the banner of the recently deposed Emperor Haile Selassie, the arch-enemy of the Galla.[33] Nor did SO2 have any more luck coordinating operations against the Italians in the Yemen and the Vichy French at Jibuti because of the general ban on sabotage activities by the Governor of Aden. SO2's operations in the Red Sea seemed to consist only of the 'cutting-out' cruise of the sloop *Saad* which, after the fall of Massawa, took the surrender of some 1,500 Italian military personnel in Eritrea, and the lone propaganda activi-ties of 'Harold'. The latter was a cashiered Iraqi policeman by the name of Hassan Fahmi.[34] He attempted to influence Saudi opinion, first in Mecca and then in Riyadh, through bribing the compilers of the official Saudi summary of broadcasts and by distributing leaflet propaganda. This aroused the ire of both the British Minister in Jedda, Stonehewer-Bird, and the Eastern Department of the Foreign Office, who feared that it would alienate King Ibn Saud and lead to his lifting of the ban on Italian propaganda in the kingdom. In an attempt to control SOE activi-ties in Saudi Arabia, the Foreign Office proposed that one of their diplomats in Jedda should work half-time for SO2. This was to prove a favourite tactic of the Foreign Office.[35]

There is no doubt that, in the Middle East as opposed to the Balkans, SO2 had little to show for the considerable investment of time, money, and personnel. Wavell's solution, in line with his establishment of the Jerusalem Bureau for the coordination of propaganda, was to advocate bringing SO2 under the direct control of GHQ, Middle East, by pairing it with G(R). This would mean, in effect, the virtual extinction of SOE in the Middle East. Not surprisingly SOE in London demurred and sent out Brigadier Taverner to replace Pollock and sort the situation out. His capture by a German patrol, following the shooting down of his Sunderland flying boat over the Bay of Biscay, delayed the investigation further and, in the interim, SOE London shackled Pollock's decision-making powers to prevent him doing any more damage to the organisation's position in the Middle East. By July 1941, however, it was clear that Pollock had completely lost the confidence of the military, the British Ambassador, Sir Miles Lampson, and the new Minister of State, Lyttleton. Therefore, the head of SO2, Sir Frank Nelson, flew out to Cairo with Pollock's new replacement, Maxwell, to restore the situation. They were presented by Lyttleton with a pretty damning account of Pollock's stewardship (the so-called 'Anti-SO2 Dossier'), which had been compiled by the 'righteous', Bible-toting, Chief of the General Staff, General Arthur Smith, from evidence provided to him by two disillusioned SOE officers, Bill Stirling and Peter Fleming, with the covert assistance of Lady Ranfurly who, working in the SO2 office in Cairo, had been asked by Wavell to purloin incriminating material from its files.[36]

Both Stirling and Fleming had been involved with the failed Yak Mission, which had been intended by London to supplement the Free Italian activities of SO1 but had ended up being misused in the debacle in Greece.[37] In a naked bid to take control of SO2 in the Middle East, Stirling condemned SO2 as 'thoroughly rotten' and morale low. This was due, in his view, to the failure of Pollock and his chief lieutenants to lead active operations themselves (there was a 'widespread delusion you can become a Lawrence of Arabia by sitting in offices and bars in Cairo and Jerusalem'), and London's failure to keep an eye on things.[38] Ironically, he thought that Pollock and his deputy, Perkins, as lawyers, had made the best case for themselves on the least evidence, whereas Fleming and Smith had, in Nelson's view, provided 'no concrete proof in this [the Anti-SO2 Dossier] of the delinquencies of members of SO2 who were mentioned thereon – if one uses the word "proof" in a legal or semi-legal sense'.[39] Yet Nelson thought that drastic action was needed to restore the confidence of the military, diplomatic and political authorities in Cairo in SO2 and proposed that both Pollock and Bailey should be replaced. Bailey, in charge of working back into the Balkans from Istanbul and broadcasting from 'freedom stations' in Jerusalem, 'had been superlatively indiscreet in his expenditure of SOE funds and in his relationship with the various evacuees in Jerusalem. He was largely responsible for the indescribably bad odour in which SOE was held.'[40] Nelson also learnt of the running feud between SO2 and SO1 in Cairo and was given as proof an 'Anti-SO1 Dossier', which implicated both Thornhill, and his deputy Colonel Metherell (the model for Sykes' evil Colonel Anstey). While Nelson recognised Thornhill's good work on Italian propaganda, he distrusted his judgement, as evidenced by his acceptance of sums subscribed for British propaganda by members of the Italian Communist Party in Egypt and applying them to equip his mission with luxurious transport.[41] He was also caught up in the Aziz el-Masri affair, which had severely embarrassed the British Embassy and the Egyptian government.[42] In order to balance the proposed purge of SO2, and prevent a collapse of morale in that organisation, Nelson advocated that Thornhill, Metherell, and Lt. Colonel Johnstone (working on Balkan propaganda) should be dismissed as well. Dalton's sanctioning of these proposals without giving Thornhill a chance to defend himself was not only resented by him but by Rex Leeper, the head of SO1 in London, who washed his hands of all further responsibility for SO1 in the Middle East. Coinciding as it did with the crisis in London leading to the formation of the Political Warfare Executive (PWE), it led to the unjustified but nevertheless real feeling that SO1 had suffered for SO2's mistakes. This was to cause resentment which was carried in the corporate memory from SO1 to PWE and was to complicate the relationship with SO2, which had inherited, by default, the title: SOE.[43]

The post-occupational planning phase, 1941–1943

With the removal of the heads of SO1 and SO2 in Cairo, the onerous task of re-organising SOE Middle East fell not to a senior trained official from London but to Terence Maxwell, a merchant banker, Territorial Officer and son-in-law of Neville Chamberlain. Until his appointment he had been unaware even of the existence of SOE and had spent only ten days in its London headquarters, with the result that he had no knowledge of its personnel or its methods.[44] London soon realised that he was 'too "academic" and "organisational"' for the job.[45] He had re-organised the Middle East Mission into four main directorates: Special Operations (DSO, which retained the cover G(R)); Policy and Agents, which became Political Advice (DPA, with the cover GSI (J)) in November 1941 and was sub-divided into two sections, for the Arab World (DPA(A)) and the Balkans (DPA(B)); Special Propaganda (DSP, with the cover GSI (K)); and Finance and Administration (DFA). Despite this, London believed that the military, through the agency of G(R), had virtually taken over DSO but were not conducting it very efficiently in the Balkans. The whole position of DSP was under siege from the Foreign Office, who criticised it not only for its handling of propaganda to the Balkans (particularly Greece), but for its plans for using Kurds, Armenians and Georgians to broadcast to the Caucasus in the event of a German occupation. By the spring of 1942, and changes at the top in London (where Dalton, Nelson and Jebb were replaced by Lord Selborne, Sir Charles Hambro and Colonel Harry Sporborg, respectively) and Cairo (where Lyttleton was replaced, temporarily, by Sir Walter Monckton, and then by Richard Casey), it was thought it was time to make a clean sweep, and replace Maxwell, as well. The case for change was made by Lord Glenconner, who pointed out that SOE activities could not be conducted

> either on big business and [*sic*] less on military lines. The success of SOE operations depends on their secrecy, the most laborious and closest attention to detail, and on the most intimate knowledge of the countries concerned. If this is not present, the patient work of months can be thrown away by one mistake or ill-judged action. Moreover, each country constitutes a different problem requiring its own treatment and solution. We should look therefore to what I may call the 'handicraft principle' as opposed to that of mass production, and to throwing responsibility as much as possible on to the officer responsible for each country section.

In other words, SOE in Cairo should be remodelled on the lines of London HQ, with the Country specialists concentrating on subversion and the paramilitary, or G(R), 'tradition, should be segregated or expelled entirely'.[46]

The story of the struggle for control of SOE Middle East between Glenconner and London, on the one hand, and Maxwell, Casey and the Cs-in-C, Middle East, on the other has been well told by Mackenzie and does not need repeating here.[47] For the purposes of this chapter, it is sufficient to say that by the compromise worked out by the warring parties in September 1942, Glenconner (who replaced Maxwell as Controller of the Middle East Mission) ceded control of operational matters (DSO) to his Chief of Staff, the belligerent Brigadier 'Bolo' Keble, and the military, subject to the re-organisation of DSO (A) and (B) along London (Country section) lines (DPA disappeared and, though DSP remained, its relations with PWE are a separate story).[48] This arrangement thus preserved the principle that SOE Middle East was a Mission primarily responsible to its headquarters in London, and also that the Foreign Office, through its May 1942 'treaty' with SOE, ultimately exercised political control over SOE activities.

Mackenzie's concentration on the battle for the soul of Middle East Mission at the highest level between London and Cairo and its aftermath, leading to the last crisis in the history of the Cairo HQ in 1943 (which was over the Balkans, so it is not covered here), meant that he made no attempt to deal with the work of Group-Captain Domville's DSO (A). He justified this 'partly because it was of little relevance to the German war after 1942, partly because the threads of its activities lead on into the post-war history of the Middle East'.[49] However, as will be seen, an examination of the activities of DSO (A), particularly in setting up post-occupational schemes in the event of successful Axis offensives in the Middle East from the west and/or the north, helps to cast light on an often neglected dimension of 'the German war'. It will also reveal some new and rather unsavoury details about how DSO (A) ensured compliance with British war aims in the region, which were to have implications for the post-war period.

While SOE had fought hard during the successive crises, in the summers of 1941 and 1942, to establish that the powers of its Middle East Mission should derive ultimately from London, it had also been essential to achieve in Cairo a very high degree of coordination, on the one hand, for its political activities and, on the other, with the plans and operations of the military. This was achieved through a new body, the SOE Sub-Committee of the Middle East Defence Committee (MEDC), which was presided over by the Minister of State with representatives from the three Services, for Propaganda and Foreign Policy, as well as the Controller of SOE. This sub-committee reviewed and approved SOE plans and operations within the general policy laid down by the authorities in London. During 1941 and 1942 the SOE Sub-Committee evolved a policy which related subversive actions to the general strategic outlook in the Middle East and the position with regard to the availability of equipment and transport. It was expected that Middle East Command would concentrate first on driving the Axis forces out of Libya and then securing that western flank before, in the spring of 1942, switching the bulk of its forces to the northern front, where it would join the troops of India Command for defensive operations in northern Persia, Iraq, Syria and possibly Turkey against an expected twin-pronged Axis offensive across the Caucasus and possibly from Thrace, through Anatolia, towards the Middle East base areas in Palestine and Egypt, at Basra and the Iraqi and Persian oil fields. After the Northern Front had been stabilised, it was intended to take offensive operations against Sicily and southern Italy, Crete and the Dodecanese. It followed that Middle East Command should try and destroy or disrupt Axis land and sea communications to the Middle East through the Balkans, Italy and across the Mediterranean, and its oil supplies from Romania. SOE's involvement in all this has been well documented but not so its activities in the Middle East proper in support of these strategic aims.[50] Here it was agreed that SOE should carry out political subversion and covert propaganda to counter Axis intrigues and encourage pro-Allied feeling; prepare guerilla forces and set up post-occupational schemes to operate in the event of an Axis invasion and, where necessary, to cooperate with the Russians and the Americans.

How then did SOE fare in carrying out these objectives? In general, it seems badly by June 1942 and the end of Maxwell's tenure, which witnessed Axis offensives into Egypt and the Caucasus. Yet it took time to lay the foundations of a subversive organisation in the Middle East, as in the Balkans. This was done under the able and industrious Wing-Commander Pat Domville (a gifted orientalist who could even sing in Arabic) and was encouraged by both Maxwell and Glenconner. Their combined efforts began to show results by the winter of 1942 when post-occupational schemes had been worked out for Syria, Palestine and Trans-Jordan, as well as Iraq, Persia and Egypt. It is noticeable that all these territories were under British or joint Allied control and military considerations were of paramount concern. In contrast in neutral countries, such as Turkey and the Yemen, political concerns, as interpreted by the Foreign Office, predominated and were to severely restrict SOE activities.

SOE had wanted to make the fullest possible preparations for a possible Axis invasion of Turkey but were prevented from doing so by the Foreign Office, who imposed a strict ban in December 1941 on their work in Turkey itself, which was even extended to propaganda in April 1942 (though it sanctioned the use of Istanbul as a base from which to work back into the Balkans). Whereas in 1941 it was feared that the establishment of an SOE organisation in Turkey would destroy good relations with the Turks and drive them into the hands of the Germans, by late 1942 it was being argued that SOE sabotage operations would prejudice the chances of bringing the Turks into the war on the side of the Allies.[51] As long as SOE did not engage in subversive or political activity in Turkey, the British Ambassador in Ankara, Sir Hugh Knatchbull-Hugessen, was prepared to see a limited number of SOE personnel maintain and develop the contacts originally made (before the ban) for work in the event of an Axis invasion. He made it clear, however, that if any of the operatives were discovered, then SOE would have to leave Turkey.[52] Despite these restrictions, the head of SOE in Turkey, Gardyne de Chastelain, engaged in pre- and post-occupational planning, with mixed results. Although SOE were to help the Cs-in-C Middle East by destroying the oil installations at Istanbul and Smyrna, sinking Axis shipping in the Sea of Marmora and demolishing key machinery at the Karabuk steel mills, de Chastelain doubted whether his organisation had sufficient staff to accomplish these tasks. He thought that pre-occupational sabotage should be left to the British military, with SOE concentrating on post-occupational work. De Chastelain had encouraged his contacts, who had been approved by Hugessen, to form small cells, mostly unknown to each other or to SOE. Their activities at this stage were confined to locating suitable sites for explosives dumps and W/T premises and recruiting suitable agents as W/T operators. These plans were dependent on sufficient explosives and devices being made available but Hugessen would only allow SOE to set up dumps at Istanbul (Therapia), Adana and Smyrna. Hugessen also successfully thwarted SOE's attempts to secure permission from the Foreign Office to use sabotage to reduce the considerable shipment of chrome to the Axis powers. He preferred to apply diplomatic pressure on the Turks who, eventually in the spring of 1944, cut off all chrome shipments to the Axis.[53] Although SOE owned five Turkish caiques for operational work along the western coast of Turkey and into the Greek islands, they were not much used in 1942.[54] Cyprus was also used as a base for caique operations against the Dodecanese. After the fall of Crete in 1941, post-occupational plans were drawn up for Cyprus which envisaged the supply by caique of three 'keeps' in the hills from which British military personnel were to carry out sabotage raids on the occupying Axis powers. 'Owing to the inherent apathy and untrustworthiness of the Cypriots, it was decided not to depend upon them for sabotage work.' SOE also ran a successful oral propaganda scheme under the direction of the Governor of Cyprus.[55]

SOE's work in Syria and Palestine also aroused the ire of the governing authorities. The local Field Commander, B. T. Wilson, operating out of Beirut, had by June 1942 recruited and trained some thirty Syrian and twenty Palestinian Jewish agents for a post-occupational sabotage network in Syria and the Lebanon, in the event of an Axis invasion, and intended to engage 160 Jews for similar work in Palestine. They were to operate under cover of a 'Home Guard' scheme, which envisaged raising local forces for resistance activities.[56] Although these schemes had been initially approved by the High Commissioner for Palestine, Sir Harold MacMichael, and the GOC Palestine Base Area, General McConnell, they soon began to have doubts about whether the small numbers of Jews involved would contribute much to the planned operations in Syria and Palestine. They also expressed concern about the security implications of delegating recruitment to the Jewish Agency, especially after the arrest by the Palestine Police of five men and one woman who were, without British knowledge, being trained by the Jewish Agency as wireless operators for the Haganah at Tel Aviv. Glenconner thought that SOE had been taken for 'suckers' and Wilson was generally blamed for not keeping a firm grip on the Jewish Agency's extra-curricular activities (he had, in any case, been dismissed in June 1942 for clashing with McConnell over lax security).[57] In the winter of 1942–1943, the Foreign Office and the Colonial Office responded by cutting off cipher and bag facilities (granted in 1940) for the Jewish Agency, ostensibly because of over-subscribed demand but in reality because of the undesirable nature of the material that was sometimes transmitted. It should be noted that when the Secret Intelligence Service had first proposed this in the spring of 1941, SOE had defeated it, arguing that it was too politically dangerous to alienate the Jewish Agency, the only 'Friends' Britain had in the Middle East at the time. There were no such qualms in the winter of 1942/1943 following the twin Allied victories at El-Alamein and Stalingrad and the turning of the tide against the Axis. The SOE training camp at Mount Carmel was also closed down and the Palestinian Jewish agents were disarmed. The Haganah retaliated in March 1943, however, by raiding the armoury and recovering the weapons (it was estimated that the theft of rifles and other equipment was running at the rate of £100,000/week in late 1942). The Security Section of SOE was also worried about the extent to which SOE in Palestine had been penetrated by the Jewish Agency; a concern which was not alleviated by the 'naïve remark' by the wife of a member of the Jewish Agency that: 'We don't hear so much of your operations now. You see we have no-one inside now.'[58] The GOC in Syria, Holmes, was equally concerned about the potentially divisive political impact of SOE post-occupational planning. He warned that if the Fighting French representative in Beirut, General Catroux, became aware of SOE activities, it would confirm his suspicion, given British pressure on him to concede Syrian and Lebanese independence, that Britain was trying to usurp France's position in the Levant.[59] Catroux would have been even more alarmed if he had known about the subversive intentions of the Office of Strategic Services (OSS) mission led by Colonel Hoskins to the Levant states in late 1942.[60] Perhaps wisely, SOE delegated responsibility for its post-occupational activities in Trans-Jordan to General Glubb because it was thought that his 'high prestige' with the bedouin best suited him to the role of resistance leader. Certainly his local contacts, and £600 in bribe-money, proved useful in preventing the tribes taking advantage of the war to revert to their old habit of raiding into Saudi Arabia and Palestine.[61]

There had been no SOE organisation to speak of in Iraq in September 1941 (SOE being reliant on SIS) but in the next eighteen months both pre- and post-occupational plans were drawn up by an ex-monk, Adrian Bishop, and after his death in a freak accident, by A. J. B. Chapman, at their Baghdad HQ, which was expanded in August 1942 into a Regional HQ embracing the newly-instituted Iraq and Persia Military Command. Their first task, following the removal of Rashid Ali's regime, was to build up the prestige of the new pro-British and anti-Axis government by funnelling money to the Regent, so that he could contribute to social welfare activities; subsidising Iraqi schoolmasters to influence their pupils in Britain's favour (a policy followed between 1921 and 1939); penetrating the army and other pro-Axis bodies and restraining the activities of the young, radical politicians who, though pro-British, regarded the existing Iraqi government as reactionary and corrupt. SOE had also to counter Axis propaganda and the activities of enemy agents. The Iraqi Director-General of Police obliged by interning Axis agents and deporting undesirable Syrians and Palestinians. SOE contributed 1,000 dinars to the religious funds of the influential Shia mujtahid, Abdel Hassan, on condition that he spread rumours on Britain's behalf.[62] While SOE left pre-occupational demolition to the Army, it concentrated on post-occupational planning. Apart from propaganda, SOE thought that the Kurds offered the best bet for resisting an Axis invasion of Iraq. Accordingly the 'Plum' Scheme was drawn up, which involved encouraging a Kurdish revolt along Axis communications through the mountains of northern Iraq. Six British officers were sent into northern Iraq in February 1942 to learn Kurdish and familiarise themselves with the terrain, under the direction of Chapman, a Kurdish expert. But overt preparations among the Kurds, including the recruitment of agents, were banned by the British Ambassador, Cornwallis, on the grounds that it would alienate the Iraqi government. SOE confined itself to identifying local personalities who would be likely to undertake guerilla work. SOE in London thought there was no hope that the British government would accede to Domville's suggestion to enhance the 'Plum' scheme by making 'a declaration at a crucial moment that at least the minimum aspirations of the Kurds would have its support'.[63] Although the Iraqi Regent and Prime Minister had agreed that Iraq should follow the example of Syria and Palestine and participate in the 'Home Guard' scheme (involving 4,000 Iraqis), their nervousness about using this as a cover for the formation of cells for sabotage severely restricted post-occupational planning. All they would agree to was the training of 'spies' at Mafraq in Trans-Jordan and the selection of twelve men for training as W/T operators who were, in the event of an Axis invasion, to provide communications between an exiled Regent and a Free Iraq government and their supporters in southern Iraq. Unknown to the Iraqi government, however, SOE encouraged the formation of a strong party of young, radical pro-British politicians, whom it was hoped would not only be able to form an alternative government in a political crisis, but could be trained in resistance techniques (they were to be provided with W/T communications). SOE also secretly set up cells in the holy Shia cities of Najaf and Karbala for the reception and onward transmission of messages, and stores and couriers were organised to operate along the smugglers' routes from Kuwait to the Middle Euphrates.[64]

In contrast to Iraq, no real progress had been made by SOE in pre- and post-occupational planning in Persia. According to Chapman:

> The British had been welcomed when they had first entered the country [in August 1941, with the Russians] and had enjoyed popularity when they had removed Reza Shah. It had been hoped that this would be followed by the disappearance of other corrupt elements, but when this had not materialised a strong reaction, helped by German propaganda, had set in against us.[65]

Both Chapman and Glenconner attributed this to the utter failure of the Foreign Office to put sufficient pressure for reform on the 'corrupt and reactionary' Persian government to remedy the situation and meet British needs. The result was that, by the winter of 1942–1943, 'Persia was a hostile country, our control was precarious, and the position was deteriorating. Such conditions made SOE work extremely difficult.'[66] Thus, very little had been done in the way of pre-occupational planning, apart from SOE's offer to the C-in-C, Persia and Iraq to sabotage the oil storage tanks at Teheran and the recruitment of a number of paid agents from the bazaar and the intelligentsia to spread oral propaganda, or 'whispers'. Unlike in Iraq, no important contacts had been made in 1941–1942 by the SOE representatives at the British Legation (Greenway, a Counsellor, then Underwood, an Assistant Military Attaché) with the police, the army, religious bodies or younger politicians. It was suggested that a new SOE Field Commander should cultivate the growing number of American advisers working in Persian government departments 'to infiltrate younger and less corrupt' pro-British nominees into high positions.[67] As for post-occupational plans, it was agreed that SOE should be prepared to 'penetrate the Persian Kurds and be ready to link them up with the Kurdish scheme for Iraq'.[68] Attempts were also to be made to establish contacts with the Bakhtari and Qashgai tribes to prepare the way for the raising of guerrilla and saboteur bands, though these were not to proceed beyond preliminary steps in order not to arouse the suspicions of the Persian and Russian governments. All efforts to appoint SOE representatives to Tabriz and Resht in the Russian zone of occupation were to be stymied by the NKVD, who regarded it as a 'sinister' British move aimed at stealing a march on the Soviets for the post-war period.[69] As for the Americans, they were perceived by Chapman as not being 'in favour of having any fifth columnists for fear of disturbing friendly relations between the Allies and the Persians'.[70] SOE's frustration in Persia from 1941 till 1943 is summed up by the later assessment that 'it was generally agreed that the Persians as a race were so gutless, that no post-occupational activity could be expected of them other than the formation of whispering and rumour groups with wireless communication'.[71] But even the Persian wireless operators (mostly Armenian) trained for this purpose were regarded as unreliable, and consideration was given to leaving behind British W/T operators. Lastly, SOE's attempt to set up a clandestine Persian radio station broadcasting from Palestine was scuppered when its existence was revealed, whether inadvertently or not is unclear, by the British chargé d'affaires in Teheran, Holman, to the Persian Prime Minister, Soheily.

Until Rommel arrived at El Alamein in June 1942, no post-occupational planning had been permitted in Egypt and SOE's activities were confined to covert propaganda and political subversion. These had been, up to the spring of 1942, in the hands of Dr Heyworth Dunne, an English Muslim convert who 'drew considerable attention to himself – and adverse comment – by wearing a tarbush when nobody could mistake him for anything other than a British national'.[72] His dealings with Sufis, Dervishes and astrologers in an attempt to discredit certain anti-British Egyptian politicians led to complaints and, when he 'became dangerous and uncontrollable', he was dismissed at the insistence of the British Embassy.[73] His successor, Roy Strange, took over the task of forming small oral propaganda cells in the main centres in Egypt in order to counter enemy and anti-British rumours and propaganda and explain the terms of the 1936 Anglo-Egyptian defensive treaty which were wholly unknown to most Egyptians. An Anglo-Jewish merchant in Alexandria, Jack Goar, was also used to bribe, through the payment of monthly subsidies, certain high-ranking Egyptian politicians and officials to garner their support for British interests and to counter any Axis activities which might undermine the British war effort. A subsidy of £E14,000 per quarter was paid to the governing Wafd Party from early 1942 up to the end of 1943 to induce their cooperation in carrying pro-British propaganda in their newspapers.[74] The leader of the opposition, Ahmed Maher, was also paid £E2,000/year as a local director of the British-controlled Ottoman Bank in order to make it worth his while to restrict his criticism of the Wafd and ensure his continued cooperation should he succeed Nahas Pasha as Prime Minister, which he did in October 1944.[75] This was just as well for Egyptian morale had collapsed following Rommel's thrust to the Alamein line and the great British panic in Cairo, which saw the evacuation of most of SOE's Middle East Mission to Jerusalem. It was against this background that the MEDC ordered the SOE Field Commander in Egypt, Colonel Stevens, to prepare a post-occupational scheme as soon as possible. Independent cells, with their own wireless communications and courier service to Advanced HQ in the Wadi el-Arish in the Sinai, were set up under Group-Captain Domville, Major Wilfrid Thesiger and Lieutenant Danby.[76] The refusal of Goar and Strange to stay behind effectively dislocated the propaganda and whispering organisations, which had to be quickly reconstructed and included in the cell organisation. A youth club for young Effendis and junior officials was set up at Shubra in Cairo, ostensibly to make propaganda but in reality in the hope that the Axis forces would close it down thus enraging some 200 trained Cairene youths.

In Libya, SOE sent parties into Cyrenaica to maintain contacts with the tribes in the expectation that those tribes would conduct guerrilla warfare against the Axis forces in concert with a British advance. SOE also gave some thought to raising the Tripolitanian tribes as the Eighth Army advanced on Sirte, but with the difference that the British would make no pledges to free the Tripolitanian Arabs from Italian rule as they had done for the Sanusis of Cyrenaica.[77] Although a committee of exiled Tripolitanian sheikhs had been formed in Cairo to plan a revolt behind enemy lines, their one attempt with SOE to organise guerrilla and sabotage activities in the Jabal Nafusa (Operation HALBEATH) came too late with the seizure of Tripoli by the Eighth Army in January 1943.[78] In the Red Sea SOE's plans to subvert the Vichy regime in Jibouti and to counter Italian influence in the Yemen through bribery and sabotage came to nothing since Jibuti rallied to the Free French in December 1942 and the MEDC preferred to seek the diplomatic intervention of the Governor of Aden and King Ibn Saud with the Imam of Yemen to expel the Axis refugees.[79]

The last crisis, 1943–1945

As the Axis forces were driven further and further away from the Middle East in 1943, the threat of invasion receded and SOE wound up its post-occupational schemes. This led to a reconsideration of the SOE's role in the region. Glenconner pointed out to Major-General Gubbins (soon to take over from Sir Charles Hambro as chief) that people were now beginning to focus on their post-war problems and ambitions:

> In all these countries, apart from anti-Jewish sentiment and the possibility of open warfare between Jews and Arabs in Palestine, there will be political turmoil and economic dislocation in varying degree, aggravated by hoarding, speculation and inflation, which the Governments in question have not the power to control. There may also be a strong reaction against the older parties whom we have supported, with whom we are identified and through whom we have ruled, and this will probably be coupled with a narrow type of nationalism and, in some cases, with anti-British sentiment. There will also be the problem of our own relations with Russia and the influence she will wish to exert,

possibly in opposition to our own. Moreover, the discontent and unrest which will prevail will be exploited by the unscrupulous for their own personal ends, and the societies and organisations which already exist in the Middle East will give excellent cover to agitators for subversive political activities in the name of nationalism, self-determination and progress.[80]

Glenconner argued that SOE, with its extensive and discrete contacts with influential figures in every Middle Eastern country, was well placed to prevent the misuse of such organisations and to steady 'often dangerously irresponsible' youth movements. It could also penetrate and neutralise terrorist groups, maintain close contacts with opposition political parties and cultivate friendships with tribal leaders. SOE could also run secret oral propaganda units, News agencies and broadcasting stations. The purpose of all this would be to discredit Britain's local and great power enemies and to build up her position in the region. The crux of Glenconner's argument was that none of these activities could be handled openly by British diplomatic or Ministry of Information representatives because they would be seen as political interference and would thus be counter-productive.

Unfortunately for Glenconner, representatives from both the Minister of State's office (Lord Moyne and Sir Arthur Rucker) and the Ministry of Information (A. P. Ryan) in Cairo, saw no reason for SOE's activities to continue in the Middle East, except in Persia where Dr Zaehner's covert propaganda organisation was proving a useful weapon for the British Minister, Sir Reader Bullard in the Anglo-Soviet battle for Persian opinion.[81] During the 'Middle East Defence Committee crisis' in September 1943, when the Foreign Office and the military tried to take over SOE Middle East, Moyne, Rucker and Ryan called for the bulk of DOS (A)'s activities to be 'parcelled out' to other departments.[82] It was felt that 'S.O.E's hands were already too full in the Balkans.'[83] Domville countered that SOE's Arab work was quite separate and unaffected by the pressures within DSO (B). Moreover SOE's 'dirt boys' were able to 'do things that Embassies and Legations could not do with propriety'.[84] As a result of Selborne's resolution and Churchill's intervention, Domville and DSO (A) survived the September crisis, along with SOE Middle East, though Glenconner, Keble and Tamplin were removed and Major-General Stawell became head of the organisation, with the cover name Force 133. A renewed attempt in the winter of 1943–1944 by the Ministry of Information, led by Sir William Croft, to garner support from the Minister of State and the Foreign Office for the transfer or winding up of DSO (A)'s activities (particularly propaganda), led SOE headquarters in London to confront the matter head-on. Colonel Sporborg pointed out, on Selborne's behalf, to Sir Alexander Cadogan that no other 'directing Department' was capable of carrying out political subversion in the Middle East as efficiently as SOE and that the status quo should be maintained until the war in Europe was over, 'when the whole future of S.O.E. work would in any event be reviewed'.[85] This duly occurred in June 1945 when an ad hoc committee presided over by William Cavendish-Bentinck (chairman of JIC) recommended that: 'SOE should become a wing of the SIS and that meanwhile every effort should be made in the interests of efficiency and economy to unify the activities of the

SOE and SIS.'[86] Under pressure from Sir Stewart Menzies, head of SIS, Gubbins accepted this proposal, which was later approved by the Chiefs of Staff, the Cabinet Defence Committee and the Foreign Office.

The next nine months is a story of increasing cooperation between SOE and SIS in the Middle East until the formal disbandment of SOE in January 1946 and its re-invention, in a much-reduced form, as the special operations branch of the new, combined secret service. The directive for SOE, contained in the report of Cavendish-Bentinck's ad hoc committee, had for the first time identified the Soviet Union as the main danger to Britain and had given the highest priority to SOE maintaining its clandestine contacts in those countries bordering on the USSR, especially in the Middle East, in order to counter Soviet subversion.[87] SOE succeeded, in collaboration with SIS, in penetrating the Yugoslav Consulate in Beirut in the early summer of 1945, 'where it is believed that certain Russian activities are centred'.[88] While Soviet press activity in Tehran declined with the folding of two Soviet-backed newspapers, in September 1945 the SOE-subsidised press maintained 'a firm attitude' and had been joined by 'neutral' papers in strongly criticising 'highhanded Russian interference' in northern Persia through the encouragement of a secessionist movement.[89] Alarmed at the anti-British activities of the pro-Soviet Tudeh Party in Khuzistan, Bullard and Anglo Iranian Oil Company instructed Colonel Underwood to organise counter-propaganda through a whispering campaign. Underwood was also involved in instigating a short-lived uprising of the local tribes in order to warn the Quvam government in Teheran to crack down on Tudeh activities or risk the breakaway of this oil-bearing south-western province under British auspices.[90] SOE were also involved, with some short-term success, in disseminating oral propaganda and whispers in the Levant states, in order to prevent anti-French nationalist feeling degenerating into conflict, and in Egypt, to allay the considerable anti-British nationalist ferment over the revision of the Anglo-Egyptian treaty, the Sudan and Palestine. But on 25 October the British Ambassador in Cairo, Lord Killearn (formerly Sir Miles Lampson), who had always been sceptical as to the utility of SOE, instructed his Oriental Secretary, Walter Smart, that SOE's oral propaganda organisation, run by Roy Strange, should be 'eliminated' and that payments to Egyptian politicians should be 'terminated'; the latter being given three months' notice, or payment in lieu, 'on the excuse of the end of hostilities'.[91] Nearly two months later, on 20 December, the Egyptian government delivered a note to the British Foreign Office calling for the immediate revision of the 1936 Anglo-Egyptian Treaty, the cornerstone of Britain's position in Egypt and the Middle East. The ensuing negotiations over the terms of a replacement treaty were to plague the post-war governments of both Attlee and Churchill, and to severely complicate the question of the defence of the Middle East. The question arises as to whether continuation of political subversion in Egypt by SOE, and later the SO branch of SIS, through covert propaganda and bribes to key Egyptian politicians, might have first averted the subsequent crisis in Anglo-Egyptian relations or at the very least smoothed the path of British diplomacy during the negotiations. Certainly SIS came to value the art of political subversion for they made good use of Dr Zaehner, formerly SOE's covert propaganda man in

Teheran, during the coup to topple Mossadegh in 1953. As Sporborg had pointed out to Cadogan:

> One could not overlook the political considerations that Arabia was not Utopia and that ways and means at the disposal of S.O.E. would continue (whether or not a threat of invasion existed) to have in practice more weight than would be the case in a country less subject to graft and political chicanery.[92]

Conclusion

It is tempting to conclude that SOE limped from crisis to crisis in the Middle East before being taken over, in a much-reduced form, by SIS in early 1946. It had consistently been out-gunned in Cairo by GHQ and the Minister of State's office and in Whitehall by the Foreign Office, PWE and the Ministry of Information. It had constantly to appease and win the confidence of these larger and more power-ful players in the bureaucratic game in order to survive and pursue its mandate for subversion. Above all, it never managed to overcome the endemic suspicion by British military, political and diplomatic officials of its activities, which threat-ened to unsettle fixed policies and procedures. As a latecomer on the Middle East scene its presence was widely resented, and its necessarily secretive nature meant that it was difficult to fit into established operating patterns. This was not helped, especially in the early years, by the behaviour of some SOE officers who, lacking knowledge or experience of the region, made a number of operational blunders and showed little political acumen. There was also the perpetual problem of London's inability to exercise anything but a partial control over its Middle East Mission. This stemmed from the difficulty of sparing and dispatching senior officials on regular tours of inspection by the short, and over-subscribed, air route through the Mediterranean to Cairo. They tended only to fly out in a crisis, usually to fire and hire Controllers, and this prevented the directors at SOE headquarters in London from keeping constantly abreast of, and having a feel for, developments in Cairo. This made them dependent on the willingness of their Controllers to keep them informed on a regular basis. Pollock proved to be particularly remiss in this respect. But even the more conscientious Maxwell and Glenconner found it difficult on occasion to convey an adequate understanding of their problems to London. The mere fact of distance meant that the Middle East Mission acted as a semi-autonomous branch of SOE.

Despite this, SOE could claim some successes in the Middle East. After a patchy start in 1940–1941, the subsequent development of the post-occupational schemes allowed SOE to make extensive and useful contacts with influential figures in all strata of society in the countries of the region. This enabled SOE to conduct covert propaganda and political subversion from 1941 to the end of the war against the Axis powers and their agents and sympathisers and in support of pro-British personali-ties and regimes. Bribery also proved to be a particularly effective tool whether in securing the cooperation of key figures among the governing class in countries like Iraq and Egypt or in persuading newspaper editors in Persia to run British-inspired articles discrediting Germany and the Soviet Union and their defenders among Persian politicians. These successes were due in part to the organisational flair, and feel for the region based on years of experience, of personnel such as Bishop and Chapman in Iraq and Zaehner in Persia. But it was also due to the rapport which they established with the ambassadors, Cornwallis in Baghdad and Bullard in Teheran, who saw SOE as a useful tool, if carefully controlled, in the defence of British interests. When SOE's station chiefs failed to achieve this rapport with British diplomatic, colonial or military authorities, as in Turkey, Palestine or Aden, they found it difficult if not impossible to operate. Credit must also be given to the overseers: Maxwell, who started, and Glenconner, who completed the post-occupational planning schemes. The latter proved to be the more effective head of the Middle East Mission, partly because he had worked in the London head-quarters and was familiar with its structure, policies and procedures, which he replicated in Cairo. His penetrating insights into his mission's problems, organisational or otherwise, and his accurate sense of what was politically possible, given the constraints on his position, also made him a skilful defender of SOE's interests. However, it was Pat Domville as director of DSO (A) who survived them all and provided the much-needed thread of continuity which enabled SOE in the Middle East to function through the succession of crises and even achieve a degree of success in its subversive aims. In defending himself and SOE's 'dirt boys' in the fetid atmosphere of wartime Cairo, he told Sir Arthur Rucker, of the Minister of State's office that if he had:

> gained the impression that he was a 'very unsavoury sort of person who is ready to adopt any methods to achieve an end' it was the result of his having spent seventeen years in the field experiencing intrigues, rebellions, plots, etc., and not that he did not think normally. He had watched British bureaucratic methods of Government being exploited to our disadvantage and felt justified in employing the same methods in retaliation.
>
> He said that he was convinced from experience that we would be assailed with the familiar situations which succeeded wars in Arab countries, and he felt what S.O.E. had built up might prove both useful and effective in dealing with such situations. He therefore hoped that full and careful consideration would be given to the question before S.O.E. in the Arab countries was just dissolved and most of its valuable contacts lost.[93]

We know that Domville's advice was heeded insofar as SOE's successor body, the SO branch of SIS, contained a section dealing with the Arab World. But to what extent this body maintained and developed SOE's clandestine contacts in the region we will not know until we have access to the files of SIS. There is no question, however, that political subversion, as evidenced by the Mossadegh coup, continued to be regarded by the Foreign Office as a useful tool in the post-war defence of Britain's position in the Middle East.

Notes

1 For a useful, recent bibliography, see M. R. D. Foot's Foreword to W. J. M. Mackenzie, *The Secret History of SOE: The Special Operations Executive 1940–1945* (London, 2000), pp. xxiii–xxvi; for North Africa, see Martin Thomas, 'The Massingham Mission: SOE in French North Africa, 1941–1944', *Intelligence & National Security*, 11/4 (Oct. 1996): 696–721. Some information on the Middle East can be culled from Nigel West, *Secret War* (London, 1992); Bickham Sweet-Escott, *Baker Street Irregular* (London, 1965); J. G. Beevor, *SOE: Recollections and Reflections, 1940–45* (London, 1981); Leo Marks, *Between Silk and Cynanide* (London, 1998); A. Cooper, *Cairo in Wartime* (London, 1996); Euan Butler, *Amateur Agent* (London, 1963); and Lady Ranfurly, *To War with Whitaker: The Diaries of the Countess of Ranfurly, 1939–1945* (London, 1994).

2 L. Atherton, *SOE Operations in Africa and the Middle East: A Guide to the Newly Released Records in the Public Record Office* (London, 1994).

3 Mackenzie, *Secret History*, Chapters 8 and 21.

4 Ibid., p. xxix.

5 'History of SOE in the Arab World', Sept. 1945; RWW/ME/4340 to RW, 23 Sept. 1945, the National Archive, United Kingdom, Public Record Office (hereafter PRO) HS7/86

6 RWW/ME/4343 to RW, 27 Sept. 1945, ref to AW/101 from AW/100 to RWW, 19 Sept. 1945, PRO HS7/86.

7 Atherton, *SOE Operations in Africa and the Middle East*, p. 7.

8 PRO HS7/85 & 285

9 They are: PRO FO371/27049, 31321A&B and 40001B. The author has asked for their status to be reviewed.

10 They are Aden/Red Sea (PRO HS3/1–3); Arab Countries (HS3/97–106, 108, 110, 112–113); Cyprus (HS3/121); Egypt (HS3/124–125); Malta and Tunisia (HS3/130, 135, 139, 142); Middle East (HS3/168, 174–176, 183–186, 188); Palestine (HS3/208); Turkey (HS3/226); Histories (HS3/87). The author has also asked for the status of these files to be reviewed.

11 Sweet-Escott, *Baker Street Irregular*, p. 73.

12 Christopher Sykes, *High Minded Murder* (London, 1944) and *The Song of a Shirt* (London, 1953).

13 Sweet-Escott, *Baker Street Irregular*, p. 73.

14 Ibid., p.74. The Arab Bureau had faced similar obstruction during the First World War, not only from its military and diplomatic rivals in Egypt, but from the Government of India, which had responsibility for Mesopotamia, the Persian Gulf and south Arabia. See Bruce Westrate, *The Arab Bureau. British Policy and the Middle East, 1916–1920* (Philadelphia, PA, 1992).

15 'Report by C.D. to S.O. on former's visit to Middle East 30th July to 20th Aug. 1941', 21 Aug. 1941, PRO HS3/193.

16 Sweet-Escott, *Baker Street Irregular*, p. 40.

17 Mackenzie, *SOE*, p. 172; M. R. D. Foot, *SOE: Special Operations Executive, 1940–1946* (London, 1999 edn.), p. 54; Marks, *Silk and Cyanide*, p. 10; CEO, 'Minute on D Activities in the Middle East', 7 Aug. 1940, PRO HS3/147.

18 D. Garnett, *The Secret History of PWE: The Political Warfare Executive, 1939–45* (London, 2002), p. 63.

19 AD to Jebb, 31 Dec. 1940, PRO HS3/147; Mackenzie, SOE, pp. 172–173.

20 'Report by C.D. to S.O.', PRO HS3/193.

21 SOE War Diary, entries for 5, 8/9, 28/29 June 1941, PRO HS7/217; Dalton to Wavell, 9 June 1941 and Wavell to Dalton, 16 June 1941, PRO HS3/147; Mackenzie, *SOE*, pp. 174–175.

22 Mackenzie, *SOE*, p. 176.

23 Sweet-Escott, *Baker Street Irregular*, p. 70; 'Report by C.D. to S.O.', PRO HS3/193; SOE War Diary, entries for 25 March 1941, HS7/214; entries for 1, 19/20, 21 Apr. 1941, HS7/215; SOE War Diary, entries for 3/4, 6, 24/25, 29/30 May 1941, PRO HS7/216.

24 'SOE in the Arab World' (note 5), PRO HS7/86; SOE War Diary, entries for 10/11, 14, 16 May 1941. HS7/216; D/HP to CD, 19 May 1941. HS3/154; Pollock to A/D1, 25 July 1941. HS3/147; L. S. Lvei-Ami, *By Struggle and Revolt: Hagana, Etzel, Lechi, 1918–1948* (Tel Aviv, 1978), pp. 154–155. l am grateful for Dr Orna Almog for drawing my attention to this and the other Hebrew sources referred to in this chapter.

25 'SOE in the Arab World', (note 5), PRO HS7/86.

26 This was the notorious sinking, by terrorist action, of a refugee ship in Haifa port on 25 November 1940, resulting in the deaths of some 240 men, women and children and twelve British Palestine Police.

27 D/HP to CD, 19 May 1941, PRO HS3/154; Pollock to A/D1, 25 July 1941, HS3/147.

28 SOE presumed that Palmer's unit perished at sea when their boat was sunk ('SOE in the Arab World', note 5, PRO HS7/86; SOE War Diary, entries for 2, 19/20 Apr. 1941, HS7/215). After the British conquest of Syria and the Lebanon, however, Moshe Shertok (later Sharett), head of the Jewish Agency's Political Department, conducted an exhaustive search and enquiry. He concluded that Palmer's unit had managed to struggle ashore at Tripoli, but that Vichy troops, alerted by an RAF raid, killed them all and covered up any trace of the massacre. Ben Tsiyonanur (ed.), *Sefer Toldot Ha-Ganah, Kerech III [The Official History of the Haganah, Part III]* (Tel-Aviv, 1973), p. 364; Yehuda Slutzky, *Kitzur Toldot Ha-Ganah [The Official History of the Haganah]* (Tel Aviv, 1978), pp. 322–323.

29 Report on Syria, 10 June 1941; Report on SO2 Activities in Syria, 12 June 1941, D/HP to CD, 15 June 1941, Edmund to S.O.2, 14 June 1941, PRO HS3/154; SOE War Diary, entries for 16/17, 28/29 June 1941, HS7/217; 'Anti-SO2 Dossier', Fergusson report, 30 June 1941, HS3/192.

30 Pollock to AD/1, 25 July 1941, PRO HS3/147.

31 SOE War Diary, entries for 10, 26/27, Jan. 1941, PRO HS7/212; SOE War Diary, entry for 6 Feb. 1941, HS7/213; SOE War Diary, entries for 7 and 19 March 1941, HS7/214; SOE War Diary, entry for 18 Apr. 1941, HS7/215; SOE War Diary, entries for 27/28, 31 May 1941, HS7/216; SOE War Diary, entries for 1, 5, 6/7, 8/9, 12/13, 16/17, 18 June 1941, HS7/217; SOE War Diary, entry for 2 July 1941, HS7/218.

32 SOE War Diary, entry for 26 May 1941, PRO HS7/216; SOE War Diary, entry for 19/20 June 1941, HS7/217; SOE War Diary, entries for 3/4, 11/12, 13/14 July 1941, HS7/218; D/HP to SO2, n.d., HS3/154.

33 SOE War Diary, entry for 27 March 1941, PRO HS7/214; entries for 9, 11, 24, 26/27 Apr. 1941, HS7/215; entry for 15 May 1941, HS7/216; entry for 11/12 Aug. 1941, HS7/219; Foot, *SOE*, p. 251; Dawn M. Miller, '"Raising the Tribes": British Policy in Italian East Africa, 1938–41', *The Journal of Strategic Studies* 22/1 (March 1999): 96–123.

34 SOE War Diary, entries for 6, 10, 14, 21 Jan. 1941, PRO HS7/212; SOE War Diary, entry for 23/24 Feb. 1941, HS7/213; SOE War Diary, entry for 18 June 1941, HS7/217.

35 SOE War Diary, entry for 31 Jan. 1941, PRO HS7/212; entry for 9/10 Feb. 1941, HS7/213; entry for 25 March 1941, HS7/214; Stonehewer-Bird to Baxter, tells. 31 & 32, 19 & 20 June 1941; Baxter to Bird, tel. 27, 6 Feb. 1941, Bird to Baxter, tel. 83, 17 March 1941, FO371/27272, E1077/1077/25.

36 Smith memo, 10 May 1941, PRO HS3/147; 'Anti-S.O.2 Dossier', HS3/192; Mackenzie, *SOE*, pp. 176–178; Sweet-Escott, *Baker Street Irregular*, p. 75; Ranfurly, *War with Whitaker*, pp. 82, 92–93, 96–97, 100.

37 HS7/219, SOE War Diary, entry for 1 Aug. 1941, HS3/197; Pollock to CD, 22 March 1941. For the Free Italy scheme, see Kent Fedorowich, 'Propaganda and Political

Warfare: The Foreign Office, Italian POWs and the Free Italy Movement, 1940–3', in Bob Moore and Kent Fedorowich, *Prisoners of War and their Captors in World War II* (Oxford, 1996), pp. 119–148.

38   HS3/192, 'Anti-S.O.2 Dossier', 'Report on Certain Aspects of S.O.2 Middle East', by Stirling, 30 June 1941 and 'Notes on organization of S.O.2 in Middle East', 30 June 1941.

39   HS3/193, CD's Report, 21 Aug. 1941 (see note 15).

40   HS7/220, SOE War Diary, 11–14 Sept. 1941.

41   Garnett, *Secret History of PWE*, p. 73.

42   CD's report, 21 Aug. 1941 (see note 15), CD to AD for Minister, tel. 4, 11 Aug. 1941, PRO HS3/193; 'Anti-S.O.1 Dossier', minutes of 12 Sept. and 1 Oct. 1941, HS3/194; the Aziz el-Masri affair involved Thornhill being duped by the fervently nationalistic ex-Chief of the Egyptian General Staff, Aziz el-Masri, into encouraging the latter to fly to Iraq in order to neutralise the Rashid Ali revolt, when in fact his real intention was to defect to Rommel's forces in the Libyan Desert and raise an Egyptian Legion to fight for Egyptian independence. His attempted flight ended ignominiously when his aircraft crashed shortly after take-off from Cairo airport and, after a month on the run, he was arrested. Aziz el-Masri's revelation of Thornhill's incautious involvement in his flight, however, effectively prevented the Egyptian government from proceeding with a trial, much to the fury of the British ambassador, Lampson. For details see Saul Kelly, *The Hunt for Zerzura* (London, 2002), pp. 160–172, 166, 168–172, 222–229, 248.

43   CD report, 21 Aug. 1941, CD to AD for Minister, tel. 4, 11 Aug. 1941, PRO HS3/193; 'Anti-S.O.1 Dossier', minutes of 12 Sept. and 1 Oct. 1941; Leeper to Dalton, 17 Aug. 1941, HS3/194; Mackenzie, *SOE*, pp. 178–181.

44   Sweet-Escott, *Baker Street Irregular*, p. 76.

45   Mackenzie, *SOE*, p. 184.

46   Ibid., p. 186.

47   Ibid., pp. 186–190.

48   Ibid., pp. 367–81; Garnett, *PWE*, pp. 154–160; Propaganda remained under DPA, which retained its cover name of GSI (K), until it was dissolved in May 1943, when it came under DSO (A). GSI (K) had propaganda representatives organising anti-Axis rumours in all DSO (A) countries. Pamphlets and written propaganda were distributed through cells. The Arab Bureau was closed down in October 1941 and replaced by an advisory committee called the Arab Panel, which was chaired by the Controller of the Ministry of Information in the Middle East and on which DSO (A) and GSI (K) were represented. While it advised on all overt propaganda to the Arabs and coordinated the work of the Publicity Officers, it also advised SOE on covert propaganda. See 'History of SOE in the Arab World', Sept. 1945, PRO HS7/86.

49   Mackenzie, *SOE*, p. 507.

50   M. Deroc, *Special Operations Explored: Yugoslavia in Turmoil 1941–1943 and the British Response* (Boulder, CO, 1988); David Stafford, *Britain and European Resistance, 1940–1945* (London and Toronto, 1980); Heather Williams, *The Special Operations Executive (SOE) and Yugoslavia, 1941–5* (London, 2002); Christina Goulter-Zervoudakis, 'The politicization of Intelligence: The British Experience in Greece, 1941–1944', *Intelligence & National Security* 13/1 (Spring 1998): 133–194.

51   SOE War Diary, 21–23 Aug. 1941, PRO HS7/219; SOE War Diary, Jan.–March 1943, HS7/268.

52   SOE War Diary, 15–20, 26–30 Sept. 1941, PRO HS7/220.

53   For details, see files PRO HS3/230 and HS3/235.

54   SOE War Diary, Aug. 1942, PRO HS7/266.

55   Memo on SOE activities in Arab Countries, Persia, Egypt and Cyprus', n.d., PRO HS7/286.

56   SOE War Diary, March 1942, PRO HS7/229; SOE War Diary, Apr. 1942, HS7/230; SOE War Diary, Aug. 1942, HS7/266.

57   SOE War Diary, May 1942, PRO HS7/232; SOE War Diary, June 1942, HS7/234; SOE War Diary, Aug. 1942, HS7/266; SOE War Diary, Sept. 1942, HS7/267; SOE War Diary, Oct. 1942, HS7/267.

58   Security Progress Report, 15 June 1943, PRO HS8/874.

59   SOE War Diary, entry for 29 Apr. 1941, PRO HS7/215; SOE War Diary, entries for 3, 4, 9 May 1941, HS7/216; SOE War Diary, Oct.–Dec. 1942, HS7/267; SOE War Diary, Jan.–March 1943, HS7/268.

60   See files PRO HS3/166 and HS3/213, and P. Baram, *The Department of State in the Middle East, 1919–1945* (Philadelphia, PA, 1978), p. 189.

61   'History of SOE in the Arab World', Sept. 1945, PRO HS7/86.

62   SOE War Diary, Nov.–Dec. 1942, PRO HS7/267.

63   SOE War Diary, Aug. 1942, PRO HS7/266; SOE War Diary, Apr. 1942, HS7/230; 'History of SOE in the Arab World', Sept. 1945, HS7/86.

64   SOE War Diary, Apr. 1942, PRO HS7/230; SOE War Diary, June 1942, HS7/234; SOE War Diary, Aug. 1942, HS7/266; SOE War Diary, Nov./Dec. 1942, HS7/267.

65   SOE War Diary, Jan./March 1943, PRO HS7/268.

66   SOE War Diary, Nov./Dec. 1942, PRO HS7/267.

67   SOE War Diary, Jan./March 1943, PRO HS7/268.

68   SOE War Diary, Nov./Dec. 1942, PRO HS7/267.

69   SOE War Diary, May 1942, PRO HS7/232; SOE War Diary, June 1942, HS7/234.

70   SOE War Diary, Jan./March 1943, PRO HS7/268.

71   'History of SOE in the Arab World', Sept. 1945, PRO HS7/86.

72   Ibid.

73   'Memo on SOE Activities in Arab Countries, Persia, Egypt and Cyprus', 1945, PRO HS7/285.

74   Ibid.

75   SOE War Diary, Nov./Dec. 1942, PRO HS7/267; SOE War Diary, Jan./March 1943, HS7/268. In examining the use of bribery as a weapon, it was calculated in Sept. 1942 that nearly two-thirds of the £300,000 authorised by the Treasury for SOE in the Arab World had been spent or earmarked for post-occupational schemes. Negotiations were then in progress for the delivery of gold bars to the National Bank of Egypt against the release of one million gold sovereigns, under the control of the Minister of State in the Middle East. Memo on 'Use of bribery as a weapon', 7 Sept. 1942, HS3/122.

76   Thesiger seemed to be everywhere at this time. He was involved with G(R) in Abyssinia in 1940–1941, with SOE in Syria/Palestine and Egypt in 1941–1942 and A (Deception) Force in 1942, where he carried out operations behind enemy lines in the Western Desert.

77   See Saul Kelly, *Cold War in the Desert* (London, 2000), p. 7.

78   SOE War Diary, Oct. 1942, PRO HS7/267; SOE War Diary, Jan./March 1943, HS7/268.

79   SOE War Diary, March 1942, PRO HS7/229; SOE War Diary, Apr. 1942, HS7/230; SOE War Diary, Oct. 1942, HS7/267; SOE War Diary, Jan./March 1943, HS7/268.

80   Glenconner memo, 'SOE's Role in the Moslem States of the Middle East', 20 May 1943, PRO HS7/285; SOE War Diary, Apr./June 1943, HS7/269.

81   For details of Zaehner's organisation and activities, see 'Memorandum on SOE activities in Arab Countries, Persia, Egypt and Cyprus', n.d. and SOE War Diary, Apr./June 1945, 'Subsidisation of the Persian Press', PRO HS7/285.

82   SOE War Diary, July/Sept. 1943, PRO HS7/270.

83   SOE War Diary, Propaganda, July/Sept. 1943, PRO HS7/284.

84   SOE War Diary, July/Sept. 1943, PRO HS7/270.

85   SOE War Diary, Apr./June 1944, PRO HS7/273.

86   P. Wilkinson and J. B. Astley, *Gubbins and SOE* (London, 1993), pp. 233–234.

87   SOE(45)34 and 43, Minutes of SOE Council Meeting meetings on 12 Sept. and 7 Dec. 1945; copy of JP(45)235, 2nd prelim. draft, PRO HS8/202.

88 SOE(45)R43, Review of Activities for May, June, July 1945, PRO HS8/247.
89 SOE(45)R45, Review of SOE Activities for Sept. 1945, PRO HS8/247.
90 SOE (45)R14, Review of SOE Activities for Aug. 1945, PRO HS8/247; R. J. Aldrich, *The Hidden Hand: Britain, America and Cold War Secret Intelligence* (London, 2001), p. 136.
91 AW100 (Cairo) to SO2, 2048, 25 Oct. 1945, PRO HS3/123; for Lampson's scepticism, see Lampson to Cavendish-Bentinck, 8 June 1945, FO371/45272/E4561/1630/65.
92 SOE War Diary, Apr./June 1944, PRO HS7/273.
93 SOE War Diary, July/Sept. 1943, PRO HS7/270.

8 'Toughs and thugs'

The Mazzini Society and political warfare among Italian POWs in India, 1941–1943

Kent Fedorowich

I

In the early days of the Second World War, when there was a chronic shortage of qualified linguists, the British government undertook a series of extraordinary measures to recruit personnel who could be used for covert intelligence and propaganda work. This included the recruitment by the Special Operations Executive (SOE) of a handful of ardent anti-fascist Italian émigrés in the United States. Their mission, under British supervision, was to conduct a political warfare campaign among the burgeoning number of Italian prisoners-of-war (POWs) who had been transported to and incarcerated in India during 1941. This policy was one of several initiatives formulated by London in its campaign to rally opposition to Italian fascism, the ultimate objective of which was the creation of a Free Italy movement.

One idea, which was first broached in August 1940 by officials who worked in SO1 (the secret propaganda branch of SOE established in June 1940), was to use Italian POWs in the propaganda war that was being waged against Fascist Italy. It was mooted that, if large numbers of POWs proved receptive to the political warfare being orchestrated in the camps, not only would this provide grist to the propaganda mill, but it could also provide the foundation of a more ambitious policy whereby POW volunteers would be recruited to fight against their former fascist leaders in a Free Italy force and serve in anti-fascist pioneer or combatant units that might be employed during the Allied liberation of Italy. As a wartime tool, therefore, POWs were deemed invaluable in the all-important psychological battle to win Italian hearts and minds, and as a potential anti-fascist fighting force.[1]

The difficulty for British propagandists was the distinct lack of any large-scale, trustworthy or coherent Italian anti-fascist association that could assist London in its covert and counter-propaganda campaigns. Indeed, the apparent desperation with which SOE pinned its hopes on the American-based Mazzini Society during the early stages of their political warfare campaign, as directed against Italy, seem remarkable. As we shall see, SOE had little choice. This chapter does not trace the largely unsuccessful efforts made by the British to indoctrinate Italian POWs in India and help forge a Free Italy movement on the subcontinent between 1941 and 1943. That story has already been told elsewhere.[2] Rather, using the Indian experiment as a backdrop, it briefly traces the origins of this little-known organization, how it became involved with SOE (and later the Political Warfare Executive), and charts how what appeared to be an admirable idea quickly soured to become one of the most farcical episodes in British intelligence operations during the Second World War. Nevertheless, this study in failure should not belittle its significance. It was one of London's first wartime attempts to employ foreign nationals in the murky world of espionage, political warfare and counter-propaganda, which despite its painful results, provided invaluable lessons for future operations. Nevertheless, before one embarks upon the examination and employment of the Mazzini Society, it is first necessary to outline briefly the British agencies involved in orchestrating the propaganda war against Italy, the policies which were formulated and the reason why Italian POWs were seen as potential weapons in the fight against Fascist Italy.

II

On 11 June 1940, the day after Italy declared war on Britain and France, Brigadier (later Major-General) Dallas Brooks of the Ministry of Information's shadowy Department EH (and predecessor of SO1), bemoaned the inadequacy of Allied propaganda operations which were being directed against Italy: 'I am unable to find either a policy or an object!'[3] Discussions had taken place in April 1940 between London and Paris for the establishment of a joint enemy propaganda committee if and when Mussolini joined the war on Hitler's side. However, nothing concrete was formulated apart from a series of broad aims and promises of greater cooperation. With the fall of France in June 1940, British intelligence officers in both Britain and the Middle East were spurred into action. Late in August, preliminary enquiries were made by Section D (an arm of the Secret Intelligence Service until its transfer to SOE in July 1940) concerning the availability among the 19,000-strong Italian community resident or interned in Britain for work as possible agents for sabotage missions overseas. This was followed up four months later when Lieutenant-Commander George Martelli of SOE's Italian section was sent to the Isle of Man to scour the civilian internment camps to see if any Italian 'thugs' were available for propaganda and espionage work.[4] His findings were disappointing. Most of those interviewed were found to be anti-fascist. Unfortunately, they were not pro-British either and were deemed by Martelli as useless for fieldwork. It was also discovered that those few internees, who were later released or recommended for release by the Loraine Committee, established in September 1940, had volunteered to serve simply to escape incarceration.[5] SOE was forced to admit that: 'Personal hostility to fascism did not mean a readiness to work for their country's enemies.'[6]

Meanwhile, efforts to establish a Free Italy Committee under the leadership of the young but little known Dr Carlo Petrone were in serious difficulties. In October 1940, Prime Minister Winston Churchill had approved the establishment of the committee and endorsed Petrone's authority. By early December, however, it had emerged that the Foreign Secretary, Lord Halifax, wanted the committee liquidated and Petrone shipped off to either the United States or Egypt. Martelli was appalled. To kill the project so soon after its creation would be a public relations disaster, especially in the neutral United States with its large Italian emigrant population. Imagine the impression this would have on the American press, argued Martelli, if Petrone arrived there with the 'story that he had been prevented from organising a Free Italy movement in England'. In addition, Rome would be handed an enormous propaganda windfall that might prove sufficient to discourage the formation of any similar movement in the United States. 'It would also have the most depressing effect on Italians here', argued Martelli, 'whose services we are already using or hope to use in various ways . . . It would, for instance, seriously prejudice the chances of raising an Italian legion.'[7]

Martelli similarly dismissed the Foreign Office's argument that by tolerating the Free Italy movement in the United Kingdom, London was forcing those Italians whose allegiances were wavering to make a choice between Mussolini's fascist regime or an alternative government. True, the French were asked to make such a choice by the Free French leader, General Charles de Gaulle: either to remain in France and submit to Nazi tyranny or abandon their country and fight for freedom. Martelli insisted, however, that no analogy could be drawn between the French and Italian situations:

> The Italians in Italy cannot take any action at the moment, so there is no question of a choice. In any case, the waverers will always waver until they see which way the cat has jumped. The object of the Free Italy movement is to encourage those who are already anti-Fascist, and I believe their number is very large, to act when the moment comes. They will never do so unless they feel they have support from outside.

Finally, he reminded the Foreign Office that the existence of a Free Italy committee in London would act as a rallying point and recruitment centre for Italian volunteers in Britain's cause against the Axis. This included the invaluable if not indispensable asset the committee would make in attracting people who could be drafted by SOE into its 'black' propaganda activities directed against Italy.[8] Growing impatient with the Foreign Office's foot dragging, Martelli launched a broadside:

> London is the centre of the Free Nations and must remain so, however small their representation here. The very fact that our Free Italians in London are exposed to German bombs and are themselves, as it were, in the front line, inevitably gives them a certain prestige and entitles them to take some precedence.[9]

Martelli's robust defence of maintaining some kind of Free Italy committee, however modest, was raised with his superiors. Dr Hugh Dalton, Minister of Economic Warfare, (who was also responsible for SOE) was told by Martelli that at this stage of SOE's strategy it was irrelevant whether or not the Free Italy committee received official British government support. The crucial factor was that

Petrone and his friends, 'none of them people with great names, should no longer be prevented from announcing the formation of a committee and carrying on press and pamphlet propaganda among Italians here and abroad'. Initially, their activities were unlikely to have any far-reaching effects, but at least it was a start from which SOE would accrue some advantages. Foremost among these was that the committee would attract a number of well-disposed Italians from which it could select personnel for overt propaganda activities. As SOE admitted: 'It has been rather difficult to get hold of suitable Italians, partly because there is no organisation to consult.' Although the Foreign Office still had deep-seated reservations about either sponsoring a Free Italy movement or allowing one to develop on its own, Halifax agreed to meet with Dalton and expedite the matter.[10]

As these ministers weighed the pros and cons of a Free Italy movement, another development was taking place in Whitehall that would have significant repercussions for SOE. In mid-October 1940, the Joint Intelligence Committee (JIC) invited Department EH to prepare a paper for the War Office's Directorate of Prisoners of War (DPW) on the supply and use of war literature, special news sheets and wireless programmes in Britain's POW camps.[11] Six weeks later SOE was asked to reconsider undertaking propaganda among enemy captives; a task first mooted for the British Council but eventually rejected by the JIC. General Brooks responded that the matter had been taken up with the director, who now agreed that SOE should be responsible for the 'education' of POWs, both with the 'long-term object of affecting their future outlook, and also with the short-term object of using them as a means of propaganda to the enemy'. Brooks informed Colonel C. T. Edwards, secretary of the JIC, that SOE were 'glad' to take on this new function with the understanding that, for the immediate future, the object would be first to prepare the ground and not to undertake any large-scale propaganda to, and through, the POWs.[12] In many respects, Brooks was articulating the ideas first raised by the military liaison officer for SO1 at GHQ, Cairo, Colonel C. J. M. Thornhill, who in August 1940 suggested that Italian POWs could be forged into anti-fascist weapons.[13]

Events soon overtook these Whitehall deliberations which inadvertently strengthened SOE's hand in justifying its support for a Free Italy committee. On 9 December 1940, General Sir Archibald Wavell, British Commander-in-Chief, Middle Eastern forces, launched his long-awaited counter-offensive against the Italian Tenth Army under the command of the dilatory Marshal Rodolfo Graziani. What began as a five-day raid quickly turned into a series of stunning desert victories for the heavily outnumbered but highly motivated British and Commonwealth forces. By early January, Wavell's men had captured 59,000 Italians and 14,000 Libyan auxiliaries. One month later, the Italians had been swept from Cyrenaica with the loss of 133,000 prisoners and vast quantities of war materiel. Equally spectacular victories in Abyssinia in early 1941 swelled Italian POW numbers even further, which by March 1941 had bulged to 160,000. Although the disposal and transfer of these captives demanded urgent attention, and were aggravating an already critical logistic situation, some senior British military planners began to see their potential either as sources of labour or as the nucleus of a Free Italy movement.

Writing on behalf of the Chiefs of Staff committee, Major-General Sir Hastings Ismay, Deputy Secretary (Military) to the War Cabinet, saw no reason why the raising of an anti-Mussolini or Free Italian force in Cyrenaica should not be considered.

> Volunteers might be called for from the hundred thousand prisoners we have taken. There must be a great many who hate Fascism. We might even rule Cyrenaica under the Free-Italian flag and treat it in the same way as de Gaulle's colonies are being treated subject to our military control . . . Can we not make this place a base for starting a real split in Italy and the source of anti-Mussolini propaganda?[14]

Churchill who presented Ismay's ideas to the War Cabinet enthusiastically endorsed the concept.[15]

The War Office, and in particular the Director of Military Intelligence (DMI), Major-General F. H. N. Davidson, did not share the prime minister's enthusiasm for the creation of these POW combat units. Even elements in the Foreign Office had their reservations about the merits of such a policy, despite the welcome support given to Churchill by his new Foreign Secretary, Anthony Eden. Nonetheless, Dalton and SOE pressed on. Dalton first took soundings from several of his field officers, who recommended that 'disgruntled' POWs be segregated into separate camps. He agreed, and urged that all Italian POWs should be 'combed in order to discover genuine and gallant anti-Fascists' who were prepared to risk their lives in order to free their country.[16] When obstacles were placed in his way, Dalton railed against the foot dragging perpetrated largely by 'knocked-kneed' officials at the Foreign Office.[17] Keen to move ahead, War Office reservations were eventually overcome when in February 1941 the JIC pushed for the prioritization in the development of enemy POWs as sources of propaganda and military intelligence. As for the Foreign Office, although some officials still doubted the value and loyalty of these combat units, the idea of creating a Free Italian force was sanctioned.

The choice of Petrone as leader was, however, a matter of growing unease within Whitehall. The debate over his suitability also reflected the deep divisions that already existed between SOE, the Ministry of Information and the Foreign Office concerning the overall conduct of British propaganda itself. The proposed Yuletide meeting between Halifax, Dalton and Duff Cooper, Minister of Information,[18] failed to materialize; in part, due to the death of Lord Lothian, Britain's ambassador to Washington, and his replacement by Halifax. Nonetheless, the Foreign Office remained cool towards Petrone and the idea of sponsoring a Free Italy movement in Britain. Dubbed a 'hot-head with very little backing' by one senior Foreign Office official, Petrone's leadership was strongly deprecated by others within the Foreign Office.[19] It opined that all arguments in favour of pursuing a Free Italy movement were solely based on reasons of propaganda. However, there were acute political difficulties and long-term foreign policy objectives, which the Foreign Office charged had been dismissed as unimportant by SO1 and the Ministry of Information.

Furthermore, the Foreign Office insisted that its views had to prevail over those of the propaganda agencies, otherwise 'we run the grave risk of seeing our foreign policy upset or at least deviated by acquiescence in proposals forced on us by other Departments'. The Foreign Office's over-riding objection to the emergence of a Free Italy movement, even of limited aims and ostensibly without official support, was that it would be interpreted as an 'artificial movement' devised by the British government. In these circumstances, it was suggested that the best course to take was one of 'masterly inactivity'.[20]

Duff Cooper and Dalton were nonetheless insistent that something, however limited, had to be initiated. Cooper suggested to Eden that Petrone be allowed to write a letter to *The Times* defining his objectives, and be given authorization to publish an Italian newspaper. The Minister of Information also tried to allay Foreign Office fears by stating that Petrone did not lay claim to the leadership of the Free Italian movement, but was 'ambitious only to provide a rallying point'.[21] Eden, after rehearsing the Foreign Office's earlier objections, now relented to the limited activities envisaged by Cooper. Not wanting to appear to always be opposing the Ministry of Information or SO1, Foreign Office officials like Sir Alexander Cadogan, Permanent Under-Secretary of State, did not see that Petrone could do much harm now.[22] On 10 February 1941, *The Times* announced the constitution of a Free Italy committee, with Petrone as secretary. Almost immediately, Petrone's shortcomings as leader were exposed. As the Foreign Office predicted, very few people had heard of him. As a result, he was going to have to become more accommodating if he was going to cultivate a wider base of support. However, far from becoming a rallying point for anti-fascist Italians, Petrone had instead attracted 'infidels, Jews, Turks and heretics' to his cause.[23] An inauspicious start to say the least, thanks, in part, to Foreign Office indifference.

In the meantime, Commander Martelli had been trying to find alternate sources of Italian volunteers for SOE's clandestine work. In January 1941, the failure to find willing internees on the Isle of Man forced him to make several visits to an Auxiliary Military Pioneer Corps (AMPC) training centre in north Devon, where several hundred pro-British Italian recruits were housed. Of the 100 potential candidates, fifty were interviewed but only nine were deemed satisfactory. Equally disappointing results were experienced at another AMPC base near Slough. Of the twenty Italians interrogated here, only one potential recruit was identified. If the local human material closest to hand was inadequate, what about potential sources overseas? Efforts were made to tap sources in Canada and Malta, but the wells were equally dry in these locations.[24] However, it was suggested that the United States – which had 4.6 million Italian-Americans residing in its borders[25] – might hold the key to SOE's recruit conundrum, as the 'toughest' type of Italian 'desperado' was 'mostly to be found in America'.[26] This Hollywood-inspired prejudice was not helpful. A crucial problem still haunted SOE: Who should they approach to facilitate recruitment?

III

Founded in New York in 1940, the Mazzini Society was one of several anti-fascist organizations that had been created by Italian political exiles who had been forced to flee overseas. The membership was largely comprised of two groups: Italian citizens who had sought political sanctuary in the United States; and American-born Italians who wanted to see Mussolini's fascist regime overthrown and replaced with a liberal-democratic government. Although the society's membership was initially small and representative of a narrow but highly educated, professional elite, the director of the Office of Strategic Services (OSS), Colonel William J. Donovan, was assured that its strengths, although less evident than its weaknesses, were nonetheless important. As John C. Wiley, a senior State Department official wrote:

> In a sense, the chief strength of the Mazzini Society lies in the total absence of any rival movement of which our government, at least up to this point, could possibly approve. Concretely, we must either accept the Mazzini Society, or have nothing to do with any group, or accept the Communist party, or accept the Fascists in the United States. The most palatable of these policies seems to be that of accepting the Mazzini Society. The enemies who attack it from several sides are one of its best reasons for existence.[27]

The society's leadership contained a number of prominent figures, several of whom would play a key role in post-war Italian politics.[28] Count Carlo Sforza, a career diplomat, pre-fascist foreign minister (1920–1921) and former ambassador to France topped the list. Although not a 'great leader', according to the Americans, he was recognized as the only leader for there seemed to be no better or alternative candidate 'around whom a corporal's guard could be rallied in [the United States] or anywhere else'.[29] Leading academics such as the Harvard historian Professor Gaetano Salvemini and the University of Chicago's Professor G. A. Borghese added an intellectual edge, while two former newspaper editors from the pre-fascist era, Alberto Tarchiani and Alberto Cianca, were the administrative dynamos driving the Mazzini Society.

Tarchiani, a member of the liberal left in Italy after the First World War, was a protégé of Professor Borghese. Editor of the *Corriere della Sera*, Tarchiani went into exile in France when Mussolini purged the Italian press. In France, he became the editor of *La Liberta* and a leader, with Sforza's closest adviser Carlo a Prato, of the exile organization called 'Giustizia e Libertà' (Justice and Liberty). With British assistance, Tarchiani and Sforza escaped during the fall of France in June 1940 and after a short stay in England proceeded to New York via Canada. Described as 'honest, high-minded, brave, and a very hard worker', Tarchiani became the prime mover in founding the Mazzini Society, served as its secretary and edited its mouthpiece, *Nazioni Unite*.[30] Cianca, Tarchiani's close friend in exile, had prior to 1922 been the editor of one of Rome's leading newspapers *Il Mondo*. While in exile, he too became a member of 'Giustizia e Libertà'. President of the New York chapter of the Mazzini Society, Cianca was the public face of the partnership. Much more comfortable working within the public sphere, his oratory skills were better than Tarchiani's and he was a better social 'mixer'.[31]

Other leaders included Randolfo Pacciardi, who had commanded the Garibaldi Brigade during the Spanish Civil War, and Dr Max Ascoli. It was Ascoli who was instrumental in building a working relationship with the Italo-American anti-fascist association in South America, 'Italia Libera' (Free Italy), which had a network of branches throughout the continent but lacked a prestigious leader.[32] Despite a promising pedigree within the vanguard, the Mazzini Society suffered from constant infighting as various leaders tried to pursue their own personal agendas. This is not the place to discuss the competing interests and intrigue that went on within the organization[33], but it is important to realize that these machinations were mirrored in the SOE/PWE mission which was eventually dispatched to India in late 1941. Another problem faced by the society, and one of its chief weaknesses, was that the great bulk of the Italo-American community in the United States was apathetic. Wiley told Donavan that most of the 'Italo-Americans are too well Americanized to care what particular movement controls Italy so long as Italy is treated fairly well and can retain [her] respect and prosperity' after the war.[34] Acute tensions also existed between the political refugees and the Italo-American community. Allen W. Dulles, section chief of the OSS mission in Switzerland, was told that the real division between the two groups was that while the primary aim of the Italian exiles was the liberation of Italy, the Italo-Americans were much more interested in preserving their stakehold in the United States as American citizens. As a result, the overthrow of Mussolini's fascist regime was not a priority for many.[35] The dissension, which existed between naturalized Americans of Italian origin and the exiles (such as Sforza, Tarchiani and Ascoli), was complicated further by the fact that there were strong fascist tendencies within large sections of America's Italian community. As Varsori has noted, Ascoli in particular was instrumental in tackling the *prominente* Generoso Pope, the pro-fascist proprietor of New York's most influential Italian language daily newspaper, *Il Progresso Italo-Americano*.[36]

IV

As we have seen, discussions had taken place concerning the secondment of Italian nationals to conduct propaganda work among their captured countrymen. Martelli wrote in early June 1941 that propaganda work should be 'conducted chiefly by Italian representatives of some recognised patriotic Italian body, in cooperation with our own organisation. We would assist and if necessary, subsidise these representatives, but they should be as independent as possible.' He also advocated that similar steps be taken in East Africa, South Africa and Australia. If the results achieved by the propaganda work in the first stages justified it, then Britain could proceed with the next step of raising a Free Italian force. This force would be put on the same footing as the other Free forces, such as General de Gaulle's Free French, and be provided with uniforms, equipment and pay. The British government, concluded Martelli, having announced its intention to raise this force, was then to make a concerted effort to obtain support of Italians world-wide, especially in the United States.[37]

As the momentum grew in Whitehall for the establishment of a Free Italian legion from among the growing number of POWs held in Egypt, the fundamental problem of leadership remained. When Clement Attlee, the Secretary of State for Dominions Affairs, briefed the Australian Prime Minister's Department on the establishment in Britain of a small, unofficial Free Italian committee headed by Carlo Petrone, he was forced to admit that no real Italian leaders had yet emerged outside Italy. Similarly, London's encouragement of 'spontaneous' free Italian movements in other countries had not met with much success either. Australia's High Commissioner in London, Stanley Bruce, was more poignant: 'Petrone is not considered here to have any standing nor is it thought that the free Italian leaders in the United States are much weightier.' 'Movement in the United States', he told the Acting Prime Minister, Arthur Fadden, was being 'closely watched' however.[38]

Despite the problems of not having a large or coherent Free Italian movement to work with, in mid-February 1941, London sanctioned the idea of using Italo-Americans for clandestine activities. The Canadian High Commissioner in London, Vincent Massey, informed his prime minister, William Lyon Mackenzie King, that the British were recruiting 'friendly' Italians in the United States to conduct political warfare work in the United Kingdom. This 'very secret movement' was being coordinated from New York by a British intelligence agent named Coit.[39] These 'friendly' Italians were in fact members of the Mazzini Society. Purported to have official US government recognition, it had been founded 'to promote among persons of foreign heritage . . . knowledge of the principles of American democratic institutions and the American way of life'.[40] The British requested Canada's assistance in the entry, housing and departure of these 200 volunteers. They would travel to Canada in small groups of between ten and twenty men over a two-month period and then be transported to the United Kingdom via Halifax, Nova Scotia. Since the United States was a neutral power, these men were to be slipped across the border into Canada without the knowledge or permission of US immigration authorities. Ottawa approved the request and entrusted this deli-cate task to the Department of Immigration and the Royal Canadian Mounted Police (RCMP). So as not to arouse suspicion or excite 'any public curiosity' the Canadian government insisted that the men travel in mufti with their RCMP escorts. Strict protocols were to be observed when handling these men. They had to be looked after and 'not be afforded opportunities to talk' outside their group while in transit. Using the cover that the men were part of an Irish(!) welfare mission, they were sent to the United Kingdom without passports, and still without the permission of their own authorities. The first – of what was to be the only batch – of twelve society members (seven Americans and five Italian subjects resident in America) travelled incognito with their Maltese-born RCMP escort on a Canadian troop ship, which disembarked at Glasgow that April.[41]

The leader of the party was an American citizen, Dr Lucio Tarchiani, a 32-year-old doctor who had studied medicine in Paris. After graduating in 1933, he established a medical practice in Normandy and worked there until the outbreak of war in 1939. He fought with the French Army, was demobilized in August 1940 and remained in occupied France until November before migrating to the United States. Described as keen and brimming with confidence, London thought highly of him. He also had the added advantage that his father Alberto was a founding member and secretary of the Mazzini Society.[42] A second officer, Dr A. R. Ingrao was fourteen years older than Tarchiani. An Italian by birth, on leaving school, he had studied medicine in Naples. War interrupted his studies, and between 1915 and 1921 Ingrao had served in the Italian Army. After demobilization, he resumed his studies and between 1924 and 1930 he practised medicine in Italy before immigrating to the United States. The rest of the party was described as a 'sundry group of Italians of a fairly low class'. Four had served with the Italian armed forces during the First World War, while the former lift attendant and native of Trieste, Carlo Fragiacomo, had served in the Austrian infantry. Most of these other rankers had left Italy in the early 1920s either to pursue gainful employment overseas or because of their staunch anti-fascist views. Fragiacomo and Luigi Galgani had also fought for the Republicans during the Spanish Civil War (1936–1939).[43]

Right from the outset there were contradictory interpretations concerning the aims and objectives of the mission. For SOE, Tarchiani's group would form the vanguard of a 200-strong para-military force and be employed in covert operations against Italy. Roughly one-third would be instructed in subversion techniques and serve as political agents in Italy. It was hoped that a few would secure employment in Italian industry providing invaluable access to technical and scientific secrets and/or conduct industrial sabotage. The remaining two-thirds were designated for pre-invasion sabotage, infiltration and raiding parties.[44] However, upon arrival, it quickly emerged that the recruits had embarked upon their mission under a misapprehension. They had been led to believe that they were proceeding to the Middle East to cultivate a Free Italian Legion from the thousands of incarcerated Italian POWs located there and 'to raise the standard of liberty on their behalf'.[45] In addition, they refused to have anything to do with sabotage, were extremely reluctant to be recruited into the British armed forces or wear the British uniform, and did not consider that they needed any training.[46]

With few exceptions, this first cohort was physically and mentally unsuited for para-military training. Six were over 40 years old, one was in his mid-fifties and several were described by one British officer as decrepit. Therefore, SOE decided that it was better to keep the group together and organize them into a self-contained propaganda section. As the two officers in charge were doctors, it was decided to designate the Mazzini team as a medical unit to disguise its real purpose as an instrument for propaganda and political warfare. In the meantime, the British agent in New York was ordered not to ship any more Italians to the United Kingdom until London could ascertain what Tarchiani's party thought they were going to do.[47]

Confusion over the aims and objectives of the mission and its future deployment were not the only problems encountered by SOE. Personal rivalries and petty bickering within the group threatened to forestall the mission before it even got underway. The chief source of discontent was Dr Ingrao. Jealous of Tarchiani's role as leader, Ingrao attempted to undermine Tarchiani's authority. With the co-operation of the New York executive, it was decided to remove the disruptive Ingrao. Using a flattering pretext that his talents were needed in America, he was persuaded to return home. However, prior to his departure, he was found guilty of further 'dangerous' but unnamed indiscretions. As his actions threatened to compromise the entire project, for security reasons he was arrested and imprisoned on the Isle of Man at a special detention facility, but without the Mazzini Society's knowledge. They were given to understand that London's plans had changed and that he was on a 'special mission' for SOE.[48] This was an ill omen, which was exacerbated further by Mario Gervasi's desire to return home which was imme-diately sanctioned in June 1941. The unit's cohesion was cracking – if indeed it ever existed – which foreshadowed future trouble.

V

Allied reverses in Libya during April–May 1941, which occurred after the recruit-ment of the Italo-American party, combined with Wavell's reluctance to consider work among Italian POWs imprisoned in Egypt introduced additional problems for the creation of a Free Italy force. This was exacerbated further by the need for a complete overhaul of SOE in the Middle East, which according to Gladwyn Jebb, SOE's Chief Executive Officer, had become muddled and ineffective. The need was for radical reform, which included the purging of the 'crooks, fools, [and] old women' currently occupying SOE's Cairo headquarters.[49] New energy and initiatives were also badly needed. Major Peter Fleming of SO2 (SOE's sabotage wing) reported that his mission to form a special sabotage training centre in the Middle East had failed. SO2's poor performance was, in part, due to Wavell's opposition because of his doubts over the quality and commitment of the POW recruits.[50] The head of SOE confirmed this in October 1941:

> [G]enerally speaking the Italian soldiers who were taken prisoner were for the most part perfectly content to remain prisoners, and showed no desire what-ever, either for money or for any other reason, to return to their country in an adventurous capacity.[51]

The future of the Mazzini mission now looked in doubt.

A faint glimmer of hope remained, however. It was suggested by Martelli, head of SOE's Italian section, that India offered a more secure environment from which to pursue the creation of a Free Italy force. SO1 needed little prompting. Dallas Brooks had already approached the Foreign Office as to whether there was any objection to sending the Italo-American party to India for propaganda work on the subcontinent. Furthermore, SOE, which had invested too much time and effort in finding these men, were anxious that this 'somewhat unfortunate and muddled affair . . . not get even more muddled and more difficult by being buried and forgotten'. In June 1941, Thornhill telegraphed Brooks that the Deputy Director of

Military Intelligence, India, had approved a plan to send the Mazzini Society team from Britain to undertake propaganda work in the POW camps.[52] The Foreign Office gave its approval later that month. Sir Orme Sargent, the Deputy Under-Secretary of State who chaired the joint meeting with SOE, was forced to admit that 'no leader or focal point' existed to which any Free Italian force could be attached. If such a force was eventually established, it would have to provide its own political leader.

As for Carlo Petrone, the Foreign Office – which had never put much faith in him or his abilities – now decided it was undesirable to cultivate him or any other Italian émigré in the United Kingdom as a Free Italian leader or as a focal point for Italian opinion world-wide. To do so would lead to a clash with any movement which might emerge from among the Italian POWs themselves. Even the Ministry of Information had become less enamoured with him. Petrone's inability to gain the confidence of his compatriots or to carry out any practical endeavour, combined with his intemperate behaviour had stretched the ministry's patience, which now found him a 'completely broken reed'.[53] The final nail in Petrone's political coffin came when Halifax reported from Washington that Count Sfroza appeared 'astonished' that a person of such 'insignificance' – a mere 'office boy' – should be considered as a suitable candidate for such a responsible position. Ascoli, who had also been consulted, was even more scathing describing Petrone as 'hardly even a vest-pocket de Gaulle'![54] Abandoned and isolated, Petrone was soon after forced off the executive of the Free Italy movement in Britain and severed all connection with it.[55]

These Foreign Office instructions made it plain to SOE that it had to refrain from recruiting captives for a Free Italian force or to promote any specific personage or particular line of propaganda among the prisoners. Moreover, anyone involved in this type of work would be expected to 'play a purely exploratory role and maintain an objective attitude'.[56] Brooks challenged what he saw as an overly cautious remit. He told Orme Sargent that enough field studies had already been carried out by Thornhill and others for the special purpose of ascertaining if there was material from which to enlist a Free Italian force. If the Middle Eastern theatre was inappropriate for propaganda activities in the POW camps there, then the best way forward was to allow SOE to send a select team of propagandists into the POW camps in India, Kenya or South Africa and gauge the mood of the prisoners incarcerated there. Brooks reinforced the experimental nature of the work. There was no suggestion at this stage of asking for volunteers for a Free Italian force. Rather, the hope was that the suggestion of raising such a force would come from the POWs themselves. If the response was favourable, a more concerted propaganda plan could be initiated. If not, a valuable lesson had been learned. Either way, the British government would not be committed to anything. Thus, there was no harm in pursuing a small-scale pilot project.[57]

There is no doubt that Brooks had the Mazzini team in mind when he drafted his response to Sargent.[58] Martelli, who had dined with Tarchiani junior in early July, reiterated both to the Mazzini Society and to all members of the mission these instructions emphasizing the investigative nature of their work. Furthermore,

Martelli impressed upon the young doctor the importance that he and his team had to confine their efforts, in the first instance, purely to the welfare side of their work and 'refrain from any overt propaganda'. Privately, however, he expressed doubts about particular members of the Italo-American party. Discipline, he forewarned, might be a problem unless these men were handled 'tactfully and firmly'.[59] This was an ominous observation.

The Mazzini party, which had been released from British Army service in order to 'volunteer' for work with the newly created Political Warfare Executive, left England in mid-August 1941. Wavell, who was now C-in-C India, was told that ostensibly the object of the visits to the camps would be as a non-political welfare mission 'to distribute comforts provided or financed by compatriots' in the United States. However, 'the real object will be to ascertain [the] attitude of prisoners and prepare a Report on [the] possibility of raising [a] Free Italian Force'.[60] The mission was escorted to India by Lieutenant F. R. Boyall and arrived in late September. Meanwhile, as Tarchiani and his party were en route to India, the British government undertook a comprehensive restructuring of its entire propaganda and political warfare machinery. The intense personal intrigue and political machinations within Whitehall need not concern us here. Suffice it to say that the creation of the Political Warfare Executive (PWE) in August 1941 – which absorbed Dalton's coveted SO1 – impacted on the Mazzini mission which now came under PWE jurisdiction.[61] In addition, key British personnel were transferred to the new agency, which had been given the sole responsibility for waging the propaganda war against the Axis powers outside Britain. For example, Thornhill, who was a personal friend of Wavell's, and had co-ordinated propaganda work among the Italian POWs in India from Cairo, was transferred, along with several of his staff, to the fledgling PWE in London. Wavell, one of the few senior military commanders who saw the real potential of political warfare and who had earlier requested direct SOE representation in India before the restructuring, no doubt welcomed Thornhill's reassignment.[62]

The PWE quickly established an India mission. All propaganda work, including the Mazzini team, was now a PWE responsibility. Two officers, Major (later Colonel) F. L. Stevens and Major I. S. Munro (both formerly of the Ministry of Information) were ordered to GHQ India to take soundings about how best to conduct political warfare, especially among the 45,676 Italian POWs so far imprisoned there. They arrived in late November 1941 and were in temporary charge of all PWE activities in India until the arrival of Thornhill in February 1942. It would prove to be a thankless task, for the ill-fated Mazzini mission almost destroyed in one fell swoop the trust and confidence the fledgling PWE had cultivated among the more sceptical elements of military intelligence and the high command in India.

The Mazzini mission to India was a fiasco from the very outset. Boyall, who claimed that he had not the slightest confidence in the mission from the start, called it a 'complete farce'. Squabbles and petty jealousies which broke out between team members during the long voyage to India reinforced this pessimism and prompted Boyall to report that such divisiveness had made it impossible to do any constructive propaganda work with such 'a gang of suspicious characters'.[63] Called gangsters by one intelligence officer in London, the Directorate of Military Intelligence tried to distance itself from the Mazzini mission. It stated that not only did it not dispatch the mission, but also that it was not concerned with 'clearing up the mess'. The idea had been 'clearly absurd from the outset and the whole conduct of the proceedings seems to have been incompetent and careless'.[64] Others, such as the DMI, India, General W. J. Cawthorn, were more scathing. Not only had the mission been an expensive, unnecessary and unfruitful exercise, it had become an embarrassing liability.[65] This was not helped by the fact that, despite the utmost secrecy from SOE, the real object of the mission may have been compromised owing to indiscretions committed by the New York executive of the Mazzini Society.[66] So what had gone wrong?

In a lengthy memorandum Lucio Tarchiani reported that right from the beginning there were inklings that certain individuals were incapable of coping with the demands of the mission. Despite the courtesy shown by the British authorities, some of Tarchiani's men grew impatient and restless as their leader attempted to persuade his British superiors of the proper course of action to take in the camps. There were obvious differences of opinion between Tarchiani and the British that had to be worked out. Meanwhile, as negotiations dragged on, inactivity among some elements of his men began to take their toll:

> [O]ne would be devoured by a morbid impatience, another would behave like a boor or a knave, [and] another would profess an open distrust of the authorities. Reports which at that time were sent weekly to London were all more or less bad and served but to increase my difficulties and to imperil the results already obtained. Everything was under the insignia of ill will.[67]

When Tarchiani departed for India the problems and disappointments encountered in England accompanied him. Boredom during the long voyage fostered personal hatreds and jealousies among the ten-member team. Several plotted to replace their long-suffering leader who lamented that upon their arrival in Calcutta the arguments and complaints not only continued but also intensified. 'All opportunities given had been ruined by a bunch of ignoramus maniacs [*sic*] and megalomaniac mugs.'[68] The already fraught situation was aggravated even more when the party was forced to stay in Calcutta for two months as Indian immigration authorities tried to discover who they were. As no passports had been provided for the men, and the only papers of identification were their Mazzini Society membership cards, the team had to stay put until GHQ India intervened. British assessments of the team's shortcomings and inadequacies confirmed Tarchiani's more colourful language.[69]

Major Munro informed the War Office that correspondence he had seen concerning the mission revealed 'a disconcerting confusion of ideas and plans'.[70] This was substantiated by Tarchiani when he admitted to his father that the situation in India was more complicated than had been foreseen in the comfortable and far removed environs of New York. It was therefore 'absolutely impossible' at the present moment to carry out any of the Mazzini Society's programme because the 'ground is not favourable at all'. He emphasized that it 'will necessitate the utmost patience before the anti-fascist elements and the fascists can be found out and separated'. Until a thorough segregation policy had been implemented, 'it would be like throwing seeds on a[n] untilled land'.[71] PWE officials had been all too aware of the inadequacies of POW segregation in India. However, these same officials were far from impressed with the maverick attitude displayed by the New York executive of the Mazzini Society. They behaved as if the British authorities did not exist. Instructions to India from New York were sent 'over the open wire'. Surely Tarchiani's father realized that the POW camps were under British jurisdiction, subject to international inspection and that any instructions to the mission could only come from British authorities? Clearly, the mission's mandate needed clarification.[72]

There was more, however, which indicated the amateurish approach that plagued the entire episode. While in Cape Town, the impetuous Galgani, described by Tarchiani as two-faced and 'the most beautiful specimen of a megalomaniac', tried to post two letters without permission to the Mazzini executive in New York complaining about the young doctor's leadership.[73] Furthermore, while in transit at Durban, the secret nature of the Mazzini mission was exposed when the purpose of their visit to India was published not only in the *Natal Daily News*, but also several leading dailies in New York. Government censors had prevented these disclosures from reaching India, but this embarrassing indiscretion could have ruined what little opportunities for success were left.[74]

Finally, to add insult to injury, when the mission was allowed to undertake work in the camps in India, an incident at the Bhopal POW facility revealed the dangers of using outsiders for such a sensitive task. Six of Boyall's party were taken into the wings of the Bhopal camp to start their work. Guiseppe Macaluso, described by Tarchiani as a 'chatterbox, [a] gossip [and a] mug . . . [with a] mentality [of] zero', was recognized by some POWs who knew him in Addis Ababa prior to the war. 'The whole party was immediately stoned', reported Stevens, and promptly evacuated.[75] The 'violent republican propaganda' which some of the more ardent anti-fascist members like Macaluso and Fragiacomo wished to indulge in was unacceptable to the prisoners. Moreover, it was the unsatisfactory conduct of these troublemakers, which had proved a considerable embarrassment to both camp authorities and the PWE.[76] This debacle forced Stevens to question the use of Italo-Americans for PWE work in India. The Bhopal incident had clearly demonstrated that if such men were introduced into a POW camp, they would at once be questioned as to where they had been captured, the regiment with which they had served and their registration number:

> Being unable satisfactorily to furnish these particulars [they] would at once become the object of suspicion by other prisoners, and if [they] made an attempt to start an anti-Fascist cell would arouse intense hostility from the Fascists elements and probably suffer personal violence. The antagonism so roused would militate against satisfactory political results.[77]

Would it not be more advantageous in the future to use POWs for this kind of work? It would certainly minimize the above disadvantages.

Undoubtedly, the Mazzini Society mission had been a complete disaster. The party was promptly disbanded in December 1941 after spending only four weeks in the camps. Six of the men, tagged by Colonel Stevens as 'absolutely useless . . . ignorant, stubborn, mistrusting fellows', were to be sent home with Tarchiani's fullest endorsement.[78] Of the ten-man team, six (five Italians and one American, Osvaldo Forlani) had proven recalcitrant throughout and upon disbandment demanded their immediate return home. The PWE wholeheartedly agreed.[79] However, Japan's entry into the war on 7 December 1941 and Italy's subsequent declaration of war on the United States made this highly improbable; and even if it had been possible to repatriate them direct to the United States, they did not have American passports or any other requisite travel documentation. As one anonymous official wrote: 'After all they <u>are</u> aliens!'[80] As for the five Italian citizens, who could 'not be allowed to wander about India', they were kept under close supervision at a camp near Bhopal. Although not interned, it was hoped that their attachment to POW Group 2 would, with time, allow these men to settle down. In fact, in December 1942 it was hoped that Andrea Albertelli and Guiseppe Poggioli could at last be transferred to the special anti-fascist camp being constructed at Jaipur in Rajasthan. The chatterbox Macaluso and the virulent republican Fragiacomo were eventually transferred to Jaipur as well. However, as one PWE official noted, these four men had only one ambition – to return to the United States. Deemed 'more of a nuisance than an assistance', it seemed these four reprobates would use any means at their disposal to get home. In early May 1943 it was reported that the four men were openly sabotaging the PWE's efforts at Jaipur and an immediate request was made for their prompt return to New York. If that was not enough, two weeks later they were accused of inciting a mutiny at Jaipur![81]

Meanwhile Galgani, a pipe fitter by trade and the fifth Italian citizen who had also spent some time at Bhopal, was sent to instruct Italian POWs employed at the United Provinces Police workshops at Sitagur. He proved unsatisfactory and was returned to the PWE mission headquarters at Delhi. As for the 'useless' American, Osvaldo Forlani, he had made a characteristically unauthorized approach to American consular officials in early 1942 revealing all the Mazzini team's activities and levelling serious allegations against Tarchiani in the 'misguided endeavour' to safeguard his own reputation at the expense of his comrades. Forlani, who had been a freelance journalist, also wrote a letter to Philip Jordan, a war correspondent, hoping to enlist his help in publicizing his plight in India. At the same time, he revealed to Jordan that the British had been training parachutist-saboteurs, which he had learnt about while in the AMPC. The possibility of trying the disgruntled Forlani under the Official Secrets Act was investigated but dropped, in part, due to the decision made by US authorities in March 1943 to repatriate him.[82]

What of the Italians who had now been interned? It was thought highly improbable that the Americans would allow these men entry into the United States as they were now classified as enemy aliens. Therefore, with the termination of the PWE mission in India that summer, it was suggested by the head of the mission,

Colonel A. C. Johnston, that they be returned to England as it was considered unfair to leave them stranded in India. The Foreign Office refused. Instead, they were interned by the Home Department of India, the PWE agreeing to reimburse the Indian government the cost of their maintenance. But it was far from over. Throughout the rest of 1943 the Mazzini Society demanded that these men be repatriated to the United States. Indeed, in May 1943, the American Consulate in Bombay had been instructed by the State Department in Washington to issue passports to the remaining members of the Mazzini mission. However, one senior PWE official, Air Commodore P. R. C. Groves became worried lest these men, upon their return home, would give as much publicity as possible to their alleged ill-treatment. Hence their internment. But even Groves's patience was wearing thin by the end of 1943. Fed up with the whole affair, the PWE decided to act Groves complained in February 1944:

> In view of the amount of trouble caused by these four recalcitrants and the endless correspondence and numerous telegrams of which they have been the subject, it would seem most desirable that action should now be taken to arrive at a final settlement of the issue. The action I suggest is that these four Italians shall now be sent to their native land [Italy] and the further demands from the Mazzini Society for their dispatch to America shall be referred to the Italian Government.[83]

The remaining four, including Tarchiani, had followed their mandate to the letter and were allowed to stay on in India, as the British had been satisfied with their hard work and dedication. Tarchiani was commissioned in the Intelligence Corps in March 1942, serving as an interpreter and liaison officer at POW camps at Bangalore and Dehra Dun. Americo Biasini, Luigi Ceccarelli and Albino Zattoni were re-enlisted in the British Army as sergeant-interpreters in April 1942 and did sterling work in the POW camps.

VI

The demise of the Mazzini mission, although an embarrassing disaster, taught British officials an invaluable lesson on the limits of using foreign operatives without first providing in-depth training in the subtle arts of subversion. Forced to re-evaluate its propaganda work in India, throughout 1942 Thornhill's under-staffed team worked hard to overcome this initial calamity into POW indoctrination. By 1943, on the surface at least, it looked as if the PWE had finally turned the corner in India. The construction of a special camp or 'rallying centre' at Jaipur, where anti-fascists could be removed from existing POW camps, seemed to secure the proper environment and support that the PWE had demanded for such a long time.[84] Unfortunately for Thornhill and his hard-working team, old problems resurfaced, and several new obstacles were introduced that by July 1943 effectively stymied the mission and led to its recall from India. At the War Office, some officials were still at a loss as to the objects of Thornhill's activities.[85] The real difficulties, however, remained with elements within GHQ, India, especially the Adjutant-General's branch. PWE officers commented repeatedly that the cooperation given them by GHQ was marred and overshadowed by the Indian military's lack of interest and understanding of political warfare. It was a new idea, and was inclined to be viewed as a 'waste of time'. The Adjutant-General's branch was singled out as the chief offender.

> Full co-operation is continually promised, but our projects are apt to be hindered by administrative difficulties, which, by the use of a little imagination, could be overcome. The Adjutant-General's Branch do not like doing anything which will disturb the even tempo of the life of the camp staffs.

The PWE were adamant that the amount of cooperation their mission had received and was still receiving from the military authorities in India left much to be desired.[86]

The failure of the PWE mission to move beyond the exploratory stage of its work was due, in part, to the fact that it had no executive authority over the Italian POWs in India. This was firmly in the hands of the Adjutant-General. As the mission was limited in scope to an advisory capacity, it had neither the executive power nor the resources to implement an effective or large-scale propaganda campaign. Segregation had been piecemeal. Therefore, despite the initial interest and support of Wavell, the effectiveness of the small cadre of PWE officials in India was constrained from the very beginning, because of their dependence on the goodwill and cooperation of the Indian military authorities. As we have seen, this was not always forthcoming. The shortage of trained personnel, in particular Italian-speaking intelligence officers (which the Mazzini mission was, in part, to help alleviate) hampered further the PWE's overall efforts in India. In the end, the immediate demands and manpower requirements of the military were to triumph over the long-term political aims of the PWE.

What of the Mazzini mission itself, ' a source of endless trouble', which seemed doomed almost from the outset?[87] It was certainly a gamble and one driven by necessity, if not desperation. The lack of suitable numbers of Italian internees in the United Kingdom or the Empire willing to participate in covert operations was a key factor in forcing London to look overseas. Coupled with the intriguing but unsubstantiated claim that the United States possessed the best type of Italian 'tough' and 'thug', the Mazzini Society provided the only avenue for SOE in its recruitment of agents and saboteurs. And although doubts as to the unsuitability of the Mazzini mission's personnel were expressed before it embarked for India in August 1941, at the time, the advantages of continuing the mission far outweighed the disadvantages. First, there was the issue of unfavourable repercussions in the United States if the men were returned without being allowed to approach the Italian POWs on the sub-continent. If they had been sent home without being given a chance to prove their worth, it would have looked as though the British had never intended to make use of them. Surely, this would have generated bad publicity in the then neutral United States, and perhaps stymied any further attempts to cultivate dissident Italian support overseas. Nonetheless, the most crucial advantage for the PWE in supporting the Mazzini mission was that it provided an all-important lever by which it could open the propaganda door to India. Therefore, the recriminations which were launched at SOE by PWE officials – that SOE had created the mess in the first place and then plunged the PWE into it – have to be balanced by the *potential* purchase it gave the PWE for its operations in India and elsewhere.[88] A farcical episode, indeed, but the escapades of 'a newsvendor, a lift attendant, a boot black and a motor mechanic',[89] taught British propaganda and political warfare officers an invaluable lesson they would never forget.

Notes

1   See Bob Moore and Kent Fedorowich, *The British Empire and its Italian Prisoners of War, 1940–1947* (London, 2002), Chapter 5.

2   Kent Fedorowich, 'Propaganda and Political Warfare: The Foreign Office, Italian POWs and the Free Italy Movement, 1940–3', in Bob Moore and Kent Fedorowich (eds), *Prisoners of War and their Captors in World War II* (Oxford, 1996), pp. 119–148.

3   Brooks to R. J. H. Shaw, Department EH, 11 June 1940, cited in Moore and Fedorowich, *Italian Prisoners*, p. 106. For the origins of SOE, see David Stafford, *Britain and European Resistance, 1940–1945* (London, 1980), pp. 10–27. The British failure to establish a propaganda machine prior to 1939 and the pre-war machinations involved in setting up a psychological warfare strategy against the Axis powers are best analysed by Philip M. Taylor, *The Projection of Britain: British Overseas Publicity and Propaganda 1919–1939* (Cambridge, 1981). He has recently updated this work in his *British Propaganda in the Twentieth Century: Selling Democracy* (Edinburgh, 1999), pp. 114–150.

4   SOE Papers for Western Europe, HS 6/885, minute by Section D, 28 Aug. 1940; Sir Frank Nelson, operational head of SOE, to AD, 9 Dec. 1940. The National Archive, London, Public Record Office (hereafter PRO) FO 898/161.

5   JA to D/JG, 17 June 1941, PRO HS 6/884. For Italian internment policies, see Lucio Sponza, 'The British Government and the Internment of Italians', in David Cesarani and Tony Kushner (eds), *The Internment of Aliens in Twentieth Century Britain* (London, 1993), pp. 125–146; and for the Loraine Committee's activities see John Curry, *The Security Service 1908–1945: The Official History* (London, 1999), pp. 165–167. Sir Percy Loraine, who chaired the committee, had been a former ambassador to Italy (1939–1940).

6   SOE War Diary, 3, PRO HS7/58.

7   Martelli to P. B. B. Nichols (Foreign Office), 7 Dec. 1940, PRO FO898/161.

8   Ibid.

9   Martelli to Ion S. Munro, head of Ministry of Information's Italian Section, 11 April 1941, PRO FO371/29936 R4059/G.

10 Memo. entitled, 'Free Italy Committee', 17 Dec. 1940; Halifax to Dalton, 18 Dec. 1940, with enclosed memo on pros and cons of launching a Free Italy movement, PRO FO898/161.

11 JIC(40)325, 'General Treatment of Prisoners of War', 18 Oct. 1940, PRO CAB81/98; JIC(40)63, minute 1, 25 Oct. 1940, CAB81/87.

12 JIC(40)71, minutes 1 and 2, 3 Dec. 1940, PRO CAB81/88; JIC(40)422, Brooks to Colonel C. T. Edwards, secretary of JIC, 17 Dec. 1940, CAB81/99; JIC(40)73, minute 1, 24 Dec. 1940, CAB81/88.

13 'Memorandum on Anti-Fascist Propaganda in the Middle East', by Thornhill and Miss Freya Stark, Assistant Information Officer, Ministry of Information, Aden, 15 Aug. 1940, PRO FO898/110.

14 Minute by Ismay, 11 Feb. 1941, PRO PREM 3/242/8.

15 WM19(41)12, 20 Feb. 1941, PRO CAB65/11; WP(41)51, 'The Formation of a Free Italian Movement in the Italian Colonies', 6 March 1941, CAB 66/15.

16 Secret minutes 'I' and 'II', Dalton to Gladwyn Jebb, SOE's Chief Executive Officer, both dated 23 Jan. 1941, PRO HS6/903. This was reiterated by the ever-zealous Martelli several months later. See 'The Free Italy Movement and the Raising of a Free Italian Force', 24 March 1941, FO 371/29936/R 5642.

17 Dalton to Sir Robert Vansittart, Chief Diplomatic Advisor, Foreign Office, 24 Aug. 1940, British Library of Political and Economic Science (BLPES), London School of Economics, Dr Hugh Dalton Papers, 7/3.

18 For Cooper's unhappy time as minister, see John Charmley, *Duff Cooper* (London, 1986), pp. 141–153. For Dalton's pugnacious tenure as head of SOE, see Ben Pimlott, *Hugh Dalton* (London, 1985), pp. 299–345.

19 Minute by Pierson Dixon, 17 Jan. 1941, PRO FO371/29935 R409.

20 Ibid.; minute by Nichols, 9 Jan. 1941.

21 Ibid., Cooper to Eden, 15 Jan.1941, which also included a short memorandum on the consultation between Cooper and Dalton earlier that month.

22 Ibid., Eden to Cooper, 27 Jan. 1941; minutes by Cadogan and Eden, 18 and 20 Jan. 1941.

23 *The Times*, 10 Feb. 1941; Minute by Sir Orme Sargent, 6 March 1941, PRO FO 371/29935 R2707; Martelli to Munro, 11 April 1941, FO371/29936 R4059/G. For the intrigue surrounding the Free Italy committee, see Lucio Sponza, *Divided Loyalties: Italians in Britain during the Second World War* (Berne, 2000), pp. 173–181.

24 Moore and Fedorowich, *Italian POWs*, pp. 107–108; Sponza, *Divided Loyalties*, pp. 95–151; SOE War Diary, 9d, PRO HS7/265.

25 In January 1942, 600,000 Italian-Americans were given enemy alien status. This ruling was overturned in October–November 1943 after Italy surrendered that September. Conversely, 400,000 Italian-Americans served in the US armed forces during the Second World War. Louis E. Keefer, *Italian Prisoners of War in America 1942–1946. Captives or Allies?* (Westport, CT, 1992), pp. 41–42.

26 Martelli to Nelson, 19 Dec. 1940, PRO HS6/885.

27 Wiley to Donovan, 8 June 1942, National Archives and Records Administration, College Park, MD (hereafter NARA), Records of the Office of Strategic Services, RG 226, W. J. Donovan's OSS Records, microfilm series, M 1642, roll 70, frame 588. Wiley was a career diplomat, who, prior to his assignment to the State Department in 1940, had been the American minister to Latvia and Estonia (1938–1940).

28 Antonio Varsori, 'Max Ascoli oppositore del fascismo la "Mazzini Society"', *Nowua Antologia*, 2136 (1980): 106–124. For Sforza's role also, see Antonio Varsori, 'Sforza, La Mazzini Society e gli alleati (1940–1943)', in Antonio Varsori (ed.), *L'antifascismo Italiano negli State Uniti durante la seconda guerra mondiale* (Rome, 1983), pp. 129–154. A heartfelt thanks to my colleagues Effie Pedaliu for pointing me in the direction of the Varsori material and Joe Dunthorn for translating these two very insightful pieces.

29 Wiley to Donovan, 8 June 1942, NARA, RG 226, M 1642, roll 70, frame 587. According to Roosevelt's personal representative in French North Africa, Robert D. Murphy, Churchill's assessment of Sforza, made during the negotiations surrounding the Italian surrender in 1943, was particularly brusque. To the British prime minister, Sforza was 'a foolish and played-out old man, incapable of facing let alone riding the storm', cited in J. G. Beevor, *SOE: Recollections and Reflections 1940–1945* (London, 1981), p. 138, and is from Robert Murphy's *Diplomat Among Warriors* (New York, 1964), p. 201. Alexander Cadogan did not have respect for Sforza either, calling him a 'dud'. David Dilks (ed.), *The Diaries of Sir Alexander Cadogan 1938–1945* (London, 1971), p. 564 (2 Oct. 1943).

30 Varsori, 'Sforza', p. 129; Biographical notes on Mazzini Society, 18 June 1942, NARA, RG 226, Entry 92, Box 66, Folder 14.

31 Biographical notes on Mazzini Society, 18 June 1942, NARA, RG 226, Entry 92, Box 66, Folder 14.

32 Beevor, *Recollections*, p. 137; Varsori, 'Max Ascoli', p. 115. For one of the first editorial forays made by Ascoli announcing the aims of the Mazzini Society, see the *New York Herald Tribune*, 29 Nov. 1940.

33 H. Gregory Thomas to Allen W. Dulles, 10 June 1942, NARA, RG 226, Entry 92, Box 66, Folder 14.

34 Wiley to Donovan, 8 June 1942. Ibid., M 1642, roll 70, frames 586–587.

35 Thomas to Dulles, 10 June 1942. Ibid., Entry 92, Box 66, Folder 14.

36 Varsori, 'Max Ascoli', p. 110; Thomas to Earl Brennan, 20 July 1942, NARA, RG 226, Entry 92, Box 103, Folder 33. For an excellent examination of the internal US dimension, see J. E. Miller, 'A Question of Loyalty: American Liberals, Propaganda, and the Italian-American Community, 1939–43', *The Maryland Historian* (Spring 1978): 49–70. A revealing insight into Sforza's initial contacts with senior US officials and the interplay between the competing factions in America is described by the Secretary of the Interior, Harold L. Ickes in *The Secret Diary of Harold L. Ickes*. vol. 3 *The Lowering Clouds 1939–1941* (London, 1955), pp. 319–320 and 462–465 (15 Sept. 1940 and 6 April 1941).

37 Minute by Martelli, 7 June 1941, FO371/29947 R6065.

38 Attlee to Canberra, circular D102, 28 Feb. 1941; Bruce to Fadden, 3 March 1941, National Archives of Australia (Canberra), NAA, Commonwealth Record Series (CRS), A981/1, ITA 9.

39 Massey to King, 12 Feb. 1941; Department of Mines and Resources memo. initialled RNM, 19 Feb. 1941; Norman Robertson, Under-Secretary of State for External Affairs, to RCMP Commissioner S. T. Wood, 20 Feb. 1941, National Archives of Canada (NAC), RG 76, vol. 467, f. 710220. Robertson later wrote to Wood commenting that Coit had been disappointed with the response for recruits in the United States. This had not surprised Robertson, who thought the response by the anti-Fascist Italians in the United States had been rather 'meagre and guarded'. Robertson to Wood, 24 March 1941, NAC, N. A. Robertson Papers, MG 30 E163, vol. 14, file 160.

40 'Articles of Incorporation of Mazzini Society', included in letter sent by an ex-internee, Paolo Sonnino, to W. Ashley Wynes, Department of External Affairs, 4 Sept. 1942, NAA, CRS A 981/1, ITA 9. Sonnino was an Italian Jew who had fled Italy only to be interned by the Australians when Italy entered the war. He was released in August 1941. A year later he suggested to Canberra that a Free Italy movement be undertaken in Australia, but he was told by W. R. Hodgson, Secretary, Department of External Affairs that it was best not to press the matter. Ibid., Hodgson to Sonnino, 29 Oct. 1942. His tribunal case files can be found in NAA, CRS A 367/1, items C54839 and C18000/265.

41 Department of Mines and Resources memo. initialled RNM, 19 Feb. 1941, NAC, RG 76, vol. 467, f. 710220; Mr Logie (probably Ministry of Information) to Philip Broad (Ministry of Economic Warfare), 11 Feb. 1941; J to CD and A/D1, 18 March 1941; 'Italian Volunteers from USA', 23 April 1941; memo. entitled, 'American Recruits', 30 April 1941, which describes arrival and processing of party, PRO HS 6/886; Report on the Italo-American party submitted to Air Commodore P. R. C. Groves, Political Warfare Executive, by Lieutenant A. Trower, Royal Artillery, 4 Feb. 1943, PRO FO939/372.

42 Tarchiani profile, PRO HS6/886; SOE War Diary, 19. HS7/265.

43 Member profiles, PRO HS 6/886.

44 'Italian Volunteers from USA', 22 April 1941; D/JG to Nelson, 6 June 1941. Ibid.

45 AD/A to M, 22 April 1941. Ibid.

46 Ibid.

47 Ibid.

48 D/JG to Nelson, 6 June 1941; AD to Jebb, 5 Dec. 1941; JA to A/D1, 10 Dec. 1941. Ibid.; SOE War Diary, 21, 24–26 and 29, PRO HS7/265. For an insight into one of the Isle of Man facilities, see Oliver Hoare (ed.), *Camp 020: MI5 and the Nazi Spies: The Official History of MI5's Wartime Interrogation Unit* (London, 2000).
49 Jebb to Dalton, 12 Aug. 1941, BLPES, Dalton Papers, 18/2.
50 SOE War Diary, 31, PRO HS7/265.
51 Extracts from the history of the Italian section war diary written by CD, 15 Oct. 1941, PRO HS7/58. For an insider's view on the SOE muddle in the Middle East, see Bickham Sweet-Escott, *Baker Street Irregular* (London, 1965), pp. 70–99; William Mackenzie, *The Secret History of SOE: The Special Operations Executive 1940–1945* (London, 2000), pp. 167–190.
52 CD to D/JG, 5 June 1941, PRO HS6/886; SOE War Diary, 31 HS7/265; secret cipher from Dalton to Wavell, 18 July 1941, FO898/111.
53 Oliver Harvey, Director, Enemy and Enemy-Occupied Countries Division, Ministry of Information, to Nichols, 16 April 1941; minute by Nichols, 19 April 1941, PRO FO371/29936 R4081.
54 Ibid.
55 Meeting at the Foreign Office with SOE officials to discuss the raising of a Free Italian force among Italian POWs, 25 June 1941, PRO HS6/886; Brooks to Sargent, 30 June 1941, FO898/111; SOE War Diary, 56, HS7/265; Alfred Stirling, External Affairs Officer, London, to Hodgson, 8 Oct. 1941, NAA, CRS A981/1, ITA 9.
56 Meeting at the Foreign Office with SOE officials to discuss the raising of a Free Italian force among Italian POWs, 25 June 1941, PRO HS6/886; SOE War Diary, 56, HS7/265.
57 Brooks to Sargent, 30 June 1941, PRO FO898/111.
58 SOE War Diary, 94–95, PRO HS7/265.
59 Draft instructions to Mazzini team, 5 and 8 July 1941, PRO HS6/886; draft telegram, 9 Jan. 1942, HS6/887; SOE War Diary, 56, HS7/265; Minute by Martelli, 7 Dec. 1941, FO939/373.
60 Secret cypher from Dalton to Wavell, 18 July 1941, PRO FO898/111.
61 Fedorowich, 'Propaganda and Political Warfare', in Moore and Fedorowich (eds), *Prisoners of War and their Captors*, pp. 119–148. A very useful insight into the internecine warfare in Whitehall over control of propaganda operations can be found in Michael Stenton, *Radio London and Resistance in Occupied Europe: British Political Warfare 1939–1943* (Oxford, 2000), pp. 22–40.
62 Dalton to Jebb, 13 Aug. 1941, PRO HS3/195; Dalton to Wavell, 5 Jan. 1941; Rex Leeper, head of SO1, to Dalton, 5 Dec. 1940, HS3/189.
63 Boyall to Munro, 14 Jan. 1942, PRO WO208/3039.
64 Ibid., minute by Major D. Talbot-Rice, General Staff (India), 24 Feb. 1942.
65 Ibid., Cawthorn to DMI, London, 21 Jan. 1942.
66 L. S. Amery, Secretary of State for India, to Marquess of Linlithgow, Viceroy of India, 18 Nov. 1941, PRO HS6/886; War Office to C-in-C India, 13 Nov. 1941, PRO FO939/373.
67 Report by Tarchiani, 27 Dec. 1941, PRO WO208/3039.
68 Ibid.
69 Ibid., Boyall to Munro, 14 Jan. 1942.
70 PWE written report no. 1 by Munro, 27 Nov. 1941, PRO FO898/111.
71 Tarchiani to his father, 27 Dec. 1941, PRO WO208/3039.
72 Unsigned draft memo., 16 Jan. 1942, PRO HS6/887.
73 Tarchiani to his father, 27 Dec. 1941; translation of Galgani to Tarchiani's father, 16 Sept. 1941 in Boyall's report to Munro, 14 Jan. 1942, PRO WO208/3039.
74 Wavell to War Office, 8 Nov. 1941, PRO FO898/111; SOE to New York, cypher no. 2932, 13 Nov. 1941, HS6/886.
75 Tarchiani to his father, 27 Dec. 1941; Stevens to Munro, 8 Jan. 1942, PRO WO208/3039. David Garnett, *The Secret History of PWE: The Political Warfare Executive 1939–1945*

(London, 2002), p. 138, incorrectly states that these men were never sent to the POW camps. But he was correct when he stated: 'Had they been allowed in Ps/W camps they would probably have been lynched.'

76 Unsigned memo., 14 Jan. 1942, PRO HS6/887.

77 Stevens to Groves, 4 March 1942, PRO FO898/112.

78 Addenda to Stevens's report on Boyall's party sent to Munro, 23 Nov. 1941, dated 27 Nov. 1941, PRO WO208/3039.

79 Flight Lieutenant H. G. Crawshaw, PWE, to Martelli, 20 Dec. 1941, PRO HS6/886.

80 Unsigned draft memo. entitled, 'Points for Mazzini Society', 10 Jan. 1942, PRO HS6/887.

81 Trower report, 4 Feb. 1943; C-in-C India to War Office, cipher from Thornhill, 31 March 1943; copies of telegrams from Colonel A. C. Johnston, Thornhill's replacement as head of PWE mission in India, sent to War Office via C-in-C India, 3 and 16 May 1943, PRO FO939/372.

82 SO London report, no. 754, 12 Jan. 1943, and no. 965, 8 Feb. 1943; copy of cypher telegram sent to New York by Tarchiani, 15 April 1942, PRO HS6/887; personnel statement on Mazzini mission, n.d. (probably mid-1942) HS6/894; SOE War Diary, 87–88, HS7/265; Trower report, 4 Feb. 1943, FO939/372. The SOE assessment of Forlani makes interesting reading. A widower, Forlani had spent most of his time in the hotel and restaurant business. 'In spite of his age [he] has shown that he is courageous, cheerful and sincerely eager to learn. Should be a useful man given the right job.' How wrong they were! Forlani profile, HS6/886.

83 SOE War Diary, 253–254, PRO HS7/265; Groves to H. C. Bowen, Ministry of Information, 21 Feb. 1944, FO939/372.

84 Fedorowich, 'Propaganda and Political Warfare', p. 57.

85 War Office to D. F. Howard, Foreign Office, 1 Dec. 1942, PRO WO208/841.

86 PWE mission progress report, 28 Apr. 1943; Groves to Brooks, 22 May 1943, PRO FO939/363.

87 Groves to Sir Robert Bruce Lockhart, Deputy Under-Secretary of State in charge of PWE, 8 April 1943, PRO FO939/373.

88 Martelli to Stevens, 7 Dec. 1941; Stevens to Leeper, 8 Dec. 1941, PRO FO939/373; Garnett, *Secret History*, pp. 138–139.

89 Trower report, 4 Feb. 1943, PRO FO939/372.

9 'Against the grain'

Special Operations Executive in Spain, 1941–1945

David A. Messenger

The neutral states of wartime Europe in many respects were crucial to the military strategy of the Allied nations in the Second World War. Great Britain, fighting alone after the French defeat in June, 1940, faced years of recovery from the initial successes of the German attacks in central and western Europe and was in no position to launch an offensive campaign on the continent. Even the arrival of the United States on the Allied side in December, 1941, did not bring instant relief. American forces too had to prepare for engagement on the Continent. Thus Allied strategy in Europe from 1940–1942 largely focused on the 'containment' of Nazi advances. Keeping neutral states out of the war was a significant part of this, and nowhere were the challenges greater than in General Francisco Franco's Spain.

A state with ties to local as well as German and Italian fascism, but one still recovering from three years of civil war, Spain by the end of 1940 was in the middle of an internal debate about whether or not to remain neutral or join the Axis.[1] Eventually an interim status of 'non-belligerency' was chosen, a choice that did not reassure the British since Benito Mussolini had declared the same before joining the war in June 1940 alongside Nazi Germany. Indeed, an offer of Spanish belligerency was made to Nazi Germany in the summer of 1940, albeit with a number of territorial and material conditions attached.[2] Throughout the war, the Franco regime was 'repeatedly on the edge' of a decision to join the Axis in war.[3] Even as Franco began to make a shift towards the Allies and speak of true 'neutrality', in autumn 1943, significant assistance to the Axis cause was maintained through to the end of the war.[4] This assistance ranged from general trade of strategic materials to the use of the Spanish merchant marine to assist Germany, the supply of German submarines from Spanish ports, acceptance of the activity of Gestapo and German intelligence agents on Spanish soil, and a full range of pro-Nazi propaganda throughout Iberia, some of it from official German sources, some inspired by Spanish admirers of Nazi Germany.[5] As a result, all the resources of the British Government were utilized in an effort to encourage, cajole, and force Spain to remain as true as possible to the obligations of neutrality, which meant limiting German influence on the Iberian Peninsula and combating German efforts to exploit Spanish resources, material and otherwise, for their own gain. Special Operations Executive (SOE) was deployed on the Iberian Peninsula to assist in this endeavour.

Strategically, a German invasion of Iberia or Spanish entrance into the war on the side of the Axis threatened Great Britain's Mediterranean position, and raised the possibility of delaying a planned American landing in North Africa.[6] Britain's goal became to do everything possible to prevent Spain from entering the war, and/or encourage Spanish opposition in the case of a German move into the peninsula. The primary means for pursuing such a policy was diplomatic. Ambassador on 'Special Mission', Sir Samuel Hoare, sought to affirm British acceptance of the Franco Government, often using a variety of economic and other incentives.[7] From May 1942 and increasingly after the success of Operation TORCH, the American invasion of French North Africa on 8 November 1942, he also pressured the Franco government to eliminate or limit Nazi influence by taking actions such as expelling German agents operating in Spanish territory.[8] For such pressure to be effective, the resources of British intelligence were necessary. What information could be gathered about Spanish contacts with Nazi Germany, about Franco's assistance to the enemy's armed forces, particularly its U-boats operating in the Atlantic and Mediterranean, or about economic ties that furthered the German war economy? Both covert and overt sources provided details about Hispano-German trade and smuggling, and about the presence of Axis agents in Spain. Hoare and his staff could then use such revelations in order to demand that Spain conform to a position of strict neutrality or else risk losing British aid. Intelligence in Spain had to serve in a complementary role to the Foreign Office's campaign to preserve Spanish neutrality and dampen pro-German sentiments within the Franco government and simultaneously develop a workable British-Spanish relationship.

The purpose of Special Operations Executive, as envisaged by the Prime Minister, Winston Churchill, was to 'organize, arm and control the European underground movements on a large-enough scale' so as to be of assistance to British military aims.[9] H Section, the SOE division responsible for Spain, Portugal and Spanish Morocco, was created in 1941 in part to assist the movement of SOE agents and French Resistance figures across the Pyrenees into occupied France.[10] It was also part of H Section's mission, however, to ensure that contact was made with various groups that might be capable of resisting a German invasion or occupation of Spain.[11] Indeed, H Section's mission was linked to the Chiefs of Staff's planning for a possible German invasion and/or occupation of the Iberian Peninsula by virtue of the importance given by the latter to the mobilization of local resistance and guerrilla units.[12] Once the success of TORCH and various diplomatic efforts began to bear fruit, however, the likelihood of a German move into Spain sometime in 1943 was thought to be negligible by the Chiefs.[13] Therefore British intelligence in Spain came to operate in a manner that first and foremost required it to serve the diplomatic mission of the embassy rather than any larger military plan.

The combination of Hoare's prioritization of diplomacy and the predominance in Madrid of other British intelligence organizations, especially the Special Intelligence Service (SIS), are often cited as reasons for the lack of any significant role for SOE in Spain.[14] Moreover, all intelligence activities in Madrid, in order to conform with Hoare's diplomatic goals, were placed under the supervision of Alan Hillgarth, naval attaché, who was sent to Madrid, as was Hoare, at the request of

Prime Minister Churchill.[15] A tendency to favour SIS operations soon became apparent within the embassy. SIS activities in Spain focused on the uncovering of German intelligence operations, most famously unearthing Germany's infrared surveillance system located in the Western Mediterranean, codenamed BODDEN. Information about BODDEN obtained by SIS and Naval Intelligence was used by British embassy officials from May 1942 through the end of the year to shame the Spanish government into reining in German covert activities in the Iberian Peninsula.[16] These protests eventually led to the dismantling of BODDEN, if not an end to German activity in the region.[17] Most significantly, the use of intelligence in the pursuit of diplomacy appeared to work well in the context of Spain, and thus cemented the relationship between SIS and Hoare's staff.[18] Kim Philby, one of the SIS operatives in Iberia during the war, reflected on the unusual fact that the Foreign Office and Hoare 'had less than its usual crop of inhibitions' when it came to using intelligence in a diplomatic protest to the Franco Government.[19] Thus, when intelligence came to matter in Spain, it was intelligence gathering done by the SIS, and not the sabotage and resistance work of SOE, that emerged as predominant.[20]

However, an examination of the archives of Special Operations Executive reveals that while initially stifled, H Section consisted of a small yet determined group who were required to pursue different and distinct roles for their organization in Spain, and who achieved some limited success in doing so. Two significant types of activities were developed for SOE operations in Spain. Beginning in 1941 and through 1943, contacts were developed with potential Spanish resistance to Nazi invasion or occupation, including a group within the Spanish military known as the Traditionalists. In conjunction with this, sabotage plans were made against German targets inside Spain, and many of these plans continued to be worked on even after the possibility of a German invasion had been downgraded. In this first path, then, the traditional goals of SOE were followed with enthusiasm, although in practice more planning than actual sabotage or resistance activity occurred. The reality was that the opposition of Hoare and the Foreign Office to military operations in a neutral state effectively shut SOE out of its mandated arena. While it could be conceded that this alone made SOE's efforts in Spain minimal, if not completely a failure, frustration over the lack of success led SOE operatives in Spain to find work they could do. Thus, a second role for SOE was developed. In the realm of intelligence gathering, particularly as it related to economic intelligence, SOE in Spain did achieve some success and carved out a limited role for itself in assisting Britain realize some of its aims in wartime Spain.[21] This chapter will survey the history of SOE in Spain by outlining some of the major activities in these two realms. While SOE was often a planning rather than an active organization so far as sabotage in Spain was concerned, this fact did not diminish the contributions made to the overall war effort in the field of intelligence gathering. SOE in Spain went 'against the grain' of its mandate but proved it could still play a role.

As planning for TORCH proceeded, and the threat of Axis or Spanish military opposition to TORCH on the Iberian Peninsula itself loomed, H Section was revitalized with the appointment of Major L. J. W. Richardson as head in October 1942. At that point in time, H Section consisted of a small staff of three or four in

London, with additional agents in Madrid, Seville and Barcelona, as well as in Gibraltar, Lisbon and Tangier. The initial Madrid mission dispatched in 1941 was led by D. Babbington Smith and assisted by D. F. Muirhead. These two made up the entire SOE team until January 1943, when George Neale joined them in Madrid under cover of the Ministry of Economic Warfare. In March 1943, E. E. Montgomery arrived under cover as the vice-consul in Seville and R. P. Pinsent at the Consulate General of Barcelona. 22 The head of the Madrid Mission for SOE from December 1943 was H. F. G. (Harry) Morris, Third Secretary of the British Embassy and formerly head of mission in Gibraltar; Babbington Smith stayed on as his assistant.

For the most part, the work that SOE performed in Spain over the course of 1941–1943 was linked with the fear that Nazi Germany might invade or occupy the Iberian Peninsula. As a result, the task of preparing for the possibility of resistance and sabotage was given to SOE. This activity was to be limited to planning; the Foreign Office made it clear that 'the interests of their foreign policy are predominant and that S.O.E. will carry out no operations and will take no active steps prepatory to operations except with the knowledge and consent of the Head of the local diplomatic mission'.[23] As noted, Hoare gave the task of making sure SOE complied with this directive to Captain Alan Hillgarth of Naval Intelligence. Fortunately, as H Section Head Richardson commented in April 1943, Hillgarth was 'prepared to take the maximum risks as regards the preparation of S.O.E. work in Spain'.[24]

H Section's work in 1941–1943 was quite diverse, and achieved 'good results within the limitations imposed upon them by the Foreign Office policy'.[25] Concerning the Spanish opposition to Franco, British contacts already existed. From 1939 through 1940, Section D of SIS maintained communications with an organization of Spanish Republican exiles in southern France, the *Alianza Democrática Española*.[26] Once the possibility of Spanish entry into the war appeared more likely, in late 1940 and through 1941, a series of activities involving British intelligence and anti-Franco Spaniards occurred in both Spain and London. SOE developed plans for the training of exiled Spanish Republicans in England for use in potential sabotage operations, though these were never acted upon.[27] Similar contacts with former Spanish Republican army officers working with Charles de Gaulle's forces were made by the SIS and uncovered by Spanish intelligence.[28] In Gibraltar, Harry Morris created an operation meant to serve as a 'feeder' of supplies and aid to a potential resistance movement in Spain. A fleet of smuggling ships was employed to ferry individuals out of Spain and carry people and supplies into Spain if needed; stores of weapons and explosives for Spanish operations were also maintained.[29] The Gibraltar mission was twice augmented by additional personnel before the launch of TORCH, first between April–August 1941 and, again, just prior to Operation TORCH in November 1942.[30]

Direct and active sabotage operations were also considered. One of the most extensively planned efforts was codenamed WARDEN. Intelligence from Las Palmas, Canary Islands, in spring of 1941 indicated 40,000 tons of enemy shipping docked in the harbour, consisting of German, Italian and Danish freighters. SOE planners proposed sinking seven and stealing the eighth, a Danish ship whose captain was known to be pro-British. This operation was to be carried out by Polish naval officers trained by SOE.[31] By 19 July, training under the command of Naval Special Operations was underway and the records indicate that the plan was forwarded to the chief of SOE for approval by 26 July.[32] Since the operation was effectively taken over by Naval Intelligence, however, there is no indication in the SOE files that it ever took place. Encouraged by the Governor of Gibraltar, General Noel Mason-Macfarlane, H Section also developed contacts with Naval Intelligence over the possibility of sabotage against BODDEN.[33] While SOE did not plan for operations here at the same level of detail that they did for WARDEN, the assistant director of planning insisted that extensive intelligence concerning BODDEN had to be shared with H Section in advance of the TORCH landings in order that some planning for sabotage could be done, for agents in Spain 'did not want to be thrust into taking action at short notice'.[34]

Despite these activities, Hoare's expressed wish to avoid SOE activity in Spain was reiterated prior to the launch of Operation TORCH, and as a result some operations were short-circuited before they could get underway. Special Operations Executive made plans to contact Spanish opposition groups in southern Spain from Gibraltar and organize armed resistance in the event that the Allied landings prompted Spanish entry into the war on the side of the Axis. Hoare refused even to consider such a scheme.[35] London supported its ambassador and SOE officials reluctantly concluded that the organization had been banned from giving any assistance to military operations that might occur in Spain or Spanish Morocco.[36] After TORCH, in March 1943, the Chiefs of Staff gave Hoare's wishes official expression in the 'Special Operations Executive Directive for 1943' which stated that, in Spain and Portugal, 'You should take no action in either of these countries other than the maintenance of your existing contacts and communications into Axis controlled countries.'[37] Wireless sets were allowed to be distributed to members of a potential resistance movement from 1942 onwards, but there were few cases of success and one prominent incident in Navarre where the local operator, a priest, was arrested in May 1943 and under interrogation exposed some of SOE's activities to the Spanish regime.[38]

In the end, British plans for a Spanish resistance movement in the case of Axis occupation in Iberia were entirely secondary to the general British approach to Franco's regime. Yet the SOE Mission in Spain was expanded after TORCH, increasing from two representatives to five (three in Madrid) by the time of Morris' appointment as head in December 1943. This alone suggests that H Section was not standing still. Despite directives from Hoare and the Chiefs of Staff, plans for resistance and sabotage in Spain continued apace, and new avenues for SOE activity were opened up.

The commitment of SOE to preparing for organized resistance to a potential German invasion did not diminish after TORCH, even though many American and British officials argued that Spain's newfound commitment to neutrality meant that even in the face of a German invasion Spanish resistance would be assured.[39] By March 1943, it became clear that most in the British military dismissed the possibility of any German invasion.[40] Nonetheless, H Section continued its work in planning for a German invasion. In February, twenty British agents, twenty-eight Spaniards and four individuals of other nationalities underwent training for use in Spain in case Germany invaded.[41] Richardson, in his review of H Section activities in Spain in April, stressed that while the Chiefs of Staff were sceptical of a future German invasion of Iberia, 'H Section should be prepared for the unexpected.'[42] Discussions with Air Force Intelligence about what SOE could do to prepare the ground continued: the contacts made, supplies stored and plans drawn up for a Spanish resistance movement to Nazi occupation were maintained.[43]

The most important initiative in this respect was Operation REPROACH, a programme of established contacts between SOE and the Traditionalists. The leading members of this movement, Generals Antonio Aranda and Alfredo Kindelán, and later General Luis Orgaz y Yoldi were all important military leaders, although the group by no means represented the majority of Spanish officers.[44] These generals vowed to resist with arms any German invasion of their country, and had moved from individual resentment of Franco's close ties to the Axis to a more organized planning for resistance against Germany and the overthrow of Franco in October 1941.[45] Working with Babbington Smith and Hillgarth, they sought to develop a potential resistance movement within the Army that would be activated in the aftermath of a German attack, the period in which the German Army would attempt to consolidate their rearguard and organize occupation policies.[46] Begun well before TORCH, REPROACH even included plans that would see the British send arms to the Traditionalists in underwater containers.[47]

The ties H Section and Hillgarth made with Spanish generals went back to 1940, when Hillgarth had been intimately involved in Britain's scheme to win over support for neutrality from Spanish generals through the payment of cash.[48] While the immediate fear of Spanish entry into the war on the Axis side encouraged British interest in the Traditionalists, the general sense that, as members of the government and monarchists, they provided a longer-term, moderate and non-revolutionary alternative to Franco's regime also inspired British efforts.[49] On the part of SOE, Richardson was a strong proponent of REPROACH. He initially hoped that the forces gathered by the generals 'might be organised and equipped so as to constitute a compact resistance force capable of holding a front against aggressors on lines comparable with Jugoslav guerillas', but eventually accepted that this force would engage in smaller-scale resistance activities such as attacking lines of communication, destroying strategic objectives, and engaging in industrial sabotage.[50] Even as late as April 1943, with the chances of a German invasion fading, Richardson emphasized the need to keep the REPROACH group 'intact and our connection with it secret so that it can operate in full force as soon as possible after [a German invasion]'.[51] Although REPROACH represented the most significant contact with anti-Franco Spaniards, it was not the only one. H Section's cultivation of an agent in Asturias, Emilio Baras Canal, a former socialist who had been conscripted into Franco's forces during the Spanish Civil War, led to indirect contact with potential resisters in the major cities and towns of the region and with a band of 2–3000 anti-Franco guerrillas in the mountains.[52]

Despite the continuation of such activities, SOE operations in Spain after TORCH primarily took a form other than sabotage and resistance, notwithstanding the official mandate of the organization. By mid-1943 the organization came to accept the fact that 'the threat of an Axis invasion of the Peninsula has disappeared' and 'specific S.O.E. preparations to meet an Axis invasion can now be discontinued'.[53] Moreover, the primary goal of British policy in wartime Spain was to keep Spain out of the war, not encourage a coup. This objective motivated policy, and thus worked against any sort of active encouragement of the anti-Franco Spaniards.[54] A draft directive for future policy, prepared at the end of July 1943, therefore moved H Section away from its focus on the agents of a potential Spanish opposition and prioritized its activities in two areas. The first priority was given to the main-tenance of lines of communication from Spain to occupied Europe, particularly to France but also the Low Countries; the second area of emphasis was the 'intensification of sabotage of Axis politico-military and economic interests'.[55] A variety of activities were considered to fall within the realm of economic sabotage. Naturally, actual sabotage or destruction of Axis economic stocks was considered, in line with SOE's mandate. Indeed, Basque operatives on both the Spanish and French side of the border were considered for sabotage operations to be carried out on French territory in 1944. The potential targets were trainloads of illegal German shipments of wolfram. In this instance, as with many SOE operations developed before TORCH, planning did not lead to action due to opposition from Hoare and SOE's French section.[56] Thus, other, subtler forms of sabotage were considered in the new policy as primary H Section tasks. These included persuading exporters to slow down shipments; pressuring neutral traders to stop their trade with the Axis; suborning shipmasters in order to intercept ships transporting goods to the enemy; fomenting strikes among dockworkers loading ships engaged in Axis trade; 'in general attacking or interfering with Axis interests by "unacknowledgeable" methods'.[57]

The change in policy was prompted by the dissatisfaction H Section and others had experienced with the *attentiste* nature of British policy in Spain. SOE argued that the Foreign Office policy since the start of the war had been one of 'appease-ment' toward the Franco regime. This not only meant that SOE did not actively pursue its various schemes with anti-Franco Spaniards, but also that Britain's policies had allowed the enemy to 'gain a tremendous foothold' in the Iberian economy. In light of that fact, the Ministry of Economic Warfare (MEW), SOE's supervisory body, appreciated that SOE was in a position 'to continue the struggle against Axis economic interests at the point where they must abandon it because only "unacknowledgeable" methods remain'.[58] Indeed, MEW and SOE repre-sentatives in Portugal together pressed for an expanded SOE role in Iberian economic warfare over the course of summer 1943 as the SOE investigated possible options for future action.[59]

The new direction in policy would see the combined resources of SOE and MEW work together to uncover sources of Axis economic interest; MEW would work with the Foreign Office and the Embassy to pressure the Spanish Government; SOE would seek other ways to weaken Axis influence and control of the Iberian market.

Intelligence gathering in the name of possible subtle sabotage operations became as important, if not more important, than support of resistance activities in the daily life of SOE's H Section. Moreover, intelligence gathering specifically as it related to economic intelligence was made part of the SOE mandate. In reality, this was not as drastic a change in H Section's operations as it might at first appear. In the maintenance of potential resistance contacts in 1941–1942, H Section had already become involved in intelligence gathering. Spaniards contacted by SOE were asked to monitor military activities and German and Italian involvement in Spain. As Harry Morris revealed, in spending more time collecting intelligence rather than planning for resistance activity, these agents were 'at present largely of use to [SIS]', yet they were on SOE's 'books' and it made little sense to let them go.[60] At the time, the head of H Section, Richardson, disagreed with Morris for he considered the maintenance of contacts to be primarily for the purposes of allowing Britain to know who the 'dissidents' were in the event of a German invasion and collection of intelligence was thus purely secondary.[61] In any event, by 1943, it was clear that the experience of intelligence gathering by SOE and its agents in Spain meant that a transformation of SOE's focus from resistance planning to gathering intelligence to assist potential economic warfare operations did not require the creation of a new organization from the ground up.

By September 1943, H Section's new directive to engage in economic intelligence gathering had been approved by the Foreign Office and MEW.[62] The MEW representative at the Madrid embassy, Hugh Ellis-Rees, was informed that the new directive was part and parcel of 'a full scale economic offensive against Axis commercial and economic activities in the Peninsula' and that the 'Foreign Office have now agreed that the stage has been reached where more drastic methods may be resorted to, and for this purpose S.O.E. are permitted to enter the field to assist and reinforce the overt activities of M.E.W.'[63] SOE was authorized to expand its activities in Spain, but in a way that was 'complementary' to the activities of Ellis-Rees and carried out with the full knowledge of the ambassador.[64] SOE's mission had changed, but it was not to be without the oversight of Hoare and the partnership of Ellis-Rees. The appointment of Morris as head of mission and the expansion of SOE personnel in Spain followed approval of the new directive.

One of the most significant areas of economic exploitation of the Iberian Peninsula engaged in by the Axis was in the acquisition of wolfram. Wolfram (or tungsten) is a metal of great strength, and over the course of the war, it became extremely valuable for the production of gun barrels and shell casings, as well as for aircraft parts. Wolfram mined in Spain and Portugal became vital for Nazi Germany, and the Allies worked furiously in both countries to deter the shipment of this mineral to the Axis, primarily through the means of pre-emptive purchasing and diplomatic and economic pressure on the two neutrals.[65] Even before the new directive for H Section was approved, SOE itself had targeted intelligence gathering about, and possible sabotage against, German illegal smuggling of wolfram as a major part of any economic warfare role it could play.[66]

The initial visit of an SOE agent, Major Mandestan, travelling under MEW cover, indicated that wolfram was primarily being smuggled from Portuguese and Spanish mines to France via the railway line running through the Spanish border town of Irun, where a major German storage facility (holding 800–1000 tons of wolfram) was located. Smuggling led to the total of actual German wolfram purchases in Spain being 500 tons in excess of officially negotiated limits. Irun and the surrounding area, therefore, seemed to be an excellent target for intelligence gathering and the 'unacknowledgeable' methods of subtle sabotage.[67]

Mandestan's report of August 1943 cleared the way for the creation and acceptance of the new directive and for the dispatch of Morris to Madrid. Yet Mandestan underlined that SOE's frustration with Foreign Office 'appeasement' of Spain had not disappeared, nor was it likely to. Hoare feared that any act deemed to be sabotage could 'seriously indispose the Spanish authorities towards us'. Even Ellis-Rees, MEW's Madrid representative, was hesitant about any 'active' plans, and speculated about a possible Spanish reaction to British interference with government or other officials, the most likely of which would be sanctions against Britain's 'pre-emptive' purchasing of Spanish wolfram.[68] Despite the fact that British Intelligence already had interfered in internal Spanish affairs, through the bribery of major-generals, fears about SOE's 'unacknowledgeable' activities remained. The Spanish government thus continued to trade legally and illegally in the belief that Britain would not force its hand and reduce what was in effect its biggest export-earning commodity.[69]

Nonetheless, by autumn of 1943, SOE-run networks of agents began to assist Ellis-Rees by providing information concerning German efforts to trade and smuggle wolfram out of Spain and into occupied France. At the end of December 1943, Morris arrived in Madrid to coordinate information gathering on wolfram with Ellis-Rees and the British government's official purchasing agent for wolfram, the United Kingdom Commercial Corporation (UKCC). By 1944, Anglo-American negotiations with Spain and the American oil embargo imposed on Spain in order to enforce a settlement seemed to offer the prospect of ending or limiting wolfram shipments to Germany.[70] Yet in the minds of many, a successful conclusion to negotiations only increased the likelihood that Germany would resort to underhand methods in order to secure wolfram, 'probably with the connivance of the Spaniards'.[71]

Hugh Ellis-Rees was clearly of this mind, and emphasized SOE's value as an intelligence-gathering organization.[72] In February 1944, he told Morris that while he still needed SOE to track any potential wolfram smuggling, the organization was to refrain from both sabotage operations and bribing Spanish officials. In fact, Ellis-Rees told Morris that when information regarding smuggling was in hand, 'all he has to do is to report the facts to the [Spanish] authorities who will take necessary action; no action by us is required'.[73] Adopting the methods of Hoare, using intelligence information to form the basis for diplomatic protests, Ellis-Rees changed the mission of H Section. This new-found confidence in Spanish attitudes towards German smuggling, combined with Hoare's long-standing view that SOE should do nothing to threaten good relations with Spain, reinforced the fate that H Section had long feared; there would not be any sort of 'active' role for this small group of agents who had signed up with the impression they would help 'set Europe ablaze'. Ellis-Rees eventually requested that Morris, in his capacity as Third Secretary of the Embassy, be given greater resources in order to act as Ellis-Rees' assistant responsible for wolfram, adopting an overt as well as a covert role in British efforts against smuggling. In the mind of the MEW official, such a position would maintain Morris, 'in the work he was meant to do'.[74] Whether or not Morris saw it this way, Ellis-Rees had started down the path toward advocating a new role for Special Operations Executive, one that gave new emphasis to the significance of economic intelligence gathering in neutral states.

The reinvention of SOE as an intelligence agency did not satisfy its agents' thirst for action. Harry Morris, for one, did not give up the idea of potential sabotage. He attempted, unsuccessfully, to coordinate his intelligence gathering with sabotage carried out by SOE agents inside France and continued to foster a network of Basques who might be willing to destroy rail and communication lines.[75] Intelligence gathering of the sort Ellis-Rees wanted done in the service of diplomacy represented for Morris 'pinpricks' against German smuggling, not significant 'opportunities' for the destruction of German wolfram stocks that sabotage would provide.[76]

Nonetheless, the work of tracking German wolfram smuggling did employ a number of SOE agents and sub-agents throughout northern Spain and was ongoing from the end of 1943. Moreover, in Morris' estimation, SOE agents were 'on the spot [and were] the only people in a position to know what is happening' with the wolfram situation in Spain.[77] While Morris organized his agents with the purpose of preparing for the eventuality of sabotage, Ellis-Rees and MEW were content to use intelligence as a lever in diplomatic talks with the Spanish Government. By February 1944, the five major roads from Irun to the French border were all being watched by SOE for German transports. In addition, plans were in the works to set up watching posts for the major roads from wolfram mining areas into Irun and attempts were being made to recruit informants and collaborators in Spanish Customs who might hold up German shipments of wolfram on the border. Subagents employed in the Irun area were primarily drawn from the underground Basque Nationalist movement, although they did not know they were working for the British Government in their scouting missions.[78] Contacts made with the Spanish customs service eventually identified officials responsible for all exports crossing into France from Irun. German agents paid these Spanish customs agents 5–10 pesetas per kilo of wolfram they allowed through; in response, British agents simply 'outbid' the Germans and halted such smuggling.

Eventually British agents in Irun were able to communicate with Spanish customs agents on a frequent basis. During one such visit they learnt of a major smuggling operation that occurred on 28 May 1944, when some 40 tons of wolfram were transferred from Irun to France over an unused bridge that crossed the border near the village of Behobia. At the time, this consignment represented the largest confirmed breach of the Allied-Spanish agreement on wolfram signed earlier in May and led the lead SOE agent in Irun, most likely Eric Picquet-Wicks, to conclude that the Franco government 'has no intention of implementing its bargain'.[79] This particular incident led Ellis-Rees to take diplomatic action in Madrid. He forced the Spanish customs authorities to admit that the incident had indeed occurred and the result was that the official German wolfram quota from Spain for June was cancelled.[80] This episode demonstrates on a small scale the importance of SOE operations to Allied economic warfare success in Spain.

SOE was not the only intelligence agency in Spain engaged in tracking wolfram smuggling. The Office of Strategic Services (OSS) of the US government also tracked shipments of wolfram across the French border, in addition to its many other intelligence-gathering activities similar to SIS work.[81] SOE and OSS had reached an agreement in June 1942 that limited OSS activity to French North Africa and Spanish Morocco, leaving Spain itself for the Foreign Office to set the terms of engagement, which limited SOE activities as described above.[82] Yet the OSS doubled the size of its Iberian operation in 1943, adding a number of agents in Spain itself, and these agents were involved in breaking up a number of smuggling rings, in cooperation with their 'British counterparts', presumably SIS as well as SOE.[83] The records of H Section suggest that there was some degree of coordination with OSS in the field, although it is impossible to assess how extensive or organized this was. American wolfram observers were involved in most Irun operations, and in the case of the Behobia smuggling incident, Morris expected to see reports from 'the American observer' at Irun, presumably an OSS agent, in addition to those from its own agents.[84] SOE's own agent in Irun implied that field coordination was common by describing in one report how he went out alone one night at 1 a.m. to track a smuggler, since 'at this hour it might be difficult to advise the American'.[85] The OSS also was able to receive reports from German sources about wolfram smuggling from its operation in Switzerland.[86] Undoubtedly the wolfram campaign was developed jointly by the United States and Great Britain as were other aspects of economic warfare in Spain, but beyond such suggestive reports, it is impossible to conclude anything definite about the scope and comprehensiveness of that cooperation.

The importance of economic intelligence in the fight against German wolfram acquisition is in many ways difficult to establish, given the lack of sources outside the records of H Section itself. In addition, intelligence was by no means the only aspect of Allied wolfram policy in 1943–1944, nor the most significant. Pre-emptive purchasing of wolfram by the United States and Great Britain remained the most significant way, over the course of 1943, in which German supplies were limited by Allied action.[87] Moreover, negotiations with the Franco government to limit Germany's ability to purchase wolfram, were pursued by both Allies, despite some significant disagreements between them, in the early part of 1944.[88] Yet as part of MEW's overall effort to ensure Spanish compliance with agreements made with the Allies after May 1944, SOE's intelligence was useful, and thus a judgement of the constructive value of SOE's contribution to Britain's wartime effort in Spain can be made. From within the files of H Section, the repeatedly positive assessments given SOE by Ellis-Rees, Britain's top wolfram expert in Madrid, are very convincing. Information gathered by SOE formed the basis of Ellis-Rees' diplomatic protests to the Spanish Government. The official British history of economic warfare notes that Allied negotiators in Spain made full use of the 'good information from their secret sources.'[89] Later, the intelligence gathered was used openly, in meetings between British and Spanish officials, in order to enforce the wolfram agreement. Although the sources are limited primarily to SOE's own files, arguably they point to an achievement on the part of H Section.

Not all of SOE's work was in the traditional cloak-and-dagger form of intelligence gathering. A significant part of SOE's wolfram work was done in the open. For example, Harry Morris worked openly as Ellis-Rees' assistant for economic warfare. In northern Spain, the lead agent, 'VS', desired an appointment as vice consul in Pamplona and Allied wolfram observer in Navarre. Such a position would allow him to engage in both 'official' and 'unofficial' activities aimed at curtailing smuggling. As a recognized British vice consul, he hoped to 'launch out as an official nuisance' given rights to inspect wolfram warehouses on a weekly basis, verify official road control papers at all regional checkpoints, and generally pressure local and provincial officials to do their job and prevent smuggling.[90] This particular appointment was blocked by the Spanish Ministry of Foreign Affairs, who deemed VS 'not suitable' for a position that put him so close to the French border.[91] Nonetheless, the incident again demonstrates the growth of economic intelligence work as a tool of diplomacy, and the growing acceptance of H Section to participate in such activities.

Despite the usefulness of such work for Great Britain's Spanish policy, it must be emphasized that SOE 'fell into' the world of economic intelligence gathering somewhat accidentally. Economic intelligence gathering in Spain had been initiated with the hope of 'discovering a means of interrupting the German wolfram supplies within the limited scope of S.O.E. activities permitted in Spain': it was soon discovered however, as an internal SOE memo put it, that SOE's information was 'an extremely valuable weapon in the hands of the representatives of M.E.W. in Madrid'.[92] Despite the importance of its intelligence work, H Section never completely abandoned the desire to engage in active sabotage, maintaining contact with the Basque movement on both sides of the border in the hope that destruction of German transports could be achieved.[93] In the weeks after the Allied invasion of France in June 1944, both sabotage plans and intelligence-gathering activities wound down as the Liberation of France made wolfram smuggling miniscule and not worthy of further pursuit by SOE.[94]

Special Operations Executive had carved out a valuable, if limited, role in the Allied wolfram campaign through the development of useful means to collect economic intelligence for use by British officials. Such a conclusion does not overlook the fact that the restrictions imposed upon SOE in neutral countries by the Foreign Office and other government agencies led to a sense of failure among most SOE operatives in the neutral and non-belligerent states.[95] Nor does it ignore that it was the course of the war, the German defeat in France, which ended illegal wolfram shipments from Iberia. Moreover, in the effort to break up Nazi smuggling, the Allies first and foremost pursued two policies – pre-emptive purchasing and direct negotiations with the Franco Government. Even if not of primary importance, however, intelligence gathering of the sort carried out by H Section was useful to the mission of MEW and the Foreign Office in Spain. For SOE, though, success, even on a small scale, was to be fleeting. Intelligence gathering, strictly defined, was the responsibility of SOE's rival agency, SIS, and conflicts did arise, forcing Ellis-Rees at one point to return to London in order to defend the work of H Section in support of MEW's wolfram mission.[96] A more serious challenge to SOE's economic intelligence-gathering apparatus was made by SIS when H Section made a claim for involvement in SAFEHAVEN, the Allied plans for the uncovering of Nazi Germany's hidden assets throughout neutral Europe. From August 1944, SOE officials in London and Madrid saw a unique opportunity to build on the experience of wolfram tracking that would result, they hoped, in a definition of a post-hostilities economic intelligence role for SOE.[97] Yet opposition from SIS resulted in SOE intelligence-gathering operations being placed under the authority of an SIS station chief in Madrid and led, by January 1945, to an almost non-existent role for H Section in Spain.[98] On 19 July 1945, Special Operations Executive in Iberia was wound up.[99]

The conditions that neutral Spain found itself in during the Second World War, and the constraints imposed upon Special Operations Executive by British policy towards the Franco regime, forced H Section to exist in a state of constant flux. Drawn to Spain by the necessity to prepare for possible Resistance and sabotage operations in the same way that SOE sections across Europe took their mandate to 'set Europe ablaze' to heart, H Section started out with many ambitious pro-jects. Yet the realities of the diplomatic path pursued by the British ambassador Samuel Hoare and the Foreign Office and the absence of any German invasion or occupation of the Iberian Peninsula meant that for the most part contacts made were not mobilized for direct action. Thus H Section found itself needing to move away from the strict definition of its mandate and develop new operations and new roles, to find a way to survive even if it meant going 'against the grain' in terms of its own organizational mandate. The most successful of these came in the realm of economic intelligence gathering, primarily in support of the Allied campaign against German smuggling of wolfram from Iberia. Even here, success was frustrating, marginal and ultimately short-lived. In the end, Harry Morris concluded that SOE's intelligence gathering would not stand up in comparison with the work of SIS; at best, SOE would only seem like a 'poor relative at the rich man's table'.[100]

Acknowledgements

The author would like to acknowledge the support of the Faculty Development Fund at Carroll College in preparation of this chapter. For assistance, suggestions and thorough and constructive comments, I am grateful to Lorne Breitenlohner, Denis Smyth, Neville Wylie and the anonymous referees of *Intelligence & National Security*.

Notes

1   Paul Preston, *Franco: A Biography* (London, 1995), p. 404.
2   Elena Hernández-Sandoica and Enrique Moradiellos, 'Spain and the Second World War, 1939–1945', in Neville Wylie (ed.), *European Neutrals and Non-Belligerents During the Second World War* (Cambridge, 2002), pp. 251–253.
3   Javier Tussell, *Franco, España y la II Guerra Mundial: Entre el Eje y la Neutralidad* (Madrid, 1995), p. 13.
4   Preston, *Franco*, p. 500; Manuel Ros Agudo, *La guerra secreta de Franco* (Barcelona, 2002), p. 331.
5   For the extent of German involvement in Spain, see Ros Agudo, *Guerra secreta*; for the activities of pro-Nazi Spaniards, see Wayne H. Bowen, *Spaniards and Nazi Germany: Collaboration in the New Order* (Columbia, MO, 2000).
6   Denis Smyth, *Diplomacy and Strategy of Survival: British Policy and Franco's Spain, 1940–41* (Cambridge, 1986), p. 3.
7   Ibid., p. 4.
8   Denis Smyth, 'Screening "Torch": Allied Counter-Intelligence and the Spanish Threat to the Secrecy of the Allied Invasion of French North Africa in November, 1942', *Intelligence & National Security* 4/2 (1989): 342.
9   Anthony Cave Brown, *'C': The Secret Life of Sir Stewart Graham Menzies, Spymaster to Winston Churchill* (New York, 1987), p. 295.
10 W. J. M. Mackenzie, *The Secret History of SOE: The Special Operations Executive, 1940–1945* (London, 2000), p. 241; M. R. D. Foot, *SOE in France: An Account of the Work of the British Special Operations Executive in France, 1940–1944* (London, 1966), p. 94.
11 Mackenzie, *SOE*, p. 322.
12 David Stafford, *Britain and European Resistance, 1940–1945: A Survey of Special Operations Executive, with Documents* (London and Toronto, 1980), p. 55; see also Neville Wylie, '"An Amateur Learns his Job?" Special Operations Executive in Portugal, 1940–2', *Journal of Contemporary History* 36/3 (2001): 443.
13 Report on Spain, Portugal and North Africa, Richardson to Hambro, 10 April 1943, The National Archive. United Kingdom, Public Record Office (hereafter PRO) HS6/957.
14 Stafford, *Britain and European Resistance*, p. 56; and Nigel West, *Secret War: The Story of SOE, Britain's Wartime Sabotage Organisation* (London, 1993), pp. 60, 100.
15 Denis Smyth, 'Les Chevaliers de Saint-George: La Grande-Bretagne et la corruption des généraux espagnols (1940–1942)', *Guerres mondiales et conflits contemporains* 162 (1991): 36.
16 Ralph Erskine, 'Eavesdropping on "Bodden": ISOS v. the Abwehr in the Straits of Gibraltar', *Intelligence & National Security* 12/3 (1997): 110–129.
17 Ibid., p. 123.
18 Kim Philby, *My Silent War* (New York, 2002 edn.), p. 56.
19 Ibid., p. 57.
20 F. H. Hinsley and C. A. G. Simkins, *British Intelligence in the Second World War*. Vol. IV *Security and Counter-Intelligence* (Oxford, 1990), p. 161.
21 David A. Messenger, 'Fighting for Relevance: Economic Intelligence and Special Operations Executive in Spain, 1943–1945', *Intelligence & National Security* 15/3 (2000): 33–54.
22 Report on Spain, Portugal and North Africa, Richardson to Hambro, 10 April 1943, PRO HS6/957.
23 Ibid.
24 Ibid.
25 Ibid.

26 Mackenzie, *SOE*, pp. 32–33.
27 Stafford, *Britain*, p. 56.
28 'Acción que el Intelligence Service prepara con militares rojos que collaboran con de Gaulle', 12 September 1941, in Fundación Nacional Francisco Franco, *Documentos Inéditos para la Historia del Generalissimo Franco*. vol. II-2 (Madrid: Fundación Nacional Francisco Franco) 1992), pp. 339–340.
29 PRO HS6/957, Report on Spain, Portugal and North Africa, Richardson to Hambro, 10 April 1943.
30 Stafford, *Britain*, p. 56.
31 PRO HS6/931, Memo for Assistant Director of Planning, 15 July 1941.
32 PRO HS6/931, Minutes of Meeting, 24 July 1941, forwarded to Chief of SOE 26 July 1941 (marginal notes).
33 For a brief description of BODDEN and British debates concerning sabotage, see Smyth, 'Screening "Torch"', pp. 338–344.
34 PRO HS6/963, AD/P to L/B.2, 16 May 1942.
35 PRO Special Operations Executive/North Africa (HS3), 203, Hanbury Williams to Morris, 4 Sept. 1942.
36 PRO HS3/203. Letter to Chiefs of Staff, 29 Sept. 1942; Memo to Hanbury Williams, 1 Oct. 1942.
37 PRO C[hiefs] O[f] S[taff] (43)142(0) in CAB 80/68. Cited by Stafford, *Britain*, p. 255.
38 Mackenzie, *SOE*, p. 323.
39 Tussell, *Franco: España y la II Guerra Mundial*, p. 362.
40 Hambro to Col. Capel-Dunn, 15 March 1943, PRO HS6/963.
41 SOE Reports 15 March 1943, PRO CAB121/307.
42 Report on Spain, Portugal and North Africa, Richardson to Hambro, 10 April 1943, PRO HS6/957.
43 D/AIR to Deputy Chief of SOE, 13 April 1943, PRO HS6/963.
44 David J. Dunthorn, *Britain and the Spanish Anti-Franco Opposition, 1940–1950* (London, 2002), pp. 21–22.
45 Ibid., p. 21.
46 Report on Spain, Portugal and North Africa, Richardson to Hambro, 10 April 1943, PRO HS6/957.
47 Richardson letter, 16 Jan. 1942, PRO HS6/932.
48 Denis Smyth, 'Les Chevaliers de Saint-George'.
49 Dunthorn, *Spanish Anti-Franco Opposition*, p. 38.
50 Report on Spain, Portugal and North Africa, Richardson to Hambro, 10 April 1943, PRO HS6/957.
51 Ibid.
52 'Statement of Services Performed by Emilio Baras Canal, Sept–Dec. 1941', 1 Jan. 1942. PRO HS6/932.
53 'Draft Directive for Future Policy', 25 July 1943, PRO HS6/963.
54 Dunthorn, *Spanish Anti-Franco Opposition*, p. 39.
55 'Draft Directive for Future Policy', 25 July 1943, PRO HS6/963.
56 Messenger, 'Fighting for Relevance', pp. 40–41.
57 'Draft Directive for Future Policy', 25 July 1943, PRO HS6/963.
58 Ibid.
59 Report of Colonel Franck on Mission to Portugal, included in Hambro to Mockler-Ferryman, 5 June 1943, PRO HS6/981.
60 Morris to Richardson, 18 Dec. 1942, PRO HS6/932.
61 Richardson to Morris, 17 Jan. 1943, PRO HS6/932.
62 Richardson to Deputy Chief of SOE, 9 Sept. 1943, PRO HS6/963.
63 Selborne to Ellis-Rees, 10 Sept. 1943, PRO HS6/963.
64 Ibid.

65   For Allied and Axis policies concerning Iberian wolfram, see Christian Leitz, *Economic Relations between Nazi Germany and Franco's Spain, 1936–1945* (Oxford, 1996), pp. 170–199 and 'Nazi Germany's Struggle for Spanish Wolfram during the Second World War', *European History Quarterly* 25/1 (1995): 71–92; James Cortada, *United States-Spanish Relations, Wolfram and World War II* (Barcelona, 1971); W. N. Medlicott, *The Economic Blockade*, vol. II (London, 1959), pp. 305–313, 557–581; Donald G. Stevens, 'World War II Economic Warfare: The United States, Britain and Portuguese Wolfram', *Historian* (Spring 1999): 539–556; Douglas L. Wheeler, 'The Price of Neutrality: Portugal, the Wolfram Question and World War II', *Luso-Brazilian Review* 23/1 and 23/2 (1986): 107–122, 97–111.

66   Mandestan to Richardson, 14 Aug. 1943, PRO HS6/981; see also Messenger, 'Fighting for Relevance', pp. 37–38.

67   Mandestan to Richardson, 14 Aug. 1943, PRO HS6/981.

68   Ibid.

69   Leitz, *Economic Relations*, p. 185.

70   Ibid, pp. 188–190.

71   'SOE Monthly Report'. Jan. 1944, PRO CAB121/207.

72   Ibid.

73   Morris to Richardson, 7 Feb. 1944, PRO HS6/981.

74   Ellis-Rees to Selborne, 21 March 1944, PRO HS6/981.

75   Messenger, 'Fighting for Relevance', pp. 39–41.

76   Morris to Head, 18 Jan. 1944, PRO HS6/981.

77   Morris to Head, 7 Feb. 1944, PRO HS6/981.

78   Morris to Head, 10 Feb. 1944, PRO HS6/981.

79   VS to Morris, 18 June 1944, PRO HS6/982; Eric Picquet-Wicks is identified in HS6/982 'Notes on Removal of Wolfram from Irun to Madrid', n.d.

80   Wolfram Coup', Memo, 25 July 1944, PRO HS6/982; see a brief description of this episode in Medlicott, *Economic Blockade*, p. 580.

81   National Archives and Record Administration, College Park, MD (hereafter NARA), OSS Records- RG226, 313, Frank T. Ryan, 'OSS Activities in the Iberian Peninsula', April 1944–July 1945.

82   Dunthorn, *Spanish Anti-Franco Opposition*, p. 37.

83   NARA, RG 226, 313, Frank T. Ryan, 'OSS Activities in the Iberian Peninsula', April 1944–July 1945.

84   Morris to Head, 21 June 1944, PRO HS6/982.

85   VS to Morris, 4 July 1944, PRO HS6/982.

86   See, for example, NARA RG 226/Microfilm M1642, Donovan to Roosevelt, 24 July 1944 and Donovan to Dunn, 6 July 1944.

87   Leitz, *Economic Relations*, p. 180; Medlicott, *Economic Blockade*, pp. 559–560.

88   Leitz, *Economic Relations*, p. 190, Medlicott, *Economic Blockade*, pp. 563–576.

89   Medlicott, *Economic Blockade*, p. 579.

90   VS to Morris, 18 June 1944, PRO HS6/982.

91   Morris to Head, 21 June 1944, PRO HS6/982.

92   'Wolfram Coup' Memo, 21 July 1944, PRO HS6/982.

93   Messenger, 'Fighting for Relevance', p. 42.

94   Head to Morris, 17 Aug. 1944, PRO HS6/982.

95   Wylie, 'An Amateur', pp. 456–457.

96   Messenger, 'Fighting for Relevance', pp. 43–44.

97   Ibid, pp. 45–46.

98   Ibid, pp. 49–50.

99   Gubbins to Blake, 19 July 1945, PRO HS6/929.

100   Morris to Mockler-Ferryman, 24 Nov. 1944, PRO HS6/929.

10 SOE's foreign currency transactions

Christopher J. Murphy

The subject of SOE's dealings in foreign currency during the Second World War has become inextricably tied to the name of Walter Fletcher. Fletcher has acquired a reputation as SOE's financial wizard in the Far East, who was single-handedly responsible for the acquisition of foreign currency to such an extent that SOE ended its life firmly in the black. In one of the first works written on SOE, Professor William Mackenzie noted that Fletcher was 'responsible for all SOE's vast and curious dealings in foreign currencies', while more recent accounts, assisted by material included in the first set of SOE papers released to the Public Record Office in June 1993, have effectively cemented the subject within the geographical context of SOE's Far Eastern operations.[1] Yet Walter Fletcher's dealings in the Far East were but one, admittedly significant, facet of SOE's foreign currency transactions. By the time Fletcher's fertile mind had dreamt up the 'Remorse' operations, which began in earnest in 1944, SOE already had a considerable history of foreign currency dealings, masterminded by its Director of Finance, John Venner, which earned it the appreciation of both the Bank of England and the Treasury.

The outbreak of war was accompanied by new legislation governing the acquisition and use of foreign currency, as the important role foreign currency would play in Britain's war effort was quickly made apparent with the shortage of American dollars for the purchase of essential supplies. As Churchill wrote to President Roosevelt in 1940: 'The moment approaches when we shall no longer be able to pay cash for shipping and other supplies.'[2] Such a shortage came as little surprise to the Bank of England which, from 1938, had concerned itself with the availability of various foreign currencies and how these could be replenished in a wartime scenario. It had developed a reputation of being 'quick to warn – and upon occasion to act – when it thought that Britain's exchange reserves were being frittered away'. The Bank continued to impress its concerns upon Whitehall during 1939 through its representative on an inter-departmental Exchange Difficulties and Essential Materials Committee, who urged 'stronger pronouncements on exchange shortages'. Little action, however, appears to have been taken until war was imminent. The Bank had long foreseen that, in the event of war, foreign currency would 'have to be severely rationed from the start', and on 25 August the Defence (Finance) Regulations were passed.[3] Amended on 3 September, the Regulations restricted dealings in foreign exchange, certain authorised banks being allowed to issue foreign exchange to traders, 'according to certain standard principles designed to limit sales to essential needs', while those in possession of foreign currency were required to hand it over to the authorities.[4] In addition, following the outbreak of war, the Cabinet established an inter-departmental Exchange Requirements Committee, with responsibility for approving all requests for expenditure by government departments that involved the use of foreign currency.[5]

While the dollar problem was overcome through Lend-Lease, supplies of various other foreign currencies inevitably continued to dwindle as the war continued, despite measures to ensure that Britain's reserves of these currencies were not used unnecessarily. By 1942, needs for such currency were causing concern at the Bank: an internal memo noted that the problem was not 'providing small amounts of . . . dollars or escudos for persons travelling on official Government missions', but rather 'the demands of Service Departments and various secret organisations', the main buyers of foreign currency notes for 'special purposes' being the War Office, Admiralty and what the memo described as 'three distinct groups of "special friends"'.[6] While the exact nature of these 'special purposes' is obscure, it is clear that foreign currency was needed in particular to provide 'purses' for escape purposes, which required considerable amounts in small denominations.[7] Although the problem of replenishing supplies of foreign currency was not new in 1942 (as early as August 1940, the Bank encountered particularly difficulties in acquiring Danish kroner[8]), it was only at this stage of the war that Whitehall began to appreciate the extent of the Bank's difficulties. An internal Bank memo of January noted the belief that the problem had been caused in large part by a lack of foresight on the part of government departments themselves:

> We have already experienced in this war the consequences of lack of imagi-
> nation; in the early days Reichsmark notes were in plentiful supply in this
> country but, in spite of advice to the contrary, they were turned down by the
> thousand by various Government Departments because they had no immediate
> use for them. There is now, and has been for some time past, a constant demand
> for them – they can still be got but they cost gold and dollars.

In addition to the difficulty in obtaining foreign currency, the memo expressed the Bank's unhappiness with the procedure for its distribution among the main buyers, which was complicated by secrecy:

> The secrecy question appears to play such an important part that it actually
> happens from time to time that I have to buy notes from one Department
> in order to sell them to another! . . . It seems to me that a very useful purpose
> would be served if we could centralise the business here and cut out much of
> the 'left hand not knowing what the right hand is doing'.[9]

In May, Charles Lockitt of the Bank's Dealing and Accounts Office prepared an estimate of the likely demand for foreign currency for 'special purposes' in the short term, indicating where demand would overtake supply. He noted that the Bank held adequate reserves of French francs (approximately 65 million), with estimated requirements for the next six months standing at 35 million. Lockitt described the Bank's holding of Norwegian kroner as 'negligible', but pointed out that the War Office had 'been able to make their own arrangements with the Norwegian Government and other demands on us are not likely to be very heavy'. The deterioration of the position regarding Dutch florin was a cause of concern, as Lockitt did not believe that any action could be taken to rectify this situation:

> Our biggest demands come from the War Office who usually require their notes in denominations of 10 florins and, unfortunately, the Royal Netherlands Government which is our only source of supply, have now virtually run out of notes of this denomination.

Lockitt considered the Belgian franc position to be 'quite satisfactory', going on to note that 'Reichsmarks, Italian lire and Danish kroner have all been covered by the Service Departments themselves. Swedish kroner is a rather hand to mouth business but I know of no potential demands of any size.' A 'steady demand' was still received for Spanish pesetas, and it was unclear whether a recent attempt to purchase one million pesetas had been successful; even if it had, Lockitt did not believe such an amount would last very long. The greatest problem concerned Portuguese escudos, where the position was 'very difficult':

> We now have only a holding of 120,000 escudos and it is only a month since we asked the Banco de Portugal to send us half a million on the old plea of travellers' requirements, etc. The War Office have just given us an order for one and a half million, of which we only executed 600,000. I understand they are likely to require the balance some time or another and it is difficult to know where they can be obtained, especially as it would not be wise to increase our demands on the Banco de Portugal.[10]

The position regarding the acquisition of Danish kroner to 'certain friends of ours' began to concern the Bank in June, as existing channels were drying up. A secret memorandum noted that 'the people concerned have, I gather, got enough to last them for another three or four months, but the outlook beyond that is not good'.[11]

The War Office began to take a greater interest in the foreign currency situation later in the month, its implications having hit home due to the fact that the Dealing and Accounts Office had been forced to tell the War Office 'that the day was rapidly approaching when we should be unable to execute their orders for unstamped guilder notes of low denominations'. The War Office proceeded to prepare a paper on the subject, which outlined the problems being faced by the Bank, its main purpose being 'to see whether a meeting of the parties concerned could not be held in order to obtain as concrete an idea as possible of future requirements in order to enable the necessary steps to satisfy these requirements to be taken in good time'.[12] That the War Office was beginning to appreciate the situation must have come as some relief to the Bank, where a further secret internal memo noted that the 'special channel whereby we were able to exchange Norwegian kroner notes of large denominations . . . for notes of smaller denominations, for which there is always a demand for special purposes' had dried up, prompting the gloomy fore-cast that 'the time is coming when the Norwegian kroner situation will be as difficult as that of the Dutch guilder'. Yet demands for Norwegian kroner continued to be received: an official at the Dealing and Accounts Officer noted the latest estimated orders for the currency: 'requirements for my "special friends" over the next three months amount to about half-a-million kroner and, in addition, War Office requirements for normal expenditure will probably approach this figure'.[13]

Hope of new avenues whereby Norwegian kroner could be obtained was provided by SOE's Director of Finance, John Venner. Prior to the war, a chartered accountant at Edward Moore & Sons, John Franklyn Venner joined SOE in October 1940 and quickly proceeded to take firm control over the organisation's financial affairs. On 29 October, he wrote to CD, Sir Frank Nelson, proposing that henceforth all applications to the Treasury for funding should be channelled through him, a move with which Nelson concurred.[14] By May 1942, Venner was responsible for SOE's expenditure of over £2 million per year.[15] He was assisted by a small staff which, by the summer of 1942, consisted of three further chartered accountants, an RAF accounts officer and a secretary.[16] Venner played a highly significant role in nurturing financial confidence in SOE. His name became known 'throughout all the Government Departments, the Bank of England and the Treasury', and he was 'highly respected and trusted'.[17] In June 1942, when interviewed as part of the investigation into SOE carried out by John Hanbury-Williams and Edward Playfair, a representative of the Bank of England stated that the Bank 'had con-fidence in Venner and trusted him', while the note of an interview with a Treasury official recorded that the Treasury was 'quite satisfied on the financial side' of SOE under Venner.[18]

Venner contacted the Bank's Dealings and Accounts Office in June and informed them that he had the opportunity 'of acquiring Norwegian kroner notes in Stockholm', requesting their permission to go ahead with the transaction.[19] This contact acts as a prelude to SOE's considerable involvement in providing a more stable, long-term solution to the problem of obtaining foreign exchange. Venner later recorded that an inter-departmental meeting was held in July 1942 – pre-sumably a result of the War Office intervention noted above – of 'all those who were concerned in the acquisition of foreign currency notes for their particular purposes with the view to the co-ordination of purchasing, the building up of reserves and the fair distribution between the users'. Venner acknowledged the Bank's concern that, while departments were capable of assisting each other 'from time to time in a somewhat haphazard fashion', for the most part they were, 'through absence of co-ordinated effort, necessarily competing against each other in neutral countries which provided sources for obtaining currency'. As a consequence of the meeting, further monthly meetings at the Bank of England were inaugurated, at which 'the available stocks, the sources for purchasing and the individual requirements of each Department' were discussed. Very soon SOE, which Venner noted had proved capable of dealing 'efficiently with its own needs' up to this point, emerged as the department responsible for 'obtaining through devious means in neutral capitals . . . those currencies of which no stocks existed in this country and which could not be obtained through any normal channel'. The currencies in greatest demand were Dutch gulden, Danish kroner, Norwegian kroner, German reichsmarks, Spanish pesetas and Argentine pesos. The need for specific denominations was as important as the currency itself; small denominations were in great demand, a particular requirement of purses. As such, SOE 'had to set its mind on developing and increasing the machinery, already created for supplying its own needs, to the extent necessary to cope as far as possible with the demands of all'.[20] An internal Bank of England memo dated 25 July highlights the immediate results of SOE's involvement:

> Since the arrangement recently made that purchases in 'black' markets should be concentrated with Venner's organisation we have obtained:
>
> (a) Escudos ½ million at a rate of 100 against sterling payments in London, (partly to resident account and partly to a Sterling Area Account). (Cost £5,000).
> (b) Florins 50,000 at a rate of 19.60 (these were bought against further escudos purchased as in (a) above. (Cost £2,550).[21]

Further details of the positive impact SOE made on the situation are to be found in reports prepared by Venner. In July 1943, Venner noted that 'apart from small denomination notes of certain occupied countries which are required by air crews, which need cannot be satisfied even from all the sources available and fully exploited, the needs of all have been adequately met'.[22] He provided a breakdown of the amounts SOE had obtained:

Argentine Pesos	500,000
Danish Kroner	127,150
Dutch Gulden	1,879,325
French Francs	3,000,000
German Reichsmarks	4,456,150
Norwegian Kroner	1,458,162
Portuguese Escudos	1,100,000
Spanish Pesetas	7,366,387
Swedish Kroner	207,990[23]

A further success concerned the cost in sterling of the transactions. Venner noted that £391,000 had been spent in total, a figure that should have been considerably higher, as in 'practically all cases' the currency had been obtained and sold 'at rates far below the official or "fixed" rates':

> the Dutch Gulden were obtained for £95,000 representing an average rate of nearly 20 to the £ as against the 'fixed rate' of 7.28 to the £, a sterling difference

of over £150,000, and the Spanish Pesetas were obtained for £96,000 at an average rate of over 75 to the £ as against the 'free market' rate of 40.50 to the £, a sterling difference of over £80,000.[24]

Problems with the system began to emerge in the spring of 1943, as efforts by various exiled governments to secure foreign exchange in Lisbon came to the attention of the Bank of England. An internal memo written in April noted that 'we must endeavour to keep the Allies right out of the Lisbon market by undertaking ourselves to provide them so far as possible with the currencies they require', 'Uncoordinated competitive bidding for increasing quantities on a narrow market', it concluded, 'is the very best way of ensuring that nobody will get all he wants when he wants it. It is also the best way of buying currencies at the wrong price.'[25] The Bank had its way. Venner recorded that during the summer of 1943 efforts were made to extend the pooling system 'so as to embrace all the activities of the Allied Governments, certain of which have continued to obtain their requirements in neutral countries thus competing with purchases on behalf of the "Bank of England Pool"', and acknowledging that this would inevitably mean 'an expansion of the business for which S.O.E. is at present responsible'.[26]

It is clear, then, that SOE's dealings in foreign currency were not limited to the Far East, as the existing literature suggests. While the practical details as to how such financial transactions took place have not entered the public domain (if these papers have survived), a broad outline of the procedure, written by Venner, has been released to the PRO in edited form. The first step was to obtain neutral currency, which there was 'little or no chance of obtaining . . . other than by unacknowledgeable means which disclosed no evidence of breaches of the laws of, or existing Agreements with, the States concerned'. This was then exchanged for the currency required. Details of the main means by which SOE went on to exchange this neutral currency have been blanked out, but in addition to these, SOE also employed 'various commercial and financial transactions whereby the currencies are obtained against payments in sterling or other currency easily obtained', including 'the purchase of Reichsmarks smuggled into Turkey by Chinese refugees against payment of Rupees in India to the Chinese Consul and the acquisition of Argentine Pesos through New York and Uruguay necessitating the use, as cover, of what purported to be a Land Company in the latter country'.[27]

While Venner dispatched orders to SOE officers in Stockholm, Lisbon and Tangier, it is likely that Lisbon proved to be the most significant area in which SOE carried out its currency transactions, much of the work falling upon its Iberian (H) section. An indication of the Section's growing responsibility for obtaining foreign currency can be seen in its accounts for 1942. Entries for Foreign Currency appear from January onwards, although at this point the acquisition is limited to pesetas and French francs. The accounts for May–June reveal the purchase of 25,000 Dutch guilder for Venner, while during June–July 87,515 Dutch florins were obtained, along with 597 Norwegian kroner and 360 Danish kroner.[28] The difficult position of the Bank of England was highlighted in a letter from the Head of SOE's Portugal Mission, P. W. Homberger (HA) to the Head of H Section in June

1942. The Bank of Portugal allowed the Bank of England to purchase escudos only at a privileged rate and 'on the express condition that they are exclusively applied in payment for goods or services originating in Portuguese territories'. The Bank of England was not 'entitled to buy escudos at the unfavourable free rate outside the terms of the agreement' in order to obtain foreign currency. As such, there was 'no legitimate method' whereby the Bank could satisfy the demands being made upon it by government departments.[29] Homberger wrote further on the subject in July, when he drew attention to the difficulties created by the ever watchful eyes of the Bank of Portugal:

(a) All drawings of escudos through an Embassy or Legation account are looked on with great suspicion by the Portuguese because on the face of it they have a political flavour.
(b) All transactions by any bank in excess of £50 have to be reported to the Bank of Portugal. Consequently any big transactions for the account of any foreign bank or any private individual are reported to the Bank of Portugal.
(c) The Bank of Portugal is trying to prevent inflation and is not in favour of any transactions which involve increasing the note circulation in Portugal by any substantial amount. There is in practice (though not, I believe, in law) a rationing system for escudo drawings and consequently Embassies, Legations and institutions such as the United Kingdom Commercial Cooperation (U.K.C.C.) are limited in their drawings.[30]

Homberger was concerned for the future acquisition of escudos:

(d) Owing to this rationing system all departments who are in need of escudos for any purpose, whether clandestine or otherwise, are really competing against each other. If U.K.C.C. of Ministry of Economic Warfare draw a million pounds' worth of escudos over a particular period it automatically makes it harder for other departments to get their requirements.
(e) The vast majority of escudo drawings for clandestine purposes has nothing to do with Portuguese problems but is destined for the purchase of foreign currencies, such as Reichmarks, French francs, Swiss francs, Belgian francs, Moroccan francs or pesetas.
(f) I believe that the problem will get worse rather than simpler in future because the War Office and other service departments are likely to place big orders for foreign currencies, particularly with a view to a possible second front.

While Homberger noted that SOE's own needs in terms of escudos were 'comparatively small', he emphasised that existing procedure would not work on the larger scale necessary if SOE was to provide for the needs of other government departments: 'In considering large scale transactions it must be remembered that they are viewed with suspicion by the Portuguese . . . if they are to be done through some official channel some reasonable explanation must be given.'[31] As such, more devious methods were required; later in the month, Homberger wrote of the need to establish or acquire a 'firm or company to assist in financial operations, including running an account for purposes of foreign exchange'. A member of the Lisbon Mission, T. P. M. Waite (HY), came to an arrangement with Graham Jr & Co, a 'large port firm who also dabble in general export and import'. While Graham himself was considered to be 'slightly indiscreet', Waite noted that it was worth taking a chance as the sums obtainable were 'considerable'. It is clear that transactions with Graham's took place, beginning a useful relationship whereby SOE acquired escudos. Waite wrote to Venner on 8 July, attaching 'a letter from W/Graham Jnr. & Co. confirming the agreement entered into'. He noted that, 'I have been promised another £10,000 for the end of this month but after that there will be a lull of about two months owing to the slack season here but there will thereafter be, if all goes well, transactions of some £20,000 monthly.' Venner was satisfied with the arrangements, noting that 'it seems to me that the existing sources which HY has found for obtaining Escudos in Lisbon against sterling will, if all goes well, amply supply our Escudo needs including those for buying certain foreign currencies as we require and which are available in Lisbon'.[32] Waite, however, did not rest, noting that he would continue the search for further firms who would agree to 'supply our requirements both so admirably and so discreetly'.[33]

As noted above, acquiring escudos was but the first step towards obtaining foreign currencies. On the second step, the exchange of escudos, information is more vague. Waite informed Venner of some of the practical details concerning the acquisition of such currency on 31 July, referring to his contacts simply as 'the racket':

> The racket's office here, on receiving an order, cables either Sweden or Switzerland or both to find out the quantities available and the rate, the latter depending upon the demand and also upon the possibilities of their reimbursement . . . There is no question of the office here haggling about the rate offered by their Swedish or Swiss office. They either have to take it or leave it, which is understandable if one takes into account the risk entailed in smuggling the currencies out of their countries of origin to Sweden or Switzerland, and then smuggling them through to here.

Waite noted the obvious point that 'If one of their lines gets blown the price of the affected currency naturally increases'. He went on to note that: 'The racket is usually beaten down a tostao (Esc.0$10) by us on large amounts purchased when it does not even make the customary 1% profit which is taken for granted here on all dealings in foreign exchange.'[34]

While there is no evidence with which to pin down the identity of 'the racket', it is clear that SOE's Escape Section, DF, was also involved in the acquisition of foreign currency.[35] DF Section established a financial network in Lisbon, which was primarily concerned with the 'distribution of money inside occupied Europe, according to instructions originating from London' – the smuggling of money on behalf of various Country Sections to their agents. However, the Section also carried out further work for Venner, a reference being made to foreign currency dealings which were carried out by DF Section 'as agents of the financial specialist at H.Q.'. While H Section was concerned with the acquisition of escudos, it can be suggested that DF Section took at least partial responsibility for using these to acquire further foreign exchange, such dealings being described as 'more or less straightforward foreign exchange transactions between two banks in two neutral countries who are willing to deal in foreign exchange without insisting on a written contract'.[36]

Venner made efforts to ensure that the considerable success achieved by SOE in terms of foreign currency dealing was not overlooked by the upper echelons of SOE.[37] In July 1943, he prepared a paper for Lord Selborne 'in connection with foreign currency purchases during the past year'. Venner took the opportunity

> [to] record the high tribute which I think is due to those S.O.E. personnel in the Field who, in addition to performing the duties primarily laid down for their Missions, have carried out with such admirable results these financial transactions in accordance with the directives received from London.

He went on to note that:

> These activities of S.O.E. hardly see the 'light of day' but I can assure you that they are very highly appreciated by the Treasury, the Bank of England and those who participate in the results, and that the Bank of England have learnt that when something is required which can only be obtained by some means of which they would have to be ashamed or which would involve them in the loss of their good name they have only to send for S.O.E.[38]

Venner saw the activity as one that was to SOE's credit, and pressed for its inclusion in Selborne's reports to Churchill. He wrote to Selborne's Private Secretary on 29 December, referring to 'our conversation yesterday regarding the possible inclusion in S.O's report to the Prime Minister on S.O.E.'s activities during the quarter ending 31st December 1943 of a paragraph regarding the obtaining of foreign currencies for the Bank of England pool'. Venner complained that 'no reference to such financial activities has appeared in previous reports'. To rectify the situation, Venner set out a short paragraph detailing all activity during the final three months of 1943:

> The quarter was, in fact, a record one and S.O.E. were successful in procuring for the Bank of England pool . . . foreign currency notes to the value of up- wards of £275,000, for which neutral currencies had first to be obtained in the form of cash. The currency notes delivered to the Bank included 75-million French Francs, 2-million Danish Kroner and 2¼-million Norwegian Kroner. S.O.E. was also able to supply the War Office, prior to the actual operation and with the maximum degree of security, with 3¼-million Escudos required in connection with the landings in the Azores.[39]

The paragraph was not included in Selborne's quarterly report, which retained its traditional geographical breakdown, however, Selborne was soon able to put the information to good use, in the aftermath of the Joint Intelligence Committee enquiry into SOE which followed the revelations of enemy penetration in Holland. As Foot notes, events in Holland had 'provided an excuse for SOE's enemies . . . to combine to try to crush it': enemies which included SIS and Bomber Command.[40] An inquiry into SOE by the JIC followed which produced a highly critical report. In response, Selborne prepared a paper for the Defence Committee which balanced the JIC's negative appraisal by highlighting the successes SOE had achieved. Here, SOE's involvement in the acquisition of significant sums of foreign currency was given special prominence – not least, because SOE's 'enemies' were among the main recipients of the foreign currency obtained. Selborne noted that:

> As I have shown in sections 18 and 19 of the Annex, S.O.E. has done much useful work of a non-military character at the request of other Government Departments, and it would be folly to scrap the possibility of this being continued. I would particularly like to draw the attention of my colleagues to sections 18, 19 and 20 of the Annex.[41]

Section 19 of the Annex dealt with the acquisition of foreign currency, the details having been provided by Venner.[42] Selborne emphasised the importance of this particular SOE activity to the war effort:

> S.O.E. have been the principal and in many cases the sole suppliers of foreign currency notes which are either in short supply or non-existent in this country, and which are needed urgently by the Service Departments, S.I.S. and others, the principal users being the Air Ministry who require large quantities of small denomination notes for 'purses' for air crews for escape purposes.

Following a detailed breakdown of actual amounts SOE had obtained, Selborne emphasised the fact that SOE was collecting substantial amounts of small denominations. 'The difficulties of obtaining them clandestinely', he added, 'and ensuring their safe delivery by secret means to this country cannot be too strongly stressed'.[43]

Following Selborne's rebuttal, SOE was now forced, quite literally, to put its money where its mouth was. It seems somewhat more than coincidental that SOE was *immediately* faced with the greatest foreign currency demands, set in large part by the Air Ministry, that it had ever received. D/Fin informed CD on 14 January that at the monthly meeting at the Bank of England held the previous day, SOE was asked to supply a number of

> urgent demands which cannot be met from the available resources of the 'Pool'': 1 million Danish Kroner in 50's and under, 1 million Norwegian Kroner in 100's and under, 1 million Dutch Gulden in 25's and under, 10 million Belgian Francs in 100's and 50's, 250 million French Francs in 100's and 50's, 90 million French Francs in 5,000's and 1,000's.

With the exception of the 90 million French francs, the sums were required 'for purses for air crews, and the magnitude of the demands is, of course, consequent upon the stepping up of the bombing operations over enemy and enemy-occupied territories'.[44] Venner was acutely aware of the enormity of the task: 'we have been asked to carry out the impossible'. The operation would first necessitate the acquisition of between £500,000 and £600,000 in neutral currencies, and, because of the small denominations required, mean transporting 'several tons of paper' across Europe. Nevertheless, Venner concluded that 'we shall do our best, and the necessary telegrams have been dispatched to Stockholm, Lisbon and Tangier'.[45]

The task did not turn out to be an impossible one. In July, Venner wrote to CD, noting that the January requests had since been 'substantially increased', with 'large fresh orders' placed at subsequent meetings at the Bank of England, and provided further details of the revised orders (Table 10.1).

He went on to note that, not only had the original orders been fulfilled, but that SOE had also 'gone a long way in meeting the further increased and fresh demands'. He remained confident that despite problems of transportation across Europe, SOE would 'be able to complete all orders in the near future'. The money had been acquired 'in the denominations asked for', despite the fact that 'the bulk delivered has been enormous'.[46]

Following its inclusion in the rebuttal of the JIC enquiry into SOE, and no doubt influenced by Venner's continued success, the issue of foreign currency began to make appearances in Selborne's quarterly reports on SOE to Churchill. In the report for April–June 1944, Selborne noted that SOE had 'the honour of being H.M.'s principal procurer of foreign currency in the black markets of Europe and Asia', and that since January 1944, 'over £1,700,000 worth of foreign currencies including 445,000,000 French francs in notes of small denominations' had been handed over to the Bank of England. The July–September report noted that currency purchases had continued, with 700,000,000 francs being obtained 'for purposes connected with OVERLORD', while currency was also being acquired 'to finance British requirements in China'.[47] Selborne pointed out that these transactions were

Table 10.1 Revised orders for foreign currency, July 1944

Total orders received since Jan. 1944	Delivered or about to be delivered to Bank of England	Sterling equivalent of cost in currencies of acquisition
Belgium Francs (24 million)	18,269,575	71,417
French Francs (462 million)	445,073,000	474,632
Swiss Francs (£20,000 worth) 340,000 (approx.)	200,000	11,700
Dutch Gulden (6 million)	4,996,090	123,752
Reichsmark (2½ million)	1,500,000	12,909
Norwegian Kroner (1 million)	1,000,000	74,006
Danish Kroner (1 million)	1,001,270	
US Dollars (8 million)	4,000,000	993,788
Total		£1,762,204

Source: D/Fin to CD (Copy to A/CD (for L/WAD)), 3 July 1944, PRO HS8/354.

'effecting saving for H.M.G. at the rate of about one million pounds sterling per month as against the official rate. In fact at the moment, S.O.E. is being run at a profit!'[48] In the October–December report, financial matters were subsumed within the section dealing with the Far East, Selborne noting that 'An S.O.E. black market trading organisation provides currency at a low rate of exchange for all British establishments in China. So far some £10,000,000 has been saved to the Treasury by these methods.' He concluded that: 'Thus during 1944 S.O.E. can claim to have been run at a large profit to H.M.G. – a rare achievement in any Government Department!'[49]

While there is undoubtedly truth in Foot's contention that 'there was infinitely more to SOE than can be set out on a balance sheet, or reduced to pounds and dollars, francs and gulden, roubles and dinars, drachmae and yen',[50] SOE's success in foreign exchange dealings can best be set down in such a fashion. While precise details remain vague, it is clear that SOE's Iberian Section was heavily involved in acquiring the large sums of foreign currency so desperately needed by the Bank of England to supply the demands of the service departments, SIS, etc. As such, it comes as something of a surprise to see that H Section has been viewed largely as a failure, with Foot dismissing its work by noting that in Spain 'nothing in fact got done', while Mackenzie's *Secret History of SOE* simply notes that Jack Beevor's removal from Lisbon in 1942 'virtually ended SOE activity in Portugal itself'.[51] More recently, the subject of foreign currency transactions has been briefly touched upon in two articles on SOE activity in Spain and Portugal. However, the con-clusions of both articles in terms of H Section's achievements remain largely negative. Discussing Portugal, Wylie notes that following Beevor's departure, staff of the Lisbon mission 'had to confine themselves to combating German propa-ganda and purchasing foreign currency on the black market'. Messenger notes that 'SOE in Spain felt deprived of their true mission, sabotage': a statement based upon the words of an H Section agent, who felt 'lost in the gap between intelligence and action, a gap that SOE as an "active" service was not accustomed to'.[52] The current study goes some way towards illustrating the limitations inherent in such geographically 'isolationist' accounts of SOE activity; it is not difficult to under-stand why, even with access to the papers of H Section, the subject of foreign currency transactions has not received greater attention from historians, due to the fact that the surviving Country Section papers play down the activity – seen as little more than an 'extra', being carried out for the Finance Directorate in London – while there is considerable material emphasising the sense of disappointment among members of H Section that they could not engage in 'regular' irregular activities. However, the importance London ascribed to the currency transactions in which H Section was involved necessitates a revision of this attitude towards SOE activity in the Iberian Peninsular as a whole, and Portugal in particular.

Since the first release of SOE Country Section files into the public domain in June 1993, little work has appeared that attempts to use these to do anything other than examine SOE activity in a given geographical region, effectively continuing both the insularity favoured by Country Sections for carrying out their work, and the pattern later set by the Official Histories: following in the footsteps of *SOE in*

France, the file material has been used as the basis for articles dealing with SOE on a geographical basis.[53] Due to SOE's organisational structure, and the primacy given to the operational role of the Country Section, the logic of such an approach is indisputable. However, no matter how much any given Country Section saw itself as the centre of SOE's universe, there were other Sections in the organisation, such as Security and Finance, whose work was not bound by geographical constraints. Some of the more recently declassified SOE material allows us to examine the work of these Sections, and there is potential for an article on SOE to be written that does not name a country in its title. However, this appears to have become so firmly entrenched as the manner in which SOE should be approached that there is a danger that anything that does not fit more or less within geographical/operational boundaries will be overlooked. While research into SOE is inextricably bound up with the National Archives, with no other archive able to compete with the sheer volume of material it holds, historians of SOE currently appear to be in danger of exemplifying Aldrich's 'flabby research posture', in terms of research methodology, in microcosm.[54] Hopefully, this chapter will highlight the value of looking, occasionally, at SOE outside the confines of its Country Sections.

Notes

The author would like to thank Philip Murphy and Neville Wylie for their advice and comments on early drafts of this article.

1 William Mackenzie, *Secret History of SOE* (London, 2000), p. 722; Ian Dear, *Sabotage and Subversion: Stories from the Files of the SOE and OSS* (London, 1996) Chapter 13; Richard Aldrich, *Intelligence and the War Against Japan* (Cambridge, 2000), pp. 286–287; Robert Bickers, 'The Business of a Secret War: Operation "Remorse" and SOE Salesmanship in Wartime China', *Intelligence & National Security* 16/4 (2001): 11–37. Charles Cruickshank, *SOE in the Far East* (Oxford, 1983), Chapter 9. Bickham Sweet-Escott briefly raised the subject, noting that it was the 'fertile brain' of Walter Fletcher that saw SOE's Force 136 engage in currency transactions: 'no C.B.E. was better earned than Walter Fletcher's'. *Baker Street Irregular* (London, 1965), p. 254.
2 Quoted in A. P. Dobson, *The Politics of the Anglo-American Special Relationship 1940–1987* (Sussex, 1988), pp. 20–22.
3 R. S. Sayers, *The Bank of England 1891–1944*, vol. 2, (London, 1976), pp. 588–589.
4 *A Bank in Battledress: Being the Story of Barclays Bank (Dominion, Colonial and Overseas) during the Second World War 1939–45* (London 1948), p. 10. For further information on the origins of the Defence (Finance) regulations, see the National Archive, United Kingdom, Public Record Office (hereafter PRO) T/231/188.
5 For further details of the establishment of the Committee, see PRO T196/1.
6 Bank of England Archive (hereafter BoE), C43/853, Memorandum: Provision of Foreign Currency Notes for Government Departments, 6 Jan. 1942. Further Bank of England papers reveal contacts with both SOE and SIS, while the identity of the third 'special friend' remains unclear, although it was probably MI9. Foot and Langley note that in the summer of 1940 MI9 was allocated 'up to £5,000 in foreign currency, most of which was spent in providing aircrew with purses containing about £12 a man among their other escape needs. More was provided when it was needed.' M. R. D. Foot and J. M. Langley, *MI9: Escape and Evasion 1939–1945* (London, 1979), p. 39.
7 Some idea of the money involved can be found in papers detailing the purses used by Combined Operations. These purses were colour-coded: Red (2,000 French francs);

Yellow (1,000 French francs, 350 Belgian francs, 20 Dutch guilder); Black (100 Norwegian kroner, 150 Danish kroner); Mauve (105 Norwegian kroner); Green/Blue (1,000 French francs) (PRO WO208/3267, 'Contents of Purses and Aid Boxes', Jan. 1943.

8 At this point, the Bank strongly advised the War Office to make a request to the Bank to 'obtain now any that happen to be available'. The War Office complied and made a request for 26,000 kroner. Charles Key to V. C. Tong, 31 Aug. 1940, BoE C43/429. A note scribbled on the top of the letter notes that 'No opportunity of obtaining these arose'.

9 Memorandum: Provision of Foreign Currency Notes for Government Departments, 6 Jan. 1942, BoE C43/853.

10 'Requirements & Foreign Currency Notes for Special Purposes', 13 May 1942, BoE C43/853.

11 Secret Memorandum, Dealing & Accounts Office, 1 June 1942, BoE C43/853.

12 Secret Memorandum, Dealing & Accounts Office, to Mr Gurney, Mr Beale, 30 June 1942, BoE C43/853.

13 Ibid.

14 PRO HS8/344, D/FIN to CD, 29 Oct. 1940.

15 PRO HS8/130, Draft letter from The Minister to Sir A Sinclair, 12 May 1942.

16 PRO HS8/1017, D/FIN to DCD, 22 May 1942.

17 PRO HS9/1524/7, CD to SO, 23 June 1942.

18 PRO HS8/1016, 'Note of a Conversation with CFC at the Bank of England, 04.06.42'; 'Notes of Talks at the Treasury, 02.06.42.'

19 BoE C43/853, Secret Memorandum, Dealing & Accounts Office, to Mr Gurney, Mr Beale, 30 June 1942.

20 'Foreign Currencies: Review of S.O.E.'s Activities', 4 July 1943, pp. 1–2, PRO HS8/354. The meeting was attended by representatives of SOE, SIS, the Treasury, Foreign Office and War Office.

21 Memorandum: Foreign Currency Notes Purchased Abroad, 25 July 1942, BoE C43/853.

22 'Foreign Currencies: Review of S.O.E.'s Activities', 4 July 1943, p. 3, PRO HS8/354.

23 Ibid.

24 Ibid., p 4.

25 Lithiby to Fraser, 19 Apr. 1943, BoE C43/853.

26 'Foreign Currencies: Review of S.O.E.'s Activities', 4 July 1943, pp. 4–5, PRO HS8/354.

27 Ibid., p 2.

28 Statements of Accounts for the months ending 20 Feb. 1942, 20 Mar. 1942, 20 Apr. 1942, 20 May 1942, 20 July 1942 and 20 Aug. 1942, PRO HS6/958.

29 HA to H, 8 June 1942, PRO HS6/958.

30 HA to A/DP (Copy to D/FIN and A/DW), 2 July 1942, PRO HS6/958.

31 Ibid.

32 D/Fin to HM, 6 Aug. 1942; HA to D/IP, 24 July 1942; HM to D/Fin, 28 July 1942; HY to H, 4 July 1942; HY to D/Fin (Copy to H), 8 July 1942, PRO HS6/958.

33 HY to D/Fin (Copy to H), 8 July 1942, PRO HS6/958. The need for further firms soon became apparent as the arrangement entered into with Grahams ran into difficulty. Waite warned London that 'Grahams are reluctant to give us any more money because of the delay in effecting the sterling payment of the last £10,000.' He noted that he would 'point out that it was really the Bank of England which was the bugbear but that all future transactions should be effected promptly', and appeared confident that he would be able to 'talk them round'. HY to H, 19 Aug. 1942, PRO HS6/958.

34 HY to D/Fin, 31 July 1942, PRO HS6/958.

35 DF Section was 'entrusted with the clandestine sale, in the Peninsula, of diamonds, in order to obtain large sums of foreign currency'. See 'Schedule "H": Clandestine Communications', p 7, PRO HS7/163. 'Clandestine Communications Section, Resumé

of Activities – 1st Jan to 31st Dec 1943', PRO HS8/192. However, the sale of diamonds was fraught with difficulties, for while they were easier to smuggle than cash, they required 'the recruiting of a neutral who is prepared to carry the stone and can be trusted by us to sell it at a fair price and deliver the proceeds to a cut out address'. Such agents were difficult to find, and 'the fluctuation of the market coupled with the difference between official and black market rates of exchange' meant it was difficult to decide on 'a reasonable price, acceptable to both parties of the transactions'. 'Creation and Organisation of Clandestine Communication Section', p. 33, PRO HS8/151.

36 'Creation and Organisation of Clandestine Communication Section', pp. 31–32, PRO HS8/151. The account of DF Section activity noted that the transfers took place 'by registered post between two neutral countries', the money being insured and 'therefore should it be lost, stolen or stopped by the censorship the loss is borne by the insurance company and not by S.O.E.' Ibid., p. 33.

37 Upon receipt of Mackenzie's first outline for his *History of SOE*, Venner complained that the work of his Finance Directorate had not been properly acknowledged. He wrote to Mackenzie, noting that although discussions with the Treasury had arrived at the conclusion that 'no reference whatever should be made to the amount of expenditure from the Secret Vote' reaching SOE, he was keen to ensure that this would not mean the total absence of SOE's financial dealings from the main narrative: 'I think that covert financial operations are just as much operations as, for instance, political subversion and should therefore be included in the body of the *History* rather than in an Appendix.' Venner rewrote Mackenzie's outline paragraph on finance since he felt it 'desirable to include some account of the financial operations (Foreign Exchange transactions etc.) carried out by the Organisation over a long period. These lie somewhat apart from S.O.E.'s normal work but they were of great importance to many Departments' (PRO HS8/430, D/FIN to Mackenzie, 27 Nov. 1945). Venner's suggestions were not taken on board. Although Venner intended to write a brief history of the directorate to guide Mackenzie's *History*, the pressure of other work appears to have prevented him from fulfilling this task (D/Fin to D/His.1, 12 Dec. 1945, PRO HS7/163).

38 D/Fin to SO (through CD), copies to V/CD, A/CD, L/WAD, 4 July 1943, PRO HS8/354.

39 PRO. HS8/354, D/Fin to AD/S.W, 29 Dec. 1943, PRO HS8/354.

40 M. R. D. Foot, *SOE in the Low Countries* (London, 2001), pp. 204–205.

41 'S.O.E. Operations in Europe: Memorandum by the Minister of Economic Warfare', 11 Jan. 1944, PRO HS6/749.

42 'For incorporation in a letter being prepared by D/Plans to be written by S.O. to either Chiefs of Staff or Prime Minister in answer to a J.I.C. paper', 8 Jan. 1944, PRO HS8/354. The paper included an up-to-date record of the amounts of foreign currencies obtained: 85 million French Francs; 2¾ million Dutch Gulden; 2½ million Danish Kroner; 2½ million Norwegian Kroner; 7¾ million Spanish Pesetas; 4¼ million German Reichsmarks; ½ million Swedish Kroner; ½ million Argentine Pesos. Venner concluded by emphasising that: 'Having regard to the fact that these notes have to be for the most part in small denominations, the difficulties of obtaining them clandestinely and ensuring their safe delivery by secret means to this country cannot be too strongly stressed.'

43 Annex: Comments on J.I.C.(43) 500 (0) and 517 (0), 11 Jan. 1944, PRO HS6/749.

44 D/Fin to CD, 14 Jan. 1944, PRO HS8/354.

45 Ibid.

46 D/Fin to CD (Copy to A/CD (for L/WAD)), 3 July 1944, PRO HS8/354.

47 'S.O.E. Activities: Summary for the Prime Minister. Quarter: April to June 1944', PRO HS8/899.

48 'S.O.E. Activities: Summary for the Prime Minister. Quarter: July to September 1944', PRO HS8/899.

49 'S.O.E. Activities: Summary for the Prime Minister. Quarter: October to December 1944', PRO HS8/899.

50 M. R. D. Foot, SOE: *An Outline History of the Special Operations Executive 1940–1946* (London, 1999 edn), pp. 360–361.

51 Foot, *SOE: Outline History*, p. 328; Mackenzie, *Secret History of SOE*, p. 324.

52 Neville Wylie, '"An Amateur Learns his Job?" Special Operations Executive in Portugal, 1940–42', *Journal of Contemporary History* 36/3 (2001): 441; David Messenger, 'Fighting for Relevance: Economic Intelligence and Special Operations Executive in Spain, 1943–1945', *Intelligence & National Security* 15/3 (2000): 42.

53 E. O'Halpin, '"Toys" and "Whispers" in "16-land": SOE and Ireland, 1940–1942', *Intelligence & National Security*, 15/4 (2000): 1–18; E. D. R. Harrison, 'British Subversion in French East Africa, 1941–42: SOE's Todd Mission', *English Historical Review* 114/456 (1999): 339–369; E. D. R. Harrison, 'The British Special Operations Executive and Poland', *The Historical Journal* 43/4 (2000): 1071–1091; Gerald Steinacher, 'The Special Operations Executive (SOE) in Austria, 1940–1945', *International Journal of Intelligence and Counter Intelligence* 15/2 (2002): 211–221. The combination of geographical area with a broader theme can be seen in Ian Herrington's 'The SIS and SOE in Norway 1940–1945: Conflict or Co-operation?', *War in History* 9/1 (2002): 82–101, while Philip H. J. Davies has examined the demise of SOE and its incorporation into SIS: 'From Special Operations to Special Political Action: The "Rump SOE" and SIS Post-War Covert Action Capability 1945–1977', *Intelligence & National Security* 15/3 (2000): 55–76.

54 Richard Aldrich, '"Grow Your Own": Cold War Intelligence and History Supermarkets', *Intelligence & National Security* 17/1 (2002): 148.

Index